GETTING GOOD GOVERNMENT

CAPACITY BUILDING
IN THE PUBLIC SECTORS OF
DEVELOPING COUNTRIES

Harvard Studies in International Development

Other volumes in the series include:

Volumes published jointly with the International Center for Economic Growth.

HARVARD STUDIES IN INTERNATIONAL DEVELOPMENT

GETTING GOOD GOVERNMENT

CAPACITY BUILDING
IN THE PUBLIC SECTORS OF
DEVELOPING COUNTRIES

Edited by Merilee S. Grindle

Harvard Institute for International Development
Harvard University

Distributed by Harvard University Press

Published by Harvard Institute for International Development

Distributed by Harvard University Press

Editorial Management: Don Lippincott
Editorial Assistance: Jolanta Davis
Design and production: Desktop Publishing & Design Co., Boston, MA

Library of Congress Cataloging-in-Publication Data

Getting good government : capacity building in the public sectors of developing
  countries / edited by Merilee S. Grindle.
       p.   cm. -- (Harvard studies in international development)
    Includes bibliographical references (p. 465) and index.
    ISBN 0-674-35417-6 (cloth). -- ISBN 0-674-35419-2 (paper)
    1. Administrative agencies--Developing countries.   2. Civil service--Develop-
ing countries--Personnel management.   3. Government productivity--Developing
countries.   4. Political planning--Developing countries.   I. Grindle, Merilee
Serrill.   II. Series
JF60.G49   1997   97-13510
352.3'09172'4--dc21   CIP

To the memory of

Michael Roemer

A colleague deeply committed to
good government throughout the world

Table of Contents

Contributors

William G. Bikales is a former Research Associate with HIID's Strategic Intervention in Support of Economic Reform Project (1993–1994) in Ulan Bator, Mongolia. A development economist who specializes in banking, trade, and industrial development, he has held consultant positions in economic policy in the People's Republic of China, Hong Kong, and Taiwan. He received his Ph.D. in economics from Harvard University.

Bruce R. Bolnick is a Development Advisor at the Harvard Institute for International Development. He is currently working in Lilongwe, Malawi, as Senior Economic Advisor to the USAID-financed Malawi Economic Management and Reform Project. From 1991 to 1994, he served as Economic Advisor to the Ministry of Finance in Lusaka, Zambia, specializing in macroeconomic stabilization and tax policy. His research focuses on monetary, fiscal, and financial-market policies in developing countries. Dr. Bolnick holds a Ph.D. in economics from Yale University.

Martha A. Chen is a Research Associate at the Harvard Institute for International Development and a lecturer at the Kennedy School of Government. Her areas of specialization are rural development, poverty alleviation, non-governmental organizations, and women in development. She is editor of *Beyond Credit: A Sub-Sector Approach to Promoting Women's Enterprises* (1995), and coeditor of *Speaking Out: Women's Economic Empowerment in South Asia* (1996), and has written extensively on development issues. Dr. Chen has long term resident experience in Bangladesh and India. She received a Ph.D. in South Asia regional studies from the University of Pennsylvania.

John M. Cohen is an Institute Fellow at the Harvard Institute for International Development. His areas of specialization include administration of agriculture and livestock sectors, design and implementation of rural development projects and programs, and decentralization and participation. He has worked for the governments of Ethiopia and The Yemen, and served 11 years in Kenya on HIID advisory and training projects in the Ministries of Agriculture and Livestock Development, Planning and National Development, and Finance. The author of more than 50 books, book chapters, and journal articles, he holds a Ph.D. in Political Science from the University of Colorado and a J.D. from the University of Michigan Law School.

Manuel E. Contreras is Deputy Director of the Harvard Institute for International Development's Human Resources for Development Project at the Universidad Catolica Boliviana (UCB), and a lecturer in UCB's Masters in Public Policy and Management Program. Previously, he served as the first director of Bolivia's Social Policy Analysis Unit (UDAPSO). Contreras is interested in the evolution of Bolivian education reform, and has recently published a book chapter on Bolivian higher education policy. His current writing focuses on early twentieth century Bolivian economic history. He received his doctorate in economics from Columbia University.

Stephen E. Cornell is an Associate Professor and the Chair of the Department of Sociology at the University of California, San Diego, and Co-Director of the Harvard Project on American Indian Economic Development at the Kennedy School of Government. He has extensive experience working with Indian nations in the United States and Canada on economic development and tribal government issues. Prof. Cornell is coauthor of two books, the forthcoming *Constitutions, Culture, and the Wealth of Nations* and *Constructing Ethnic and Racial Identities: A Global Perspective*, and author of *The Return of the Native: American Indian Political Resurgence*. He holds a Ph.D. in sociology from the University of Chicago.

Graham Glenday is a Fellow of the Harvard Institute of International Development, and the Senior Resident Advisor in Tax Policy and coordinator of HIID's Tax Modernization Programme. He has advised the Ministry of Finance of the Government of Kenya on tax policy since 1986, and also provides advice on local government finance and intergovernmental fiscal relations under Kenya's Local Government Reform Programme. An expert in the appraisal and financing of capital investment projects, he has served as a tax policy advisor in Lesotho, Brunei, Nepal, and Ukraine. He received his Ph.D. in public policy from Harvard University.

Clive S. Gray is an Institute Fellow at the Harvard Institute for International Development and a lecturer at Harvard's Department of Economics and Kennedy School of Government. He is the coauthor of *Introduction to Project Appraisal*, 2nd ed. (1993) and *Primary Health*

Care in Rural Africa: The Mali Rural Health Project, 1978–1982 (1990), and the author of numerous book chapters, papers and articles on development economics. He has served as a consultant in Kenya, Indonesia, Ethiopia, Colombia, Morocco, Uzbekistan, and Mongolia. He holds a Ph.D. in economics from Harvard.

Merilee S. Grindle (editor and contributor) is the Edward S. Mason Professor of International Development at Harvard University's Kennedy School of Government, and a Fellow of the Harvard Institute for International Development. A specialist on the comparative analysis of policy making in developing countries, she currently focuses on governmental effectiveness in supporting development. She is the author of *Challenging the State: Crisis and Innovation in Latin America and Africa* (1996), and coauthor, with John W. Thomas, of *Public Choices and Policy Change* (1991). At HIID, she has participated in projects based in Southeast Asia, Latin America, and Central America. She holds a Ph.D. in political science from MIT.

Mary E. Hilderbrand is a Development Associate at the Harvard Institute for International Development. She specializes in the political economy of development and the international relations between developing countries and advanced industrial countries. She has research interests and project experience in Africa and Latin America, and has written on the political economy of implementing economic adjustment programs, institutional capacity building, and technical cooperation. Currently, she manages an HIID project establishing a master's program in public policy and management in Bolivia. She holds a Ph.D. in political science from Harvard.

Joseph P. Kalt is the Ford Foundation Professor of International Political Economy and co-director of the Harvard Project on American Indian Economic Development and the National Executive Education Program for Native American Leadership. In addition, he is chair of the Economics and Quantitative Analysis program at Harvard's Kennedy School of Government. He is the coauthor of *What Can Tribes Do? Strategies and Institutions in American Indian Economic Development* (1992), and has written extensively on Indian development economics. He received a Ph.D. in economics from the University of California at Los Angeles.

Donald F. Lippincott, III is the Publications Officer at the Harvard Institute for International Development, in which capacity he oversees public relations as well as management and production of the institute's book series, working paper series, and biennial report. He previously served for seven years as an Academic Counselor in HIID's Training Office, where he advised and worked closely with government officials from a number of developing countries. The author of several international case studies, he has written a case study on training management issues for the Indonesian state banks, *Training Director's Dilemma*. He holds an M.A. in law and diplomacy from the Fletcher School of Law and Diplomacy at Tufts University and an M.B.A. from Boston University.

Charles N. Myers is an economist working on health, education, and labor market policy in developing countries. He was the Harvard Institute for International Development's Resident Advisor and Project Manager at the Thailand Development Research Institute (1985–1991) and at the Social Policy Research Unit in Bolivia (1994–1995). Previously, he served as Coordinator of HIID health projects and an analyst in the Philippines Health Finance Development Project. In 1996, he began working with the United Nations Development Programme to help establish a policy analysis network in Southeast Asia. He holds a Ph.D. in economics from Princeton University.

Stephen B. Peterson is a Project Associate at the Harvard Institute for International Development and the Chief of Party of the Ethiopian Decentralization Support Activity Project, which was developed to strengthen Ethiopia's budget and expenditure management systems. A specialist in comparative public administration, public sector management, and financial management and planning, his research involves computer-based information system applications in these areas. He is the author of numerous articles and papers in his field. He holds a Ph.D. in political science from the University of California, Berkeley.

Jonathon L. Simon is a Development Associate at the Harvard Institute for International Development and the Principal Investigator and Project Director of the Applied Research on Child Health (ARCH) Project, a global program to support applied health research on priority issues in child survival. Mr. Simon has written on research capacity strengthening and the development of programs to make applied, policy-relevant health research available to policy makers. His other research interests include urban health in the developing world. He is now finishing his doctorate in population sciences and international health at Harvard.

Johannes U. Sommerfeld is a Research Associate at the Department of Tropical Hygiene and Public Health, Ruprecht-Karls-University of Heidelberg, Germany, and a former Research Associate with HIID's Applied Diarrheal Disease Research Project. He has written extensively on the topics of capacity building in the health social sciences, anthropology of international health, and anthropological aspects of infectious disease. As a consultant for Save the Children, GTZ, and Kreditanstalt für Wiederaufbau, he has travelled throughout Africa, Indonesia, and Pakistan. He holds a Ph.D. and M.P.H. in medical anthropology/epidemiology from the University of Hamburg.

James A. Trostle is Director of the Five College Program in Culture, Health, and Science and Five College Assistant Professor of Anthropology at Mt. Holyoke College. A former Research Associate with HIID's Applied Diarrheal Disease Research Project, Trostle studies public health issues including international health epidemiology, domestic and international research capacity, and medication usage. His recent writing concerns the influence of research on health policy in Latin America; his chapter "Beliefs about Epilepsy: Perception of Stigma," appeared in Engel and Pedley's *Epilepsy: A Comprehensive Textbook*, (1997). Trostle received a Ph.D. from the University of California, Berkeley,

John R. Wheeler is an Overseas Development Administration Advisor on public investment programming in Kenya's Ministry of Planning and National Planning. A specialist in decentralized planning systems, land resource assessment, and capital budget portfolio planning, he served as a Harvard Institute for International Development advisor for Kenya's Resource Management for Rural Development and Budget and Economic Management Projects. He earned his degrees in land use and natural resource planning from the University of Newcastle-on-Tyne and the University of East Anglia.

Albert R. Wight is a World Bank consultant and a former Project Associate for HIID's Russian Privatization Center in Moscow. His primary interests and professional experience are in organizational and institutional development, training, conflict resolution, learning and memory. Dr. Wight's "Cross Cultural Analysis as a Training Tool," will appear in Fowler and Mumford, eds., *Intercultural Sourcebook: Cross-Cultural Training Methods*, Vol. II (May 1997). He has country experience around the globe, including Russia, Pakistan, Micronesia, Brazil, and Zaire. He received his Ph.D. in organizational/industrial psychology from the University of Utah.

FOREWORD

One of HIID's key strengths always has been developing relationships with senior policy makers and managers—those who actually make and implement real choices. The Institute has done this by providing resident advisors and short-term consultants to assist institutions in developing countries. Through daily collaboration with colleagues in host countries, HIID advisors prepare policy analyses for discussion with senior officials. Since these working relationships are often long term, the advisors generally assist in the implementation of policy decisions as well.

In conjunction with such close collaborative policy analysis, which is generally based on substantial research efforts, building capacity in government and quasi-governmental organizations has been an important, parallel activity. In fact, one of the things that has characterized HIID has been its emphasis on preparing local researchers, managers, and political leaders with whom we work to perform their jobs more effectively after HIID staff have returned home.

This well-integrated collection of analytical studies and case histories bears testament to the wealth of experience the Institute—and its collaborating counterpart organizations—has under its belt. As editor, Merilee Grindle has deftly woven together the many far-flung strands of capacity-building activities in which HIID and its staff have been engaged. The chapter authors, most of whom have extensive experience working and residing in developing countries, have shared with one another their experiences and solutions that benefited the capacity-building efforts on which they have worked. As such this book will be a valuable addition to the library of those interested in both the process and the applications of capacity building in the public sectors of developing countries.

Jeffrey D. Sachs
Director, HIID

Preface

For the thirty-five years of HIID's and its predecessor's existence, HIID personnel have participated in policy reform initiatives as advisors to government decision makers around the world. They have also done extensive research and publication on development issues and have taught numerous courses on the subject. Underlying all of these efforts has been the belief that our job was not primarily to come up with the best policy outcome or the most polished research article in an academic journal. Our task was first and foremost to work with developing countries to help them to develop their own capacity to carry out this work.

Most foreign technical assistance has local capacity building as a primary objective, but the reality is often quite different. It is easy for foreign advisors to get so caught up in day to day policy crises that they never find time to support capacity-building efforts. But even when there is time and a sincere commitment to capacity building, there is not a great deal of received wisdom about how that objective is to be achieved. Knowledge of how to build sustainable capacity in the public sector is particularly weak. To some scholars and politicians, economic and social reforms involve little more than reducing the role of government and turning its functions over to the market. But as HIID and others learned long ago, an efficient market system requires a well-functioning government in many critical areas. But how does one help build the government institutions that make for a well-functioning government?

It was for the purpose of better understanding our own experience with capacity building that HIID decided to hold a conference in the spring of 1995. If we understood our own experience better, we would be more effective as advisors in the future. The great range of our experience, we felt, could also be of use to other scholars and practitioners. To make that experience accessible, we decided to ask a number of our HIID colleagues to write research papers based on their efforts to help build capacity in various parts of the world. The result, led from the start by Professor Merilee Grindle, is this volume.

Dwight H. Perkins
Director, HIID
1980–1995

Acknowledgments

The editor would like to thank Dwight Perkins, who encouraged and supported the conference at which this work was first presented, and Ellen Pigott, who encouraged and supported the contributors with skill and patience through the revision, the editing, and production of this volume. I am grateful to the contributors, who continued to labor over their chapters long after the conference, not least of all to Don Lippincott, who helped ensure the publication of our research. Others who assisted him in the management of the production process include: Jolanta Davis, who helped in moving the manuscript along; Sarah Newberry, who designed several of the figures; Sharon Hogan, who copy-edited the book; Diane Benison, who prepared the index; and Allison Blyler and Elena Patino, who worked on the text at its early and latter stages, respectively.

Merilee S. Grindle
Editor

Introduction

1 THE GOOD GOVERNMENT IMPERATIVE

HUMAN RESOURCES, ORGANIZATIONS, AND INSTITUTIONS

Merilee S. Grindle

The truth is that we have simultaneously too much state and too little state.

—João Guilherme Merquior

In this reflection about his native Brazil, João Guilherme Merquior captured a dilemma faced in many countries around the world in the mid-1990s.[1] "Too much state" acknowledges that, for many, the development history of the past several decades meant interventionist and often intrusive state-led development strategies combined with an emphasis on centralized political control. Too frequently, this history resulted in stagnant and inefficient economies and political regimes that were unresponsive, authoritarian, and corrupt. Ironically, "too little state" points to the reality that these large and intrusive public sectors often showed little effective capacity to formulate policy, implement it, and perform routine administrative functions. This condition frequently added up to a pervasive inability to carry out even the most basic tasks required of modern states. In short, while many governments claimed a central role in leading the process of development, they demonstrated remarkable incapacity to plan and pursue it.

The response to problems created by "too much state" occupied the development agenda for much of the 1980s and early 1990s. In changes triggered by debt and fiscal crises, international pressure, and loss of support for centralized and authoritarian regimes, this period was marked by dual transitions. Many governments committed themselves to market-oriented approaches for generating economic growth at the same time that civil societies organized to press for democratic elections and greater participation in decision making. In both economic and political terms, pressure was exerted to eliminate or strictly limit government control and intervention. Throughout this period also, development specialists joined in an attack on the state for having "grown too large, intervened in economic interactions too energetically, and mismanaged policy making and implementation too regularly."[2] An almost universal focus on state minimalism—on cutting down on the size, expense, and responsibilities of public sectors—was a clear response to decades of too much state.

The response to "too little state" took much longer to emerge. For much of the 1980s, intense concern about reducing state involvement in the economy overwhelmed the policy agendas of international financial institutions, which often took the lead in such initiatives, and reformist policy elites. Stabilizing macroeconomic conditions, liberalizing domestic and international trade, deregulating the market, privatizing state-owned industries, and reducing the size and fiscal drag of central bureaucracies were the first priorities of economic reformers. Similarly, democratizing initiatives, driven by both domestic and international advocates, focused primary attention on dismantling the structures of control and corruption that had held discredited regimes together. Initially, economic and political reformers alike were convinced that the state must shed functions in order to enhance opportunities for dynamic growth and political freedom.

For a considerable period, then, reform initiatives were blind to the critical importance of having capable states, not just minimal ones, if markets were to perform effectively and citizens were to be assured of basic rights and freedoms. Only after a decade of experimentation with reducing government did economic reformers become more explicit about the importance of strengthening government by infusing it with the capacity to be efficient, effective, and responsive, and with the capacity not only to manage macroeconomic policy, but also to regulate some forms of market behavior.[3] In this regard, "the rediscovery of the market" as a basis for economic policy eventually produced "the rediscovery of the state," as Moisés Naím has written.[4] Democratic reformers similarly grew to recognize the importance of well-defined and functioning institutions of governance for the stability and legitimacy of new modes of participation and conflict resolution.

By the mid-1990s, good government had been added to the development agenda precisely because of greater awareness that neither markets nor democracies could function well—or perhaps function at all—unless governments were able to design and implement appropriate public policies, administer resources equitably, transparently, and efficiently, and respond efficaciously to the social welfare and economic claims of citizens. Although a general consensus developed about the imperative for good government, how to get good government has not been at all clearly understood. This volume is part of a larger search for understanding how governments can be encouraged or induced to perform better and how state capabilities can be developed in ways that allow markets and democracies to flourish.

DEFINITIONS AND DEBATES

In attempting to analyze initiatives to promote good government, contributors to this volume had to address, individually and collectively, a series of debates. Early on, we had to consider definitional problems: What is implied by the concept of capacity building? Should we draw distinctions among capacity *building*, capacity *development*, and capacity *strengthening?* Simiiarly, we had to address a debate about the site of capacity-building initiatives: Is good government a result of changes focused primarily on the public sector or of broader sets of actions affecting the private sector and civil society also? We also faced a set of questions related to what needs to be done in order to build—or develop or strengthen—capacity: Should capacity-building initiatives focus primarily on efforts to improve the quality of human resources, on efforts to make organizations work better, or on efforts to alter the institutional context within which individuals and organizations function? Finally, a debate about the process of capacity building had to be addressed: Does technical assistance help or hinder such initiatives? What is the role of the foreign expert in capacity building? Considered as a whole, the volume "takes sides" in these debates, although the authors of individual chapters at times dissent from a general consensus.

Definitional concerns have long characterized discussions of what is being attempted in capacity-building initiatives. Our use of the term *capacity building* is intended to encompass a variety of strategies that have to do with increasing the efficiency, effectiveness, and responsiveness of government performance. Our use of these terms is straightforward: efficiency relates to the time and resources required to produce a given outcome; effectiveness relates to the appropriateness of efforts undertaken to the production of desired outcomes; and responsiveness relates to the link between the communication of needs and the capacity to address them.

Some development specialists prefer the terms *capacity development* or *capacity strengthening* to signal that the task is one of strengthening existing capacity rather than constructing capacity that does not yet exist.[5] In Chapter 3, for example, the authors self-consciously adopt the term *capacity strengthening* to emphasize that "it is more important to understand…present roles and limitations [of existing human resources and organizations] than it is to suggest new organizations and new strategies."[6] More generally, however, contributors to this volume use the terms capacity *building, development,* and *strengthening* interchangeably. We believe this use of the terms reflects conditions actually encountered in many developing and transitional countries, where it is difficult to isolate whether the need is for creation, reform, or support of activities and structures that result in good government.

Debate also surrounds the question of appropriate sites for capacity-building activities. Particularly where scarce development resources are at stake, it is a matter of some concern whether efforts to get good government should be focused primarily on government itself or should also include activities to strengthen the capacity of private sectors and organizations of civil society, such as nongovernmental organizations (NGOs), political parties, unions, and public interest groups. At issue here is whether how government functions is primarily a reflection of internal government operations or is produced by an organized, educated, and vigilant society.

Most of the contributions to this volume take government personnel, activities, or structures as their focal point. This focus suggests considerable bias toward a "supply-side" understanding of how good government is achieved. Despite this apparent bias, however, most contributors would agree that for government to be efficient, effective, and responsive, demand-side pressures are extremely important; moreover, development itself requires diverse kinds of capacity to be broadly available in societies and their economic and political systems. It also requires effective and continuous interaction along hypothetical boundaries among the state, society, and economy. This view is represented in Chapter 9 by Martha A. Chen, in which she argues that NGOs need to improve their policy analytic and research skills if they are to be effective participants in policy discussions and advocates for the reform of public sector policies, organizations, and institutions.[7] Similarly, in Chapter 10 on the institutional underpinnings conducive to economic development, Stephen E. Cornell and Joseph P. Kalt explore the nature of societal values and attitudes toward authority.[8] Our primary focus on the operation of government reflects the vocations of most of the contributors (most are actively engaged in promoting internal improvements in government performance) rather than an assertion of convergence on a "supply-side" theory of governance.

The debate about the site of capacity-building initiatives raises related issues about what it is that governments should be responsible for. Contributors to this volume would certainly agree that getting good government often begins by making hard choices about what government should be responsible for and what activities it ought to abandon through deregulation, privatization, or downsizing. In general, however, we assume that these kinds of choices have already been made through a political process. We therefore do not engage much of the debate about what government "ought" to do. Rather, we focus instead on ways in which activities considered to be the responsibility of government—for philosophical, political, and historical reasons related to the development of each country—can be improved.

Given a principal focus on the public sector and on the activities that are considered the proper domain of government, the question remains as to what needs to be done to strengthen the ability of governments to perform efficiently, effectively, and responsively. Answers to this question have changed over time, reflecting changing needs as well as frustration with prior intervention strategies for their inability to "fix the problem."[9] As outlined by Peter Morgan, efforts of the 1950s and 1960s tended to focus on *institution building*, involving initiatives to put in place basic public sector institutions that would allow postindependence governments to deliver on promises for rapid economic and social development.[10] By the late 1960s and early 1970s, however, concern for *institutional strengthening* indicated growing concern that institutions already in existence were falling far short of expectations. Then, the idea of *development management* was adopted to emphasize the importance of the developmental responsibilities of government, particularly in addressing the needs of the poor majority. *Institutional development* reappeared in the 1980s as a concern for the broader structures and activities considered important to the process of change, including the contributions of private sectors and NGOs to the process of development. Over time, then, the definition of what needs to be done to build capacity grew to include actions and processes that link the public sector, the market, and civil society; the new definition suggests that capacity building is synonymous with the concept of development.[11]

We believe that this formulation is too broad to allow for productive discussion of concrete initiatives to get good government. Through iterations of the draft chapters and discussions at a conference at which the papers were presented, contributors instead came to share a conviction that good government is advanced—although by no means ensured—when skilled and professional public officials undertake to formulate and implement policies, when bureaucratic units perform their assigned tasks effectively, and when fair and authoritative rules for economic and political interaction are regularly observed and enforced. In our view, then, good government has much to do with the quality of human resources, organizations, and institutions in the public sector. Getting good government means, among other things, efforts to develop human resources, strengthen organizations, and reform (or create) institutions in this sector. Table 1-1 indicates that these three dimensions of capacity focus primarily on personnel, management, or structures and imply distinct activities if they are to be developed, strengthened, or reformed.

Individual chapters focus more attention on one dimension of capacity building or another. Some contributors, for example, assert the importance of focusing capacity building primarily on human resource development, whereas other authors focus more on organizations or institutions. The organization of the volume reflects these distinct emphases, with sections devoted to each of the three dimensions. Nevertheless, close reading of any chapter will confirm that these three dimensions of governance are interrelated and that efforts to improve the efficiency, effectiveness, and responsiveness of government often must address all three.[12]

A final set of issues that concerned us as the volume took shape was that of the role of technical assistance in capacity-building initiatives. As will become evident, many of our cases of human resource development, organizational strengthening, and institutional reform were based on donor-funded projects. In the 1990s, some individuals

TABLE 1-1
Dimensions and Focus of Capacity-Building Initiatives

Dimension	Focus	Types of Activities
Human resource development	Supply of professional and technical personnel	Training, salaries, conditions of work, recruitment
Organizational strengthening	Management systems to improve performance of specific tasks and functions; microstructures	Incentive systems, utilization of personnel, leadership, organizational culture, communications, managerial structures
Institutional reform	Institutions and systems; macrostructures	Rules of the game for economic and political regimes, policy and legal change, constitutional reform

and some international financial institutions became highly critical of such initiatives because extensive investments apparently produced little in terms of the increased capacity of public sector officials or organizations to perform efficiently, effectively, and responsively.[13] They questioned continued dependence on expatriates for performing centrally important functions in government and on specially funded donor projects that often rob government of its most committed and high-quality talent. Contributors to this volume are not so certain that technical assistance is unproductive in capacity-building initiatives, but they emphasize that the design of such projects and the context in which they are carried out are primary determinants of success or failure. In this regard, they would agree that getting good government in many cases means getting good technical assistance projects in the sense that they are well designed, appropriately staffed, and sensitive to context.

Problems of "Too Little State": Lessons of Experience

Indeed, context is important in all of the chapters presented here. As they demonstrate, human resource development, organizational strengthening, and institutional reform are affected by a wide range of economic, political, and social conditions, such as the impact of international economic conditions on domestic economies, historically embedded relationships within civil society and between the state and society, and the orientations, skills, and support coalitions of public leaders. Nevertheless, while acknowledging that analyses and prescriptions for reform must be attuned to the unique character of economic, political, and social conditions in each country, we are primarily concerned with drawing comparative lessons from specific efforts to enhance human resource development in the public sector, strengthen organizations that contribute to the public purpose of government, and reform the institutions that set the formal and informal rules for economic and political interaction. This set of concerns is organized into three sections in the volume. Part 1 presents analytic frameworks for understanding and designing capacity-building interventions; Part 2 contains case studies of human resource, organizational, and institutional capacity development; and Part 3 considers the role of technical assistance in capacity-building efforts.

PART ONE
ASSESSING CAPACITY-BUILDING NEEDS: CONCEPTUAL MAPS

The chapters in Part 1 present contrasting approaches to specifying the kinds of information that is important to have in considering where capacity gaps exist, what kinds of interventions can respond to these gaps, and how such initiatives can be strategically managed. These frameworks differ primarily in terms of their focus. In Chapter 2, Mary E. Hilderbrand and Merilee S. Grindle present a comprehensive framework for assessing capacity in the public sector based on five levels of analysis. Capacity is rooted in conditions that exist at each of these levels and efforts to build capacity must first assess the constraints that exist in each of them in order to understand where and how to attack the problem. In contrast, in Chapter 3, James A. Trostle, Johannes U. Sommerfeld, and Jonathon L. Simon present a framework based on a dynamic process of change, in which actors, actions, and events interact. They explain how capacity-strengthening projects unfold. While Hilderbrand and Grindle focus on context, Chapter 3 presents a process-oriented approach to analysis. Both frameworks are implicit in most of the case studies presented in Parts 2 and 3, in which analysis often moves back and forth between considerations of the context in which capacity-building initiatives take place and the dynamic processes through which they are carried out.

More specifically, in Chapter 2, Hilderbrand and Grindle are concerned with understanding public sector capacity—and capacity-building initiatives—in terms of the causes of existing conditions. Too often, they argue, capacity-building initiatives do not fully assess the roots of constraints on performance, tending to focus instead on the most concrete expressions of *in*capacity—officials who do not fulfill their responsibilities and organizations that do not perform their assigned functions well. The problem, of course, is that poorly performing officials and organizations may only be symptoms of dysfunctions rooted more deeply in political, social, and economic contexts. They indicate that prior to the design of specific interventions to improve performance, it is imperative to assess the action environment, the institutional context of the public sector, the task network surrounding the accomplishment of particular functions, the organizations most central to achieving specific objectives, and the nature of the human resources involved in the task. Their framework is accompanied by a methodology for carrying out such an assessment and is directed toward revealing the origin of constraints and the most appropriate focus of capacity-building efforts. Capacity-building activities can be focused on any level or any combination of levels, but a broad analysis is essential in order to identify those factors that most constrain the ability to perform well.

The Hilderbrand and Grindle framework was applied in a comparative analysis of six developing countries, and the results of this study lead them to question the underlying assumptions of many capacity-building initiatives. For example, their findings suggest that effective utilization of professional and technical personnel is often a more important constraint than lack of training in specific skills; that administrative structures and control regimes within organizations are often less important to performance than organizational culture, managerial styles, and communications networks; that the performance of public officials is most affected by the kinds of jobs they are assigned, the professional norms they hold, and the performance expectations on them than by their job descriptions or their training in specific skills.

Trostle, Sommerfeld, and Simon take issue with the Hilderbrand and Grindle framework. They argue that although the framework provides a map of sites for analyzing constraints on capacity-building initiatives, its contextual focus is too static to provide an understanding of the way in which such initiatives develop. Instead, they propose a framework focused on process and the actors, actions, and events that actually shape how capacity-strengthening activities unfold over time. They identify four phases in the life of capacity-strengthening initiatives—program design, project implementation, capacity acquisition, and capacity performance. The framework asserts that the relative influence of various types of actors—donor agency personnel at headquarters and field level, government ministries, implementing agencies, program administrators, and consultants, for example—over program outcomes alters according to these phases. Equally important, actors at each phase take specific actions that shape subsequent program activities and outcomes. Knowledge of the actors, their influence during particular phases of a program, and the implication of their actions for succeeding choices is essential to the strategic management of capacity-development initiatives. Just as important, a series of events—often unrelated to the program itself—can affect the influence of different actors and shape the actions they undertake.

Actors, actions, and events are the analytic building blocks for the process-oriented framework that Trostle, Sommerfeld, and Simon use to describe the history of a program to strengthen scientific research capacity in areas related to diarrheal and other diseases fatal to children in developing countries. They show how numerous actors in this donor-funded initiative made sequential decisions that ultimately defined the mission, beneficiaries, and accomplishments of the program. The authors encourage sensitivity to the need to identify actors, the predictable phases that programs and projects undergo as they move from design to implementation to results, and the choices that define what is to be done, who is to benefit, and what is to be the outcome of time and resource investments. They recommend ways that capacity-strengthening efforts can be improved through strategic management.

PART TWO
STRATEGIES FOR CAPACITY BUILDING

The concepts and contrasting emphases presented in the two frameworks introduced in Part 1 underlie many of the case studies that constitute Part 2 of this volume. Some focus primarily on efforts to diminish or maneuver around the constraints on capacity, while others give greater attention to process-oriented analyses. In most cases, however, contributors must deal both with contextual constraints and dynamic processes as they explore cases of human resource development, organizational strengthening, and institutional reform in a diverse set of countries. In doing so, they suggest that neither analytic framework is fully useful without considering the other.

Developing Human Resources

Initiatives to develop human resources generally seek to increase the capacity of individuals to carry out their professional and technical responsibilities. Such initiatives seek to overcome the educational and skill constraints set by the social and economic conditions of underdevelopment and to redress constraints set by the nature of public sector employment. Training and changes in remuneration scales and conditions of work, for example, are aimed at the underlying goal of preparing, attracting, and retaining dedicated, capable, and performance-oriented professional and technical talent in the public sector. Over the years, much investment in human resource development has been carried out through investments in on-the-job training and study leaves for domestic and international degree and nondegree training. Most of these activities are important components of larger programs to strengthen the capacity of organizations to carry out specific tasks; as such, they attest to the interrelated nature of capacity building along the dimensions we have identified.

Two chapters take a critical look at training initiatives and raise questions about the assumptions underlying them, how they are most effectively organized, and whether they address the most critical constraints on the effective performance of professional and technical roles in government. These chapters concur that training and skill-building investments tend to be more easily accomplished than utilizing professional and technical personnel appropriately. Ultimately then, and among other insights generated in these cases, their authors question whether the constraints on human resource development in the public sector have been properly identified.

In Chapter 4, Donald F. Lippincott presents several models used for overseas training initiatives. He describes targeted, narrowly focused efforts to produce the right number of people with specified skills for the functions assigned to particular agencies or ministries; approaches that seek to increase the overall number of people with specific skills in government; and initiatives to "pick winners" to send abroad for training in the expectation that these individuals will return to take on leadership roles in the sponsoring institution. He then presents an alternative model that was successfully followed by the ministry of finance in Indonesia. "Saturation training" involves a major initiative within a particular agency to "flood" the organization with new knowledge and appropriate skills by sending large numbers of officials overseas for training. It is hoped that they will return to staff middle and upper levels in the ministry with highly qualified human resources.

Exploring the Indonesian experience, Lippincott finds the saturation model to be an effective, if costly, way to develop the human resource capacity of a ministry or agency. Indonesia's oil wealth was clearly an important facilitating factor in enabling several hundred finance ministry officials to be trained abroad, largely in the United States. The in-house capabilities of the ministry, however, were greatly improved as a result of this training. The chapter also suggests that when newly trained officials return from overseas, their jobs and career opportunities do not always reflect the increased level of skill they have. Thus, the constraints on replicating the model are not only financial; they are organizational in the sense that the effective utilization of professional and technical personnel is an organizational and managerial responsibility.

The origin of constraints on human resource development is pursued in Chapter 5 on the training and retention of technical and professional personnel in Kenya. John M. Cohen and John R. Wheeler review the experience of six technical assistance projects that sent Kenyan officials abroad for training. Despite the current widespread expectation that such overseas training programs do not lead to public sector capacity development because those trained find more lucrative employment in the private or international sectors, these researchers found a surprisingly high retention rate for the Kenyans trained. In attempting to explain this outcome, they present additional evidence about the characteristics of those who return to government service and those who leave and about those who return to their sponsoring agency and those who move elsewhere in government. Given the constraints embedded in the nature of public sector employment in Kenya, it is not surprising that Cohen and Wheeler found that a large portion of the professional and technical personnel who were trained abroad did not find their positions in government to be either financially or psychologically rewarding. Interviews with returned trainees indicated that they believed they were capable of assuming much greater responsibility and performing much more effectively if given a chance to do so. Why, then, did they remain in the public sector, particularly when opportunities elsewhere were available to them?

Cohen and Wheeler indicate that, in fact, returned trainees made rational choices to remain in the public sector despite low pay and poor conditions of work. A primary motivation for continuing to work in the public sector, even when other opportunities were available to work in the private sector or for international agencies, was that government employment made it possible for them to receive a steady, if small, income for doing very little and thus freed them to pursue other activities that were more financially rewarding, such as consulting or running a business "on the side." The disturbing implication of this finding is that skilled human resources, although articulating a desire for more meaningful jobs, might not really welcome changes in the direction of greater utilization of their talents which might then rob them of the time to pursue other economic opportunities. Cohen and Wheeler indicate that civil service reform initiatives cannot be successful in getting better performance from professionally and technically trained personnel unless salaries are simultaneously improved to compensate for the opportunity costs of encouraging greater productivity.

Strengthening Organizations

The case studies of human resource development are explicit in recognizing the link between training (a personnel issue) and utilization (an organizational management issue). This link directs attention to the challenge of organizational strengthening, a second focus of capacity-building initiatives. Widely recommended means to achieve such ends are activities such as improving recruitment and utilization of staff, introducing more effective incentive systems, restructuring work and authority relationships, improving information and communication flows, upgrading physical resources, introducing better management practices, and decentralizing and opening decision-making processes. Four chapters in this volume address the question of how organizational capacities can be strengthened, assessing lessons from Africa, Thailand, Bolivia, and Bangladesh. In each case, the authors are concerned with sketching the constraints of organizational development at the same time that they explore the characteristics and process of relatively successful initiatives in this direction.

In Chapter 6, Stephen B. Peterson draws a distinction between the hierarchical bureaucratic structures that are central to Western organization theory and the largely informal networks that are the culturally constructed ways in which bureaucratic activities are undertaken and pursued in Africa. Thus, he focuses attention on the processes through which actors engage in decision making and actions are performed. Peterson argues that African societies are not primarily organized around hierarchies of impersonal structures and rules. They are instead organized around interpersonal networks that are composed of kin, clan, friends, and professional identities. When organizations are constructed to reiterate Western notions of structures and rules, their form may endure but their content will be subverted by the underlying networks and processes that are socially familiar and sanctioned. Previewing the institutionalist argument presented by Stephen E. Cornell and Joseph P. Kalt later in this volume, Peterson indicates that although similar problems may exist in many distinct contexts, they must find culturally specific solutions within their specific contexts.

If networks are the basis of social *and* official interaction within bureaucratic organizations, he argues that they should be the basis on which bureaucratic organizations and capacity-building interventions are designed. In a specific application of this perspective, he indicates that information technology is an effective means of taking advantage of formal and informal networks to increase productivity within African bureaucratic organizations. Information technology can be designed to be specific to tasks and to networks already in existence. Equally, information technology can bring task networks into existence by linking individuals within a given span of control in the performance of specific tasks. Peterson indicates that building on "what is" in terms of socially conditioned forms of interaction rather than on "what ought to be" in terms of Western organization theory is more likely to produce effective and efficient bureaucracies in the African context. This is a major challenge to most theories underlying organizational design reforms.

In Chapter 7, Charles N. Myers develops more universalistic principles for the development of specific kinds of organizations. He is concerned with how policy research institutes are created and sustained and explores this problem through the experiences of the Thailand Development Research Institute and the Bolivian Social Policy Analysis Unit. Research institutes such as these, developed in asso-

ciation with the public sector, face particular challenges and constraints in being able to provide useful and timely input into policy
decision making. As Myers indicates, they need to be concerned that
they are neither too far nor too close to government, that they are
seen as neutral purveyors of data and analyses to inform policy choice,
that they respond to both short-term and long-term needs for research and advice, and that they can survive politically, economically,
and intellectually.

Policy research institutes in Thailand and Bolivia successfully met
these challenges over the course of their first several years of existence. Myers compares the dynamics behind their creation, how they
attracted and motivated staff, how they defined their research programs and worked with international partners and assistance agencies to expand their capacities, and how they ensured their viability
and continued capacity to influence policy discussions in financial,
political, and intellectual terms. He relates the success of these organizations to their initiation under unusual circumstances and the ways
in which they met internal and external challenges. He argues that
the development of such institutes holds great promise for improving policy making in many countries and for introducing and sustaining innovations in public sector development initiatives. Persistence, effort, and luck are necessary for such institutes to survive and
to fulfill their promise, however. The context in which they must be
developed is often fraught with political risks and they are vulnerable to the quality of actors, actions, and events that surround their
creation and early development.

In Chapter 8, Manuel E. Contreras, an economist who became
responsible for assessing the efficiency, effectiveness, and equity of
social service provision in a very poor country, and the first director
of Bolivia's Social Policy Analysis Unit, reflects on the importance of
"getting off on the right step." Linking analysis of context and process and adopting the perspective of an "insider," Contreras focuses
on the external environment in which the policy unit was created
and sustained as well as on the nature of the internal incentive and
management systems put in place to encourage good performance
within the unit. In terms of the external environment, strong political support, the availability of the "godfathers" that Myers also refers
to, and the capacity to impress policy-relevant publics with the quality and relevance of research findings are central to Contreras' analysis.

Turning to the internal factors that contributed to the successful initiation of the policy unit, Contreras emphasizes the importance of organizational rules and management systems that reflect the kinds of tasks that organizations need to carry out. Thus, he argues, the quality of and commitment to research activities are enhanced when time pressure to produce results is high but rules about attendance and reporting relationships are flexible, when people work in teams, and when managers encourage links to broader research communities to promote skill development and a sense of community. Contreras confirms the findings of the Hilderbrand and Grindle study that management style, organizational culture, and nonmonetary rewards are important ingredients in the successful performance of public sector entities and suggests that they may be particularly critical factors in research units. He emphasizes the importance of the quality of strategic management decisions that Trostle, Sommerfeld, and Simon explore. He also adds further insight to the problematic nature of retention introduced by Cohen and Wheeler by demonstrating the positive benefits for government of high turnover in the research unit as young professionals sought overseas training opportunities and experienced professionals moved on to high-level positions in government.

In Chapter 9, Martha A. Chen adopts the framework presented by Hilderbrand and Grindle and extends the discussion of research capacity to NGOs. She notes the heightened interest in these organizations and the role they play in development as well as the contributions they make to issues of governance. For them to fulfill the high expectations that many have for the NGO sector, however, she argues that they must develop greater capacity to engage in policy debate and discussion and enhance their advocacy role. In order to do this, they must develop greater capacity to do policy-relevant research. This capacity building involves strengthening their technical and strategic skills to improve their own performance, provide information on the impact of policy on diverse constituencies, and become influential "players" in policy discussions about topics such as poverty, the environment, and gender inequalities.

In building policy analysis skills and research capacity, Chen finds that NGOs face the same constraints as the research units in government discussed by Myers and Contreras. Human resource development issues related to training, organizational management issues involving incentives and appropriate systems, and finding the institutional "space" to present and defend their perspectives are among the most important challenges they confront. She uses the case of the Bangladesh Rural Advancement Committee (BRAC) to argue that in addition to the problems associated with research institutes on a generic level, NGOs face a series of special challenges that have to do with the kinds of research they are able to undertake, the identification of appropriate (and often complex) analytic frameworks for research, and the hiring and retention of appropriately trained personnel for guiding and carrying out social science research. The task for those involved in building research capacity within the NGO sector, she concludes, is particularly important, particularly urgent, and particularly difficult.

Reforming Institutions

The foregoing chapters on efforts to strengthen organizations indicate that this task often involves redressing problems that originate outside individual organizations, such as cumbersome civil service rules, low pay scales, the counterproductive activities of other organizations, or the lack of systems that link several organizations in accomplishing complex tasks. Few can have witnessed or participated in capacity-building initiatives without being impressed by the extent to which organizations are deeply embedded in their environments and the extent to which this larger context must be considered in addressing their capacity. For this reason, capacity development often requires addressing problems of institutional reform.

Institutional reform means altering the rules of the game in which organizations and individuals make decisions and carry out activities. In this volume, we have adopted Douglass North's definition of institutions as "the rules of the game in a society; ...the humanly devised constraints that shape human interaction...[and] structure incentives in exchange, whether political, social, or economic."[14] Thus, capacity building through institutional reform would involve initiatives such as the development of legal systems, policy regimes, mechanisms of accountability, regulatory frameworks, and monitoring systems that transmit information about and structure the performance of markets, governments, and public officials. At the broadest level, institutional reform involves the structures that affect economic and political interaction and the way states relate to markets and civil society.

As indicated, much of the emphasis of capacity-building initiatives traditionally has focused on human resource development and on the organizations (or projects) that carry out specific tasks. In the 1980s and 1990s, however, as development concern shifted to greater awareness of the importance of the policy framework for development, the institutional aspect of capacity building began to acquire greater attention. Moreover, because so many efforts of the 1990s to strengthen government performance were driven by the objective of enhancing the operation of markets and the sustainability of democracy, major institutional reforms were undertaken in many countries. Their success or failure relates not only to the quality and acceptability of the new rules of the game, but also to their appropriateness to time and place, as subsequent chapters indicate. Three chapters address the question of the institutional reforms that affect the nature of public sector performance and the capacity of governments to undertake development-relevant activities. They describe the contexts and processes that contribute to capacity building.

In Chapter 10, Stephen E. Cornell and Joseph P. Kalt present an arresting case for the congruence of institutions of governance with more deeply embedded social or cultural notions of legitimate authority. Drawing data from American Indian tribes, the authors assess institutional forms that are effective in controlling rent-seeking behavior and solving collective action problems. In economic development, they argue, some societies provide legitimate institutions that create opportunities for the efficient production of public goods; others fail to produce such institutions or such outcomes. The difference, Cornell and Kalt argue, is in part the nature of the institutions—they must enable government to be a neutral and authoritative enforcer of rules. Equally important, however, is the extent to which such institutions are accepted as legitimate by society. Among American Indian tribes, although there are significant differences in institutions and governing principles, the authors indicate that economic development is facilitated when institutions are effective in controlling rent-seeking and enforcing rules and when there is a "fit" between culturally embedded notions of legitimacy and historically derived institutions of governance.

Cornell and Kalt assess institutions for self-government among two tribes that have been relatively successful developers, especially when their performance is compared to the large bulk of tribes that have failed to grow economically and that account for the poorest minority in the United States. The two tribes differ markedly in the structure of their formally constituted governments—one is a parliamentary democracy, the other is a traditional theocracy. What unites them is the extent to which their governing institutions have been effective in solving problems of collective action and in producing socially sanctioned rules of conduct for economic actors. That is, their institutions are culturally legitimate and supported by broader sets of societal norms. Cornell and Kalt's findings suggest that the search for efficient and effective rules of the game that contribute to sustained economic development must be simultaneously concerned with universally encountered problems of authority—encouraging coordination and enforcing stable rules of the game—and with culturally specific contexts that define norms of legitimate authority. The result of the search will lead, they argue, to different solutions to similar problems of governance.

In Chapter 11, Bruce R. Bolnick takes up a much more specific institutional problem. What kinds of rules are available and enforceable in a situation of almost complete fiscal collapse of government? Using Zambia as a case in point, he describes and assesses a new system for imposing fiscal discipline in a government threatened by hyperinflation and with no tradition of effective control of public expenditures. In this case, new rules for budgetary control that were imposed throughout the public sector helped the government to achieve some discipline in its monetary management and to improve the informational base for decision making about macroeconomic policy. The new rules sought to determine the actors involved in the process of fiscal control, control their actions as much as possible, and anticipate events that could undermine the discipline of the new system. The introduction of the cash budget system was a draconian measure, which Bolnick argues should not be maintained over a long time period, that was appropriate for the severe economic crisis the government was facing in 1993. It not only brought greater capacity to manage the macroeconomy, it increased public and investor confidence that the government was in control of the situation, despite severe cutbacks in public expenditures that were widely felt.

Bolnick describes how the cash budget system worked, the rules of the game that it imposed on fiscal management, and the ways in which this institutional innovation increased the capacity of the Zambian government to stabilize an economy. He also demonstrates how the side effects of the cash budget increased demand for information and focused attention on the poor revenue performance of the government. He provides an assessment of the costs of imposing a cash budget principle, including its impact on long-term policy and investment planning and the demands placed on the budget office and the central bank. He concludes, however, that the cash budget provides a simple and direct institutional innovation that can be applied to countries that, like Zambia, have experienced long-term economic decline and severe macroeconomic imbalances.

The cash budget was an institutional innovation that had systemwide repercussions. In a similar way, reforms in revenue generation, such as the tax modernization program analyzed by Graham Glenday in Chapter 12, require changes in a broad array of organizations and have systemic implications. Using the case of such a program in Kenya, Glenday argues that capacity-building efforts should be output-oriented in that they assess the value of inputs by their effectiveness in promoting specified outcomes, such as increased government revenue. He shows how developing an effective tax system requires multiple capacity-building interventions—from the creation of new legal and regulatory frameworks, to the design of computer-based information systems, to reforms in budgetary, personnel, and administrative systems. Because such projects deal with introducing new systemwide processes, they require choices about whether reforms will be general or specific, comprehensive or partial, and how they will be sequenced.

In the analysis of the Kenya Tax Modernization program, Glenday demonstrates that an output-oriented capacity-building intervention is most effective when it is specific, comprehensive, and properly sequenced. This adds layers of complexity to the reform, but, with initiatives that are built of multiple levels of capacity, comprehensiveness and coordination among multiple interventions are a key to success. Issues of sequencing, timing, and pacing of capacity-building efforts were critical to the enhanced revenue-generating capacity of the Kenyan government, particularly because reforms at various levels—training, organizational and administrative improvements, and legal and regulatory changes—reinforced each other and led to greater sustainability. Glenday concludes that systemwide reforms such as that undertaken in Kenya require a significant investment of time, a requirement that is frequently not met in donor-assisted programs. This conclusion provides a logical bridge to the final part of this volume, which focuses on the issue of technical assistance in developing public sector capacity.

PART THREE
THE ROLE OF TECHNICAL ASSISTANCE

This volume is the product of an initiative by the Harvard Institute for International Development (HIID) to assess the impact of many of its projects on capacity building in particular countries and to explore the more general lessons that could be derived from these and other experiences. As a result, most of our case studies reflect experiences of HIID in its more than thirty years of development advising and applied research. Over the years, HIID has worked in several countries, often on a sustained basis within individual countries. The core of these activities was always focused on the imperative to get good government, in the sense of developing human resources, strengthening organizations, and reforming institutions. Appropriately, then, this volume concludes with chapters that address an ongoing debate about the utility of technical assistance in capacity building.

Authors of the case studies in Part 3 assert that the design of technical assistance projects is an important factor in determining whether investments pay off in terms of increased capacity. Although this observation may appear self-evident, they find considerable cause for criticizing the design of the projects they have been involved in, which were often a result of processes of interaction and decision making explored in the Trostle, Sommerfeld, and Simon framework. Just as important, however, is the context within which the technical assistance project is carried out—the human resource capacity, the organizational characteristics, and institutional environment with which it must work. In each chapter, the authors look inward to the project and its underlying assumptions and processes of decision making and outward to the context within which it is embedded to assess the positive and negative contributions of such investments. Far from agreeing with those who attack technical assistance for capacity building as a waste of money and energy, the authors nevertheless caution against the easy assumptions of success that are all too often incorporated in project-level activities.

In Chapter 13, Albert R. Wight explores the difficult process through which recipients of technical assistance develop ownership and commitment to the goals of organizational development. He indicates that although participation in development projects has become an "apple pie" topic, acclaimed as an obvious benefit by all, few have focused on the way in which participation is encouraged and self-reliance and responsibility developed. Drawing on the literature in management, organizational behavior, training, and counseling, he assesses two projects in Pakistan in which extensive efforts were undertaken—even at the cost of immediate project pressures to "get the job done"—to encourage organizations and their managers to assume ownership of needed reforms. This chapter is significant in part because Wight provides a clear, process-oriented description of how the projects developed over time.

Wight concludes that development assistance projects focused on building capacity in developing countries are more in need of facilitators than they are of the kind of project managers who, all too often, focus narrowly on project outputs but ignore the deep cultural and incentive changes that need to be made for sustained development. The desire to improve the performance of organizations or projects in developing countries, he argues, must begin with recruiting and training different kinds of technical assistance staff and consultants. Narrow technical specialization, which is often sought in those who lead and carry out technical assistance missions, must be eschewed in favor of skills that have to do with communication, interaction, and process facilitation.

In Chapter 14, citing repeated failures of technical assistance to build capacity in the domain of policy analysis and implementation, Clive S. Gray is also cautionary about expectations in this regard. While reminding us that capacity building is usually not the sole and often not even the primary objective of technical assistance (providing direct policy advice may have a more direct and even more durable impact on a country's development), Gray insists it is or should be a key objective, and creative steps must be taken toward its fulfillment.

Questioning the "measurability" of technical assistance's contribution to capacity building, Gray raises issues of retention and utilization earlier discussed in chapters by Lippincott, Cohen and Wheeler, and Contreras. He goes on to stress the pervasive lack of interest and support for capacity building on the part of political leaders and agency managers pursuing short-term, opportunistic agendas. As a general rule, effective local demand for capacity building is unpredictable and even ephemeral. Hence, according to Gray, purveyors of technical assistance should take a flexible view of their mandate, pursuing targets of opportunity by assisting those agencies where demand emerges and investing in talent wherever it can be found, in or outside the nominal host agency.

In Chapter 15, William Bikales is also critical of the technical assistance for capacity building. He takes the case of macroeconomic management in a transitional economy, Mongolia, and demonstrates the ways in which donor-assisted programs can become part of the problem rather than part of the solution. In a country undergoing a transition from a planned to a market economy, he argues, conditions should be promising for effective technical assistance. The nature of all government activities is being fundamentally reassessed; recipient governments are more willing than usual to accept the advice of outsiders, having initiated the process of change themselves; and training activities are likely to be unusually effective because of the generally good level of educational development achieved under socialist governments of the past. Because of such conditions, Mongolia and other transitional countries can serve as test cases of the utility of technical assistance.

Despite many favorable expectations, Bikales found that the urgency of reform was undermined by donor interventions that drew time and effort away from the central concerns of economic policy reform in Mongolia. In addition, he found that the nature of the reform program remained contentious among individuals and organizations within government and ideological and stakeholder resistance undermined the progress of reform. Moreover, rivalries over policy and institutional "turf" among agencies and donors and the frequent failure to locate projects in the most appropriate organizations contributed to the strengthening of opposition to reform. In addition, donors were often driven by their own goal of maintaining influence in the reform process, which undermined their capacity to channel resources most effectively. To be more successful, capacity-building initiatives must center on organizations that are ideologically supportive of reform and foreign assistance must be carefully assessed in terms of the political impact it will have in promoting or hindering reform. Bikales joins Clive S. Gray in indicating that technical assistance projects should seek counterparts on the basis of reform commitment and maintain flexibility for dealing with failure, moving assistance activities to alternative organizations if reform commitment is not maintained, and focusing attention on committed reformers wherever they are found in government.

CONCLUSIONS

The creation of capable states is a challenge confronting several countries around the world. Although many adopted significant economic and political reforms in the 1980s and 1990s, most continued to suffer from a lag in the capacity of the state to carry out functions that are required by market economies and political democracies. In the wake of the economic and political reforms of the past decade or so, development specialists became increasingly interested in the need to improve government performance. Getting good government became a more explicit imperative.

Chapters in this volume focus on efforts to build state capacity in support of markets and democracy. They leave little ambiguity about the difficulty of the process of change, however. Getting good government requires time, commitment, innovative ideas, consensus building, changed behavior and norms for those who work in the public sector, new rules of the game, efficient design and resource allocation in technical assistance, and probably considerable good luck. As many contributors to this volume demonstrate, interventions to develop more capable states require analytic tools that explore the roots of poor performance and that provide insights into the process of change. They also demonstrate that building state capacity also requires effective efforts to develop human resource capacity, particularly among technical and professional staff; organizational strengthening initiatives, particularly those focused on incentive and managerial systems; and institutional reforms, particularly those that address underlying constraints on government to contribute more effectively to the development of a country. Additionally, some contributors stress the positive role that technical assistance projects can play in building public sector capacity, but they are clear that these interventions can be effective only when the projects themselves are well designed and the environments in which they are introduced are conducive to change. Getting good government is a lengthy, laborious, and multifaceted process, fraught with opportunities for failure and misspent resources.

In contrasting many of the economic reforms of the 1980s and 1990s with the imperative to improve government performance through a second generation of reforms, Moisés Naím has written that "the heroes of the next wave of reform will not be a handful of powerful technocrats well versed in the complexities of macroeconomic management. Rather, they will be a myriad of midlevel public managers adroitly building the indispensable organizational structures and logistics to run the state."[15] These "heroes" need to be supported by development specialists, both academics and practitioners, who design and implement capacity-building interventions to improve the performance of government in a wide range of activities. Their work will probably not be as well noted as the high-profile activities of the economic technocrats who played critical roles in the first generation of reforms, but ultimately, their contributions will be as important in improving the potential for sustainable development of countries in all regions of the world.

NOTES

1   João Guilherme Merquior, "A Panoramic View of the Rebirth of Liberalisms," *World Development* 21,8 (1993):1265.

2   Merilee S. Grindle, "Sustaining Economic Recovery in Latin America: State Capacity, Markets, and Politics," in Graham Bird and Ann Helwege, eds., *Latin America's Economic Future* (London: Academic Press, 1994): 304.

3   Ensuring greater efficiency and effectiveness—improving the link between cost and impact—is perhaps the most frequently cited need for public sectors that are often characterized by high cost and low achievement. Governments, however, particularly those that claim to be democratic, must also be capable of being responsive to the needs of citizens and encouraging their participation in the design and delivery of public goods. On public sector performance more generally, see Milton J. Esman, *Management Dimensions of Development: Perspectives and Strategies* (West Hartford, CT: Kumarian Press, 1991). See also Arthur Goldsmith, "Institutions, Planned Development, and Socioeconomic Change," *Public Administration Review* 42,6 (1992).

4   Moisés Naím, "Latin America's Journey to the Market: From Macroeconomic Shocks to Institutional Therapy," *ICEG Occasional Paper* 62, International Center for Economic Growth (San Francisco: ICS Press, 1995). See also Tony Killick, *A Reaction Too Far: Economic Theory and the Role of the State in Developing Countries* (London: Overseas Development Institute, 1989); and Paul Streeten, "Markets and States: Against Minimalism," *World Development* 21,8 (1993).

5   See Esman, *Management Dimensions of Development*.

6   See Chapter 3 of this volume, James A. Trostle, Johannes U. Sommerfeld, and Jonathon L. Simon, "Strengthening Human Resource Capacity in Developing Countries: Who Are the Actors? What Are Their Actions?"

7   See Chapter 9 of this volume, Martha A. Chen, "Building Research Capacity in the Nongovernmental Organization Sector."

8   See Chapter 10 of this volume, Stephen E. Cornell and Joseph P. Kalt, "Successful Economic Development and Heterogeneity of Governmental Form on American Indian Reservations."

9   For a useful review of this history, see Peter Morgan, "Capacity Building: An Overview" (paper prepared for a workshop on capacity development at the Institute on Governance, Ottawa, Canada, November 22-23, 1993). See also Esman, *Management Dimensions of Development.*

10 See Morgan, "Capacity Building."

11 For additional insights into the progression of thinking about government capacity, see Mick Moore, *Institution Building as a Development Assistance Method: A Review of Literature and Ideas* (Stockholm: Swedish International Development Authority, 1995).

12 For a divergent opinion, see John M. Cohen, "Capacity Building in the Public Sector: A Focused Framework for Analysis and Action," *International Review of Administrative Sciences* 61,3 (1995).

13 See especially, Eliot J. Berg, *Rethinking Technical Cooperation: Reforms for Capacity Building in Africa* (Washington, DC: United Nations Development Programme/Development Alternatives, Inc., 1993); and Edward V. K. Jaycox, "Capacity Building: The Missing Link in African Development" (transcript of address to the African-American Institute Conference, African Capacity Building: Effective and Enduring Partnerships, Reston, VA, May 20, 1993).

14 Douglass North, *Institutions, Institutional Change and Economic Performance* (Cambridge: Cambridge University Press, 1990), 3.

15 Naím, "Latin America's Journey to the Market," 12.

PART I

ASSESSING CAPACITY-BUILDING NEEDS
CONCEPTUAL MAPS

2 BUILDING SUSTAINABLE CAPACITY IN THE PUBLIC SECTOR

WHAT CAN BE DONE?

Mary E. Hilderbrand and Merilee S. Grindle

Why have many countries been unable to promote and sustain economic and social development over extended periods of time? In recent years, one response to this question has been emphatic: because governments have failed to fashion appropriate roles for the state in development; they have been unable to organize and manage systems that identify problems, formulate policies to respond to them, implement activities in pursuit of policy goals, and sustain these activities over time. Development has not occurred, many have argued, because governments have hindered rather than promoted development.[1]

Reflecting an analysis that singled out the state as the culprit in the poor performance of many developing countries, policy prescriptions of the 1980s emphasized the need to reduce radically the extent of government action in the economy; a minimalist notion of the state, largely defined in terms of what it should not do, characterized much of this decade. Experience in implementing these policies, however, indicated that while state minimalism responded to real problems of overcentralized decision making, overzealous regulation, inappropriate incentives for public sector enterprises, and distorted markets, it failed to give enough attention to the need for *capable* states if markets are to operate effectively and efficiently.[2] Moreover, with the publication of the first *Human Development Report* by the United Nations Development Programme (UNDP) in 1990, and with mounting pressure from developing countries and nongovernmental organizations (NGOs) to attend to the social consequences of economic crisis and structural adjustment measures, the notion of a social agenda for the state gathered increased support.[3] The importance of legitimizing new democracies added further weight to the arguments for responding to social needs. Similarly, the notion of sustainable development underscored the need for states that could take action to protect the environment, regulate markets, and promote social policies to alleviate poverty.[4]

Effective government performance thus became central to a changed definition of the role of the state in development and to its ability to create the institutional conditions for market-oriented economies, secure and productive populations, and democratic political systems. Despite these imperatives, knowledge about how to improve public sector capacity remains uncertain; research indicates that large numbers of capacity-development initiatives have produced only meager results. In fact, in recent years, a variety of international agencies have produced reports indicating that investments in capacity-building initiatives have not paid off in terms of improved effectiveness overall or higher levels of organizational or individual performance.[5]

The general paucity of positive capacity-building experiences derives in part from a set of implicit assumptions that underlie many such initiatives: that organizations or training activities are the logical site for capacity-building initiatives; that administrative structures and monetary rewards determine organizational and individual performance; that organizations work well when structures and control mechanisms are in place; and that individual performance improves as a result of skill and technology transfer through training activities. These assumptions need critical examination.

Are organizational strengthening or training activities the most efficient means to develop capacity? Capacity-building initiatives focusing on organizations and training activities typically rest on the belief that the binding constraints on performance can be effectively addressed by organizations or their employees.[6] Yet organizations and trained individuals do not perform in a vacuum; their ability to carry out assigned responsibilities is deeply affected by the broader contexts within which they operate. Moreover, the degree and type of constraints on organizational and individual performance vary from country to country and over time for any given country. Indeed, in some countries, performance problems diagnosed at the organizational or individual level may be so deeply embedded in economic, social, and political deficiencies that efforts to improve performance must focus primarily on these conditions. Although the importance of the broader contextual setting for organizational and individual activities may seem obvious, many capacity-building initiatives are in fact designed without regard for this environment.

Are administrative structures and monetary rewards effective determinants of public sector performance? Capacity-building initiatives that focus on civil service and public employment reform often give particular attention to structures such as pay scales and conditions of employment. In recent years, these reforms have generally been undertaken for reasons of fiscal discipline.[7] Even where they have been undertaken to improve performance, however, they rest on the belief that performance will improve when public servants are well paid, have well-defined responsibilities, and work within well-structured hierarchies, rules, and procedures. Nevertheless, recent research indicates that such reforms do not result in improved output unless they restructure public sector management systems to be performance- and results-oriented. This has become an important starting point for "reinventing government" in the United States and other industrialized countries, but has yet to influence civil service reform efforts in developing countries.

Do structures and control mechanisms within organizations contribute to good performance? Ultimately, of course, capacity-building initiatives must be reflected in organizations that are better able to carry out the responsibilities assigned to them. Typically, interventions designed to raise organizational performance focus on improving systems for accomplishing particular tasks, introducing new technology, increasing monetary incentives for personnel, and strengthening accountability and control mechanisms. However, organizational culture is more important as a determinant of performance than structures for remuneration and control. Most organizations that perform well are ones that have cultures stressing flexibility, problem solving, participation, teamwork, shared professional norms, and a strong sense of mission. Moreover, despite the evidence that the roots of performance deficits often lie outside the purview of specific organizations charged with accomplishing particular tasks, organizational culture can compensate for constraints that are rooted in more general problems.

Does training focused on skill and technology transfer lead to better performance among public servants? Typically, training activities focus largely on increasing skill levels, particularly those skills necessary for the adoption of new technologies.[8] Yet public servants in a broad range of countries and organizations regularly complain that they do not have meaningful work to do, that the skills they have are not effectively employed in their jobs, and that the quality of their performance is irrelevant to their career development. These complaints suggest that human resource constraints are more likely to derive from the failure to provide people with meaningful jobs and to utilize their skills effectively than from problems related to training per se. Again, the assumptions underlying many capacity-building initiatives may focus attention on interventions that do not generate the most payoff in terms of improved performance.

Each of the assumptions discussed above is called into question by the findings of research carried out in six countries and reported in this chapter. The purpose of the research was to test an analytic framework for identifying capacity gaps and designing intervention strategies. In the following pages, we describe a framework, or conceptual map, that emphasizes the "embedded" nature of training activities, organizational performance, and administrative structures in the public sector. When it was applied in the six case-study countries—Bolivia, the Central African Republic, Ghana, Morocco, Sri Lanka, and Tanzania—the framework proved useful in identifying capacity gaps and in providing a tool for the strategic design of interventions that are sensitive to the roots of performance deficits.[9]

FRAMEWORK FOR ASSESSING CAPACITY GAPS

For our study, we defined capacity as the ability to perform appropriate tasks effectively, efficiently, and sustainably. In turn, capacity building refers to improvements in the ability of public sector organizations, either singly or in cooperation with other organizations, to perform appropriate tasks.[10] Beyond a basic set of irreducible public sector functions—establishing law and order and setting the rules of the game for economic and political interaction, for example—we did not specify a universal list of what such tasks are. Appropriate tasks are those defined by necessity, history, or the situation in specific contexts. Thus, in putting the concept into operation for research, tasks must be specified and assessed for their appropriateness within a given country.

Similarly, measures of effectiveness, efficiency, and sustainability must be specified. Because many factors affecting the outcome of public sector activities are beyond the control of particular interventions, indicators of capacity need to be identified in terms of a series of task-specific questions: Was the task effectively identified? Were appropriate actions put in place to achieve the task? Were skilled human resources assigned to accomplish the task? Were resources used efficiently to accomplish the task? Was the ability to accomplish the task sustained over time? These are difficult questions to answer in most cases, but they are much more tractable to deal with than questions such as whether the gross national product grew or infant mortality declined in response to specific interventions.

Tasks can be defined very narrowly and involve the actions of one organization or organizational unit. Many public sector tasks important to development, however, require the coordinated action of several organizations. In this case, we refer to networks of organizations involved in performing particular tasks. Research on the capacity to perform a particular task often focuses on the activities of a particular organization, but such an effort must include a map of the range of organizations involved in a task network.

Our framework identifies five dimensions, and correspondingly, five levels of analysis, that affect capacity and capacity-building interventions. They incorporate a panorama of factors that affect the ability of organizations to achieve specified goals. The five dimensions are presented schematically in Figure 2-1. As indicated, these dimensions of capacity are interactive and dynamic.

■ The *action environment* sets the economic, political, and social milieux in which governments carry out their activities. The performance of development tasks can be significantly affected by conditions in the action environment such as the rate and structure of economic growth, the degree of political stability and legitimacy of government, and the human resource profile of a country. Figure 2-1 indicates several of the factors that are most likely to have an impact on public sector capacity. Interventions to improve conditions in an action environment take a long time to

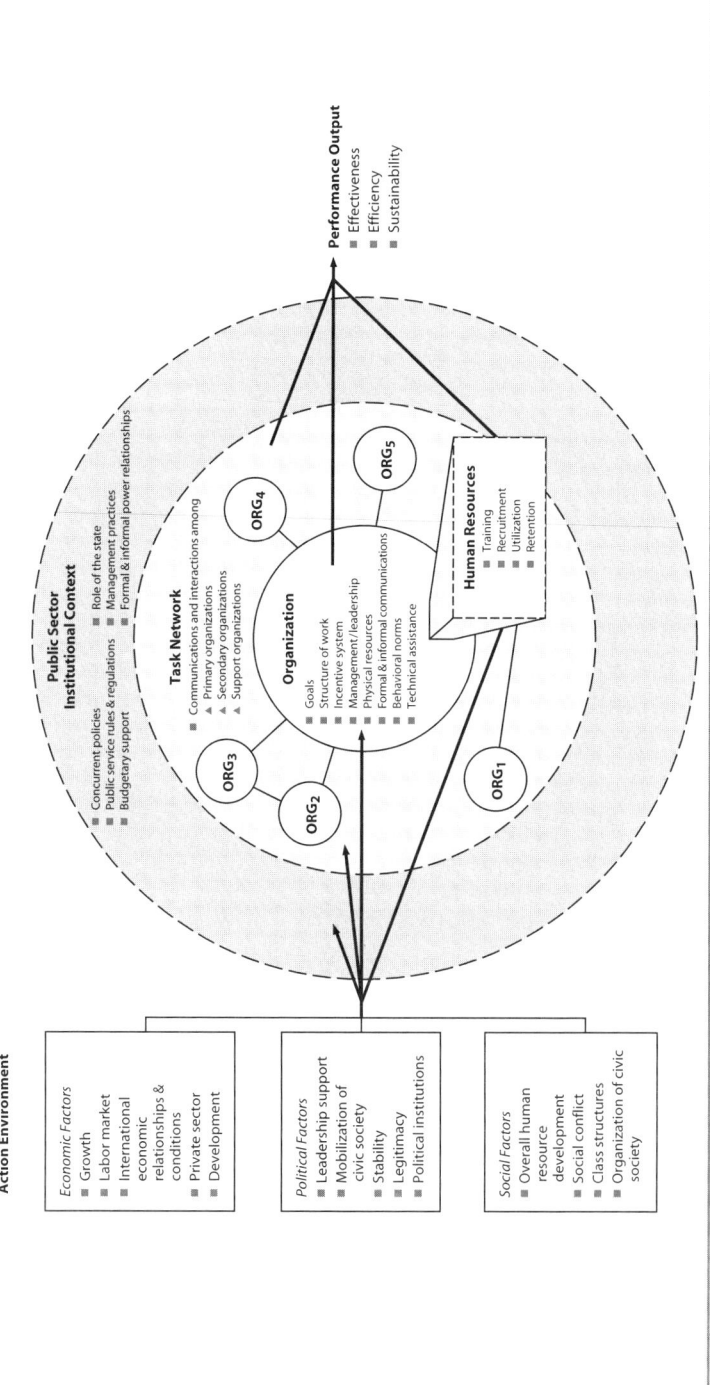

FIGURE 2-1
Dimensions of Capacity

produce results because they attempt to alter basic economic, political, and social structures.

■ The *institutional context of the public sector* includes such factors as the rules and procedures set for government operations and public officials, the financial resources government has to carry out its activities, the responsibilities that government assumes for development initiatives, concurrent policies, and structures of formal and informal influence that affect how the public sector functions. This context can constrain or facilitate the accomplishment of particular tasks.

■ The *task network* refers to the set of organizations involved in accomplishing any given task. Performance is affected by the extent to which such networks encourage communication and coordination and the extent to which individual organizations within the network are able to carry out their responsibilities effectively. Networks can be composed of organizations within and outside of the public sector, including NGOs and private sector organizations. Primary organizations have a central role in performing a given task; secondary organizations are essential to the work of the primary organizations; and supporting organizations provide important services or support that enable a task to be performed.[11]

■ *Organizations* are the building blocks of the task network and the vantage point from which diagnostic research is usually carried out. The structures, processes, resources, and management styles of organizations affect how they establish goals, structure work, define authority relations, and provide incentives structures. These factors promote or constrain performance because they affect organizational output and shape the behavior of those who work within them.

■ A fifth dimension of capacity focuses on how *human resources* are educated and attracted to public sector careers and the utilization and retention of individuals as they pursue such careers. This dimension focuses particularly on managerial, professional, and technical talent and the extent to which training and career trajectories affect the overall performance of a given task. Figure 2-1 illustrates the interconnectedness of organizational performance and human resources.

In Bolivia, the Central African Republic, Ghana, Morocco, Sri Lanka, and Tanzania, national researchers assessed how and to what extent factors at each level affected the ability to perform particular tasks. We identified the tasks to be studied by first selecting two broad functions that governments are called upon to perform—management of the macroeconomy and delivery of services. For each, we further specified tasks that must be performed if the overall function is to be carried out. For the macroeconomic function, researchers assessed the capacity of the six governments to formulate a budget. For the service delivery function, they assessed the capacity of the governments of Ghana, Morocco, and Sri Lanka to deliver agricultural extension services and the ability of the governments of Bolivia, the Central African Republic, and Tanzania to deliver maternal and child health services. Our concern was to identify factors that constrained or facilitated the ability to perform these development tasks effectively, efficiently, and sustainably and to be able to assess what kinds of interventions would be most efficient in correcting for capacity gaps.[12]

The research process involved a series of steps that were common to all six country cases. For each task, researchers first developed a map of the organizations involved in accomplishing particular tasks. Then, the researcher looked outward from this task network to assess the contextual factors that were important in affecting how the task was performed. This assessment involved an analysis of the public sector institutional context and the broader action environment. As a third step in the research, at least two organizations within each task network were selected for study, based on their centrality to the performance of that task. Once the organizations were selected, research focused on them and their human resources. Then, the researchers returned to assess the institutional context and the action environment in terms of their influence on the organizations studied and their ability to maximize available human resources. The studies used a variety of methodologies, including interviews with key informants, documentary research, and organizational mapping.

FINDINGS: CAPACITY GAPS AND REMEDIES

The studies demonstrate the extent to which performance can be constrained by a wide variety of factors. They also indicate the extent to which the five dimensions of capacity are interdependent. In general, interventions to improve performance are most difficult to make and take the longest time-horizon to demonstrate results at the broadest level of the action environment. Constraints that occur at the level of the organizational network, the organization itself, or the preparation and use of human resources are likely to be much more tractable and remedied more quickly. Nevertheless, an important finding of the studies is that remedies introduced at the human resource, organizational, or interorganizational level may not produce improvements if constraints along other dimensions of capacity are more binding. We will indicate the findings of the case study research for each of the dimensions and their implications for capacity-building intervention strategies.

Action Environment

Development tasks are carried out within complex environments; this fact often is acknowledged but frequently overlooked in the design of capacity-building interventions. The case studies clearly indicate that the action environment is a critical dimension in constraining or facilitating the ability of governments to perform development tasks. Our studies cover a range of possibilities. In Morocco, a relatively high level of economic development, a far-reaching educational system, and a stable and legitimate political system worked together to create an environment conducive to relatively effective performance by government. In contrast, in the Central African Republic, a series of repressive, patrimonial regimes and successive military coups, a very low level of human development, and extended periods of economic stagnation created conditions in which the potential for effective public sector performance was nonexistent. Sri Lanka's postindependence investment in education and human development led to the creation of a highly qualified pool of human resources for the government. Beginning in the 1970s, however, ethnic conflict, a lowering of educational quality, and increasing politicization of the public service undermined this traditionally strong public sector capacity.

Our studies confirmed what is widely documented elsewhere in terms of the impact of the economic crisis of the 1980s on public sector capacity. All six countries were hurt, though to varying degrees, by falling real income levels for government employees that resulted in a combination of brain drain and siphoning off of time and energy devoted to government jobs.[13] Governments' inability to pay for supplies, equipment, and vehicles for the work that needed to be done also hurt performance. In Ghana, low salaries and salary compression led to the loss of many of the best public officials and seriously constrained the government's ability to train new entrants into the public service. In Tanzania, loss of qualified people and diversion of officials' attention and energy to additional income-generating activities had a direct negative impact on the capacity of the public sector. Brain drain was a major problem in Ghana, Sri Lanka, and Tanzania.

Our cases also point to several broad political factors, less well documented in other studies, that had a substantial impact on capacity. The Central African Republic was a case of extreme political dysfunction, in which even the most routine and simple tasks could not be carried out because of instability and illegitimate and ineffective political institutions.[14] Ghana's years of military rule, marked by numerous coups, similarly had a negative effect on the capacity that had been built before and just after independence. In Tanzania, a low level of participation by society in public decision making severely limited the ability of the government to design and implement appropriate programs. The six cases also suggest a mixed relationship between democracy and capacity. In postindependence Sri Lanka, broad participation in the political system was consistent with building a capable public service and making long-term investments in human development. In contrast, however, the cases of Bolivia and the Central African Republic showed that democracy is also compatible, at least in the short run, with high levels of politicization and inefficiency. Potentially positive effects of political liberalization on the environment for capacity building might be anticipated, but only over a longer period of time. In addition, individual political leaders in the Central African Republic, Sri Lanka, and Tanzania had a direct impact on strengthening or weakening public sector capacity.

The cases confirm that a low level of human resource development and extensive social conflict are among the most important causes of large capacity gaps. It is hard to escape the comparison between Morocco and Sri Lanka, on the one hand, where long traditions of investing in health and education resulted in strong human development profiles and higher levels of capacity, and the Central African Republic and Bolivia on the other, where there was an equally strong tradition of poorly funded and ineffective investment in human development and much greater difficulty in finding good professionals for the public service. Similarly, where human resource development was higher, populations were more able to demand effective performance from government. High levels of social conflict were extremely detrimental to capacity, as evidenced by the case of Sri Lanka, in which long-existing capacity was undermined, and the case of the Central African Republic, which never was able to develop such capacity.

As might be expected, the factors that contributed to poor and good performance tended to "go together" in the sense that low growth, political instability, and low human resource development were found in those countries with the weakest overall performance and the best performers had much more positive profiles along all these dimensions. In addition, we also found that conditions in the action environment were not static, but could and did change over time. In particular, economic crisis and stagnation caused capacity to deteriorate. On the other hand, in Bolivia, Ghana, and Tanzania, increased political stability, political liberalization, and changes in political leadership were creating new opportunities for capacity building.

Most important to assessing capacity gaps, the case studies indicate that the action environment was much more important as a constraint in some countries than in others. The Central African Republic left little doubt that until basic conditions of economic development, political commitment, and social stability are put in place, little can be done along other dimensions that would contribute to improving public sector performance. In Morocco, by contrast, capacity-building initiatives would not need to pay much attention to improving a generally positive or at least benign action environment. In the other cases, while the action environment was far from ideal, interventions at other levels could do much to redress the capacity gaps that were identified.

Where the action environment is particularly dysfunctional to development, improving conditions at this level is a vital first step. In countries such as the Central African Republic, effective capacity development may be limited in the foreseeable future to actions that contribute over the longer term to the creation of human resources, the development of social consensus, and the potential for the private sector and NGOs to perform functions that government cannot accomplish.

Even where the action environment is not fully binding on public sector performance, its contributions to capacity gaps must be assessed and intervention strategies along other dimensions designed with an eye to how such contextual factors can affect or even derail those interventions. Moreover, adverse conditions in the action environment generally have very immediate implications for public sector performance: they limit the financial and human resources available to even well-intentioned and stable governments. Ultimately, all countries will build sustainable public sector capacity only when they promote broad-based economic growth strategies, invest adequately in human development, and develop stable and legitimate political institutions that are effective in mediating economic and social conflict. Assessments of the action environment can also identify factors that are particularly supportive of capacity-building interventions, such as the existence of favorable labor market conditions or reformist political leadership.

Institutional Context of the Public Sector

We were not surprised to discover that all six countries shared problems connected with the nature of public sector employment: low salary levels in the public service as a whole, lack of effective performance standards, inability to fire people, too few rewards for good performance, recruitment procedures that did not attract appropriately trained people, and promotion patterns based too much on seniority or patronage and too little on performance. These conditions have been widely documented in discussions of public sector failure in recent years. Changing them, as opposed to finding ways to compensate for or maneuver around them, requires action at the level of public sector institutions in general.

The case studies show quite clearly that inadequate budgetary support affected capacity primarily through its impact on both public sector salary levels and funding for operating expenses and investment. Even in Morocco and Sri Lanka, where salaries had not fallen as seriously as in the other cases, researchers noted that salary erosion was important in undermining previously existing capacity. The vast systems and programs required for service delivery to the grassroots suffered severely from shortages of funds for programs, vehicles, buildings and maintenance, equipment and supplies of needed materials, along with salaries and incentives for employees. The findings of the Tanzanian case are particularly telling; a national infrastructure suitable for delivering basic health services to a large part of the population lay wasted and little used for lack of personnel, medicines, vehicles, and equipment. In several countries, there were large performance discrepancies between regions or tasks that had donor support and ones that had to rely on the government budget.

Economic reform programs were a major component of the public sector institutional context in all six countries, but they had mixed effects for capacity. Financial stabilization policies included a combination of budget austerity, which held down public sector salaries, and price and exchange rate policies, which tended to increase prices for the urban middle class. Austerity meant tight budgets for ministries' operating expenses and investment.[15] At the same time, however, the reforms emphasized improving the policy framework for macroeconomic management and strengthening the capacity of organizations that contribute directly to the ability to manage the macroeconomy or, in some cases, high-priority sectors such as agriculture. In Morocco and Ghana, in particular, the preparation of the budget improved significantly under structural adjustment programs and donor assistance. Similarly, the delivery of agricultural extension services improved in these two countries. In contrast, low-priority areas in all the countries, often including the delivery of social services, were neglected, and thus weakened.

Traditionally, development administration has paid much attention to setting up the rules, regulations, and procedures that define and structure public sector activities and conditions of employment. Our cases, however, indicate that the impact of rules, regulations, and procedures on supporting or constraining performance is two-edged. On the one hand, effective rules and procedures for getting things done and getting them done right are essential for day-to-day functioning and for being able to confront longer-term development challenges. Bolivia, for example, had a poorly evolved public administration that had considerable difficulty managing the daily operations of government. On the other hand, these rules and procedures can lead to inflexibility and unduly complicated requirements that actually stand in the way of accomplishing important tasks. Morocco was caught in this dilemma, with a highly developed public administration that at the same time was often "seized up" by its rules, regulations, and hierarchy. It worked, but slowly, ponderously, and not as well as it should have.

Our case studies confirmed the findings of several other studies in terms of the impact of administrative reforms such as cutting back on the size of the public service.[16] They had important and often negative consequences for public sector capacity. Voluntary and incentive-led retirement programs, for example, tended to result in the loss of the best people in government, as those with the best chances of finding good employment on the outside opted for the incentive. This problem was particularly serious in Sri Lanka. Moreover, continual increases in the numbers of planned layoffs contributed to a climate of uncertainty and low morale in other countries, especially Tanzania. Although diminishing the size of the public service may be important to improve performance, in the case-study countries cutbacks were carried out primarily to generate a net improvement in the budget deficit, not to develop capacity.

Public sector capacity in the six countries was affected in important ways by changes in roles assigned to the state. For example, privatization of crop marketing and seed provision changed the context for agricultural extension and encouraged greater attention to the central task of extension. In Ghana and Morocco, these changes and a renewed emphasis on agricultural production allowed the extension services to focus more directly on assistance to production. Nevertheless, incomplete consensus on newly defined roles for the state contributed to slow institutional change in some countries.

Conditions in this context clearly set parameters for what organizations can and cannot accomplish. In some of our cases, these parameters were so constraining that little could be done unless they were first addressed. Tanzania was one such case. In other cases, the parameters were wide enough that concerns about capacity could be attacked at other levels, if changing this context was a particularly onerous task. Bolivia might fit this situation. In Sri Lanka, Morocco, and Ghana, the institutional context could be addressed at the same time that other levels of intervention were considered. In all cases, however, some attention needed to be given to strengthening this context.

Much conventional practice has focused on creating detailed sets of rules, procedures, and other mechanisms to control the activities of public organizations and the behavior of public officials. In contrast, our research suggests the utility of focusing on a very few basic conditions that affect performance in the public sector institutional context. First, salaries must be provided that will attract qualified, capable people to the public service. At a minimum, public servants must know that they will make enough money to live on, regardless of any other benefits of working for the public sector.[17] Salary levels alone do not necessarily attract qualified people to the public sector, however; alternatives for employment and the degree of status and professional identity associated with government work are also important factors. Second, some minimal level of structures and processes must be in place. Organizational structures, job descriptions, hiring procedures, reporting relationships, supply lines, and information systems must exist at some basic level before other kinds of interventions will "pay off" in terms of improved performance. Mindful of the considerable potential for public administrations to become "seized up," rigid, and unresponsive, however, the emphasis should be on creating the basic infrastructure of the public sector in terms of a minimum set of structured relationships.

Beyond these basics, our studies indicate that changes in the public sector institutional context should focus efforts on initiatives that will improve performance at individual and organizational levels. Although many recent reforms have focused on size of the public service, pay scales, and conditions of employment, these issues appear to be necessary but not sufficient conditions for improved performance. In terms of encouraging public officials to become more efficient and effective in their positions, standards for good performance need to be set and then used consistently as instruments of personnel management. Organizations need greater autonomy to hire and fire personnel within general standards set for the public service. Recruitment procedures and norms for professional behavior need to be developed that confer status and identity on public servants and that allow organizations to monitor, evaluate, and enforce such standards. This strongly implies movement away from patronage-based or formalistic merit criteria in recruitment, assignment, and promotion and away from highly centralized systems. It suggests that specific skills, managerial talent, "fit" to the position, and record of performance must become the criteria for admission and advancement in public sector careers and that organizations should be the implementers of these criteria. To improve organizational commitment to performance, rules must be straightforward and consistent to ensure transparency and fairness, but they must also provide organizations with clear performance standards, room to maneuver in solving problems, and control over decisions that are central to producing the results they are responsible for.

Task Network

In the six cases, complex networks for task performance involved many public sector organizations and international agencies such as the World Bank, the International Monetary Fund, donor agencies, and donor projects. At times, they also included private sector organizations and NGOs—both local and foreign. They involved organizations at the center and units at lower levels of administration, as well as regional or provincial government organizations. Weaknesses in these networks that constrained performance came from two sources: the absence of organizations to fill needed roles for any given task, or inadequate performance of those roles; and the lack of effective interactions among organizations in the network.

For example, the budget process in several countries was severely hampered in the central budget office by the inability, or the varying abilities, of operational ministries to provide accurate spending information or formulate budget proposals. This problem was significant in Bolivia, Ghana, Morocco, and Tanzania. In the latter case, the weakness of ministries reporting to the ministry of finance was further compounded by the inability of regional and local governments to produce budget proposals or to monitor expenditures. In Tanzania, these weaknesses were so extensive that the budget process was a mere "house of cards."

We found that lack of effective interaction among organizations in the task network could occur with regard to many different interactions that are important to performance. Coordination among those individuals who set policy and those who implement it is critical if an overall policy framework is to guide development tasks. In service delivery in particular, coordination is required if the service is to reach its intended beneficiaries. Coordination among different providers, including separate government programs, private organizations, and donor projects presents particular challenges. In addition, the quality of human resources can be affected by interactions between training institutions and the organizations that need well-trained staff.

In agricultural extension and maternal and child health, the lack of effective links between center and field, policy and implementation, intent and resources, and training and skill needs were in evidence in all the countries we studied. In Ghana and Morocco, inadequate coordination plagued agricultural extension. In Sri Lanka, decentralization caused a temporary breakdown in the delivery of extension services, as newly responsible units had to create a new task network to ensure that activities were actually accomplished.

Often, the problem was that communication within a task network occurred in one direction only. This problem characterized maternal and child health care in the Central African Republic and

Tanzania, where a central organization transmitted directions to lower-level units and did not allow them any input into decisions about program design and implementation. Training and recruitment functions did not allow for input from client organizations in budget formulation in Bolivia and Morocco or maternal and child health programs in Bolivia and Tanzania. In contrast, the ministry of agriculture in Morocco helped shape what was included in the curriculum of its training programs, and it also had a better capacity to match job openings with the qualifications of recruits. As a result, extension services were supplied with staff with more appropriate training.

Just as weaknesses in the task network can impede performance, effective interactions can support good performance. To remedy a coordination problem in Ghana, agricultural extension services were reorganized to clarify reporting relationships and emphasize coordination among numerous service providers in the public and private sectors. Greater coordination between policy and implementation was also stressed. A communications and training unit was established to coordinate research, extension, and training. In Morocco, multidisciplinary teams were created to facilitate links between the center and lower levels of the extension services through mentoring, supervision, and transfer of technical expertise.

Capacity-building interventions at the level of the task network are more easily targeted than those that focus on the public sector as a whole. Furthermore, such interventions do not necessarily have to encompass an entire task network to make a difference, but can target those parts of it where specific weaknesses have been identified. Thus, efforts to strengthen task networks should target the most critical weaknesses: Does an overall policy framework specify objectives and mechanisms for particular tasks? Which are the weakest organizations in the task network and how important are they to the performance of the task? Where do communication and coordination break down in the interactions among organizations?

Where serious problems exist in the coordination and communication among organizations, our studies strongly indicate that tinkering with organization charts will not produce effective results. Capacity builders need to create active mechanisms for interaction and coordination. Formal means of communication and coordination can be created, such as high-level and technical-level coordination committees, interlocking boards of directors or advisors, joint workshops and seminars, and relocating offices or improving technology so that communication is physically easier. Informal communications can be stimulated to supplement and support these formal interactions. "Turf battles," particularly those stimulated by the focus of donor funding on some activities but not on others in the same network, were clearly counterproductive to improved performance in our cases. Friendly competitions, on the other hand, were effective in stimulating more effective interactions.

Mechanisms to promote greater coordination must be task specific. For example, greater coordination within the budget function could be stimulated by oversight committees that bring high-level officials together to discuss progress and problems or by joint training activities among technical staff. Coordination of service delivery tasks can be facilitated by stimulating the organization of client groups and by more intense "visiting back and forth" between field offices and ministry headquarters. An important objective of all such mechanisms is that communications become multidirectional and dense, and focused on task performance and problem solving.

Organizations

The framework emphasizes the embedded nature of organizations. Because of many factors outside their control, failures in organizational performance cannot always be laid on their doorsteps. Nevertheless, one of the most important sets of findings from our studies is the evidence that relates organizational performance to the strength and orientation of its organizational culture. The country studies provided us with twenty-nine organizational case studies. Some of them performed relatively well, whereas others, even within the same country, performed poorly or only adequately. Our findings focus on the characteristics that set the good performers apart from the poor performers, especially when these outcomes could not be explained by extra-organizational factors.

In explaining why some organizations performed better than others, our cases indicated the importance of a problem-solving orientation within an organization and a dynamic interaction between human resources and how those resources were oriented, deployed, and rewarded. An organizational culture that stressed commitment to a mission and results-oriented performance was fundamental to establishing these positive interactions and enabling some organizations to be productive despite constraints at other levels indicated in the framework.

Without exception, the organizations that performed well were able to inculcate a sense of mission and commitment to organizational goals among staff, whereas those that were poor performers did not provide the same sense of mission. In several of the technical units involved in the budget process in Bolivia, Ghana, Morocco, and Sri Lanka, for example, professionals shared a sense of elite status, pride in how hard and professionally they worked, and commitment to the importance of the task they were performing. In Bolivia, a clear difference among several health care organizations was their degree of commitment to a mystique about their mission. In the agricultural research institutes in Ghana, Morocco, and Sri Lanka, a sense of elite status as scientists was coupled with links to international communities of scientists and enhanced commitment to high performance standards. Across the board, a sense of professional integrity among middle- and upper-level staff was associated with higher levels of performance.[18]

Contrary to what is often suggested in assessments that link productivity to remuneration, commitment to organizational goals was at times independent of salary levels. In the case of Bolivia, for example, salaries of public sector and NGO health professionals were quite similar, although commitment and sense of mission varied significantly. Elsewhere, in the economic agencies involved in the budget process, elite units often benefitted from higher salaries than groups in other parts of the public service. Just as frequently, however, being part of elite organizations, sharing a sense of importance to national development, and sharing a tradition of prestige associated with a particular organization, such as the Central Bank in Sri Lanka, were major factors in encouraging better performance, even when salary levels declined. Efforts to build a culture of enhanced prestige, professional integrity, and organizational mission might compensate for some of the constraining factors introduced by an economically strapped or rigid public sector institutional context.

The structure of work, authority relationships, communications, and behavioral norms also emerged as factors that differentiated good performers from poor performers at the organizational level, and these also were linked to characteristics of organizational culture. For each of these factors, the better performers demonstrated management styles that emphasized equity, participation, and flexibility. In Bolivia's NGO health organizations and Sri Lanka's agricultural research institutes, professionals clearly valued and responded to the opportunity to have some input into organizational decisions. In an agricultural research institute in Ghana, informal dialogue about policies and problem-solving teamwork enhanced performance. Politicization of assignments and favoritism by managers were singled out as counterproductive to effective performance in the less effective organizations.

The link between organizational culture and management style, then, including factors such as setting a good example, collegiality, openness to participation in decision making, consultation, and encouragement, was regularly in evidence in the better performing organizations. Organizational culture and management style were also in evidence in the incentive systems of the good performers. Although many incentives were not within the power of management to alter, as when salary levels were set by a civil service or where recruitment and promotion were centrally managed, the cases provide considerable evidence that nonmonetary incentives were as important as monetary ones.[19] Opportunities to study abroad, a sense of organizational mission, promotion for good performance, being singled out for excellent performance, a sense of professional community, friendly competitions to achieve performance goals, involvement in teamwork, and other such practices were in evidence among the better performing organizations. Moreover, incentives for good performance were often matched by disincentives for poor performance in the better units, and staff were aware that dismissal was a cost of consistently poor performance.

The strength and orientation of organizational culture also appears to have had some impact on how important physical resources were to the performance of particular organizations. Of course, among the poorest performers were organizations that were located in old, run-down, and abused buildings; that had little access to modern technology or transportation; and that had significant deficiencies in basic office amenities such as desks, pencils, and light bulbs. Better performers tended to have much more pleasant and convenient offices in which to work. In a few cases, however, staff who were performing well and finding their work psychologically rewarding contributed to preserving and even upgrading their physical environment. Clearly, organizations cannot perform at optimum level if they do not have equipment or necessary vehicles. Nevertheless, some highly motivated organizations found ways to compensate for poorly provided physical resources.

The cases indicate that the constraints organizations face often have less to do with structuring work, defining missions, and describing jobs—the focus of many public administration strengthening projects—than they do with providing meaningful jobs and incentives for goal-focused performance, inculcating an organizational mystique among professional staff, and encouraging a problem-solving orientation toward work.

Based on the findings of our case studies, among the most important features of an organizational culture are those that inculcate a mission-focused mystique about the organization. Such a mystique is built in several ways. Induction training can include a strong component of mission-focused curriculum and discussion. Managers can stress the importance of contributing to organizational missions in performance reviews and in evaluations of team, office, and project activities. Work carried out in teams can also help build and promote an organizational mystique. The participation of clients in service-oriented organizations can help reinforce a sense of mission and commitment to it.

A strong component of effective organizational cultures is the capacity to send clear messages that "performance counts." For example, open and competitive recruitment procedures emphasize that those selected for employment will have "won" a competition on the basis of their merit; they will understand that the organization uses performance as a measure of professional merit.[20] Similarly, job descriptions and rules about recruitment, remuneration, and promotion can send messages about performance expectations; when consistently applied, they indicate what must be done in order to be retained, promoted, or given salary increases.

Our cases indicate also that focused induction training can and should be used to inculcate desirable organizational norms and performance expectations. Probationary periods for newly hired personnel and timed and renewable contracts linked to performance reviews are other ways that messages about performance are communicated within organizations. Promotions, recognition, and monetary and nonmonetary incentives are important ways to reward good performance. In addition, excellent performance can be singled out for recognition and reward just as poor performance must be acknowledged and punished.

Organizations must be able to provide professional and technical personnel with meaningful work and encourage them to share commitment to professional norms of behavior.[21] Building professional identities can also encourage ethical behavior among staff and build commitment to mission-driven activities. Professional and technical staff can be encouraged to join or create professional associations. Links to international reference groups also encourage a strong sense of professional identity and the importance of the work of the organization.

The capacity to create a performance- and results-oriented organizational culture is enhanced when organizations have some autonomy or "room for maneuver" that provides greater scope for leadership. In addition, organizational missions can be defined in ways that encourage active problem solving and creative adjustment to changing circumstances. Managers and staff can be trained in analytic methods that encourage problem identification and assessment of options for resolving them. Working in teams to identify problems and solutions is often used as a means of encouraging this kind of culture.

Organizations respond to managers who know how to inculcate performance-oriented cultures. Such managers are oriented toward finding solutions to problems and providing incentives for good performance rather than toward exercising authority by applying rules and regulations. They are able to negotiate effectively within the organization and between the organization and its environment. They also encourage participation in decision making and responsiveness to client needs. At times, they must be able to shield their organizations from some of the negative influences of very unsupportive environments.

Organizations also respond to the external demand for effective performance. Organizations need to be told by those outside the organizations that to achieve these larger goals, their performance will be monitored in terms of taking credit for success or sharing blame for failures. Clients can be mobilized to put pressure on organizations to provide effective and timely services. Similarly, demand for information can improve its availability and accuracy. Organizations should know that their constituencies have means to communicate to important "others" when they encounter good and poor performance or when individual public officials are responsive or unresponsive to their needs.

Human Resources

Training of human resources varied widely across the case studies. One significant difference among countries was whether universities and technical training prepared people well for the kinds of jobs they were going to undertake. In some cases, low or inappropriate professional training led organizations to compensate for it with in-house training programs. At the same time, in-service training programs varied significantly in effectiveness. Induction training, particularly when it was task-specific and clearly linked to inculcating an organizational mystique, was usually a successful method of preparing people for their responsibilities. Ongoing and programmed professional upgrading was also generally successful as a form of in-service training. Less successful, and at times counterproductive to good performance, were in-service training programs and workshops scheduled on an ad hoc basis. Similarly, the usefulness of study leaves varied by organization and country. They were most successful when individuals were awarded study leaves for good performance and when they were closely connected to professional career development and obligations to return to the organization.

A clear pattern emerged in the case studies linking open and competitive recruitment procedures to employee performance. Without exception, the organizations that were best able to recruit appropriate talent were those that had public announcements and competitions for applicants; rigorous examinations or interviews, or both; and some kind of review board to ensure objectivity. In these cases, new recruits were most likely to be eager to share in the organization's mission and to participate effectively in its culture and work toward its goals. In addition, recruitment worked best to improve performance when it was managed by the organization rather than by the civil service or some other public sector entity.

Our cases indicate that while training and recruitment are important aspects of developing capacity, effective utilization of human resources within organizations is the most important factor in determining whether public officials are productive or not. Thus, the human resource problem for organizations was often not so much the availability of well-prepared personnel, but how they were utilized once they were recruited into an organization. It is clear in several of the cases that professionals were very sensitive to whether their jobs were meaningful and appropriate to their level of training. To the extent that they believed they were using their talents to accomplish tasks they considered meaningful, they were more motivated to contribute to the organization. When such people were idle or tied down with routine administrative tasks or kept from their activities because of a lack of vehicles or computers, they lost motivation.

Utilization was clearly related to the ability to retain qualified personnel. Salary levels played some role in explaining the ability to retain good people, but more important was the sense of organizational mission and involvement, job satisfaction, professional identity, and recognition for good performance. In fact, these factors made it possible for some organizations to retain staff even when salary levels declined or job security was uncertain. Length of contract was related to retention of well-qualified personnel in counterintuitive ways. One-year renewable contracts clearly linked to annual performance reviews led consistently to good retention records. On the other hand, civil service employment guarantees, often coupled with promotion practices based on seniority rather than performance, tended to mean that only poor performers were retained, whereas good performers moved on to more rewarding or interesting responsibilities. Highly politicized environments diminished the link between performance and employment and therefore had deleterious impacts on retention. Overall, then, retention appeared to be highly sensitive to performance rewards and job satisfaction. This finding is useful because it suggests that even where financial resources are very constrained, retention can be improved through efforts to create effective organizational cultures and to improve management practices within organizations.

Much of the "problem" of human resources, then, is a problem of utilization—what jobs individuals are assigned and what kinds of incentives shape their behavior in those jobs. In addition to focusing attention on performance, incentive systems, job satisfaction, problem solving, management, and demand creation, the case studies suggest several additional insights about how capacity builders can overcome human resource constraints.

They indicate, for example, that it is important to build links between institutions that train professional and technical resources and the organizations that recruit and use such talents. This is not a particularly onerous activity to stimulate. Officials of universities and training institutes can meet regularly with managers of organizations that recruit from their institutions. If appropriate, positions on the boards of training institutions can be filled by prominent leaders of the recruiting organizations. Graduates of training institutions who are recruited into the public sector can be provided with channels for feedback to leaders and faculty about the adequacy of their training.

A somewhat more difficult task is to orient curriculum in training institutions to emphasize employment-relevant skills. Emphasis on analytic techniques, management development, and problem-solving skills in particular need to be emphasized. In addition, considerable organization-specific thought needs to be given to assessing how and when additional training for professional and technical staff is most appropriately offered. Opportunities for domestic and international study leaves should be clearly linked to organizational as well as to individual needs. Professional and technical personnel must develop or upgrade their management skills as well as—and in some cases instead of—their profession-related skills, and additional training must be linked to job performance. Similarly, high-prestige training opportunities, such as overseas training, should be linked to some means of ensuring commitment to return to the sponsoring organization.

Conclusions

The conceptual map presented in this chapter is a comprehensive framework for assessing the factors that affect the capacity of government to perform development tasks. The case studies indicate that it is a useful tool for sorting out where the most important constraints are to creating more capable states. They also indicate that these constraints are interrelated within countries and vary considerably among countries. Interventions, therefore, need to be strategic; they need to vary and be sensitive to the interrelationships among the different dimensions of capacity sketched out in the framework. In a few countries, the only effective course of action may be to attack "the root causes of bad government" by working to develop conditions for basic economic, political, and social stability.[22] In most cases, however, intervention strategies can be more targeted on conditions within the public sector and designed to focus primary attention on what appear to be the most binding constraints on effective performance.

Earlier, we suggested that many capacity-building interventions begin with a set of assumptions about where such activities should be focused and what kinds of activities are most effective in creating or strengthening capacity. The research summarized in this chapter raises questions about the utility of these assumptions and suggests some alternative ways to begin thinking about where and how to intervene to develop capacity.

■ Where should capacity-building initiatives be focused? Selecting a site that will most constructively address the problems of poor performance must follow from an assessment of a relatively broad set of factors, including the action environment in which all such activities take place. In many cases, the traditional focus on organizations or training may not be the site for action that most effectively addresses the problem.

■ What kinds of incentive structures and interactions contribute to good and poor performance? Based on our research, we would argue that it is appropriate to assume that effective public sector performance is more driven by strong organizational cultures, good management practices, and effective communication networks than it is by rules and regulations or procedures and pay scales.

■ Where and when is training an effective means of enhancing performance? Our case studies indicate that individual performance is more affected by opportunities for meaningful work, shared professional norms, teamwork, and promotion based on performance than it is by training in specific skills. Effective training activities will most likely take place within contexts in which these other aspects are in place or are being simultaneously developed.

Building effective state capacity means continuous development and effective utilization of human resources, constructive management of task-oriented organization, institutional contexts that facilitate problem solving, and economic, political, and social conditions that help sustain such capacity. These are inevitably long, difficult, and frustrating processes, as punctuated with failure as they are with the potential for success. There are no easy solutions to getting better government. There are, however, approaches and strategies that are more effective than others and specific kinds of interventions that are likely to lead to better results than many that have been followed in the past. The framework and the results of the case studies begin to suggest what some of these are.

NOTES

A version of this chapter originally appeared in *Public Administration and Development* 15, no. 5, 1995. It is reprinted with the permission of John Wiley and Sons Limited (Chichester, Sussex, UK).

This chapter is part of a larger research project funded by the United Nations Development Programme (UNDP), Project INT/92/676. It appeared in *Public Administration and Development* 15, 5 (December 1995):441-463. We are grateful to Gus Edgren and Sheila Smith of the UNDP and Nimrod Raphaeli of the World Bank for inviting us to carry out the study. Guillermo Pacheco Revilla of Bolivia, André Nzapayeke of the Central African Republic, Ghulam Adamu of Ghana, Abderrahmane Haouach of Morocco, Nimal Sanderatne of Sri Lanka, and Rwekaza Mukandala of Tanzania carried out effective case study research in their countries. Lisa Garbus, Dale Johnson, and Ellen Pigott provided excellent editorial assistance for the project, and Dan Seimann, Sarah Dix, and Sarah Newberry facilitated its completion. We very much appreciate their efforts.

1   See, in particular, Jagdish N. Bhagwati, *Foreign Trade Regimes and Economic Development: Anatomy and Consequences of Exchange Control Regimes* (Cambridge, MA: Ballinger, 1978); David C. Colander, ed., *Neoclassical Political Economy: The Analysis of Rent-Seeking and DUP Activities* (Cambridge, MA: Ballinger, 1984); Anne O. Krueger, "The Political Economy of the Rent-seeking Society," *American Economic Review* 64, 3 (1974); Deepak Lal, "The Political Economy of the Predatory State," *Discussion Paper* 105 (Washington, DC: Development Research Department, World Bank, 1984); T. N. Srinivasan, "Neoclassical Political Economy: The State and Economic Development," *Politics and Society* 17, 2 (1985); and World Bank, *Towards Sustained Development in Sub-Saharan Africa* (Washington, DC: World Bank, 1984). An alternative explanation for the failure of many countries to thrive emphasizes the negative impact of the international political economy on developing countries.

2   The "orthodox paradox" identified by Miles Kahler called attention to the problematic need for a relatively effective state apparatus to carry out the reforms required by the minimalist solution to the role of the state. See "Orthodoxy and its Alternatives: Explaining Approaches to Stabilization and Adjustment," in Joan Nelson, ed., *Economic Crisis and Policy Choice* (Princeton, NJ: Princeton University Press, 1990), 55. By the late 1980s, some development specialists began to acknowledge that the emphasis on minimalism had been "a reaction too far" and to note that effective state action was important to the promotion of equitable growth. See especially Tony Killick, *A Reaction Too Far: Economic Theory and the Role of the State in Developing Countries* (London: Overseas Development Institute, 1989); Peter Evans, "The State as Problem and Solution: Predation, Embedded Autonomy, and Structural Change," in Stephan Haggard and Robert Kaufman, eds., *The Politics of Economic Adjustment* (Princeton, NJ: Princeton University Press, 1992); Paul Streeten, "Markets and States: Against Minimalism," *World Development* 21, 8 (August 1993). Research on development success stories in East Asia underscored that states could be as central to explaining success as they could be to explaining failure. See Robert Wade, *Governing the Market: Economic Theory and the Role of Government in East Asian Industrialization* (Princeton, NJ: Princeton University Press, 1990). Others looked to the experience of Western market

economies to suggest that the notion of a minimalist state was a misreading of the historical record. The "new institutional economics" showed that institutions created or enforced by public authority—such as rights of private accumulation and the sanctity of contracts—were essential to the development of capitalist economies of the West. See Douglass C. North and R. Thomas, *The Rise of the Western World* (Cambridge: Cambridge University Press, 1973) and Oliver E. Williamson, *The Economic Institutions of Capitalism* (New York: The Free Press, 1985).

3   This agenda emphasized that levels and degrees of poverty could not be reduced, nor could economic growth be sustained, unless governments committed themselves to invest in human resource development, particularly in health, education, and social safety nets. See the UNDP's *Human Development Reports* (New York: Oxford University Press) for 1990 through 1993 and the World Banks's *World Development Reports* (New York: Oxford University Press) for 1990 (on poverty) and 1993 (on health). See also Nancy Birdsall, David Ross, and Richard Sabot, "Inequality and Growth Reconsidered" (paper prepared for the American Economics Association Meeting, Boston, MA, January 1994).

4   See *World Development Report 1992*, which focuses on the environment. See also the "Brundtland Commission" report, World Commission on Environment and Development, *Our Common Future* (New York: Oxford University Press, 1987); Richard Sandbrook, "Development for the People and the Environment," *Journal of International Affairs* 44, 2 (1991); and Maurice F. Strong, "ECO '92: Critical Challenges and Global Solutions," *Journal of International Affairs* 44, 2 (1991).

5   See Eliot J. Berg, *Rethinking Technical Cooperation: Reforms for Capacity Building in Africa* (Washington, DC: United Nations Development Programme/Development Alternatives, Inc. , 1993); Edward V. K. Jaycox, "Capacity Building: The Missing Link in African Development" (transcript of address to the African-American Institute Conference, African Capacity Building: Effective and Enduring Partnerships, Reston, VA, May 20, 1993); C. Gray, L. Khadiagala, and R. Moore, *Institutional Development Work in the Bank: A Review of 84 Bank Projects* (Washington, DC: World Bank, 1990). Analysts have pointed to the continued reliance of many governments, particularly those in Africa, on expatriate advisors and consultants to carry out basic functions of government or to provide the expertise for formulating and implementing effective public policies. See John M. Cohen, "Foreign Advisors and Capacity Building: The Case of Kenya," *Public Administration and Development* 12, 5 (1993). Evaluations of technical assistance projects are in general agreement that efforts to strengthen institutions and build capacity are the least effective type or component of technical assistance. On public sector performance more generally in developing countries, see Milton J. Esman, *Management Dimensions*

of Development: Perspectives and Strategies (West Hartford, CT: Kumarian Press, 1991).

6 See Mick Moore, *Institution Building as a Development Assistance Method: A Review of Literature and Ideas* (Stockholm: Swedish International Development Authority, 1995), for a good review of how strategies for improving organizational performance have changed over time.

7 For experience with such reform initiatives, see David L. Lindauer and Barbara Nunberg, eds., *Rehabilitating Government: Pay and Employment Reform in Africa* (Washington, DC: World Bank, 1994); Mamadou Dia, *A Governance Approach to Civil Service Reform in Sub-Saharan Africa* (Washington, DC: World Bank, 1993); and L. Adamolekum, "A Note on Civil Service Policy Reform in Sub-Saharan Africa," *International Journal of Public Sector Management* 6, 3 (1993).

8 For an overview, see Derek Brinkerhoff, "Technical Cooperation and Training in Development Management in the 1990s: Trends, Implications and Recommendations," *Canadian Journal of Development Studies* 20, 3 (1992).

9 The six case-study countries were selected by the UNDP and the World Bank. For the full reports, see Ghulam Adamu, *Ghana: Pilot Study of Capacity Building* (Cambridge: Harvard Institute for International Development, 1994); Abderrahmane Haouach, *Morocco: Pilot Study of Capacity Building* (Cambridge: Harvard Institute for International Development, 1994); Rwekaza Mukandala, *Tanzania: Pilot Study of Capacity Building* (Cambridge: Harvard Institute for International Development, 1994); Guillermo Pacheco Revilla, *Bolivia: Pilot Study of Capacity Building* (Cambridge: Harvard Institute for International Development, 1994); Andre Nzapayeke, *Central African Republic: Pilot Study of Capacity Building* (Cambridge: Harvard Institute for International Development, 1994); and Nimal Sanderatne, *Sri Lanka: Pilot Study of Capacity Building* (Cambridge: Harvard Institute for International Development, 1994). For a more detailed presentation of the framework and analysis of the findings, see Mary E. Hilderbrand and Merilee S. Grindle, *Building Sustainable Capacity: Challenges for the Public Sector* (Cambridge: Harvard Institute for International Development, 1994).

10 Our definition lies between the broadest view that equates capacity with development and the narrowest perspective that equates capacity with the training of human resources. See, for examples of both, Peter Morgan, "Capacity Building: An Overview" (paper prepared for a workshop on capacity development at the Institute on Governance, Ottawa, Canada, November 22–23, 1993), and John M. Cohen, *Building Sustainable Public Sector Managerial, Professional, and Technical Capacity: A Framework for Analysis and Intervention* (Cambridge: Harvard Institute for International Development, 1993).

11 In the budget formulation process, for example, the budget office of the ministry of finance is often a primary organization for getting a budget produced; a macroeconomic or statistical unit in the central bank is a secondary unit that provides important input for the budget office; and a computer training unit of a national training institute could be a supporting organization.

12 In selecting the tasks to be studied, we chose those that involve substantial human resource capacity and depend on interactions among several different organizations. Budget formulation requires regular coordination of numerous organizational units, typically including the offices of the finance ministry, units within planning ministries and the central bank, the functional ministries, and statistical and other technical support agencies. This task also requires trained economists, accountants, budget specialists, and effective managers, along with experts in information systems and other technical fields. Budget formulation, which is important for the public sector and the economy as a whole, is a defined process with a specific output and performance capable of evaluation. Maternal and child health care and agricultural extension require trained personnel and involve the interaction of a range of institutional units, from headquarters offices that make policy to research and training institutes to field offices. Often these units also involve shared responsibility among different levels of government and sometimes with private actors, such as NGOs or commercial enterprises. Outputs of each of these activities can be measured using various indicators.

13 For several cases confirming this experience, see Lindauer and Nunberg, eds., *Rehabilitating Government*; and David C. Chew, "Internal Adjustments to Falling Civil Service Salaries: Insights from Uganda, *World Development* 18, 7 (1990).

14 In this regard, the Central African Republic comes close to the definition of a "collapsed state." See William Zartman, ed., *Collapsed States: The Disintegration and Restoration of Legitimate Authority* (Boulder, CO: Lynne Rienner, 1995).

15 For a discussion of the impact of structural adjustment policies on public sector performance, see David Hirschmann, "Institutional Development in the Era of Economic Policy Reform: Contradictions and Illustrations from Malawi," *Public Administration and Development* 13 (1993).

16 See Lindauer and Nunberg, eds., *Rehabilitating Government.*

17 In many countries, this salary level need not be as high as that in the private sector, but it must be at least high enough to ensure that public officials can put food on their tables. At reasonable levels of remuneration, people are attracted to public sector professional and technical positions for reasons beyond compensation, such as professional prestige and op-

portunities to work on important issues and, sometimes, by nonsalary benefits such as housing, which in some countries are substantial enough to outweigh the salary level itself, especially for higher-level officials. In order for governments to be able to provide a level of budgetary support that allows salaries to be paid consistently and that covers necessary operating expenses and investment, they will need to make choices about what activities are most important to carry out and then focus on building capacity in these areas. This focus will allow for better use of scarce financial and human resources and will encourage governments to devolve some activities to private or NGO sectors.

18 See Moore, *Institutional Building,* 29, on the importance of professional norms and actions, and their undervaluation in discussions of public sector performance in developing countries.

19 Moore, *Institution Building,* suggests that greater attention has been given to incentive systems in recent capacity-building approaches. Nonmonetary rewards are less often considered than monetary ones, however.

20 See Judith Tendler and Sarah Freedheim, "Trust in a Rent-Seeking World: Health and Government Transformed in Northeast Brazil," *World Development* 22, 12 (1995) for a discussion of this finding.

21 See David K. Leonard, "Professionalism and African Administration," *IDS Bulletin* 24, 1 (1993).

3

STRENGTHENING HUMAN RESOURCE CAPACITY IN DEVELOPING COUNTRIES

WHO ARE THE ACTORS? WHAT ARE THEIR ACTIONS?

James A. Trostle, Johannes U. Sommerfeld,
and Jonathon L. Simon

Efforts to help less developed countries construct independent functional state institutions after World War II began with notions of "institution building" in the 1950s and 1960s, moved to a focus on "institution strengthening" of existing institutions in the 1960s and 1970s, and then evolved into more narrowly focused concerns with "development management" and "institutional development" in the 1980s.[1] In the mid-1980s and 1990s, a concern for "capacity building" emerged, as donors and citizens realized that prior investments in public sector institutions had often failed to bring about the intended major improvements in their ability to predict, recognize, prevent, or manage development problems.[2]

Much as the institutional development literature moved from a focus on building to a focus on strengthening, so too should the future literature on capacity *building* come to stress capacity *strengthening* instead.[3] This is the term used in this chapter, unless we refer to authors who have specifically used the term *building*. In short, we assume that, more often than not, organizations and human resources already exist in less developed countries. It is more important to understand their present roles and limitations than it is to suggest new organizations and new strategies.[4] We are making a strategic choice to emphasize that capacity often can be increased more effectively by reinforcing existing structures than by building new ones.

The term *capacity building* has been defined in many different ways in the development literature. Some relate capacity to development of skills and human resources, whereas others associate it with strong institutions. For example, Cohen defines human resource capacity as the ability of public sector institutions to carry out assigned functions, operationalized through institutional roles filled by individuals carrying out their tasks.[5] More generic definitions of capacity have also been developed: In Chapter 2, Hilderbrand and Grindle define capacity as "the ability to perform appropriate tasks effectively, efficiently, and sustainably."[6] They present five dimensions of capacity building in the public sector (the action environment, institutional context, task network, organization, and human resources), and present a framework that maps these dimensions. Mapping dimensions rather than actors, actions, and events potentially diverts analytic attention away from the catalytic events and strategic nuances of how people respond to external and national development initiatives.[7]

Our concern with the Hilderbrand and Grindle framework, and others like it, is that they represent sites of action better than they represent actions themselves. This is partly a question of written representation, because actions are usually put into models through a series of complex arrows that obscure more than they reveal. It is more than that, however. The Hilderbrand and Grindle framework should be complemented by descriptions and categories of interaction.[8]

We contend that strengthening public sector capacity requires a map of sites of action, but it also requires an understanding of structural engineering (the study of the distribution and control of tension and compression forces through structures).[9] Maps help focus attention on relevant pathways, but they do not chart paths of adaptation or resistance. For example, people in organizations engage in specific processes and tactics when selecting themes, countries, organizations, and individuals. They negotiate between competing forces and make compromises to account for and control or manipulate various tensions. We highlight this decision-making process because it plays an essential role in determining what is defined as capacity and whose capacity is strengthened. These dynamic steps appear to be missing from the Hilderbrand and Grindle framework. Depending on the results of such tactical and strategic decisions, differing types of training and technical support components will be relevant. A focus on different levels of capacity will result in different mixes of types of assistance: degree training and skill development will be more appropriate for individual capacity; planning and budgeting assistance more appropriate for organizational capacity.

This chapter therefore describes not only the structure but also the processes of human resource capacity strengthening. We first present a general process-oriented framework applicable to less developed countries. The framework focuses on actors, actions, and events as the critical forces within structures and institutions. We then use this framework to explain the design and functioning of the Applied Diarrheal Disease Research (ADDR) project, a project undertaken to build and strengthen research capacity in the health sciences.

We offer this framework as a structural engineering complement to Hilderbrand and Grindle's map of the dimensions of capacity. They suggest that their framework "can be used to assess constraints, capacity gaps, and opportunities and also as the basis for developing intervention strategies to build more effective capacity to achieve development tasks."[10] We suggest that their framework provides an important set of organizing principles to guide discussions of different dimensions of capacity, but that the development of interventions requires a framework with greater specificity, and greater attention to the origins and the vectors (in both the mathematical and the biological sense) of power and influence.

Framework for Conceptualizing Human Resource Capacity Strengthening

Figure 3-1 illustrates our framework of human resource capacity strengthening. The framework depicts actors, actions, and events at various stages of the capacity-strengthening process. It emphasizes and categorizes the relationships among people, their actions, and structural forces acting upon them in shaping the course and outcomes of programs designed to strengthen human resource capacity.

We think this framework complements that proposed in the previous chapter because it focuses on human resources rather than public sector institutions and gives a more dynamic portrayal of the capacity-strengthening process. Performance of appropriate tasks at appropriate levels of quality is the final demonstration of acquired capacity. Successful performance, however, is also the final outcome

FIGURE 3-1
Actors, Actions, and Events in Programs Aimed at Strengthening Human Resource Capacity

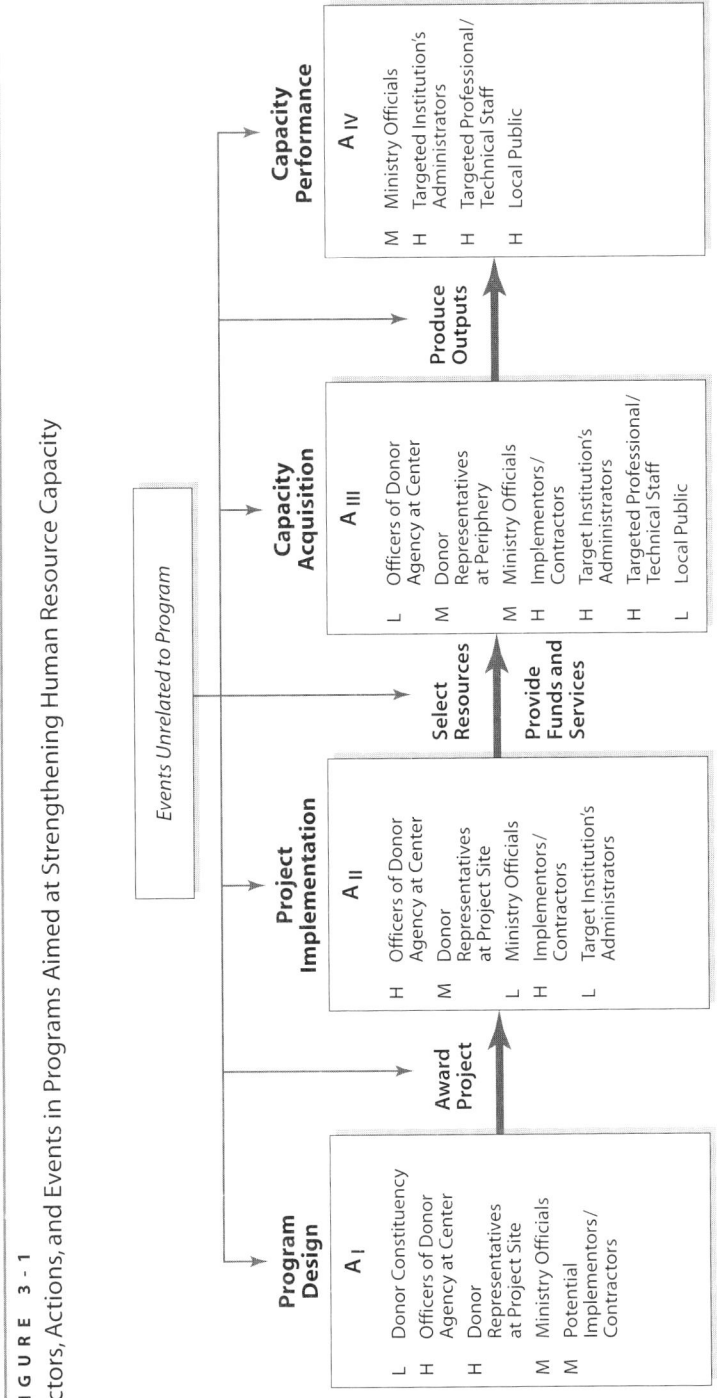

Key: *Sets of Actors:* A_I–A_{IV} *Actors' level of influence:* Low (L), Medium (M), High (H)

of a long series of interactions and negotiations among members of different interest groups, and of outside events often unrelated to any particular program of capacity strengthening.

There are many forms and sources of capacity strengthening. Our framework refers specifically to those capacity-strengthening activities begun by external donors and implemented through specific programs. We recognize that most capacity-strengthening activities are not undertaken by external donors, and may not be organized as specific programs designed to build capacity; they are instead the result of individual initiative (sending a child to school to get a degree, either at home or overseas) or local organizational initiative (running a training course in computer use). These activities are informal, often ad hoc, and not designed to be distributed, though, so they are at once more difficult to see, influence, and evaluate. The framework is designed to be relevant, with a few adjustments, to special programs organized by formal national ministerial initiatives (e.g., a ministry of education's design of a new scholarship program or a medical research council's support of a national research grants program) or other internal programs organized by what might be called internal donors. It is also relevant, with a few more adjustments, to everyday activities undertaken by specific institutions (government curricular reform, agricultural extension work, primary education). We are highlighting the external donor example because it is the base of our experience, and because it highlights more starkly a set of phases within which actors, actions, and events interact.

Figure 3-1 identifies four basic phases in the process of strengthening human resource capacity through organized programs. These include a design phase (resulting in, for example, a specific donor or government initiative), a project implementation phase (a contractor or administrative unit is selected to implement a program, and begins to do so), a capacity acquisition phase (various training and other actions take place and informal experiences build new skills), and a performance phase (capacity is manifested in task performance and is evaluated). Though these phases are diagrammed in linear fashion in the figure, the process on the ground is complicated by feedback loops and evolutionary changes. For example, information about poor performance by trainees might change the content of the personnel selection or training activities included in the capacity acquisition phase, or new donor concerns might change how an existing project is being implemented.

The term *actors* in the framework refers to people in specific organizations or other contexts rather than to organizations themselves. We contend that a conceptual focus on human resources rather than organizations is important to stem the further dilution of the concept of capacity building "by definitional expansion."[11] The list of relevant actors in programs aimed to strengthen human resource capacity is long (Box 3-1), and will vary according to type of capacity being strengthened (e.g., research versus communication or budgeting) and sector (e.g., health, education, finance, agriculture).

The framework shows that the list of involved actors can change at each phase of a capacity-strengthening project, and that the same actors can have different levels of influence in different phases. For simplicity in the model, these are presented schematically in the figure as high, medium, or low levels of influence. For example, directors, deans, and bursars in target educational institutions have less influence at the project implementation phase (when contractors are selected) than they do during the acquisition phase, when their staff are gaining skills or performing new tasks. In contrast, officers of the donor agency often have strong influence in setting the agenda at the

---

BOX 3-1

Actors in Programs that Strengthen Human Resource Capacity

- Donor constituency (e.g., for international organizations such as the World Health Organization [the World Health Assembly comprised of member states]; for public donors in the United States, the people of the United States or their congressional representatives; or for a private foundation, the board of trustees)
- Officers of the donor agency in the originating country
- Officers of the donor agency at the project site
- Relevant government officials at the project site (usually federal ministry, but also sometimes provincial or local officials)
- Staff of implementing agencies (contractors) responsible for carrying out the program
- Administrators at the target institution (directors, presidents, deans, or bursars)
- Professional staff within the target institutions (scientists, teachers, or other technical staff)
- External or national consultants (hired by the donor agency, the implementing agency, or the local government)
- Local public at the project site

design phase, but far less during the acquisition phase, when a recipient of support might be performing experiments, analyzing data, or obtaining specific credentials. Actors in capacity-strengthening projects respond to different incentives at different phases of the project, and evaluations of projects will need to choose different methods and criteria for success depending on which phase is being assessed and which actors are involved.

The various actors involved in each phase of the capacity-strengthening process negotiate and make decisions based on their individual and institutional power, perspectives, and incentives, resulting in specific *actions. Actions* refer to manifestations of deliberations and decisions within different phases of a project's life. They include awarding a project after defining the problem and negotiating the program's focus and methods; allocating funds; selecting resources to be strengthened; and carrying out the various activities designed to build or strengthen capacity (degree and nondegree training, donation of equipment or supplies, improvements in communications, and the like).

Events refer to occurrences that determine or influence the course of a capacity-strengthening program. Such events are often external, or unrelated, to specific capacity-strengthening programs. These events include replacements of key staff, closures of liaison offices, wars and civil unrest, changes in bilateral politics, changes in government because of elections or coups, natural disasters, and other important, often unanticipated, changes. The framework suggests that such events can play critical roles in determining the success or failure of capacity-strengthening initiatives, quite aside from the efficacy or appropriateness of the methods themselves.

Figure 3-2 emphasizes the contingencies in the capacity-strengthening process. Each phase of project development, and even some decisions within phases, can include multiple possible sets of actors. Thus each decision leads to a specific set of actors, fosters certain actions, and *precludes* others. For example, a donor may decide to implement a specific project through a university, an NGO, or a private consulting firm. Each of these will in turn bring different sets of actors into play when selecting target institutions and grantees. Similarly, a university selected to implement a capacity-strengthening program may focus its actions on helping individuals to acquire research skills, but may thereby preclude increasing the skills of administrators who need to manage finances, do long-range planning, or create linkages to other organizations.

FIGURE 3-2
Decision Making During Design and Implementation of Capacity-Strengthening Programs

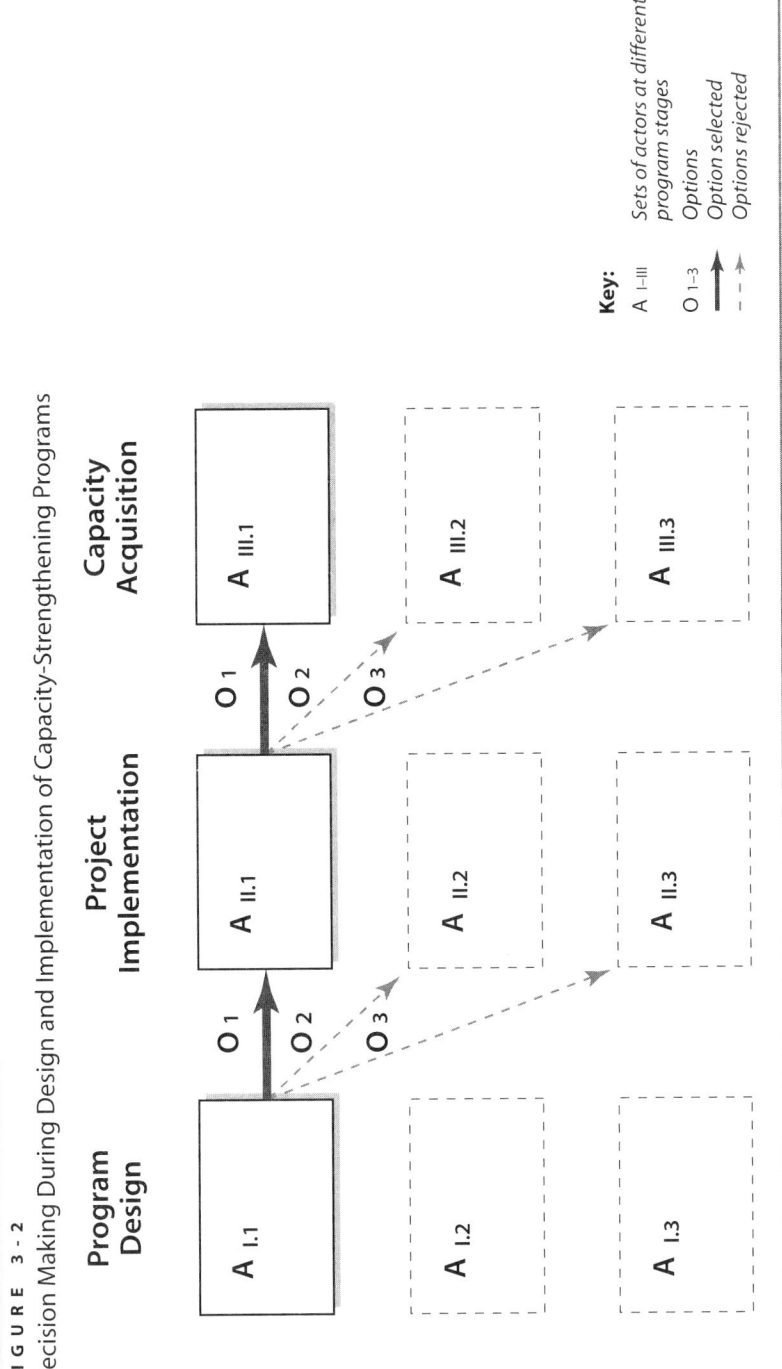

**Program
Design**

**Project
Implementation**

**Capacity
Acquisition**

Key:

A I–III   *Sets of actors at different
program stages*

O 1–3   *Options*

⬆ *Option selected*

⇢ *Options rejected*

Following a discussion of research capacity strengthening as a specific form of human resource development, we will use this framework to explain the development of a project with a specific mandate to strengthen research capacity in the health sciences.

RESEARCH CAPACITY STRENGTHENING AS A SPECIFIC FORM OF HUMAN RESOURCE DEVELOPMENT

Professional and technical skills are one important component of human resource capacity. Such skills are a critical part of a nation's ability to describe its problems and to develop appropriate plans, policies, and programs to confront them. Research capacity strengthening is a relatively new idea in development discourse, and is becoming an important component in attempts to improve the quality of science in low-income countries. It is assumed to have both economic and broader social benefits.[12] In this volume, Chapters 7, 8, and 9 present case studies of research capacity development; these case studies attest to its increased importance in discussions of national development.

We define *research capacity* as a subset of human resource capacity particularly concerned with the sustained ability of individuals, organizations, and nations to identify important basic and applied problems and to collect, process, analyze, and disseminate information that addresses them. This capacity is important for three objectives: providing useful information in a timely fashion, transmitting the skills required to create and use such information, and increasing the depth and complexity of human knowledge. Our definition of research capacity emphasizes the concrete steps needed to identify and implement research studies, and to link those studies to important national issues. Having research capacity means being able to sustain over time these processes of identification, implementation, and linkage.

Thus, research capacity is more than just the ability to answer questions. It also comprises the ability to create new questions so that a research community can respond to new challenges and question its own assumptions. Following the production of answers to questions, it also includes the ability to use those answers for specific purposes. Thus, research capacity includes the ability to recognize how information might be employed, and the skills and linkages to bring that information to bear in relevant problems and sites.

Donors investing in research capacity building or strengthening have developed a diverse set of definitions. For example, the United Nations Development Programme (UNDP)/World Bank/World Health Organization (WHO) Special Programme for Research and Training in Tropical Diseases (TDR) has, since the late 1970s, supported a diverse set of activities designed to strengthen the capabilities of developing country scientists to carry out high-quality research. In the mid-1980s, TDR narrowed its focus to activities more directly linked to research and research training, and human resource development.[13] However, it thereby paid less attention to organizational issues of financial management, long-range planning, and linkages between researchers and policy makers. TDR defines research capability strengthening as:

> ...a phased process of individual and collective development...focused on three levels....Support at the individual level responds to basic stages of individual achievement and career development. At the institutional level, support responds to the need to build strong research groups and to solidify research activities through well-planned programs. Collaborative links with other productive groups are an important element in this phase of RCS. As strong core groups emerge from this level, further support is provided at the network level to enable these groups to contribute fully to the Programme's global collaborative R&D activities...[14]

While these definitions reflect donor priorities, they highlight the same conceptual confusion evident in broader definitions of capacity building. As one analyst has put it, "the study of institutions still remains fragmented with no comprehensive theory acceptable and relevant to different types of institutions in different development contexts. Specifically, there is no integrated theory of institutional analysis and development for research institutions for developing countries."[15] Because definitions are used to develop evaluation criteria, a diverse set of definitions limits the ability to make comparisons across programs.

Although the framework we presented in Figure 3-1 is generic to program-based human resource capacity strengthening, it also has specific relevance to research capacity strengthening. For example, actors at the program design phase decide what type of research to support, in what countries and what types of institutions, who should distribute funds, what should be spent on the overall enterprise, and what type of technical assistance should be provided. Actors at the project implementation phase decide who should receive funds, in what amount, for what specific activities (degree versus nondegree training, single site versus multicenter research designs, what specific research topic). Actors at the capacity acquisition stage determine what type of knowledge and skills are transferred, what incentives are developed to assist or sustain these projects, and what knowledge is actually transferred or acquired. Actors at the performance stage determine which elements of research infrastructure (field sites, laboratories, computer facilities) and which research projects are sustained through time, which are taken up for local rather than external support, and what criteria are used to determine the success of capacity-strengthening efforts.

The types of actors engaged in different phases of the research capacity-strengthening process, and the nature of their social prestige and power, vary by sector and national site. For example, much work in financial research capacity strengthening focuses on economists, a local professional elite with quite strong connections to government in most countries. Research capacity strengthening for health often involves physicians, actors with sometimes weaker ties to government, whereas such work among teachers engages actors potentially even more distant from the centers of power. There is variability in these rankings across nations. Such evaluations of power and influence are important because of their relevance to the types of networks actors can form, the levels of financial and other support available for research from national governments, and the types of linkages that are available between researchers and decision makers.

Finally, though some types of events (wars and political unrest, natural disasters) may influence all capacity-strengthening activities at once, other events may have a different impact on strengthening research capacity than they have on strengthening communications or budgeting capacity. For example, a regime's commitment to its universities is closely linked to its commitment to research; therefore, a change in regime might have a specific impact on education investments and on research that it might not have on communications or budgeting.

Research capacity strengthening requires coordinated action in multiple dimensions. Social context, the status and productivity of science, and the prestige of research organizations all must be taken into account when choosing appropriate methods. We use our generic framework to present the organization of the ADDR project, which is one example of such choices.

ACTORS, ACTIONS, AND EVENTS INFLUENCING THE DEVELOPMENT OF THE APPLIED DIARRHEAL DISEASE RESEARCH PROJECT

Between 1985 and 1996, the ADDR project funded and supported approximately 150 research studies by local scientists in sixteen developing countries. The ADDR project was a science development project, a small-grants program financed by a government agency (United States Agency for International Development [USAID]). It was directed toward research on child survival issues (diarrhea, acute respiratory infections [ARI], and micronutrient deficiencies). During this period, the ADDR project was run by a consortium of three U.S. academic institutions (Harvard Institute for International Development, New England Medical Center, and Johns Hopkins School of Hygiene and Public Health). During its ten years of existence, the ADDR project spent approximately $17 million, provided research opportunities to more than 300 principal and co-investigators, and research and field staff of approximately 1,000 others, hired more than 150 scientific consultants and reviewers, and generated more than 200 scientific articles by the end of 1995.

Project studies yielded new, inexpensive, locally available diets for use in treating sick children; new methods to reduce inappropriate prescribing by physicians and pharmacists; new community-based education programs; and descriptive studies of disease magnitude and cause useful for health planning. ADDR project-funded scientists created formal researcher-community linkage programs in Nigeria, developed new national disease control strategies in Mexico, formed national reference centers in Indonesia, and assisted in developing national ARI policies in Pakistan. These resources of knowledge and policy are the project's most important contributions to health.

The ADDR project was mandated to strengthen national research capacities through a disease-specific grants program. This broad mandate required constructing a complex project that responded to the issues of structural engineering in the sense used earlier. ADDR aimed to increase research skills and improve research careers (human resources), develop research organizations and research networks, link research to the policy environment, and contribute to influencing the societal organization of science. The following sections show how actors, actions, and events combined to create specific outcomes during each of the phases in our organizing framework.

Program Design: Selecting Countries, Organizations, Investigators, and Research Themes

Research capacity-strengthening projects must develop a set of tactical strategies to decide which countries, organizations, investigators, and themes to support. Because these strategies determine all subsequent actions, they are a critical dimension of capacity from the perspective of project design and implementation. Yet these strategies are often invisible to those receiving support. Sometimes they are developed through compromises between representatives of project implementors (e.g., a university or grants-making program) and their funding sources (e.g., project officers in bilateral donors such as USAID or the International Development Research Centre in Canada, or in private foundations). Other times they are developed by project implementors to justify existing personal and organizational relationships between donors and recipients.

Select Countries

Projects to strengthen or build research capacity must first decide in which countries they will invest their funds and organize their activities. This is particularly true for those projects funded by bilateral development agencies, which mix foreign policy with humanitarian concerns. On one extreme lie so-called advanced developing countries with well-developed research establishments. These countries often need more expensive and complex projects to continue their development, because their research involves expensive laboratory facilities, or large-scale intervention designs, or complicated experimental designs. On the other extreme lie least developed countries with quite limited research communities and scientific traditions, where even small initial investments in research projects may create dramatic new resources. Somewhere in the middle are countries with small but established research communities, with a need and ability to do research using both simple descriptive and more complex experimental methods. Investments in any of these countries may still be overwhelmed by social constraints such as civil unrest or economic instability.

The ADDR project began with a list of countries eligible to receive funding from USAID and a mandate to include countries from Latin America, Asia, and Africa. Countries were selected through negotiations between USAID and ADDR project personnel based on criteria including the extent of the diarrhea problem, the personal and organizational linkages of the members of the ADDR project consortium, and the receptivity of national scientific communities. The project also looked for structural support for applied research on diarrheal diseases, for example, whether government control of diarrheal disease (CDD) programs or important NGOs in the country expressed interest in conducting such research, whether USAID had a history of sustained research support in a country, and whether the country USAID mission was interested in ADDR activities. Following direct consultation with USAID field staff and any field visits to research organizations, ADDR funded projects in eight emphasis countries: Bangladesh, Thailand, Indonesia, Pakistan, Kenya, Nigeria, Mexico, and Peru. Ecuador, Guatemala, Cameroon, Côte d'Ivoire, and Ghana became emphasis countries later, and single projects were funded in Zaire, Senegal, and Costa Rica.

Following country selection, changing political agendas within donor agencies and national governments influenced the project's ability to sustain its activities. For example, ADDR's cooperative agreement with USAID compelled the project to obtain concurrence from USAID/Washington as well as local AID missions on all funded studies and all country travel. Thus, the ADDR project was often constrained by shifts in U.S. foreign policy. In Pakistan, the project was unable to continue research efforts in the aftermath of the policy changes that prohibited further financial and technical assistance to the country. In Cameroon and Côte d'Ivoire, the project had to limit its research portfolios because both USAID missions closed. In other instances, the political and economic context put ADDR's efforts to strengthen capacity at risk. The ADDR project's program in Nigeria was forced to close early in 1995 because of restrictions on USAID assistance based on the absence of a democratic government. Similar restrictions took place in Thailand after a coup d'état in 1991. On the other hand, the ADDR project was able to continue its funding in Peru throughout a period of extended turmoil (1988–1992). Because many donors withdrew from Peru during this period, the project's funding became a major source of support for some local research organizations.

Select Organizations and Investigators

Following country selection, organizations and investigators must be identified. The ADDR project selected many of its key organizations using a subset of the criteria for selection of countries. Especially where ADDR project staff and advisors had no personal knowledge, they asked: Were researchers likely to serve as catalysts for future public health research? Did the organization have a critical mass of diarrheal disease investigators? Did it offer an environment conducive to research? Was it capable of being linked with other research organizations? If not, did it still represent an important real or potential base for research activities?

In other instances, the project relied on previous relationships between U.S. academic and foreign research investigators and organizations. The members of the ADDR project's technical advisory group were instrumental in locating potential grant recipients in early years of the project, based on their own international experience. Organization linkages were also important. This was the case, for example, with the Institute for Nutrition Research in Lima, which had had a long history of collaborative research with the Johns Hopkins University School of Hygiene and Public Health. These types of long-term relationships can increase the sustainability of a local organization's research capacity, because collaboration extends through many short-term research projects.

Local organizations were also recommended by other research funders, local USAID missions, or individual scientists. The ADDR project decided to fund some investigators from high-status organizations which, in most cases, were the outcome of previous capacity-building efforts. These organizations included the Kenya Medical Research Institute, University College Hospital in Nigeria, Chulalongkorn University in Thailand, the Institute for Nutrition Research in Peru, the National Nutrition Institute in Mexico, and the Noguchi Institute in Ghana. The project also funded research at less renowned organizations. In some instances this was done to increase the geographical breadth of funded projects in a single country, in other cases to support ethnic minorities disadvantaged in the competition for national research funds.

Select Research Themes

Who decides what themes merit additional research? Examining the sources of ADDR's scientific themes provides an overview of the various influences. The ADDR project's early focus solely on diarrheal diseases reflected the importance of these diseases in causing child mortality and the underutilization of adequate treatments. It also reflected the existence of U.S. congressional earmarks for child survival programs, of which diarrheal diseases formed an important part, and the belief that vertical disease control programs like those for diarrhea and years later for ARI were important ways to organize services. The ADDR project's focus on case management, foods and fluids, and particular research in persistent and invasive diarrheas reflected research themes of importance when the project began. Prevention was added as a research theme in 1989, cholera in 1991 following the epidemic's onset in Latin America, and ARI and micronutrient research in 1991. These last three themes were pushed by specific U.S. congressional earmarks to annual USAID budgets, showing the continuing influence of the donor constituency in project design. ADDR project staff added an emphasis on professional prescribing practice research; this shows the influence of implementors themselves. These themes then were reinterpreted by national researchers according to their own interests during the acquisition phase.

In summary, these examples from the ADDR project illustrate how project officers and their funding sources decide where to focus their efforts. This decision, in turn, determines what topics and countries receive emphasis and, consequently, who has the opportunity to increase their research capacity.

PROGRAM IMPLEMENTATION PHASE

The ADDR project faced a specific training challenge in providing technical assistance to researchers in developing countries. To function independently over time, these researchers required skills that were not sufficiently emphasized in their degree programs. These skills included how to select a good research question, design a research proposal, formulate a budget, find scarce financial and other resources, implement studies in the field, and analyze and apply research results.

The ADDR project's response to this training challenge yielded a specific set of implementation strategies and engaged specific sets of actors. The following discussion illustrates how decisions were made to take specific types of actions, which actions were contested, and how groups of actors came to be included in later phases.

Emphasize Local Design and Application

The ADDR project's main objective in strengthening research capacity was to provide basic training in research methodology through designing and conducting an applied research project. This effort involved enabling researchers, in their local settings, to face a series of concrete steps. They needed to identify research questions relevant to their own national health policy or to international policy. They had to figure out how to train their field workers, keep them paid, organize field-work logistics, and manage the many other parts of carrying out a research project. Finally, having finished collecting data, they needed to analyze data, write up the findings, disseminate them, and work to apply them to the chosen issue or policy.

For the first six years of ADDR, the staff debated, and rejected, using model research protocols and multicenter research designs. Opponents argued that this would negate the project's central interest in helping researchers identify their own questions and develop their own studies, and would lead instead to researchers capable of implementing projects designed elsewhere, but weak in design, dissemination, and application. Supporters argued that this was the best way to build comparability into global research questions that could not be answered in any other way, and that this was the path being taken by science in advanced developing countries. In its final four years, the project undertook a few limited multicenter studies using model protocols. The model protocols were revised in workshops and were adapted within limits to local research interests. These attempts to maintain investigator initiative seemed to have only limited success in developmental terms, however. Many researchers included in these projects felt they were implementing studies designed elsewhere. On the other hand, the results from these projects did convince various international agencies to change their policies, so their international impact was significant.

This debate illustrates how an early strategic project decision to focus on local investigator autonomy precluded certain types of results (international comparative data) and emphasized a particular type and scale of research work. Smaller research projects were preferred to larger ones, and local innovation and application were valued over international comparison. The list of actors for these projects was thus more heavily weighted toward national scientists and less heavily weighted toward international agencies or foreign scientists. (See the similar attention to participation expressed in Chapter 13.)

This debate also illustrates the relevance of outside events during the implementation phase, and some of the ways in which local actors adjust to the external constraints of donors. At the international level, changes in USAID's focus and funding caused ADDR project interest in research themes to wax and wane: it was difficult in the beginning of the project to fund researchers who wanted to study both diarrhea and ARI, yet by the end of the project it was politically desirable to do so. Researchers interested in comparing treatment of diarrhea and ARI responded to the project's early inflexibility by obtaining small quantities of additional funds aside from their ADDR project grants. They could thereby use project funds to pay the major costs of their project, yet justify that their expenses for nondiarrhea research came from other sources.

International funding priorities also caused ADDR project interest in research strategies to shift over time. USAID's growing interest in global research priorities created incentives for the project to invest later in international multicenter studies, though such study designs had been discouraged by project staff earlier.

Combine In-Country Training with External Technical Assistance

The decision to focus heavily on the development of local scientists at home was taken after the design phase was completed and the project funds were awarded to HIID and other universities in the ADDR project consortium. The overall design from the donor (USAID) specified that a research grants-making process was to be established, but it did not specify the qualifications of grant recipients or the manner of their support. These issues were left for the implementing agency to work out. Many other research capacity-strengthening projects have focused on foreign degree-based training, mentor relationships with foreign scholars, or grant support with little technical assistance. The ADDR project, in contrast, combined in-country training with external technical assistance throughout the research project.

Use the Peer Review Process and Emphasize Quality

ADDR project staff faced national policies that often neglected health research as a national priority, leading to limited human and financial resources for public health research. Some countries lacked the political will and capital to fund significant research projects, even when they had official national research councils. In some cases there was no national competitive proposal selection process, and grant funds were distributed based on selection criteria unrelated to the scientific content and quality of the proposal. In these instances research funding was explained more by the status of the researchers than by the merits of the study.

The ADDR project's proposal development methods included submissions of preproposals, reviews of proposals, and participation in proposal development workshops. Many researchers who submit research proposals to international funding agencies expect to receive final negative or affirmative responses rather than methodological and conceptual critiques with requests for resubmission. This iterative process of resubmissions therefore came as a surprise to some investigators. Some chose not to resubmit; others went through as many as five drafts before receiving funding. This method itself helped to select those researchers most committed to their projects.

The project's implementation plan included investigators at various stages of their careers. The project funded both junior and senior investigators from both established and new groups. Weaker research groups from less well-known universities were funded in addition to stronger teams, so local researchers confronted their own national divisions. In one country, for example, the ADDR project funded a project led by a public health nurse, who, at the beginning, thought she could not possibly "compete" with her highly reputable colleagues at a project workshop. Thus technical assistance needed to be provided at various levels to satisfy various needs: some researchers needed training in descriptive statistics, and others lacked only computers to carry out the complex multivariate analyses they had learned previously.

The model of research support ultimately developed by the ADDR project extended from problem identification through proposal design, data collection, and analysis, to dissemination and application of results. This phased model of research support offered an opportunity to collaborate closely with a research team over a period of two or three years. In the twenty cases where follow-up proposals were funded, ADDR project collaboration with researchers extended over more than four years.

Provide Varied Forms of Technical Assistance

Capacity-strengthening programs organized by external donors must decide at what level and with what staff to support their target candidates. The ADDR project experimented with many patterns to provide technical assistance. Over 10 years, we used "in-house" interdisciplinary project staff expertise as well as approximately 150 external technical consultants and reviewers. We placed long-term full-time resident advisors, hired nationals as long-term part-time consultants, and relied on several expatriates living in the country as part-time resident advisors and as short-term consultants.

Technical assistance by the ADDR project was provided at numerous stages in the research process. The project tried to match the research team with an appropriate external consultant who advised the team during the entire project. Project staff or consultants were often involved in the preliminary steps of problem identification, refining research questions, or reviewing first drafts of proposals. To maintain project control in the hands of the national research team, the consultant was asked to function more as a mentor than as a co-investigator. Consultants' communication skills were just as important as their technical skills.

The project experimented with various forms of longer-term technical assistance as well. It sent resident advisors to two countries for two-year periods and employed local expatriates as part-time advisors in another five countries.

The ADDR project had limited experience with using local consultants in their own countries. Using nationals potentially led to higher sustainability but in some instances created resentment and rivalry among colleagues. As in the case of foreign consultants, this response was caused more often by communication problems than by technical faults. Hiring nationals as facilitators for project workshops in four countries was seen as an important sign of collaboration and collegiality between institutions in the south and the north. It also helped increase local knowledge about the technical content and administration of ADDR project workshops. At least four national participants in ADDR project workshops subsequently organized similar workshops in their countries based on the project model.

The ADDR project also experimented with south-to-south consultancies using project researchers or highly qualified local staff to consult for the project in other countries. For example, a group of cholera experts from south Asia were sent to Latin America in 1991 at the beginning of the cholera outbreak there. Some of their hosts were pleased that they could learn from staff who had treated thousands of cases already; others felt that Asian children and health systems were too alien to provide lessons for Latin America.

Selecting different actors to provide technical assistance yields varying results. The choice of each type of actor (for example, foreign-resident advisor, short-term foreign consultant, short-term national consultant) further shapes the assemblage of actors who receive training or other capacity-strengthening strategies and influences the political and scientific linkages among these actors. These issues are explored further in Chapters 4, 5, and 14.

CAPACITY ACQUISITION PHASE

Adapt Project Methods to Local Culture and Constraints

Human resource development in the ADDR project was structured to allow short-term intensive training of researchers through designing and carrying out all steps of a research project. This design entailed working around a series of constraints in the process of grants making, and it required experimenting with different types of technical assistance during the funded studies themselves.[16]

While providing support to funded research studies, ADDR project staff found that they needed to adapt the dominant Western model of science and scientific development for use by some foreign scientists from different cultures because the organization and practice of science in some cultures differed from that in the West.[17] For example, the project received an application to Harvard's Ethical Review Committee from a research team in southeast Asia. This application specified that the informed consent of people in the community to participate was not required because the governor of the province had already given his permission for the research to proceed. Though this rationale was not a familiar one to the Harvard ethics committee, it chose not to contest it. In a similar fashion, the project came to recognize that local incentives for promotion in some Asian countries caused researchers to print and distribute voluminous reports instead of publishing them in national or international scientific journals.[18] The ADDR project tried to improve the quality of these publications and to interest researchers in also writing for policy audiences, rather than trying to convert all products into articles for journals.

Strengthen Organizations as well as Individuals

The ADDR project was designed to focus on human resource development, but the project also aimed to strengthen research organizations and the policy and research environment. In fact, though diagrams of public sector capacity can place individual career enhancement and institutional strengthening on two separate dimensions, in practice these often take place simultaneously.

Some methods used by the ADDR project worked on both levels at once. For example, the proposal development and data analysis workshops provided skills to individual investigators, but they also increased communication within and between organizations, provided models for ways organizations could provide such services to others, and increased the prestige and legitimacy of researchers. Helping investigators learn how to influence local policy and emphasizing this action as a legitimate part of the research process had benefits for the investigators and their organizations.

ADDR project staff attended to a limited subset of organizational issues. The most important of these were attempts to minimize organizational constraints on careers, provide physical resources, encourage cross-disciplinary and interdepartmental collaboration, improve financial management, and develop ethical review committees.

Career Constraints

During the acquisition phase, the ADDR project experimented with several methods to counter or minimize the structural constraints on research careers in developing countries. The project invested financial and technical resources in a limited number of key organizations in each country. This investment provided relatively long-term funding to a department or organization and helped build or sustain a critical mass of investigators. Where interdisciplinary teams were assembled, sustained funding gave the team more time to explore new research areas, get to know the strengths and weaknesses of different disciplines and individuals, and discover new ways to organize research and analysis. This strategy thus affected not only the number of actors participating, but also the range of specializations they represented.

The ADDR project created incentives for scientists to continue a research career, focus on local issues, and maintain residence in their country. These incentives included the research opportunities themselves, salary support, access to foreign literature and consultants, opportunities to travel to scientific meetings, and assistance in analysis, writing, and dissemination. Through providing multiple grants to a limited number of research teams, ADDR helped scientists in Mexico, Peru, Nigeria, Pakistan, Indonesia, and Thailand to sustain their research interests over a period of up to five years. This history of sustained research itself subsequently assisted the researchers to obtain funding from sources other than ADDR.

Physical Resources

The project also tried to improve the physical resources and enabling conditions conducive to research. Institutions of higher education in developing countries usually suffer from a chronic lack of physical resources. Except for elite research centers, libraries are rarely able to purchase basic research literature, particularly scientific journals. Especially in Africa, research institutes often do not have access to recent computer hardware and software. The ADDR project gave limited assistance to research organizations by providing selected books, journal articles, computers, software, and links to the Internet. These resources, especially those related to computers, were not always tied to a specific grant.

Cross-Disciplinary Collaboration

Applied research is often hampered by lack of communication and coordination between disciplines. Where interdisciplinary teams did not form naturally, the ADDR project encouraged researchers to make appropriate links to other departments and campuses. An imposed collaborative model sometimes worked, especially at ADDR project workshops, or between a research team and its consultants. The project hoped to assess how many of these teams continued to function during the capacity performance stage, when they were no longer dependent on ADDR project support.

Financial Management

Managing external funds can be a challenge. In countries where foreign currencies are scarce, institutional incentives exist to delay disbursements and manipulate exchange rates. Slow bureaucratic procedures within some institutions caused problematic disbursement of grant monies from institutional accounts to individual investigators. In one country, bursars at several universities were quite uncooperative in locating and disbursing grant monies. In another, researchers were initially very concerned about the project transferring funds to the university account because they rightfully feared that these monies would never be accessible.

The project was able to work more closely with university financial managers in the two countries where it had placed resident advisors. Ease and frequency of contact allowed greater trust between bursars, project staff, and scientists. The resident advisors were able to disburse funds in local currency from local banks; this hastened the availability of funds and removed incentives to capture benefits from foreign exchange rate fluctuations. In country programs without resident advisors, intermittent contact with ADDR project staff and use of dollar checks made financial management more difficult.

As if local delays and corruption are not enough, every donor has its own rules. For example, 10 percent of the total ADDR project grant served as an administrative fee to support accounting staff, rent, power, maintenance, and other indirect costs of research projects. Some organizations had not managed such funds before, whereas others had established indirect cost rates in excess of 10 percent based on the calculations by international accounting firms. In some organizations, particularly those with weak financial management procedures, this 10 percent became a potent source of conflict. It was not tied to specific budget categories, so it became a premium to be contested.

Ethical Review

Efforts to strengthen the research capacity of organizations also required emphasizing the ethical conduct of research. However, most research institutions in developing countries do not have ethical review committees to adequately monitor the design and implementation of research. The ADDR project therefore emphasized the importance of such committees in the process of proposal development. USAID mandated that Harvard University review the potential risks of human subjects' participation in project-sponsored research. Realizing the limitations of this process and the need to sustain local ethical review boards, the project also stressed the importance of establishing institutional review committees in appropriate organizations.

Build Linkages

The ADDR project, through various strategies, aimed to improve linkages between research networks and disease control programs and policy makers. The Project workshops generally offered good opportunities to present research findings to a larger policy audience. Final presentations at ADDR project data analysis workshops were attended by national policy makers and representatives of international organizations. The ADDR project also organized separate workshops that brought together policy makers and researchers to discuss the constraints and incentives for using health research in making policy. Policy makers could be quite unreceptive to research on matters they considered politically delicate. For example, discussions of ethnic differences in disease rates and behaviors were unacceptable to national policy makers in one country, and in another country, work to develop local interventions among a neglected population was considered irrelevant to national health program objectives.

The type of assistance provided by the project changed over time as project staff learned what worked and as changes took place at local levels. This flexibility emphasizes the importance of outside events, because local changes in personnel and policy allowed different types of actions to be undertaken. At the country level, for example, there were five different directors general of health over the life of the Pakistan country program (1988–1994), with accompanying changes in policy and support for health research. In Nigeria, changes in the organization of functional responsibilities in the ministry of health caused staff there to move from complete disinterest to total support for ADDR project activities. In Mexico, the promotion of an ADDR project-supported researcher to a high-level position in the ministry of health increased the power of the diarrheal disease control program, and thus the opportunities for project research to become part of the national research agenda.

PERFORMANCE PHASE

From the donor perspective, the performance phase is the ongoing, open-ended, yet final stage of a capacity-strengthening project. This stage is when individual recipients of training or organizations that have received computers or developed research field sites with outside support proceed to use their skills, equipment, and other resources to perform more effectively, or when these efforts fail. Donors sometimes perform outcome evaluations during this phase, though few do so very long after their major assistance has ended.

From the recipient perspective, of course, this is the beginning of the process. Having learned to do some new quantitative analysis, returned home with a foreign degree, built a new laboratory, or reorganized an administrative process, the challenge for the recipient of outside assistance is to integrate these new skills and structures into a complex existing context and set of expectations.

The role of the ADDR project during the performance phase was much smaller than during the implementation and acquisition phases. This was by design: the project was conceived as a development project in five-year stages, not as a sustained effort to create a new independent research donor. (In fact, its initial design would have been far more complex, and would have involved far more actors, had this been the case.) Nonetheless, the project experimented during this phase with some forms of new assistance to help scientists sustain their research careers. It also began to assess the types of research and types of incentive structures most likely to endure through time.

Provide Dissemination Grants to Researchers

ADDR's emphasis on applied research has been discussed. As part of that emphasis, the project tried to learn how researchers disseminated and applied their research results. Discussions with researchers revealed that small grants ($1,000–2,500) for specific dissemination and application plans could be instrumental in helping researchers organize key meetings and conferences, publish and distribute key documents, or reach potential audiences more effectively. These grants were offered to researchers who had successfully completed their projects, identified their applied significance, and created a plan for dissemination and application. It is too early to tell whether these small grants were effective in changing policies, but they did lead to many special publications and extensive media coverage. More importantly, they helped researchers pay better attention to the complexities of communicating their results to colleagues, the general public, and decision makers.

Preparation of this information for formal channels like press releases, executive summaries, and journal articles also made it more available to researchers to distribute through informal channels. The well-developed anecdote and the brief presentation of compelling statistics can be just as effective at lunches and dinner parties as at organized conferences.

Form and Sustain Indigenous Linkages

ADDR project grantees usually had opportunities to interact over several years at project workshops, policy/research meetings, and national or international conferences. The project distributed travel funds for this purpose. Beyond this, ADDR project grantees formed nationwide interest groups on their own in several countries. ADDR project investigators in Nigeria created the Nationwide Network for Health, an NGO of multidisciplinary researchers. Pakistani researchers sponsored by the project to conduct research on ARIs formed a network contributing to the national ARI program. In Mexico, ADDR project researchers formed the majority of an interinstitutional working group between the ministry of health and the Mexican Social Security Institute. The group studies diarrheal diseases.

Publish in Multiple Venues

In addition to its efforts to help researchers publish and distribute their own writing, the ADDR project developed a set of its own publications to broaden the distribution of project documents. Its annual report highlighted key findings across research portfolios and included abstracts and results from all major studies. ADDR also published or distributed conference reports and assembled special issues of relevant international scientific journals. Finally, it produced special sections of newsletters that were disseminated broadly to both applied clinical and policy audiences.

ADDR staff created incentives for investigators to form multidisciplinary research teams at the design stage. Cross-disciplinarity at later stages of ADDR project-funded research studies was nonetheless often constrained by lack of disciplinary understanding, unequal roles of various members in the multidisciplinary research team, and rivalries around publication rights. Collaboration between representatives of public health or medical disciplines and those of health social sciences remained mostly multidisciplinary. True interdisciplinary or transdisciplinary science was not achieved within the project and remained a challenge for the future.[19]

Evaluate Project Efforts

Though the indicators are still being refined and assessed, our initial inquiries have led us to conclude that the ADDR project had a major impact on the ability of our grant recipients to perform technical tasks like data analysis and write-up, as well as strategic tasks like designing budgets, supervising field staff, and managing funds. We expect less impact on individuals' career pathway within organizations, because our investigators had multiple sources of support and because the impact of research funding on career pathways takes longer to see and is more difficult to measure. We expect a relatively minor effect on organizations, because our funds were primarily study-related, and we only sporadically attended to organizational structures. Finally, we expect a limited effect on governments with respect to their abilities to sustain research efforts. However, some ADDR project research results had an important impact on government policies, and other studies are expected to have a similar impact in the future.

Conclusions

This chapter presented a framework to use in analyzing programs organized to strengthen or build human resource capacity. It applied that framework to a specific project designed to strengthen health research capacity, though we would argue that the framework is not limited to this specific type of program. The presentation and analysis of ADDR project activities emphasized a few key actions in each project phase. It illustrated which types of actors were important in the different phases and how they came together to negotiate. It also illustrated how outside events influenced these actors and actions, creating some new opportunities while closing others, and engaging new actors while excluding others.

We presented a case that highlighted a capacity-strengthening approach that dealt only with research capacity and that ranked acquisition of skills and technical competence over need to reform organizational policies. It focused primarily on research capacity strengthening in health within countries with low levels of national health research. The strategies would need to be adapted to other sectors, countries, and types of human resource capacity.

Aside from the research results themselves, whatever successes the ADDR project attained were based largely on its attention to the human side of scientific research. The project preferred to strengthen existing structures before building new ones, to assess existing incentives and constraints, to develop relationships with grantees and maintain them over time, and to emphasize science as a process of communication. These processes allowed ADDR staff to see themselves as only a few among many relevant actors, and thus to develop actions that are more sensitive to local processes and constraints.

We contend that the focus on actors, action, and events is the strength of the analytic framework we have provided. Programs that hope to strengthen human resource capacity must have maps to identify relevant actors and organizations, and to understand the tensions, stresses, and competing forces that are not represented in maps, but rather must be represented in structural engineering diagrams and process flowcharts. By going beyond maps of project domains and attending to dynamic human interactions, our model can focus attention on strategic decision points. It can also increase attention to the impact of unforeseen events that are so often critical to program directions and results. These distinct types of attention can improve predictions of the potential cultural and political problems facing new initiatives and thus ideally lead to better designs in the future. The framework's attention to contingency, process, and negotiation realistically portrays the challenges of influencing human behavior.

Notes

1   P. Morgan, "Capacity Building: An Overview" (manuscript prepared for the Institute on Governance Capacity Development Workshop, Ottawa, Canada, 1993); A. A. Goldsmith, "Institutional Development in National Agricultural Research: Issues for Impact Assessment," *Public Administration and Development* 13 (1993):195–204.

2   As the concept rapidly becomes widespread, it rapidly loses its meaning. For example, in its recent reorganization, U.S. Agency for International Development (USAID) placed a series of education and international training programs under an umbrella "human capacity development center," implying the term is synonymous with training. In similar fashion, a recent newsletter from a USAID-funded health project was headlined, "Quality assurance training in Chile: A comprehensive strategy for motivation and capacity building." [*Quality Assurance Brief* 3(2), Summer 1994, Bethesda, MD: Center for Human Services].

3   See also D. Habte, "Building and Strengthening Research Capacity in Health: The Challenge to Africa," *Journal of Diarrhoeal Disease Research* 10 (1992):73–78.

4   D. Marsden, "Indigenous Management: Introduction," in Susan Wright, ed., *Anthropology of Organizations* (London: Routledge, 1994), 36.

5   J. Cohen, "Capacity Building in the Public Sector: A Focused Framework for Analysis and Action," *International Review of Administrative Sciences* LXI, 3 (1995), 409; and J. M. Cohen and J. R. Wheeler, Chapter 5 of this volume.

6   M. Hilderbrand and M. Grindle, *Building Sustainable Capacity: Challenges for the Public Sector*, report prepared for the United Nations Development Programme, (March 1994):10, and Hilderbrand and Grindle, Chapter 2 of this volume.

7   In some respects this emphasis derives from disciplinary differences between political science and anthropology: we are drawing on models that recognize both the systematic formal and informal arrangements of social relationships, called "social structure," and the reaction to circumstance, or concrete working arrangements of society, called "social organization" (R. Firth, "Essays on Social Organization and Values," *LSE Monographs on Social Anthropology* no. 28 [London: Athlone Press, Univ. of London, 1964 [1954]). As Raymond Firth wrote, "A structural principle is one which provides a fixed line of social behaviour and represents the order which it manifests. The concept of social organization has a complementary emphasis. It recognizes adaptation of behaviour in respect of given ends, control of means in varying circumstances, which are set by changes in the external environment or by the necessity to resolve conflict between structural principles." (Firth, "Essays on Social Organization," 61.)

8   G. Walt and L. Gilson, "Reforming the Health Sector in Developing Countries: The Central Role of Policy Analysis," *Health Policy and Planning* 9 (1994):353–370. Walt and Gilson provide similar emphases in this paper. They argue that health policy pays too much attention to the content of reform, neglecting actors, processes, and context.

9   Some concepts and metaphors useful for development discussions are found in *Why Buildings Fall Down*, by the structural engineers M. Levy and M. Salvadori (New York: W.W. Norton & Co., 1992). These ideas include the importance of redundancies in systems; problems of progressive collapse; the importance of continuity in building joints; resonance, or the amplification of movement; stress concentration; and the importance of plasticity.

10 M. Hilderbrand and M. Grindle, *Building Sustainable Capacity: Challenges for the Public Sector*, report prepared for the United Nations Development Programme, (March 1994):15–16.

11 J. Cohen, "Capacity Building in the Public Sector: A Focused Framework for Analysis and Action," *International Review of Administrative Sciences* 61 (1995):408.

12 Commission on Health Research for Development, *Health Research: Essential Link to Equity in Development* (New York: Oxford University Press, 1990.)

13 A. M. Pearce, ed., *Strengthening Health Research Capability: A Review and Major Policy Directions in Tropical Disease Research* (Geneva: TDR, 1992), 2.

14 Pearce, *Strengthening Health Research Capability*.

15 M. N. Kiggundu, "Managing Research Institutions in Developing Countries: Test of a Model," *Public Administration and Development* 14 (1994): 201.

16 J. A. Trostle and J. Simon, "Building Applied Health Research Capacity in Less-Developed Countries," *Social Science & Medicine* 35 (1992):1379–1387.

17 See also T. Nicholson, "Institution Building: Examining the Fit between Bureaucracies and Indigenous Systems," in S. Wright, ed., *The Anthropology of Organizations* (London: Routledge, 1994), 68–84.

18 J. Trostle, "Why Publish? Differences in Institutional Incentives to Disseminate Research Findings" (manuscript prepared for Harvard Institute for International Development Research Retreat, Kennebunkport, Maine, May 1993).

19 See also J. Sommerfeld, "Cross-Disciplinary Collaboration in International Public Health Research: A Challenge for Research Capacity Building Efforts in Developing Countries" (manuscript prepared for Harvard Institute for International Development Research Retreat, Newport, Rhode Island, May 1994).

PART II

STRATEGIES FOR
CAPACITY BUILDING

DEVELOPING HUMAN RESOURCES

4 SATURATION TRAINING
BOLSTERING CAPACITY IN THE INDONESIAN MINISTRY OF FINANCE

Donald F. Lippincott, III

One of the most important aspects of national development concerns the ways in which developing country institutions and donors formulate strategies for advanced education and training. Without skill acquisition, countries may find it difficult to shed the external consultants to whom, in many instances, they have become addicted. Nevertheless, although there is abundant literature on various higher education training programs, little work has been done to analyze the benefits and pitfalls of different approaches to such training. One lens for analyzing these pros and cons is to examine training options in ascending order of magnitude of time away from the job (i.e., on-the-job training, local short courses, local degree programs, external short courses, seminars and workshops, and external degree programs). There has been extensive debate in recent decades over which of these approaches brings the "biggest bang for the buck," what mix of training programs is appropriate in given circumstances, and what one can do with limited resources. However, most would agree that, in the best of all worlds, advanced education in high-quality academic institutions is the preferred option for promising professionals. Many—indeed most—of the external advisors who provide high-level advice to these countries possess advanced degrees from Western academic institutions; for better or worse, developing-country government officials, university professors, and other leaders may also need such degrees in order to perform and replicate a similarly complex level of advanced analysis.

The following are frequently pursued strategies for advanced external degree programs:

- Targeted, narrowly focused education and training

- The pooled-resource, multi-institution approach (e.g., the Latin American Scholarship Program of American Universities [LASPAU] and the Government of Indonesia's Overseas Training Office [OTO])

- The "hit-or-miss" approach

- The "key individuals" approach

To these, I will add "saturation training" and analyze it through the lens of one case study, the Indonesian Ministry of Finance. This strategy was adopted to solve the shortage of analytical capacity in the ministry, and its experience with such an approach can provide useful lessons for other countries. Each of these strategies has costs and benefits.

The "targeted, narrowly focused" approach is a strategy in which an institution or ministry decides that it can determine precisely what its needs will be three to five years in the future. Therefore, it predicts that at that time it will require, for example, five economists, three business majors (one in finance, one in accounting, and one in marketing), two public managers, one agricultural policy manager, and one environmental engineer. Then it can select the best qualified candidates for each of these positions and attempt to place them in the best or most appropriate graduate programs. This is a high-reward, high-risk strategy: if the projections are accurate, and three to five years later the needs are roughly the same, this is an ideal, cost-effective approach to taking advantage of overseas education. On the other hand, if plans change, for example if a new government (or minister) comes into power with significantly different plans and ideas, or if external circumstances dictate that a somewhat different emphasis is required, such training may no longer be completely appropriate, and in the worst cases, may be irrelevant. The potential reward is that governments can get precisely what they want and have planned for; the risk is that the training may turn out to be irrelevant or obsolete.

The "pooled-resource" approach brings together individuals for similar degree training from many different, but related organizations. In the Midwest Universities' Consortium for International Activities (MUCIA)/OTO project, Indonesian government officials came from several different government ministries. In the LASPAU Training for Development (TFD) program, 164 degree seekers came from twenty-three different Latin American and Caribbean university faculties to pursue master's degrees in agriculture, engineering, education, health, and social sciences.[1] The advantage of this approach is that a central repository or sponsoring agency can pool its resources, especially its capabilities in evaluation, placement, and monitoring of candidates, to achieve a rich mix of academic experiences and bring that knowledge to bear on an ongoing basis. The downside is that, unless there is exceptional diligence, the distribution of academic experiences may not be even, given availability of programs, acceptance rates in universities, and so forth. One organization may find, for example, that all of its staff were trained at only one or two universities, thus defeating in part the purpose of this approach.

The "hit-or-miss" approach is best exemplified by the strategy of sending a few key individuals from an organization to either a variety of universities, or the same university with which the institution in question may have developed a formal or informal affiliation. This approach can work well if the university/individual selection match is an ideal fit, or in the case of an ongoing relationship, if the university in question possesses the resources to handle the variety of academic needs of the selected individuals. What hampers this strategy is the low-aim, low-reward nature of depending on a few individuals both to succeed in their programs and to stay in their home-country organizations when they return.

The "key individuals" approach (in which selected "rising stars" are the focal point for training) is extremely effective if, for example, in the ministry of agriculture, three individuals are trained in three related agricultural disciplines, succeed, stay in their ministry, and then are promoted. However, this is a big "if." If only one of these individuals is still in the ministry seven years later, how significant have the rewards of this training been to the organization? That organization will probably have changed very little, if at all, as a result of this external training. Twenty-five years hence, there may even be no recollection that it ever happened. On the other hand, some would argue that even if individuals leave the ministry, they still add value to the society as a whole, assuming they remain in the country.

Saturation training is the thorough flooding of a particular organization—in this case, the Indonesian Ministry of Finance—with a pool of new knowledge. Here, that knowledge consists of relevant academic training that is planned to enhance future performance. There are many advantages to this approach for upgrading the analytical capabilities of an organization's staff.

First and foremost, saturation training is thorough; any individual who shows academic potential, effective work outputs and habits, and initiative may be eligible for such external degree training. Moreover, by having such a program in place, the organization quite naturally will attract very bright and motivated employees (as well as others who think they are).

In addition, unlike targeted training, a soundly designed saturation program will span all the relevant disciplines of a given organization rather than force individuals into areas of study to which they would not normally gravitate. By offering a range of fields to be studied, and some choice on the part of the individual, the organization plays to the strengths of the individuals being trained, thereby increasing the chances of success in graduate studies. More importantly, individuals trained are confident that the general academic and applied learning they have absorbed will be relevant to the ongoing needs of the institution, and do not need to fear the possibility (as in targeted training) that circumstances might change, and their degrees become obsolete. This, of course, mitigates the risks inherent in the targeted approach.

Another advantage of the saturation strategy is that because professional employees are made aware of these opportunities from an early stage, they are motivated to perform well in order to earn the privilege of competing with their colleagues for training opportunities. The number of opportunities is relatively large, and thus does not discourage people from competing. If the program is well designed, employees are not eligible for this privilege until they have completed a stipulated number of years of service.

From an institutional perspective, this infusion of new knowledge is sufficiently large that it not only reinforces the ambitions of those coming through the pipeline after their predecessor (often more senior) colleagues have returned, it also serves to raise the general body of knowledge of the organization as a whole. When, as in the case of the Indonesian Ministry of Finance, several hundred employees return to many different directorates and subdirectorates of an organization, their new approaches to and techniques of analysis touch many fellow employees with whom they interact, compared to the relatively few who would be "exposed" in the other training approaches. If the plans for returnees are highly developed and if the returnees are spread widely throughout the institution, this can be a very effective strategy indeed.

Last but not least, this substantial investment in human capital fosters healthy competition in the form of debates over different ideas and strategic approaches to particular problems. It does not require a great stretch of the imagination to realize that such an approach can raise analytical and management skills to levels that would have been inconceivable before adoption of such a strategy. If the program is well designed from start to finish, such goals are achievable.

Clearly, the main obstacle to such an approach is its finances. There is no question that for most countries, the luxury of the approach taken by the Indonesian Ministry of Finance is unattainable, particularly from the perspective of the number of individuals trained. However, this Ministry employs several thousand professionals and thus, in order to achieve saturation, it had to train a core of several hundred professionals. In the ministry of a smaller country, with perhaps 500 employees or fewer, the training of only thirty to fifty professionals might achieve similar (distributive or other) goals.

Another criticism of a saturation approach is that one ministry may not be able to absorb so many well-educated individuals in a relatively brief period of time. There is certainly some validity to this argument, particularly if the organization in question does not take steps to ensure that returnees are challenged and gainfully employed. One method the Indonesian Ministry of Finance employed was to train the best students to the doctoral level, and reward a high percentage of them with the most challenging and high-ranking positions. Indonesia is especially fertile ground for this approach because of the many university-educated employees working in its ministries. The general point, however, is that such an abundant supply of highly trained professional technocrats entails much more "upside" than "downside" risk, particularly if the returnees remain within the ministry. The key is planning in advance for successful absorption, while simultaneously maintaining the flexibility to place the trainees in positions that both take account of their new expertise and coincide with current organizational needs. Admittedly, that in itself is a challenge.

Although much of the academic literature on the effectiveness of training to help build capacity in developing country ministries is fairly pessimistic, the Indonesian case provides a more promising picture.[2] In contrast to other cases, such as Kenya, which is discussed in Chapter 5 of this volume, and where the results are at best very mixed, external degree recipients in this program have remained in their ministry in overwhelming numbers. Moreover, many—particularly those with doctorates—were promoted to positions of prominence, and at a much faster rate than their colleagues who did not earn external degrees; this indicates the value attached to these degree holders and the commitment of the ministry to building in-house capacity.

Indonesian Ministry of Finance Training Program

Beginning late in 1981 and early 1982, the Harvard Institute for International Development (HIID) assisted the Government of Indonesia in its efforts to build a cadre of academically trained young professionals who could perform the analysis necessary to make rational, well-informed policy decisions. (Although HIID had played a role in training and making referrals for Indonesian officials to universities on an ad hoc basis prior to this time, the formal ministry training program did not commence until 1981.) In particular, HIID became deeply involved in improving the analytical capacity of the Indonesian Ministry of Finance, with which it was most closely associated for more than a decade. The chief vehicle employed to upgrade such capabilities was external degree training in the United States. Through 1994, 348 officials sponsored under HIID contracts with the ministry had returned to Indonesia with graduate degrees earned in the United States. Twenty-four of these individuals earned doctorates, and the rest earned master's degrees. More than fifty other officials were enrolled in U.S. graduate programs—or in the pipeline—as of mid-1995.

Although the ministry had hundreds of (Indonesian) university-trained professionals, few had the ability to engage in policy analysis or planning because of both a lack of experience and a lack of education. Consequently, around 1980, key ministry leaders and HIID decided together that a more comprehensive training program, which included formal graduate education outside of Indonesia, would be most effective in improving the analytical capabilities in this large organization.[3] They agreed that master's degrees in economics would be most effective in providing the analytical skills that the brightest young ministry professionals would need in order to come back and perform effective, analytical research. Subsequently, it was determined that business administration, public administration, and law were also appropriate academic disciplines for ministry officers.

As a result, HIID established a Cambridge-based training office in 1981 to act as the lead implementer of this plan. In the first year of its operations, a dozen ministry officials came to the United States for master's degree training. In the second year, the number doubled; by the fifth year, it had doubled again, and by the peak years of 1989 through 1991, some fifty new ministry-supported Indonesian officials were coming to the United States for graduate degrees each year. Table 4-1 presents the numbers of degree earners each year, and Figure 4-1 provides the cumulative buildup of such degree earners in the ministry. A small percentage of the total number of officials—fewer than 10 percent—came from two other ministries, trade and foreign affairs.

On the surface, what seemed to be developing was the evolution of a comprehensive effort to build a cadre of professional analysts based on specific ministry or government needs. However, more probing assessment, based on discussions with government and HIID officials, firsthand knowledge gained through numerous meetings with officials from both sides, and years of written communications and analysis, supports a somewhat different conclusion. In retrospect, it appears that, despite an overarching plan to train as many individuals as possible, there was no master plan that addressed specific needs or desired outcomes.

Although there was a plan to train many individuals, the selection of trainees was based more on a combination of the success of applicants in predeparture screening programs, both in academic potential and English language competence; the initiative taken by individual supervisors in producing and "pushing" their own qualified candidates and training agendas; the willingness of (other) applicants' supervisors to release them for the two to three years typically required to earn a master's degree; and the amount of money in the pool allotted for overseas training at the particular time in question.[4]

As the project evolved, it became clear that the main goal was to educate as many professionals as possible while funding lasted. The

TABLE 4-1

Indonesian Ministry of Finance/HIID Training Project
Earners of External Graduate Degrees

Year of Return	Number Earning Degrees	Number Failing
1984	17	3
1985	11	2
1986	19	1
1987	16	1
1988	33	1
1989	35	1
1990	20	3
1991	46	2
1992	46	1
1993	68	—
1994	37	—

Universities (through 1993)

American Univ. (12)
Ball State Univ. (5)
Baylor Univ.
California State Univ., Fresno (3)
Carnegie-Mellon Univ. (16)
Case Western Reserve Univ. (2)
Claremont Graduate School (6)
College of Insurance
Colorado State Univ. (6)
Cornell Univ.
Drake Univ.
Duke Univ. (6)
Duquesne
Fordhan Univ. (3)
Georgetown Univ. (2)
George Washington Univ.
Georgia State Univ.
Harvard Univ. (5)
Killinois State Univ.
Indiana Univ. (5)
Johns Hopkins Univ. (3)
Kansas State Univ.
Memphis State Univ.
Michigan State Univ. (2)
New Mexico State Univ. (2)
New School For Social
Research (2)
North Carolina State Univ. (4)
Northeastern Univ. (2)
Ohio State Univ.
Ohio Univ. (5)

Pace Univ.
Pennsylvania State Univ. (2)
Saint Louis Univ. (12)
Southern Illinois Univ. at
Carbondale (6)
Southern Illinois Univ. at
Edwardsville (2)
Southern Methodist Univ.
Stanford Univ. (3)
State Univ. of New York at
Binghamton
Syracuse Univ. (2)
Texas Tech Univ.
Tufts Univ.
Tulane Univ. (3)
Univ. of Bridgeport
Univ. of Chicago
Univ. of Colorado at Boulder (9)
Univ. of Colorado at Denver
Univ. of Dallas (2)
Univ. of Delaware (6)
Univ. of Denver (3)
Univ. of Detroit (2)
Univ. of Hartford (18)
Univ. of Hawaii (2)
Univ. of Illinois (20)
Univ. of Kansas City (4)
Univ. of Kentucky (2)
Univ. of Maine (2)
Univ. of Maryland
Univ. of Miami (5)

Univ. of Michigan
Univ. of Nevada at Reno (3)
Univ. of New Haven (3)
Univ. of New Orleans (3)
Univ. of Notre Dame (5)
Univ. of Oklahoma City (5)
Univ. of Oregon
Univ. of Pittsburgh (6)
Univ. of Rochester
Univ. of San Diego
Univ. of Southern California (3)
Univ. of Texas at Arlington
Univ. of Virginia (3)
Univ. of Washington
Univ. of Wisconsin at Madison
Univ. of Wisconsin at
Whitewater (9)
Univ. of Wyoming
Utah State Univ.
Vanderbilt Univ. (10)
Virginia Commonwealth Univ. (2)
Wake Forest Univ. (3)
Washington Univ. (3)
Western Illinois Univ. (10)
West Virginia Univ. (2)
Williams College (2)
Yale Univ. (3)

Univ. of Birmingham,
United Kingdom

FIGURE 4-1

Indonesian Ministry of Finance/HIID Training Project
Earners of External Graduate Degrees

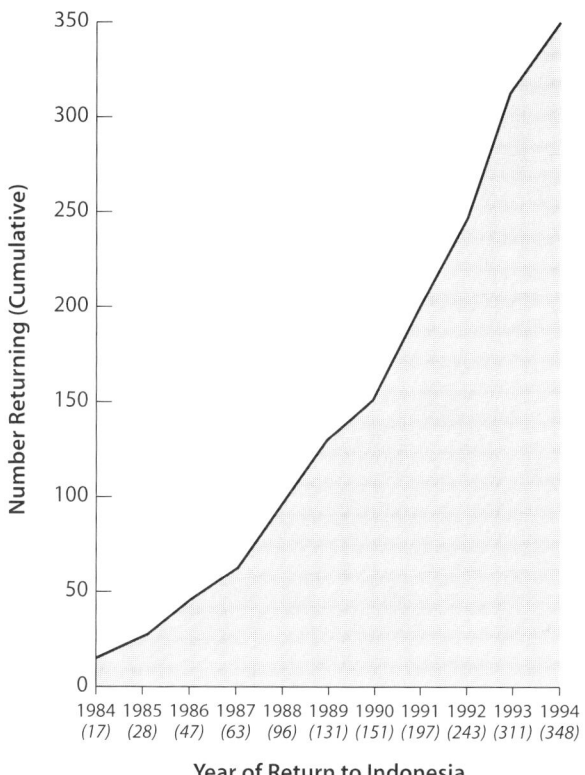

main implication of this policy (or lack thereof) is that it seemed to attain a life of its own (because of the ongoing availability of funding). What remained for project managers—both at HIID and in Jakarta—was to steer the direction of this ship in the most "common sense" approach possible.

Between 1982 and 1995, funding for training came from two main sources. In the early years, financing was available through direct contracts between the government of Indonesia and HIID. From 1989 on, the World Bank served as a major funding source, under its Professional Human Resources Development (PHRD) contract with the Government of Indonesia. Under the PHRD contract, roughly $100 million was provided to the government, about $17 million of which was allocated to the Indonesian Ministry of Finance training program. Approximately $10 million of this sum was administered through the HIID Training Office. Other PHRD funds allocated to the ministry were expended largely for training in the United Kingdom and Canada, through other international sponsorship agencies. Ultimately, some $45 million was expended for training through HIID.

Annual and Cumulative Number of Students Trained

To analyze how trained returnees have fared with respect to retention and promotions, it is useful to reduce this total group to those who graduated and returned to Indonesia by August 1993, because the latest accessible directory of highly ranked government officials was released in early 1994.[5] Between 1982 and 1993, HIID sponsored more than three hundred ministry and ministry-managed students who earned graduate degrees from U.S. universities (see Figure 4-1). Of this number, twenty-one earned doctoral degrees, all but one from a U.S. university. Eight failed in their doctoral programs. Three additional officials earned Ph.D.s in 1994, twenty-two were enrolled in doctoral programs, and some fifty others enrolled in master's programs in 1995. (See Tables 4-1 and 4-2 for numbers of external graduate degrees earned and earners of doctorates.) It is expected that the pass rate (roughly 75 percent for Ph.D.s) will be roughly the same for the group pursuing the Ph.D. in 1995; i.e., sixteen or seventeen of this group should earn their doctoral degrees.[6] In sum, approximately thirty-six professionals will have earned U.S. doctoral degrees and four will have earned U.K. doctoral degrees under this training program by the year 1998. About twenty-eight to thirty of these students will have been ministry employees, with the remainder coming from related organizations or other ministries.

Before 1982, there were at most a handful of ministry officials who had earned doctorates from Western universities.[7] Most of this first wave of Western-trained economists received Ph.D.s at the University of California at Berkeley, and have been referred to for a generation as the "Berkeley Mafia." These individuals played leadership roles—in several cases, they continue to play leadership roles to this day—in economic policy analysis and policy making. They were also instrumental in designing and pushing this training effort. Most observers attribute Indonesia's economic success to the economic policy

TABLE 4-2

Indonesian Ministry of Finance/HIID Training Project
Earners of Doctorates

Year of Return	Number Earning Degrees	Number Failing	Universities	Fields of Study
1986	2	—	Univ. of Pittsburgh	Economics (1) Public Admin. (1)
1987	4	—	Univ. of Colorado, Vanderbilt Univ., Univ. of Pittsburgh	Economics (3)
			Ohio State Univ.	Political Sci. (1)
1988	2	—	Univ. of Maryland	Economics (1)
			Univ. of Virginia	Law (1)
1989	4	1	Univ. of Notre Dame (2), Univ. of Illinois, Carnegie-Mellon Univ.	Economics (4)
1990	1	1	Univ. of Southern Calif.	Public Admin. (1)
1991	4	1	Univ. of Illinois, Southern Illinois Univ. at Carbondale, Univ. of Colorado (2)	Economics (4)
1992	2	2	Univ. of Birmingham (UK)	Public Admin. (1)
			Michigan State Univ.	Economics (1)
1993	2	3	Univ. of Illinois, Claremont Graduate School	Economics (2)
1994	3	—	Iowa State Univ., Univ. of Kentucky	Economics (2)
			Case Western Reserve Univ.	Accounting (1)
1995*	5	2		
1996*	4	1		
1997*	4	2		
1998*	4	1		

* See Endnote 6 for an update for these years

making skills of these leaders. Aside from doctorates, it is believed that there were also fewer than several dozen individuals who had earned master's degrees at that time. Thus, the number of highly educated professionals in the ministry will have nominally increased tenfold as a result of HIID's sponsorship of officials in largely U.S. programs over the life of the project.

Success of Master's Degree Students

What is particularly remarkable is the success rate of master's degree students during this twelve-year period (1982–1994). Of those students who entered graduate programs, only fourteen failed to earn master's degrees (see Table 4-1), a pass rate of 96 percent. According to knowledgeable HIID personnel, senior ministry officials, and the students themselves, several factors contributed to this remarkable success rate:[8]

■ High motivation levels of most of the students. These were generally bright, highly motivated individuals who took their academic responsibilities quite seriously. As such, they were well-selected. Their academic records in Indonesia were factored into decisions regarding potential success in the United States.

■ Diligence on the part of ministry managers in ensuring that only the most qualified and capable officers were permitted to go abroad. In particular, these managers tested for academic aptitude, English language capability, performance in simulated graduate course work in Jakarta, and psychological testing, which measured such factors as initiative, adaptability to new situations, and team orientation.

■ Well-designed preparatory course work, both in Jakarta and at several academic centers around the United States. These courses covered both substantive and English-language materials and were designed to serve as a bridge between the Indonesian civil service and the U.S. university environment. The prep programs also served as a useful, final screening hurdle before participants were allowed to attend graduate programs.

■ The ability of the HIID training office to match students with appropriate university programs. Given the wide variety of student academic and English language capabilities as well as the different relative emphases of graduate programs, this was an essential step in order to maintain low failure rates. Failure generally occurred in those few cases in which programs misrepresented their emphases or, in several instances, disguised a hidden attrition agenda.[9]

■ The close monitoring by and support from HIID's training office to ensure students were given every chance of success. A key strategy was to get to know the advisor or director of graduate studies, or both, as soon and as well as possible, to explain the goals of the program and to emphasize HIID's eagerness to learn of any academic problems at an early stage so that appropriate remedial measures (such as math tutoring, additional English course work, paper editing, or personal counseling) could be provided immediately. Similarly, training office personnel spent numerous hours on site visits or on telephone calls evaluating prospects for success, cajoling hesitant advisors, and hunting down alternative opportunities for degrees.

PROMOTION RATE FOR EARNERS OF MASTER'S DEGREES

The success rate in earning degrees was very high. However, assessing the ability of these individuals to perform policy analysis at relatively advanced levels and achieve merited promotions is somewhat difficult because such detailed data are as yet not readily available and the contributions that Echelon III and IV employees make to policy making entails some highly subjective judgments.[10] In any case, most of the master's degree earners were promoted at faster than normal rates, but only eight out of the 290 students who earned master's degrees had attained Echelon II status as of the beginning of 1994 (Figure 4-2). This is hardly surprising, because historically even the most highly qualified individuals have not attained Echelon II status until age 45 to 50 or older.

From another perspective, conservative estimates indicate that the ministry had a better than 90 percent retention rate for its returning external master's degree earners (retention is discussion later on). Thus, the pool from which it could draw many of its future leaders was a very large one. Although detailed information on the promotion rates and professional career paths of the master's students is relatively scant, the data for returning Ph.D. students are much more solid and, as a result, more revealing of the importance that ministry officials attached to individuals with advanced degrees.

DOCTORAL DEGREE STUDENTS

In the early 1980s, managers of the training program (from the ministry and HIID) actively discussed the utility of having a few select officials continue from master's to doctoral programs. At the time,

FIGURE 4-2

Indonesian Ministry of Finance/HIID Training Project
Percentage of External Graduate Degree Earners Attaining Echelon II Status
(through June 1993)

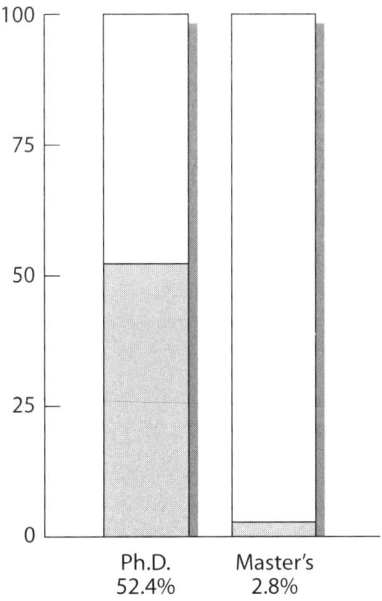

the ministry was quite top-heavy in terms of its best-educated staff. With a handful of educated elite running economic policy at the highest echelons, the ministry did not have nearly enough capacity to engage in the research needed to provide inputs into the policy decision-making processes, let alone to allow for ideas being generated from the bottom up.

In part, these discussions were motivated by several requests from students who wished to earn doctorates; but the idea of having some continue for the Ph.D. had been considered from the inception of the training program. Between 1984 and 1988 (inclusive), twenty HIID-sponsored students commenced Ph.D. programs, an average of four students per year. Although this number was somewhat larger than initially envisaged, it was within the bounds of what the ministry could be expected to absorb in a reasonable fashion and time frame. Also, most people involved believed that the attrition rate for Ph.D.s would certainly be significantly higher than for master's students.

Promotion Rate for Earners of Doctoral Degrees

The Ph.D. clearly served as a launching pad for officials within the ministry. Of the twenty-one students who earned doctorates under the ministry/PHRD training program between 1985 and 1993, eleven had attained the lofty Echelon II level by 1995. Very few had served even as high as the Echelon III level prior to coming to the United States for their degrees and most were at Echelon IV or lower. That half of the doctoral earners had moved to Echelon II is significant, because reaching this level normally would have taken between five and ten years.[11] Figures 4-1 and 4-2 emphasize the extraordinary rate at which Ph.D. earners achieved promotions to the highest levels, in comparison especially to their colleagues who earned only master's degrees (although the latter generally appeared to be receiving faster promotions than their peers who had not earned external degrees).

Most of the Ph.D. students wrote on relatively applied thesis topics that involved Indonesian situations. Many university advisors throughout the United States, especially those with experience working in developing countries, believed strongly that Indonesian Ph.D. students should write theses that were relevant to their homeland, and, if possible, on a topic dealing directly with Indonesian issues. Box 4-1 provides a sampling of thesis topics.

Thus, most returning Ph.D.s not only thought about, analyzed, and attempted to solve (or at least make recommendations about) real economic problems facing their country, but they also carved out a niche of expertise that they could often build upon after they returned home. In addition, during the course of their writings, many returned home to collect data, refine their topics, and consult with colleagues, superiors, HIID advisors in Jakarta, and others. These consultations helped keep them abreast of the latest developments and research efforts already under way, and enabled them to make useful contacts.

Some critics have questioned the level of Indonesian trainees' understanding of the economic theory required to direct research teams or policy analysis efforts. These questions have come principally from two distinct perspectives: those who wonder whether the programs in which students were enrolled were sufficiently rigorous and those who suspect there is a double standard at many graduate schools for non-English, non-Western-educated students. Answering the second question first, HIID training office personnel did in

---

BOX 4-1

Sample Doctoral Dissertation Topics

- Relationship between Indonesian Central and Local Governments: How to Develop Local Tax Efficiencies and Equitability [a]
- Fiscal Efficiency and Equity: Analysis of State Sales Taxes [b]
- A General Equilibrium Analysis of Indonesian Petroleum Tax Incidence [b]
- Burden of Excise Taxes by Income Groups in Indonesia: Case Study of Tobacco [b]
- Econometric Model for Trade in Indonesia [b]
- Development of a Theoretical Framework to Build Model of the Optimum Public Policy for Indonesia's External Debt [b]
- Effects of Taxation on the Indonesian Labor Supply [b]
- Political Economy of the Indonesian Textile Industry under the New Order Government [b]
- Political Implication of the Law of the Sea conference for ASEAN Countries [b]
- Theory and History of Indexation: Case of External Mexican Debt
- Optimal Modelling of Indonesian Internal Migration
- Effect of Foreign Direct Investment in Indonesia
- Indonesia's Real Urban Property Tax: Evaluation of Taxpayer Compliance
- Economics of Property Taxation in Indonesia

---

[a] This dissertation was written by an official who has attained Echelon I.

[b] These dissertations were written by officials who have attained Echelon II.

---

fact witness students from developing countries receiving special dispensation in the form of wide latitude in the level of analysis required, written or spoken English expression, and political naiveté and cultural lack of awareness.

All four training office counselors expressed little doubt that some sympathetic professors, particularly those who had experience working in the developing world, and who were familiar with the rote education methods that prevail in many education systems, sometimes provided extensive assistance to students who at times put in substandard performances. On the other hand, these same advisors also met with professors who not only stated that they would not cut foreign students any "slack," but that they were also not interested in having Indonesian students in their programs anymore because they couldn't develop them into U.S. university faculty members. In general, those who took longer to earn their degrees were forced to jump through more rigorous hoops because their advisors were not among those who were willing to give international, nonnative-English-speaking students special treatment.

As to the question of whether the academic programs were of sufficiently high caliber, many of the doctoral and master's students attended high-quality universities, as indicated in Tables 4-1 and 4-2. More than two-thirds of the ministry group attended universities ranked very strong, strong, good, and acceptable plus in *The Gourman Report*.[12] Seventeen percent attended universities ranked as adequate and 3 percent attended schools rated as inadequate.[13] More than one-third of all students came from the "very strong" and "strong" categories. Even more impressive is the fact that of the eleven students who earned doctoral degrees and who were promoted to Echelon II, eight attended top-ranked programs in their respective fields, according to Gourman.

This quality control stands in marked contrast to placement and achievement levels of many other students who have been placed in large groups by some other sponsors.[14]

Indonesian officials who were selected to come to school in the United States were by and large top-notch students, as evidenced by their Indonesian academic records, Indonesian-administered tests of academic potential, and their collectively very high rates of success in challenging American graduate programs. Moreover, the efforts of the HIID training office to place students in high-quality doctoral programs, in particular, were quite successful.

Barriers to Full Reintegration

Despite the apparent willingness of the ministry to promote earners of doctorates to the highest levels, the same cannot be said for its policies regarding returning master's students, as indicated in Figure 4-2. Why was the ministry so slow to incorporate the earners of master's degrees into its upper echelons? One reason is that some senior ministry officials were traditionally dependent on expatriate advisors, and had little confidence in the returning trainees.[15] In addition, however, the contributing factors were exogenous in nature, and had little to do with the increased analytical capacities of its Western-educated professional staff. Fuller reintegration would have been more likely in the absence of several barriers.

First, the ministry's role in overseeing the training program evolved historically into a mode of benign neglect. Although the early training administration was overseen in a relatively heavy-handed fashion by the "training czar" of the time, the later years were managed more loosely, as training management became a less central concern of subsequent training directors. As a result, the attention paid to appropriate placement and reintegration diminished over time.

Second, proactive measures are usually required to change—even in the smallest ways—how a bureaucracy functions. Inertia serves to counteract effective reintegration in that genuinely appropriate job and career placement of returnees requires significant effort to find the best fit and advance planning to ensure that achieving such a fit is possible. For example, it may require creation of a new job or even removal of the current occupant of the position. It is hard to imagine a more effective "inertia point" in any civil service scheme than this last one.

Third, even though HIID had a very solid record of knowing when its work was done on any given project, related, follow-on projects surfaced quite frequently. These follow-on projects created bottlenecks for turning projects over to Indonesian analysts, and, as indicated earlier, were the source of some consternation, particularly among certain returnees.

Fourth, many high-ranking ministry officials became quite accustomed to the services and advice provided by consultants. They appreciated the sound analysis and judgment provided in policy papers and recommendations, and the quick turnaround time they came to expect when asking for such analyses. Given this situation, they were apprehensive about trusting the advice of the "new kids." Still other officials wondered whether untested subordinates could really have adequate analytic skills, and they were too impatient to allow staff to learn by doing and to make mistakes as they advised. A few also worried about their staff handling confidential materials. Could they be trusted politically? Would economic information be leaked to individuals and corporations who could benefit inappropriately? Had Western ideas of democracy undermined their loyalty to the Government of Indonesia? Did they have notions of meritocracy that would erode their allegiance to a system historically built around seniority?[16] Could they lead others? In general, senior officials believed that intergenerational change needed to be managed carefully.

Fifth, especially during the first year after returning from studies (after being out of the country and the civil service from anywhere between two and eight years), trainees were often disoriented. There was little, if anything, in the way of a formal reintegration process to assist them in this underestimated difficulty. Often they were placed in positions that underutilized the skills they had acquired, with little indication that they might soon advance to positions in which they could employ what they had learned. In this light, it is even more remarkable that more flight from the ministry has not occurred. Occasionally, the opposite was true. One individual interviewed was placed in charge of an important research bureau immediately upon his return simply because his predecessor had recently retired. After being a graduate student in an American college town for more than eight years, he suddenly had a staff of more than fifty individuals and a research agenda to devise and implement. Before coming to the United States, he had had little managerial experience, and he didn't study human resources management during his graduate training. This was a setup for failure.

Sixth, returning trainees and the supervisors who sent them were all well aware that the low salaries of civil servants made it almost mandatory for the returnees to find outside work—often teaching in universities or consultancies, just to maintain a semblance of the lifestyle they had become accustomed to as U. S. graduate students. That being so, few except the most highly placed former trainees could afford to forego other, more remunerative opportunities. Thus, most were unwilling to demonstrate solid analytic judgment and put in the long hours necessary to carve out steady career advancement. Their bosses knew not to call them after 4 P.M.

Seventh, there was certainly a learning curve in applying economic and managerial theory—or even practical course work, such as case studies—to the complex problems faced in the real world by real bureaucracies. Most individuals had to go through a "trial and error" period on the job; this raised the possibility that inappropriate policies would be chosen and have dangerous repercussions in Indonesia's economy.

RETENTION

The retention rate among the Indonesian ministries administered under the Indonesian Ministry of Finance and World Bank projects was quite remarkable. It is conservatively estimated that significantly more than 90 percent of those employees who earned master's or doctoral degrees still worked for the government at the beginning of 1995.[17] In fact, it is estimated that more than 90 percent also worked for the same ministry, with only a slightly smaller proportion being employed in the same directorate.

Why did Indonesians stay in government service after returning with advanced degrees? In part, the answer falls somewhere near the point where cultural loyalty, respect for and fear of authority, and lack of alternative opportunities come together. The opening up of Indonesia's marketplace in general, and of the financial services industry in particular, may erode the pull of these factors in the future, but the long-term effects of the liberalization of the economy and the anticipation of the first changeover in the presidency had had little impact by 1995.[18]

The fact that individuals sign a "contract" with the ministry before embarking for the United States also serves to encourage high retention rates. That contract obligates students to work for five years immediately upon returning, or else be forced to pay double the cost of their education, which could easily reach six figures in U.S. dollars. Training office records indicate only one case in which an employer, a U.S. mining company operating in eastern Indonesia, grabbed a returning student away from the ministry by buying out this contract. There may have been other cases, but the steep costs plus the relatively few examples of individuals who left government service made it unlikely that many others would avail themselves of such opportunities.

In addition, being a professional civil servant in Indonesia carries significant status. Many civil servants live in subsidized ministry housing blocs, with special buses that take them to and from work, and they enjoy many other amenities. A civil servant truly believes that he or she is among the elite of the society on the occupational level. This intangible status helps keep officials in the government, according to several officials interviewed, in spite of the much greater financial rewards that could be gained in the private sector.[19]

Moreover, Indonesians working in government service demonstrate remarkable loyalty to the government, which represents, in their minds, their cultural heritage. The idea of Greater Indonesia, in which *Pancasila* (the five principles of mutual respect and cooperation) predominates, has been a major cultural theme since independence (1948), and particularly since the New Order came to power in the mid-1960s. Thus, virtually all students came of age in this culture in which they were taught to honor and take pride in their new country and to strive to make ethnic diversity work harmoniously. Moreover, they were the first generation to grow up fully in the spirit of *Pancasila* in the post-Sukarno, New Order era, in which greater acceptance—rather than polarization—of different political, socioeconomic, and cultural groups became the norm.[20] Related to their perspectives on government are trainees' attitudes of moral and ethical obligation to repay their government for giving them the privilege of studying abroad and earning an advanced degree.[21]

Another factor that enhanced retention rates appears to be cultural. The Javanese, who are the dominant ethnic group in the population, are generally stereotyped as being unwilling to do the unexpected or to rock the boat.[22] However accurate this overly general cultural characterization, few returnees in fact seemed willing to "jump ship" and leave the government employ, partly because in doing so they would be viewed as engaging in inappropriate behavior, and would risk disfavor or, at worst, ostracism. This fear is heightened substantially by the fact that a military regime is in power.

Similarly, respect for seniority seems to have limited attrition. Traditionally, Indonesian society has been guided by an overarching respect for seniority that pervades all aspects of the culture. Although this relatively passive Asian outlook has been breaking down somewhat under Western "youth culture" influences, respect for seniority was still predominant, especially in government bureaucracies, in the mid-1990s. There is evidence that meritocracy is gradually replacing seniority, however (and older, locally educated ministry officials would probably say quickly, not gradually). This evidence is supported by much of the data described in this chapter. Returning officials with degrees were promoted and moved up through the ranks much more swiftly than their "stay-at-home" counterparts. Still, the old system was not yet dead, and there are those who obstructed progress in this area quite effectively, particularly with respect to the master's trainees.

All who were sent abroad for degrees and successfully completed their programs carried with them the parting words of the training director: "We are being groomed as the future leaders of our country." That thought sustained many promising civil servants for a long time, and as they heard about and saw firsthand the rise of their colleagues who returned earlier, they continued to have high hopes for career advancement. Precisely because this proved to be true, returnees were more likely to come back eager to reap their "just rewards," and even to work hard to ensure that it happened. Of course, part of this process was self-selecting: the most ambitious and driven of the civil servants pushed themselves to achieve higher status and responsibilities, and to take advantage of overseas training opportunities in the first place.

In addition, many of the returnees took jobs on the side, often in teaching or consulting. Such work enabled them to increase their incomes greatly, thereby prodding them to remain in the civil service while they awaited the hoped-for promotions to the upper echelons, and gave them experience in other areas. Of course, as officials move higher up the ranks, moonlighting becomes more difficult to do, because ministry work becomes more important and time-consuming. Those demands are imposed on only a tiny minority of officials, however, and are apparently well worth the sacrifice of greater freedom.

Last but certainly not least, few of the Indonesians in government service had experience with higher-paying full-time positions in the private sector; most entered the civil service shortly after graduation from university. Until the mid-1980s, the financial services sector had been largely controlled by the government, and there were relatively few opportunities there. With deregulation and the entry of many new banks, financial service firms, and corporations into the marketplace, the long-term attractiveness of lower-paying jobs in the civil service may erode.

CONCLUSIONS

Over the thirteen-year life of HIID's training projects with the Indonesian Ministry of Finance, there were many accomplishments, not the least of which was the significant strengthening of the organization's human capital base. Even leaving aside the question of whether the skills and academic knowledge of the more than four hundred officials was being most effectively employed, the ministry acquired an incomparably greater analytical capability than it had in 1982. From less than a few dozen, it increased its ranks of academically well-trained officials more than tenfold.

By the mid-1990s, the resources were in place, and in many cases individuals were very well positioned to make substantial contributions. This is not to assert that all was rosy in this ministry; it was not. Traditional barriers to success remained: outdated seniority systems without regard to merit; intransigent supervisors who jealously guarded their power; political in-fighting; corruption; and other factors. Nevertheless, the civil service was moving in the direction of a stronger meritocracy.

Thus, what was new in the ministry was a cadre of officials who had received Western academic training and who, when interviewed, overwhelmingly indicated their intention of staying within the ministry both because they believed it would enhance their careers and because they honestly thought that they could contribute to the national effort to progress economically.[23] It remained for the ministry to determine how to keep this very large pool of officials gainfully employed and challenged by the work that needed to be done. The ministry clearly figured out a way to do this for its returning doctoral earners. It is not clear that it had done the same for the vastly larger pool of officials who earned master's degrees.

The ministry did several things very well in this effort to upgrade its in-house capacity. First, it committed the resources to training. Second, it set up a system and developed a selection process for this external training privilege that was truly meritocratic, encompassing such factors as work performance, academic potential, English attainment levels, and psychological preparedness. Third, it designed an informal system that allowed returning earners of doctorates largely to circumvent the age-old, culturally intransigent seniority system so diametrically opposed to meritocracy. Finally, despite the inability to move the returning master's earners up through the ranks of the hierarchy as quickly as the Ph.D.s, it managed to keep well over 90 percent of them within the ministry. For, even though those with master's did not generally advance as rapidly, many of them nonetheless progressed more expeditiously than their "stay-at-home" colleagues.

The areas in which the ministry was less successful parallel quite closely the areas of success. First, it did not develop a comprehensive system for reintegrating returning officials, in terms either of placing them in positions that most closely matched their newly gained skills or of timing their return so that they could use their skills fully. In other words, there was little coordination between training office managers and their human resource counterparts.

Second, the ministry failed to set up a system to determine what individual returnees learned or specialized in, so that it could develop a broad and simultaneously precise overview of what new skills the organization possessed, and place staff accordingly. Conducting a training needs assessment early on would have been extremely beneficial in the long term for targeting appropriate individuals for study abroad and placing officials into academic programs where the ministry needs were greatest (e.g., five monetary analysts, two public finance specialists, seven tax people, and so on).

Third, while returning master's degree recipients received some credit for earning the degree, that credit seems often to have been offset by the loss of time actually working in the ministry. In other words, a comparable system to the one developed for Ph.D.s was not implemented for 90 percent of the returnees. In some cases, permitting officers to pursue doctorates was done in part to allow senior managers to circumvent the internal seniority system, by making such officers special cases, rather than by confronting the problems of instituting the fundamental formal reforms that would have enabled the organization to take more effective advantage of its academically well-trained officers.

Finally, the ministry spent about $45 million on training these individuals, and it remained unclear what benefits the country was receiving from it. Such returns will take years, if not decades, to be realized. Yet, if many members of this group attain the upper echelons of the economic planning elite—and make wise policy decisions—dividends will accrue many times over.

At the very least, the ministry was well positioned in 1995 to take advantage of a large arsenal of trainees. At best, the ministry may have amassed a pool of talent that will prove the envy of any developing or developed country agency in the early years of the twenty-first century.

Notes

1   Maria Teresa Tatto, "An Assessment of the LASPAU/AID Training for Development Program in Latin American and Caribbean Universities," (Ph.D. diss., Harvard University Graduate School of Education, 1987), 5.

2   For example, see Elliot J. Berg, *Rethinking Technical Cooperation: Reforms for Capacity Building in Africa* (New York: United Nations Development Programme/Development Alternatives, Inc., 1993), and Clive S. Gray, Chapter 14 of this volume.

3   By the end of the 1970s, one very senior Indonesian ministry official informed an HIID advisor that things had reached the state that, if he needed to make any kind of calculation, he had to do it himself. This incident served as a real motivator for external training.

4   Officials were also administered a "psychological test," which apparently was designed (unscientifically) to measure their aptitudes, levels of initiative, and willingness to work hard both in U.S. graduate programs and for the ministry upon returning. A similar program was in effect for the Indonesian State Bank Training project.

5   See *Kabinet Pembangunan VI beserta Buku Alamat Pejabat Negara Republik Indonesia 1994,* or (Book of Addresses of State Functionaries of the Republic of Indonesia) (Jakarta: Badan Penerbit Alda, 1994).

6   As of January 1997, this prediction has so far come to pass quite accurately: in 1995 and 1996, a total of nine of this group earned doctorates (most in Economics), while three dropped out of their programs (thus, a 75 percent success rate). It is also projected that an additional eight or nine of the now-expanded group of twelve individuals will earn Ph.D.s in 1997–1998. As for the master's students, 65 officials received degrees in 1995–1996, with only one having failed in that time period. In sum, by the end of 1996, more than 400 government officials had earned graduate degrees under this program and returned to Indonesia.

7   In truth, this number may be overstating the case. The collective memory and accumulated knowledge of several HIID advisors and numerous Indonesian officials are only aware of two Ph.D. holders who were working in the ministry in 1980. If there were any others present, and this is highly dubious, they did not have positions of significant rank or influence.

8   The author personally interviewed—both formally and informally—dozens of such officials when they were graduate students in the United States and different Indonesian training managers to ascertain the key success factors described.

9   In several cases, the author interviewed senior departmental administrators in graduate schools and departments who seemed not at all displeased to be "flunking out" a foreign student. The hidden agenda was their view that this action would enhance their standing in national rankings.

10   The time that earners of external master's degrees have saved in moving up the ranks appears over the long haul to be some three to seven years, much more if they have moved higher than Echelon III. The way in which

the echelon system functions in the civil service is somewhat difficult to fathom; in a nutshell, the lower the echelon number, e.g., Echelon I, the higher the rank. Based on interviews with Indonesian officials, historically, a typical young professional who starts in the ministry after earning an Indonesian bachelor's degree takes ten years to attain Echelon IV. Assuming good luck and success, that individual can reach Echelon III after seven or eight years. Assuming more of the same, an individual may after another similar time span, reach Echelon II, at approximately age 50. Retirement looms at age 55, unless, to keep the person in the ministry, senior officials promote the individual to Echelon II before reaching age 55, in which case he or she can work to age 60.

11   As can be gleaned from the preceding discussion of how master's earners move at faster than normal speeds up the ranks, doctoral students save perhaps an average of ten years, depending on their ages, over nonexternal graduate degree recipients. This is extremely hard to quantify more precisely, especially because an "invisible hand" in the form of a high-ranking patron (who sees promise) often intervenes to circumvent normal promotion routes. The importance of personal contacts in this system cannot be underestimated. The best of all worlds occurs when a hardworking patron selects an individual for "extraordinary promotion" based on analytical contributions to the work of the ministry. Somehow, it is easier to "finger" an individual this way when the latter has a doctorate.

12   Jack Gourman, *The Gourman Report: A Rating of Graduate and Professional Programs in American and International Universities* (Los Angeles: National Education Standards, 1993).

13   Four and one half percent were from schools not listed in the directory.

14   During participation in several National Association of Foreign Student Affairs (NAFSA) conferences, and numerous site visits to several preparatory programs designed to help international students gain admission to U.S. universities, the author became well acquainted with some less than stellar approaches to placement of sponsored government officials and "private" students alike. A typical approach used by one such sponsor was to cluster whole groups of same-country nationals at the same university, both because of the lack of an ability to gain admission for them elsewhere and an unwillingness to do the legwork necessary to do otherwise. Of course, there are other organizations with strong placement records with whom it would be interesting to compare track records.

15   In recent years, the ministry has demonstrated a penchant for reducing the number of foreign advisors working in its offices, with measurable success. A core cadre of such advisors still exists, however, though reporting channels for many such advisors may be more indirect than they were five years ago.

16 Several key ministry officials and advisors historically have expressed concern as to whether important leadership qualities can be learned in traditional academic settings (whether Western or non-Western). A few have asserted that "leadership gaps" are central in capacity-building efforts they observe.

17 The "stock line" given by Indonesian officials when queried about retention rates is "Not 90 percent; more than 95 percent." Astoundingly, this seems to be a highly accurate, though unproven, assertion. This author has struggled unsuccessfully for months to locate the "mythical" Indonesian Ministry of Finance personnel directory, which would substantiate or repudiate this claim. In the meantime, we can only verify one "attritor," an individual who had psychological problems. Even the individual previously said to have been bought out by a U.S. mining company is suspected to have opted in the end for staying in the ministry.

18 In the long term, this could pose the largest threat to retention, because a more liberal and open economic system may lure employees away from the ministry. If senior officials are prudent, they will do their best to promote the most productive and brightest of these officers so that they are less tempted to jump ship.

19 Attaining Echelon III status entails benefits not greatly dissimilar to heading up a "small kingdom," according to one official. Reaching Echelon II status and working and living outside a city apparently brings on even greater perquisites.

20 See William H. Frederick and Robert L. Worden, eds., *Indonesia: A Country Study* (Washington, DC: U.S. Library of Congress, 1993), especially 47–105.

21 Between 1987 and 1994, the author interviewed dozens of individuals who professed these viewpoints with apparent heartfelt sincerity. A few members of this group seemed less sincere. In any case, because most hope to succeed in their positions in the ministry, barring significant changes or real long-term barriers to promotion, the issue of honest intentions is moot.

22 Frederick and Worden, *Indonesia*, 47–105.

23 See note 21.

5

Training and Retention in African Public Sectors

Capacity-Building Lessons from Kenya

John M. Cohen and John R. Wheeler

> *The Government must train four or five officers to retain one for a long period of time…[this] serious retention problem…is reaching alarming proportions…[it] must be addressed squarely…[efforts must be made] to change and improve the management and utilization of trained professionals in Government so as to create an environment in which graduates will enjoy a challenging and rewarding professional career in the Civil Service.*
>
> —Paul S. Haddow[1]

Since the early 1990s, African governments and aid agencies have given renewed attention to strengthening the expertise and performance of public sector personnel while reducing the amount of foreign aid expended on costly expatriate technical assistance. Pressures to read-dress these long-established objectives result from widely held perceptions that past efforts to create public sector capacities have largely failed, that bureaucracies remain weak and continue to lack skilled staff, and that an overdependence on expatriate advisors still predominates. Efforts in Kenya to build public sector capacity span nearly three decades. In this period, six externally funded capacity-building projects were implemented that focused on training public sector economists, planners, statisticians, and financial managers, while providing expatriate "gap-filling advisors" who could support public sector functions while training efforts were carried out.[2] All six projects included large programs for training to the master's level at overseas universities.

In this chapter, we provide a case study that suggests that dismissals of past capacity-building efforts should be questioned.[3] As such, we explore and demonstrate several points. First, we argue that identifying and providing training to targeted personnel is relatively easy, whereas effectively utilizing such personnel is more difficult. Second, we examine the level of retention of those trained and find that, given unconducive conditions of service, the level of retention is higher than might be expected. Third, we demonstrate that economists and planners trained to the master's level who elect to remain in government service do so for a wider variety of reasons than other studies suggest. Fourth, we illustrate less well-known but entrenched mechanisms for augmenting low salaries and promoting retention. Fifth, we contend that the focus for improving the performance of the civil service lies as much in effective utilization as it does in adequate salaries and benefits.

Capacity Building in African Public Sectors

Recent studies of capacity-building initiatives stress two interrelated points. First, they indicate that building institutional and human resource capacity contributed to the success of several Asian countries and that the failure to do so led to inadequate planning, policy making, and implementation by most African and some Latin American governments.[4] Second, they indicate that the capacity building attempted in many African countries has been dissipated by the inability of the public sector to retain trained staff, the political and financial crises that have damaged public sector institutions, and the difficulties of reforming the public service in ways that address issues of retention.[5] According to recent studies, the failure to build this capacity is the result of: economic factors that constrain government budgets, resulting in unrealistic pay levels and low morale; inadequate leadership of skilled public sector personnel by senior public servants; social disruptions that create benefits for a few and alienation for many; and political exclusion or repression that drives skilled personnel out of the public sector, and in some cases out of the country.[6]

Growing attention to African public sector capacity building arises, to a large extent, from aid agencies that fund large numbers of projects requiring public sector management. In addition, structural adjustment measures require skilled economic managers and professionals. As highlighted in an internal World Bank report, however, many projects are underperforming and many conditionalities are being poorly implemented.[7] Aid agencies contribute to this problem by acting as individual agents and treating the scarce management and professional capacity in recipient countries as if they were the "commons." Each agency assumes that the management and professional services required to carry out its projects and implement its conditions will be forthcoming. When problems in finding personnel to carry out such services arise, they call for capacity building, demanding that greater attention be given to ensuring that professionals and managers in government institutions be increased and made more effective.[8]

This demand is reinforced by studies arguing that after four decades of training investment, there are still many costly expatriate advisors and consultants in Africa.[9] Further, the numbers, range of services, and costs of such advisors may increase as aid agencies give greater attention to helping governments address their seemingly intractable development problems. Alternatively, development processes may be accelerated only if African governments are better assisted to build the sustainable personnel capacity required to set their own strategies and policy agendas, adapt them to changing circumstances, and implement them through their own structural adjustment reforms, programs, and projects, and negotiate effectively with aid agencies.[10] This change will require increased attention to building local managerial, professional, and technical capacity to carry out the activities essential to the development process and greatly reducing the number of expensive Western university and consulting firm experts who currently provide such capacity where it is missing.[11]

Unfortunately, the growing call for strengthening human resource capacity building is typically based on conventional wisdom and anecdotal evidence. Critics have few case studies to review that systematically analyze the successes and failures of training and staff retention. Hence, this chapter seeks to provide sufficient detail to generate insights and guidelines for African governments and aid agencies seeking to strengthen the managerial, professional, and technical skills of public sector personnel.

Given limited resources, the extent of the problem, and the pressing need to improve governmental performance, it is essential to target capacity building on specific types of public sector personnel.[12] Hence this chapter focuses only on projects seeking to train and retain the economists, planners, and statisticians essential to governmental efforts to define long-term national strategies for sustainable development; formulate sound policies that respond to the impact of global and regional economic trends; deal with a rapid expansion of complex information systems; absorb and benefit from international foreign aid resources; manage and strengthen budget structures and processes; design and implement projects and programs that carry out adopted policies; and assist private sector entrepreneurs and firms to identify, absorb, and adapt new growth-inducing technologies.[13]

EXPERIENCE IN BUILDING TARGETED PUBLIC SECTOR CAPACITY

Between 1970 and 1994, six projects aimed at building the capacity of targeted public sector personnel while providing advisory services were implemented in Kenyan ministries. These six projects were remarkably similar in design and focus. They provide insight into the issues and difficulties involved in training, retaining, and effectively utilizing scarce public sector personnel.

Four of the projects sought to strengthen national, sectoral, and district planning capacities in the Kenyan Ministry of Planning and National Development (MPND): the York University project (1970–1982); the Rural Planning project (RPP) (1976–1985); the Resource Management for Rural Development (RMRD) project (1986–1992); and the Long-Range Planning (LRP) project (1985–1993). The fifth project, the Technical Assistance Pool (TAP) project (1977–1994), focused on the development planning departments of the Kenyan Ministries of Agriculture (MOA) and Livestock Development (MLD). Finally, the sixth project, the Budget and Economic Management project (BEMP) (1990–1994) assisted the Kenyan Ministry of Finance (MOF) in the areas of budget and fiscal management.[14]

All six projects included extensive training programs, the supply of microcomputers and supporting equipment, and the provision of experienced technical assistance advisors. Most of the projects were invested in providing government officers with both long-term master's degree training and short-term overseas training. The projects also ran focused local workshops and seminars, particularly in the areas of budgeting, district planning, and microcomputer operations. Project advisors did not fill specific established posts. Nor did they have specific Kenyan officers assigned to work with them and eventually to replace them after training. Rather, advisors worked with the full range of officers in the units they served, from recent university graduates to senior-level officers. In carrying out their tasks, advisors were expected to provide expertise focused on introducing improved methodologies and systems while strengthening the analytical and policy formulation capacities of the officers they worked with.

CAPACITY-BUILDING OBJECTIVES AND ACHIEVEMENTS

A review of the interim evaluations and final reports published on the activities of the projects suggests that they were remarkably successful in providing gap-filling advisory services and training government economists, planners, statisticians, and managers. These reports also make clear, however, that the projects were far less successful in working with the government to ensure that those Kenyans trained were effectively utilized and retained in the ministry targeted. This experience is summarized in Table 5-1.

Several points need to be made about this table. By way of comparison, in early 1995 there were a total of 570 Kenyans filling government posts for economists, planners, and statisticians. Of this total, 315 were in MPND, with 213 at headquarters and 102 in provincial and district field offices. The remaining 255 officers were posted to other ministries and agencies, including the MOA and MLD, where the TAP was located. Although it is difficult to judge the sheer number of economists required by the government, the size of the total number employed indicates that the absolute number is not the primary problem. Rather, it is their skill levels and effective utilization.

Table 5-1 provides data on the numbers of those trained who have been retained by the ministry seeking to build its skilled personnel (target ministry). It locates those who have left the target ministry but are still working in the public sector and it identifies those who have left the public service. However, it is difficult to track accurately all these individuals because they tend to change jobs, sometimes working for aid agencies and other times for consulting firms, nongovernmental organizations (NGOs), or private sector institutions. For this reason, nonpublic sector categories were not disaggregated. The data were collected in December 1994.

Several issues arise from the data provided in Table 5-1 about which reliable and comprehensive empirical evidence is lacking. Despite this problem, it is possible to address these questions by using both the partial data available and personal knowledge gained by the

TABLE 5-1
1994 Location of Personnel Trained by Six Projects to the Master's Level in Economics, Planning, and Management

Current Location of Project Master's Trainee	Capacity-Building Projects						
	York University Project (1970–1981)ᵃ	Technical Assistance Pool Project (1977–1985)	Rural Planning Project (1977–1985)	Resource Management for Rural Development Project (1985–1992)	Canadian Long-Range Planning Project (1985–1993)	Budget and Economic Management Project (1990–94)	Total
Targeted Ministry for Capacity Building	10 23.8%	10 22.2%	5 33.3%	23 56.1%	5 26.3%	5 71.4%	58 34.3%
Other Government Ministry, Agency or Parastatal	16 38.1%	11 24.4%	2 13.3%	5 12.2%	10 52.6%	0 —	44 26.1%
Sub-Total Public Service	26 61.9%	21 46.6%	7 46.6%	28 68.3%	15 78.9%	5 71.4%	102 60.4%
Private Sector, Nongovernmental Organization, Aid Agency, or University	7 16.7%	19 42.2%	4 26.7%	12 29.3%	4 21.1%	2 28.6%	48 28.4%
Retired or Deceased	9 21.4%	5 11.2%	4 26.7%	1 2.4%	0 —	0 —	19 11.2%
Total Trained	42 100%	45 100%	15 100%	41 100%	19 100%	7 100%	169 100%

Source: Personnel data for the Scheme of Service for Economists and Statisticians reviewed by the authors in 1991 and 1995.

ᵃ The York University Project trained seventy economists, planners, managers, and engineers to the master's level, forty-two of whom were targeted for the then Ministry of Economics and Planning. The remaining twenty-eight were trained for the Ministry of Public Works, the Ministry of Transport and Commerce, the Ministry of Environment, and the Nairobi City Council. Of the forty-two trained in economics and planning for the Treasury, the authors could only track forty. It is assumed the missing two are deceased or retired.

authors as a result of their long experience with all of the projects and many of the Kenyans who were trained under them.[15] This information will generate some tentative answers that may be useful to those seeking to design more effective human resource capacity-building projects in Africa.

The most basic question is, Were these projects successful at building human resource capacity? Table 5-1 shows that across all six projects, the current retention rate of trained master's-level personnel in targeted ministries is 34.3 percent, with a range from 71.4 percent to 22.2 percent. If the broader retention within the public sector is taken, then the overall retention rate rises to 60.4 percent, with a range from 78.9 to 46.6 percent. The different retention categories are significant. In most cases the decision to leave the public service, with the exception of death or retirement, is taken by an individual and is voluntary.[16] Movement from a target ministry to another government agency is the result of transfers made by senior managers, albeit sometimes at the request of the individual. Thus, the loss from a target ministry is the result of both voluntary individual decisions and imposed managerial decisions. For example, the LRP shows a low rate of retention within the target ministry (26.3 percent) but a high rate of retention within the public service (78.9 percent); this reflects management decisions to strip the target ministry of trained personnel rather than individual choice. No ready explanation can be given for the differences among projects, other than a general one that time takes its toll. This does not explain why the retention rate for TAP and RPP are much lower than all the other projects, however.

Whether these levels indicate success is open to debate, given the lack of comparative data. However, there remains a significant presence of personnel trained under the six projects in the target ministries, and the overall retention in public service seems higher than might be expected given anecdotal evidence.

Nevertheless, are retention levels adequate to justify expensive overseas graduate school training? There are dichotomous views in regard to evaluating the success of these projects. The aid agencies that funded the six projects argue that capacity-building components are not successful if those trained are not effectively used and retained in the targeted ministries to take over functions and expertise provided by advisors. For example, a UNDP assessment of capacity building in Kenya's finance and planning ministries found:

The overall government strategy to reduce dependency on foreign experts should be based on clearly defined measurable objectives, and specifying targets and schedules over realistic periods of time depending on the institutions concerned. The strategy should explicitly address the issue of increasing the ability of national professionals to perform tasks satisfactorily without external assistance.[17]

Alternatively, senior Kenyan government officials argue that so long as there is a net addition of trained personnel to the country's human resources, the training component is successful, particularly if those who leave their targeted ministry are retained within the public sector. This point is also made by Clive S. Gray in Chapter 14. Kenyan officials argue that economists transferred from planning to sectoral ministries are still fulfilling the mandate of the planning ministry to provide the government with economic policy and analysis. Some would extend this argument to include those who leave government service for related institutions, aid agencies, or the private sector.

The narrower "replacement" definition of success should apply when evaluating individual projects. On the other hand, benefits will accrue to the capacity of government as long as a trained officer remains within the public service. However, the intention of this chapter is to examine the history of retention and to provide insights into the levels of retention that have been achieved rather than to make judgments as to the relative success of each project. Thus, it is important to take account of both "degrees of retention," that is, both within target ministries and within the public service.

Second, how long should those trained to the master's level be expected to remain in the targeted units where they were to replace expatriate advisors? Turnover must be expected in any bureaucracy, but what are the attrition rates of those trained under these projects? To answer this question, account must be taken of time decay that is a result of normal career development in a public sector desperate for skilled personnel and a civil service in which retirement is mandatory at age 55. Nonetheless, it is valid to calculate an annual attrition figure for each project that takes account of the numbers leaving over different periods of time.[18] The resulting attrition, expressed as an annual percentage that leave, is presented in Table 5-2.

Unfortunately, there are no published figures for the rate of attrition from the public sector as a whole and so it is not easy to determine what the attrition rates are for managers and professionals in

T A B L E   5 - 2
Annual Rates of Attrition of Master's Trainees for Six Projects

Project	Number Trained	Number Leaving by End of 1994	Number Of Years	Annual Attrition Rate (%)
York University Project				
Target Min[a]	42	32	19	−6.9
Govt Serv[b]	42	16	19	−2.5
Rural Planning Project				
Target Min	15	10	14	−7.6
Govt Serv	15	8	14	−5.3
Technical Assistance Pool Project				
Target Min	45	35	11	−12.8
Govt Serv	45	24	11	−6.7
Resource Management for Rural Development Project				
Target Min	41	18	6.5	−8.5
Govt Serv	41	13	6.5	−5.7
Canadian Long-Range Planning Project				
Target Min	19	14	6	−19.9
Govt Serv	19	4	6	−3.9
Budget and Economic Management Project				
Target Min	7	2	2	−15.5
Govt Serv	7	2	2	−15.5
Average All Projects				
Target Min	169	111	9.8	−9.6
Govt Serv	169	67	9.8	−4.3

Source: Personnel data for the Scheme of Service for Economists and Statisticians reviewed by the authors in 1991 and 1995.

a   "Target Min" covers master's trainees who left the targeted ministry but remained in the public service.

b   "Govt Serv" covers those who left the public service entirely.

Kenya's public sector. A partial picture of this emerges from a recent study of departures from the Scheme of Service for Economists and Statisticians (SSES) between January 1992 and June 1994.[19] During this period, 106 professionals left the SSES. Assuming that replacements equaled departures over this period, which appears to be the case, the annual attrition rate is 5.4 percent. Thus it appears that the average attrition rate of those trained under the projects (4.3 percent) is slightly less than that recorded from the whole SSES over the sample period. However, this lower figure may be explained by the larger numbers of individuals retiring from the SSES, whereas master's trainees are selected from among younger officers. Of the 106 officers resigning from the SSES during the period under review, 55 were at the grade level usually held by recently returned master's trainees.[20] The question that remains unaddressed here is what would be comparable annual attrition rates for such personnel in other African and Western public sectors.

Figure 5-1 addresses these attrition rates from a different perspective. It seeks to capture the pure effect of time on attrition.[21] It is based on the assumption that at present there is no objective standard "attrition rate" to apply to any single project for master's trainees. The nearest one can come to such a standard is to accept that time will have its impact on attrition, recognize that more recently completed projects are more likely to have lower attrition from targeted units, and analyze the kinds of data found in Table 5-1 and begin to formulate rates.

Data on the six projects are arrayed chronologically in Figure 5-1, using each project's midpoint as the year for locating data points related to its retention patterns (York = 1975.5; RPP = 1981; TAP = 1984; RMRD = 1988.5; LRP = 1989; and BEMP = 1992). Two points are included for each project: retention within the target ministry and retention in the public sector. Curves for these categories are presented. For each of these categories an envelope of "best practice" has been sketched in. This term is meant to suggest natural attrition rates that good projects would have in Kenya regardless of factors related to retention that are discussed elsewhere in this chapter. In the absence of any other criteria, it is hypothesized that if there is a normal retention rate for master's trainees in the Kenyan public sector, and retention is as good as it can be, most capacity-building projects focused on master's degree training should have retention and attrition rates lying along these curves.

Figure 5-1 suggests that three projects (York, RMRD, and BEMP) define best practice if only retention within the target ministry is considered. The only thing that appears to differentiate these three projects is their age. The RMRD and BEMP projects are the most recent and have higher retention scores than York, which is the oldest. Two

FIGURE 5-1

Attrition and Best Practice Retention for Officers Trained to the Master's Level in Economics, Planning, and Finance Management by the Six Projects

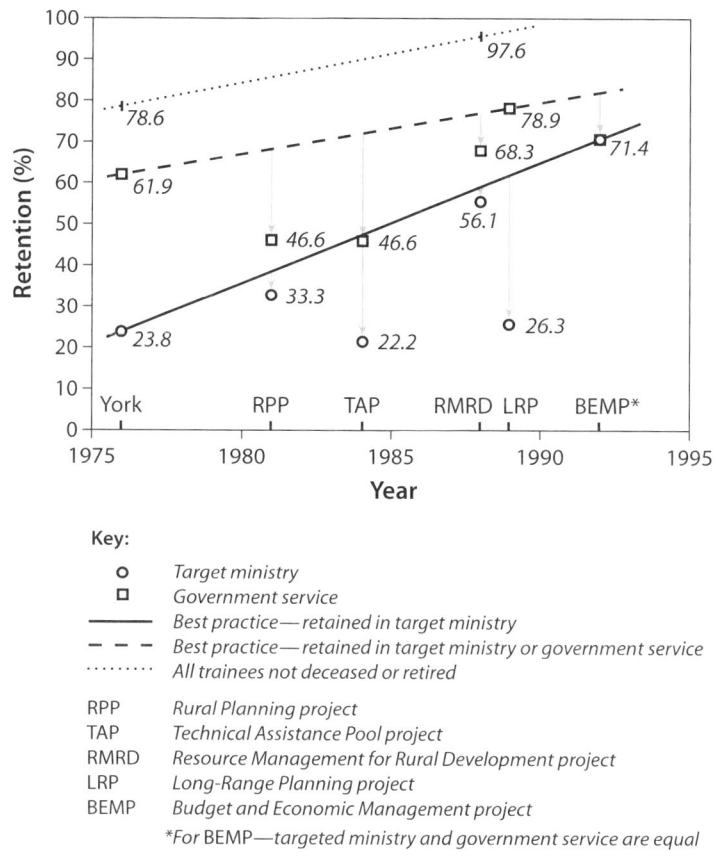

Source: Personnel data for the Scheme of Service for Economists and Statisticians

projects (TAP and LRP) come in well below this curve, which suggests that there was a significantly lower retention rate that cannot be explained by the different ages of the projects alone. If, however, the criterion for retention is defined as the master's trainees staying in the public sector, the picture changes slightly. The dashed curve suggests that the York and RMRD projects are very close to best practice but, interestingly, the LRP project looks substantially better by this criterion, whereas the RPP project looks substantially worse. Again the TAP project is deficient in retention.

By the mid-1980s, TAP advisors concluded that a five-year period was the most that returned master's trainees could be expected to stay in their target ministry, largely because of career mobility, the tendency for economists to be transferred from time to time by the head of the SSES, and the push factor generated by low salaries, inadequate benefits, and poor management. TAP advisors believed that if a cadre of experienced master's-degree graduates could be held for four to six years, they would provide a model and incentive for new B.A. graduates entering the target ministries. RMRD took a longer view, primarily because it was targeted on building systems for effective district planning and training planners to extend and embed them. For both projects, government decision makers, aid agency personnel, and advisors generally agreed that retention for less than two years meant failure. Even during implementation, however, it was recognized that 100 percent retention was unlikely and that the actual numbers were less important than achieving a level of retention that was sufficient to effectively fulfill required work programs and end or reduce dependency on expatriate advisors.

Because a prime objective of all the projects was to reduce the need for technical assistance, a second question that should be asked is whether the decline of expatriate advisors in a target ministry is an indicator of successful capacity building. If this indicator is used, the four projects in MPND have been successful because the number of such experts in that ministry declined from forty-six in 1986 to two in mid-1995.[22] A major reason for this decline appears to be that sufficient numbers of trained personnel were retained to operate the planning and microcomputer systems that advisors put in place, and that the training of Kenyan officers was sufficient to enable them to manage systems. On the other hand, the decline in advisors is potentially caused by the decision by aid agencies in 1991 to freeze project funding until the government implemented agreed-upon structural adjustment conditions, which reduced funding for advisory teams in government.[23]

A third question is whether the best and brightest of those trained stayed in or left the public sector. Our tentative answer, based on personal judgments and extensive professional contact with many of the 169 trainees, is that those most likely to leave the targeted ministries were the most talented and ambitious. A related question is whether these officers depart shortly after returning or after facing the frustrations of public service for an extended period. Tentative data suggest that the more ambitious and talented master's graduates leave relatively soon after returning from training, largely because of higher salaries and the fact that public service promotions are slow, particularly beyond middle-level positions.[24]

A fourth question that must be asked is to what extent retention levels in the targeted ministries result from the fact that the numbers sent for master's-degree training under the projects increased during the late 1980s and early 1990s. Those remaining in targeted ministries may be back too recently to have found the higher paying jobs their predecessors sought throughout the 1980s. For example, nine of the ten officers remaining in the TAP's targeted ministries were trained between 1990 and 1992. In contrast, of the twenty-three economists trained under RMRD that have been retained, twenty-one were trained before 1990. Although there is no conclusive evidence that the rates of retention are improving, the actual numbers retained have increased. If, as suggested, most of those who leave do so soon after their return, then the prospects are that a core of master's graduates has been established.

Fifth, how have retention rates of targeted personnel been affected by downturns in economic growth and privatization? During the late 1970s and early 1980s, many of those people leaving government service went to work for private businesses, parastatals, aid agencies, or consulting firms employed by aid agencies or NGOs. However, employment opportunities for economists outside the public sector were affected by the downturn in the Kenyan economy experienced in the late 1980s and early 1990s. It is therefore likely that the numbers retained during this period improved because of declining private sector opportunities for Kenyan economists and planners holding master's degrees. During this period, civil service salaries were eroded very seriously by inflation, creating prime conditions for qualified personnel to look elsewhere for employment.

Sixth, to what extent have retention rates in targeted ministries been affected by the fact that aid agencies and major NGOs have sought out qualified staff for their local offices and to what extent does this practice continue? According to data collected by the authors on the positions of trainees at the end of 1994, it appears that thirty-three of the forty-eight economists who left the public service, or 19.5 percent of the 169 trained, did so to join aid agencies or international NGOs. Moreover, fifteen of the twenty economists trained by TAP between 1977 and 1988 worked for aid agencies or international NGOs directly or for their projects.[25] Of the last twenty-two officers trained under the project, however, none had gone to work for aid agencies, although one of these officers worked in the consolidated Ministry of Agriculture, Livestock Development, and Marketing (MALD) because he received substantial salary topping up from a World Bank project.[26] The time line is probably too short to determine if this is because aid agency headquarters staff now have sufficient numbers of nationals on board, whether agencies prefer seasoned economists to recent trainees who have not been back in post for a sufficient period of time, or whether demand is declining because of the reduction of foreign aid.

Some experts contend that parastatals are the major government units poaching those trained to the master's level by capacity-building projects, largely because they have salary and benefit packages that the civil service cannot match. In fact, seventeen of the 169 government economists (10 percent) who were trained under the six projects now work for parastatals.

The higher than expected retention rates for RMRD may also be attributable to another factor. The project assigned a high proportion of trainees to field posts where the cost of living was low and they received benefits not given to headquarters staff, such as government housing. It may also be that this high retention rate results from increased rent-seeking, which augments income. District-level positions offer substantial opportunities for garnering tendering and construction project-related rents; this practice led to the 1991 suspension of the large Rural Development Fund (RDF) by Scandinavian supporters because of documented corruption by district officials. Given the RDF case and the rapid increase in corruption that has characterized Kenya's public sector since the mid-1980s, this is an altogether appropriate question.[27]

Transfers within the SSES dilute efforts to build capacities in targeted MPND units. Government policy has been to expand the numbers and seniority of economists serving in the planning units of other ministries to bolster their sectoral planning capacities. The initiative to strengthen these ministerial planning units has certainly resulted in the loss of officers trained under capacity-building projects targeted on the MPND. Those responsible might argue that the trained economists were being engaged in the best national interest, but it is questionable whether the negative results on the ministry units from which they were transferred were considered. The tendency to make such transfers is in part inherited from the British colonial service, which was based on generalists who could serve in any position. Today that heritage is used to justify transfers out of targeted units.[28]

Seventh, to what extent do the data on retention reflect the overall capacity-building success of each project? The answer depends on several additional factors. All six projects reviewed had other training components. For example, RMRD also carried out a range of other capacity-building efforts that involved training nine ministry officers in short-term, specialized external courses; holding six annual weeklong training workshops for nearly one hundred provincial and district level planners; and establishing microcomputer training courses in the planning ministry and at the Kenyan Institute of Administration. These courses trained more than a thousand senior and staff personnel. On the other hand, the LRP project funded no short-term courses and held few specialized training workshops. The BEMP project, in addition to providing master's training for seven officers, also sent sixty-five finance ministry officers to specialized short-term external training courses and held many large-scale training seminars in Nairobi over its four-year period. Clearly, a careful evaluation of the full range of training activities of a project and an analysis of utilization and retention rates for those trained has bearing on the capacity-building success of all six projects.

Eighth, are the rank and influence of those trained as important as the total numbers of those retained? For example, the York project has one of the lowest retention percentages among all projects. To a large extent this is because it is the oldest of the projects. Its annual rate of attrition compares well with all projects. However, of the ten economists remaining in the targeted finance and planning ministries, one became the permanent secretary of the planning ministry, one became permanent secretary for government investment in the finance ministry, and three others rose to positions as chief economists.[29] Again, this success is the result of the age of the project and the fact that under the Kenyan system, those who stay the course eventually do rise to higher positions. Nearly all of those trained and retained under the RMRD and LRP projects continued as junior-level economists and planners with uncertain careers and limited responsibilities in 1994. That said, in 1995 several of those trained earlier under these projects were beginning to climb the promotion ladder and entered middle-level posts and so took on increasing responsibility for policy formulation.

In sum, of those trained to the master's level under the six projects, 102, or 60.4 percent, elected to remain in government service. Although the authors know of no comparable data, this level of retention is higher than current writing on the topic would lead one to suppose.[30] Retention within those ministries targeted by the projects is considerably lower, running at 34.3 percent. Although this figure may be disappointingly low, it again may be higher than currently expected. These data generate a final question, namely, given wide perceptions of very low pay, poor management, a lack of equipment, and a demoralized civil service, why have so many individuals elected to remain?

WHY DO QUALIFIED ECONOMISTS REMAIN IN THE SERVICE?

The constraints and disincentives facing professionals in the Kenyan civil service are very similar to their counterparts in other African countries. Briefly, the list of disincentives includes low salaries and poor benefits; slow promotion and lack of reward for hard work and initiative; poorly conceived career ladders; inadequate and demoralizing management by supervisors; underemployment and lack of stimulating assignments; and inadequate and unreliable recurrent budget provisions for supplies, equipment, and transport essential to effective job performance.[31] Further, the MPND, in particular, suffered from a poor organizational structure, with diffuse responsibilities and unfocused roles. It had no ministry vision for addressing the rapidly changing economic environment and perceived roles of government. These problems were compounded by an "image problem": economists and planners were often held in low esteem. They were frequently bypassed during the policy-making process or found their opinions on particular issues disregarded. Finally, beginning in the mid-1980s, there was a marked move to politicize the civil service and increased political interference in decision making. Economic and planning analysis became subservient to short-term political demands. The civil service was weakened and could no longer be relied on to enforce regulations or procedures in a disinterested manner. As a result of these constraints, it is difficult for an officer to feel that he or she is contributing to national development or gaining other work satisfaction.

Under these circumstances it would seem understandable for motivated professional officers to look outside government for opportunities to advance their careers. Yet, nearly two-thirds of those trained under the six reviewed projects elected to remain in the SSES and the public service. To better understand this higher than expected retention, a sample of officers trained under the six projects were interviewed. Eighteen interviews were completed with "stayers," representing almost 20 percent of the total remaining in the public service.[32] Although only two interviews were conducted with persons who had left the service after their master's training, admittedly a small number to provide contrast, time did not permit a wider follow-up with "leavers."

With 1995 gross salaries ranging from about Ksh 175,000 ($3,500) a year for a deputy chief economist to just over Ksh 100,000 ($2,000) for an economist I, a major concern for all respondents was making ends meet.[33] By way of comparison, an economist at the upper end of the market in the private sector might command a gross salary up to ten times that of the public sector.[34] Although marginal pay increases had been awarded, they had not kept up with inflation, and real incomes had declined since the mid-1980s. Government allowances contribute little to gross pay with the exception of the provision of a house. Government housing is very limited in Nairobi and only one respondent benefitted. Both those posted to the field occupied government housing. In Nairobi, the provision of a house has a cash equivalent of at least Ksh 15,000 ($300) a month, compared to a housing allowance of less than Ksh 3,000 ($60). Other allowances are of marginal value and often not available. For example, budgetary limitations frequently preclude use of official travel or leave allowances.

However, only one respondent was totally reliant on a government salary. Fourteen of those with other sources of income had spouses who worked full-time, whereas twelve personally supplemented their civil service salary. It is evident that complex and well-entrenched coping mechanisms had evolved, enabling officers to augment their meager civil service pay. Although it was difficult to gauge an accurate estimate of total household incomes, more than half of those interviewed agreed that their salary was a minor component of their overall income.

Apart from the income of a working spouse, government economists typically augment their salary through running or having an interest in an outside business or undertaking consultancies, either for a local firm or on their own account. Further important sources of income, especially for more senior officers, are honoraria and generous allowances paid by aid agencies in connection with project work—for example, evaluations or workshops. The distinction between purely private consulting work and quasi-official work associated with donor projects is often blurred. The necessity and opportunity to engage in private work reflects a syndrome whereby low salaries demand it and poor management and discipline facilitate it. The opportunity to use office hours and equipment to significantly augment official salaries through private income-earning activities provides a major incentive to remain in the civil service. It was difficult to gain an estimate of the proportion of a working week spent on private business; figures ranging from more than 50 to less than 10 percent were volunteered. The portion may fluctuate quite widely but the amount of time demanded by outside work is the determinant rather than the time available. Those people exploiting these opportunities well recognized that their security of employment coupled with a regular, if small, government salary and the prospect of a pension provided a satisfactory "bottom line" to which significant additional, if sometimes erratic, income could be added. This recognition is reinforced by feelings that the private sector is a hard taskmaster that demands long hours and total commitment.

Most interviewees expressed a surprising degree of satisfaction with the status quo. They considered their quality of life comparable to their counterparts in the private sector because laxity of management and low demand for their time provided the opportunity to undertake a variety of outside income-generating activities of the individual's choice. A high value appeared to be placed on the flexibility that allowed civil servants to maximize choice. A government decision to allow voluntary retirement, with full pension, at 40 years old reinforced this perception. If the time prior to early retirement can be used to build up a business or networks for future work while receiving some steady income, then in some ways a civil servant enjoyed the best of both worlds.

This situation has major implications for any attempts to implement civil service reform and increase the productivity of government services. Any attempt to increase the output of civil servants will meet with stiff resistance unless remuneration is increased to private sector levels. Given revenue and deficit constraints, the prospects for this increase are remote and near-term attempts to revitalize the civil service are likely to be frustrated.[35]

Given the foregoing, it is somewhat ironic that the most frequently cited reason for remaining within the public service is that of work satisfaction. Over two-thirds of the respondents cited this reason as being important. The concept of work satisfaction embraced immediate reward from work completed, levels of responsibility, and the tools to do a job satisfactorily. Almost all those interviewed claimed to gain satisfaction from their work, although there were complaints that their efforts were not recognized because of slow promotion. Those working on aid agency-funded assignments were particularly satisfied. Their work was more focused, they had better access to equipment, particularly microcomputers, and they were more likely to have funds for travel and supplies. Furthermore, in many cases the aid agencies provided topping up of government allowances such as "nights out" per diem.

Two other concerns were mentioned by virtually all respondents—management and promotion. All junior officers considered that management within their ministry was poor, although a certain ambivalence was evident because they recognized better management would almost certainly reduce their opportunities to undertake private work in office hours. However, issues such as the lack of guidance and feedback and the absence of teamwork received negative comments as did the lack of clear work plans and the prevalence of "fire fighting."

The situation with regard to promotions received universal condemnation. Over half the respondents claimed to be more than two years past supposed promotion dates. Interestingly, their condemnation was couched as much in terms of a denial of recognition for work done as a denial of increased remuneration. Merit promotions are forbidden by civil service rules for fear they would be subject to tribal, religious, or personal abuse. Nor do poor evaluations hold back the promotions.[36] Promotions are merely based on "time in grade" and perfunctory annual evaluations. This system discourages efforts at achievement and lowers morale of promising officers. Promotions are also affected by the fact that the planning ministry career ladder has few steps. Younger officers may move to section head within five years. After that, promotion as head of the limited number of divisions and departments is problematic. This short career ladder discourages officers, because they know there are many in their grade and few available senior posts.

Finally, the issues of corruption and extralegal sources of income were raised at each interview. Those officers based in Nairobi claimed that they had no opportunity to obtain rents because they did not handle financial matters. There is probably a degree of truth in this, although just what constitutes corruption could be debated. The two field-based officers who were interviewed agreed the opportunity existed but that the level of rents available was often exaggerated. That said, everybody agreed that corrupt practices were pervasive in the public service, particularly at higher levels, but some excused this corruption because senior officers did not have the time to undertake outside work.

COULD THEY LEAVE?

Fifteen of the eighteen officers interviewed had, at some point since master's training, actively sought employment outside the public sector. Of these, five were doing so at the time of interview. The reason given was always a desire for a higher salary and better conditions of service. Surprisingly, job satisfaction and better supervision were not widely mentioned in the context of responses to this question. Most of those no longer looking to leave claimed that the higher salary alone was not sufficient inducement. Whether this is a genuine reason or a rationalization of past failures to secure private sector employment is open to conjecture, but it does raise the question of how realistic aspirations are for lucrative employment outside the public sector.

In mid-1995, the job market for economists was tight. As a result of the general economic recession experienced in Kenya since the late 1980s, economic activity and investment stagnated and thus private sector opportunities were restricted. There would appear to have been a similar downturn in employment opportunities in aid agencies. This downturn reflected both declining aid budgets in Kenya and, possibly, the fact that aid agencies had satisfied their demand for local staff and current incumbents had yet to reach retirement. The NGO sector was still expanding, but wage rates, particularly for local NGOs, were not significantly higher than those of the civil service. Thus, conditions existed that were in marked contrast to those of the late 1970s and early 1980s when the demand for economists was booming, the supply was smaller, and the possession of a master's degree could be viewed as a passport to a well-paid private sector job.[37]

Increasing competition for fewer jobs means that employers can be more particular and an applicant's qualifications are subject to greater scrutiny. How well would the typical government economist fare? Significantly, at graduation most of the best economics department majors are directed by the faculty to local master's courses and, if they perform well, toward teaching posts in Kenya's university system. Other top economics graduates go directly into the private sector. So the government does not get the best prepared and most talented economics students of each graduating class. Further, standards appear to have declined over time. Records reviewed by the authors show that the Graduate Record Examination scores for those receiving training in the late 1980s and early 1990s were substantially lower than those achieved by their predecessors in the late 1970s and early 1980s. Indeed, they were well below the minimum required for Western applicants by most graduate programs in the United States. Thus the RMRD project, working with Cornell University as a subcontractor, devised a training strategy that would guarantee admission for twenty-four trainees at Cornell in a one-year master's in professional studies program that was designed for midcareer professionals rather than academics.[38] This program enhanced the skills of Kenyan planners, economists, and statisticians without giving them the academic credentials that would facilitate their mobility on return.[39] Only the passage of time will demonstrate whether the strategy was successful or whether the limited academic reach of the training limits their future utility. However, the Cornell subcontract allowed officers to gain training for future government service they might not have received otherwise, leaving the public sector better off in the future.

Although based largely on selected interviews, it can be concluded that opportunities for any but the very best and most dynamic government economist to find full-time outside employment were severely constrained in 1995. At best, they might have been able to obtain consulting work or moonlight for a consultancy firm on a temporary basis. Although this situation may bode well for retention objectives, it does little or nothing to improve productivity, a point we will return to later.

Achievements, Failures, and the Future

Over a period of twenty-five years, the six projects reviewed here financed the master's training for 169 officers. That some 60 percent of those trained continued to work within the government service is an achievement that must contribute positively to building the potential capacity of the government to undertake economic policy and analytical work. During the same period, numerous expatriate advisors worked to build the planning systems and administrative procedures that would provide the framework within which government economists were to operate. The foundations would appear to have been built, although the real capacity of the government to fulfill its mandate effectively and efficiently does not seem to have materialized because of the poor utilization of those trained.

Numbers alone do not build capacity and the effectiveness and efficiency of capacity-building projects. Those trained need to be effectively utilized and productive. Unfortunately, this is not the case in Kenya.

The roles of most of Kenya's governmental units are changing rapidly in response to structural adjustment demands. Functions, strategies, and organizations of government ministries and agencies must adapt to these changes. Kenya's planning ministry is a good case in point. Decreasing, or at least changing, needs for economic planning and policy interventions were not reflected in the ministry's internal organization or staff assignments. Its departments had only hazy notions of areas of responsibility and lacked task-oriented work programs. Duplication of efforts was frequent and uncertainty existed over which unit should be responsible for specific tasks. Delegation and work assignments were haphazard and officers lacked any clear understanding of how their efforts contributed to a wider environment. Not infrequently, the skill levels of government economists and planners were not adequate for addressing the increasingly complex economic, development, and structural adjustment issues facing the government. Too often, systems, procedures, and regulations introduced to deal with such issues were not enforced, adding to frustrations and poor performance. At a more personal level, department heads and task managers often failed to instigate work programs or meaningful job descriptions for those working under them. The litany of problems did not end here but need not be described more extensively.

These problems indicate that management and staff utilization are not simply matters of common sense that will take care of themselves. Building technical capacities through gap-filling advisors backed by strong training programs is not sufficient. Governments and aid agencies must move beyond such simplistic notions and recognize that managing a work force as large as a civil service, which is responsible for such a wide variety of tasks, is a very necessary skill for which research, training, and resources must be made available. Hindsight shows that a major failing of all the projects reviewed in this chapter was that so little investment was devoted to strengthening management skills and addressing organizational problems. Although rationalization is stated as one objective of civil service reform, action has yet to be extended to the question of improving productivity, beyond a bland assumption that reducing numbers will create a slimmer, more efficient organization.

Immediate attention must be given to improving incentives and increasing the "psychic" reward for work and initiative. Enhancing career development through a more attractive scheme of service, transparent and timely promotions, teamwork and supportive supervision, and provision of microcomputers and related equipment is urgently required. Budget constraints are well recognized, but the arguments for reallocating funds to operations and maintenance activities are overwhelming. Lastly, if the best and the brightest leave the public service soon after their return from master's training, then special programs that provide enhanced responsibility could be put in place to enable returnees to apply their new knowledge and skills immediately.

However, the most pervasive constraint to increasing civil service productivity and motivating increased effectiveness remains that of low salaries. Evidence and opinion provided earlier in this chapter indicate that a massive rise in remuneration will be required to ensure that officers do not pursue outside income-generating activities that detract from their official duties. Herein lies an intractable problem, for governments simply do not have the resources to pay wages that even approach those available in the private sector. Already the greater proportion of recurrent expenditure is given over to salaries and wages. Even the most severe reduction in the numbers employed will not free sufficient resources and would involve enormous short-term costs.

Other than ignoring the problem or holding out a promise of increased pay at some time in the future, there does not seem to be a satisfactory solution. Merit pay, performance bonuses, fast-track promotion for selected officers, and other such ideas are helpful. However, motivation does not rely entirely on financial reward. Despite all the dissatisfaction with the current levels of pay, there is strong evidence that work satisfaction, involvement, and sympathetic management can be very important incentives for professional civil servants. Finally, although it may read as cynicism or sacrilege, it should not be forgotten that professional government services do continue to operate, and that the greater part of the criticism and calls for sweeping reform originate from expatriate observers.

Notes

1   Paul S. Haddow, "The Post-Graduate Training and Utilization of Professional Planners and Economists in the Government of Kenya: Recommendations to the Government and Donor Agencies" (report prepared for the Ministry of Economic Planning and Development and the Canadian International Development Agency, July 1982), ANNEX III, 118–121. Gap-filling advisors are one of six types of advisors identified by Cohen. John M. Cohen, "Foreign Advisors and Capacity Building: the Case of Kenya," *Public Administration and Development* XII 5 (1992), 493–510.

2   This type of advisor is used in projects that combine advisory and training components through the provision of needed expertise while training government officers to replace its members. Such advisors are funded by aid agencies at the request of ministries that recognize they lack professional capacity to formulate policies and forge administrative systems and want to have their own nationals trained in these skill areas. J. M. Cohen, "Foreign Advisors and Capacity Building: the Case of Kenya," 496.

3   Most notably summarized in Eliot J. Berg, *Rethinking Technical Cooperation: Reforms for Capacity Building in Africa* (New York: United Nations Development Programme/Development Alternatives, Inc., 1993).

4   E. R. Morss, "Institutional Destruction Resulting from Donor and Project Proliferation in Sub-Saharan African Countries," *World Development* XII, 4 (1984), 465–70; World Bank, "The Bank's Work on Institutional Development in Sectors: Emerging Tasks and Challenges" (paper prepared by the Public Sector Management and Private Sector Development Division, May 1991); Haven W. North, "Capacity Building and Technical Co-operation—Managing the Connection" (paper prepared for NaTCAP/UNDP, New York, June 1992); Jennifer Widner, "Reform Bargains: The Politics of Change" in David L. Lindauer and Michael Roemer, eds., *Asia and Africa: Legacies and Opportunities in Development*, (San Francisco: Institute for Contemporary Studies Press, 1994), 59–97.

5   United Nations Development Programme, "National Capacity Building: Report of the Administrator" (report on Programme Planning and Implementation Presented to the Fortieth Session, New York, January 1993), 3.

6   United Nations Development Programme, "Strategy for Assessing UNDP Effectiveness in Capacity Building During the Fifth Programme Cycle" (paper prepared by the Central Evaluation Office, Bureau for Policy and Programme Evaluation, New York, March 1993); David C. E. Chew, "Internal Adjustments to Falling Civil Service Salaries: Insights from Uganda," *World Development* XVIII, 7 (1990), 1003–1014; Robert Klitgaard, "Incentive Myopia," *World Development* XVII, 4 (1989), 447–460.

7   World Bank Portfolio Management Task Force, "Effective Implementation: Key to Development Impact," known as "The Wapenhans Report," (Washington, DC: World Bank, 1992); "Africa: World Bank," *Oxford Analytica* (June 3, 1993).

8   Arturo Israel, *Institutional Development: Incentives to Performance* (Baltimore: The Johns Hopkins University Press, 1987).

9   Approximately 100,000 resident foreign advisors work in the public sectors of sub-Saharan African countries at an annual cost of more than $4 billion, nearly 35 percent of Official Development Aid to the region. World Bank, *Sub-Saharan Africa: From Crisis to Sustainable Growth* (Washington, DC: International Bank for Reconstruction and Development, 1989), 181. Other studies put this figure in the range of 40,000. Berg, *Rethinking Technical Cooperation*, 71–77.

10 United Nations Development Programme, *Human Development Report 1990* (New York: Oxford University Press, 1991), 1–7; World Bank, "The Bank's Work on Institutional Development in Sectors: Emerging Tasks and Challenges" (paper prepared by the Public Sector Management and Private Sector Development Division, May 1991); OECD, "Principles for New Orientations in Technical Cooperation" (statement issued by the Development Assistance Committee, Paris, 1991), para. I.7; Edward V. K. Jaycox, "Capacity Building: The Missing Link in African Development" (transcript of address to the African-American Institute Conference, African Capacity Building: Effective and Enduring Partnerships, Reston, VA, May 20, 1993).

11 Beatrice Buych, *The Bank's Use of Technical Assistance for Institutional Development* (Washington, DC: World Bank, 1989), ii; J. Bossuyt, G. Laporte, and F. van Hoek, *New Avenues for Technical Cooperation in Africa: Improving the Record in Terms of Capacity Building* (Maastricht: European Centre for Development Policy Management, 1990), 3, 59; Berg, *Rethinking Technical Cooperation*; Jaycox, "Capacity Building." Others take the opposite view and call for more expatriates to assist African countries rebuild their shattered economies and polities, for example: William Pfaff, "A New Colonialism? Europe Must Go Back into Africa," *Foreign Affairs* LXXIV, 1 (1995), 2–6.

12 The importance of targeted capacity building is reviewed in John M. Cohen, "Capacity Building in the Public Sector: A Focused Framework for Analysis and Action," *International Review of Administrative Sciences* LXI, 3 (1995), 407–422.

13 United Nations Development Programme, "National Capacity Building," 7, 14–16; World Bank, "The Bank's Work on Institutional Development in Sectors: Emerging Tasks and Challenges" (paper prepared by the Public Sector Management and Private Sector Development Division, May 1991), 54; World Bank, *Handbook on Technical Assistance* (Washington, DC: Operations Policy Department, 1993), i–vi; Lawrence Whitehead, ed., "Special Issue: Economic Liberalization and Democratization: Explorations of the Linkages," *World Development* XXI (8), 1245–1393.

14 Detailed studies of four of these projects (RPP, RMRD, TAP, and BEMP), including analysis of their extensive and complex training components are found in John M. Cohen and Stephen B. Peterson, "HIID's Advisory and Training Experience in Kenya," in Dwight Perkins, et al., ed., *Assisting Development in a Changing World: The Harvard Institute for International Development (1980–1995)* (Cambridge: Harvard Institute for International Development, forthcoming 1997).

15 Cohen served as chief-of-party and training officer for TAP (1979–1982), chief-of-party and training officer for RPP (1985) and RMRD (1985–1990), and training officer for BEMP (1990–1992). Wheeler served as chief-of-party and training officer for RMRD (1990–1992) and training officer for BEMP (1992–1994). As such they have personal experience in evaluation of the capacity-building experience of all projects in Table 5-1, both with the Government of Kenya and the aid agencies funding both HIID and non-HIID projects.

16 In some cases officers are forced to retire, or retired "in the public interest," either because of improper administrative or personal actions or because of political conflict with superiors.

17 Hussein Abby, "Assessment of Capacity Building Needs for Economic Management in Kenya" (report prepared for United Nations Development Programme, Nairobi, June 1994).

18 The period of time was the midyear of project implementation to the end of 1994; e.g., the RMRD project ran from 1985 to 1992 with a midpoint of 1988. The period over which an annual compounded attrition took place was therefore taken to be six years.

19 The SSES was established by the Directorate of Personnel Management in 1974 and revised in 1985. It seeks to establish terms of service comparable to other professional groups serving in government (doctors, lawyers, engineers, and architects). See John M. Cohen, "Expatriate Advisors in the

Government of Kenya: Why They Are There and What Can Be Done About It," *HIID Development Discussion Paper 376* (Cambridge: Harvard Institute for International Development, June 1991), 23, fn. 72; and the Ministry of Planning and National Development, "Review of Individuals Departing the Scheme of Service" (Nairobi, n.d.).

20 Data held by the authors show that of these 106, 15.2 percent retired, 30.5 percent resigned, 6.7 percent took a leave of absence, 16.2 percent were seconded, 16.2 percent were on study leave, and 15.2 percent left for other reasons, most notably because of death. Of the fifty five noted, twenty eight resigned from the scheme of service during this period.

21 The authors are indebted to Michael Roemer for his suggestion that the data in Tables 5-1 and 5-2 be translated into Figure 5-1 format and for his assistance in doing this.

22 See the profile on advisors in MPND in Cohen, "Expatriate Advisors," 16–17.

23 Of particular importance in the decline of advisors in MPND was the 1992 suspension of Nordic aid to a major rural development project (Rural Development Fund) managed by MPND because of frustration over corruption in the implementation of project activities. This project alone funded eleven expatriate advisors located in the MPND's headquarters and field offices in 1986. See the profile on advisors in MPND in Cohen, "Expatriate Advisors," 16–17.

24 In early 1995 the composition of those in post and their job group (JG) was as follows: director of planning; chief economist—9 (JQ-Q); deputy chief economist—20 (JG-P); principal economist—35 (JG-N); senior economist—72 (JG-M); economist I—192 (JG-L); economist II—180 (JG-K); economist assistant—48 (JG-J); planning assistant—13 (JG-H). The numbers at each level demonstrate that although promotion to economist I is reasonably assured, promotion beyond this level is likely to be delayed.

25 For comparative purposes, four of the fifteen officers (26.7 percent) trained under the RPP project, nine of the forty-one officers (21.9 percent) trained under the RMRD project, and two of the seven officers (28.6 percent) trained under the BEMP project now work for aid agencies or for international NGOs.

26 On the practice and problems of salary topping to keep economists in public sector ministries, see L. S. Wilson, "Kenyanisation and African Capacity Building," *Public Administration and Development* XIII, 4 (1993): 489–499.

27 Jane Perlez, "Citing Corruption in Kenya, Western Nations Cancel Aid," *New York Times* (October 21, 1991), 1; Martha Mbuggus, "Kenyans and

the 'Chai' Syndrome," *The Daily Nation* (December 18, 1991), 1; "Bribery and Extortion," *Finance* (November 15, 1992), 18–23.

28 This and other disruptive practices in East African public administration are well reviewed in Jon R. Moris, "The Transferability of Western Management Concepts and Programs: An East African Perspective," in Laurence Stifel, James S. Coleman, and Joseph E. Black, eds., *Education and Training for Public Sector Management in Developing Countries*, (New York: The Rockefeller Foundation, 1977), 73–83.

29 Had the year 1991 been the basis of the Table 5-1, the York project would have had thirteen of its trainees in its targeted ministries, and those retained would have been holding such senior posts as permanent secretary, director of planning, chairman of the parastatal reform committee, and head of the rural planning department.

30 For example, note the undocumented assertions and conventional wisdom presented in Berg, *Rethinking Technical Cooperation*, passim.

31 These disincentives are expounded at length in Cohen, "Expatriate Advisors," 11–14.

32 Each confidential interview attempted to elicit views through both answers to standard questions and more informal discussion. Of the eighteen "stayers" interviewed, twelve were male and six were female. All but one were married. The length of time since their return from training ranged from nineteen to three years. Of the total interviewed, twelve were currently posted in either MPND or MOF, four were in sectoral ministries, and two were in field positions. Although a range of current levels of post were included, there was no attempt to select a statistically representative sample.

33 Average earnings of those employed in Kenya's modern sector averaged $1,120 in 1994 (Office of the Vice President and Ministry of Planning and National Development, *Economic Review 1994* [Nairobi: Government Press, 1995]).

34 Public and private sector differentials are presented in Cohen, "Expatriate Advisors," 12, 16–17.

35 The difficulties of achieving civil service reform in Africa are reviewed in Louis de Merode, "Civil Service Pay and Employment in Africa: Selected Implementation Experiences" (staff paper, International Bank for Reconstruction and Development, Washington, DC, 1991); John M. Cohen, "Importance of Public Service Reform: the Case of Kenya," *Journal of Modern African Studies* XXXI, 3 (1993), 449–476.

36 Most notations on personnel files concern administrative irregularities such as using a vehicle without an approved work ticket, taking excessive

leave, or not repaying or accounting for a travel or per diem imprest. Rarely does a senior officer place a criticism in an officer's file on the quality or timeliness of technical work. So too, memorandums of commendation are infrequently issued.

37 Economic stagnation and reduced aid levels continued into 1995, see "Kenya: Donor Alienation," *Oxford Analytica* (June 15, 1995).

38 As designed, the program sent five to seven officers each year to Cornell University where they completed a ten-month master's in professional studies degree in international development. At Cornell they took basic courses in economics, planning, quantitative techniques, and microcomputer applications. The Cornell program is described in *Kenya Training Program* (Ithaca: Institute for African Development, Cornell University, March 1989).

39 The Cornell degrees were professional rather than academic. They were of a different type, not of second class. Western professionals serving in donor agencies take a year's sabbatical to do the same degree at Cornell.

Part II

Strategies for Capacity Building

Strengthening Organizations

6

Hierarchy versus Networks

Alternative Strategies for Building Organizational Capacity in Public Bureaucracies in Africa

Stephen B. Peterson

It's not really that hard to run a large organization. You just have to think small about how to achieve your goals. There's a very finite limit to how much leadership you can exercise at the top. You can't micromanage. People resent that. Things are achieved by individuals, by collections of twos and fives and twenties, not collections of 115,000.

—General William Creech[1]

A great deal remains to be learned about effective management in Africa and any simple attempt to transfer Western managerial technologies is likely to end in failure.

—David K. Leonard[2]

The capacity of public bureaucracies in Africa can be understood by considering three dimensions: political, individual, and organizational. Previous work on the political dimension of capacity has shown that there is a lack of political will to demand high performance in many bureaucracies and that public service is often compromised by political elites who use the state for personal gain.[3] Research on the individual dimension of capacity has revealed that staff have limited skills, are poorly managed, and lack resources.[4] These factors, in combination, undermine individual motivation and performance.

A third dimension of capacity, and the subject of this chapter, relates to the design of organizational processes, or process design.

Process design refers to how an organization does its work. Understanding process design and how it can be improved in the context of African bureaucracies is critical for enhancing public sector efficiency and reducing costs, centerpieces of many reform strategies.

This chapter presents three theses related to process design in public bureaucracies in Africa. First, in most public bureaucracies in Africa, procedures and thus formal hierarchies are compromised. Second, information technology can play an important role in process redesign and management. Third, the organizing principle of networks provides an effective alternative to hierarchy and can serve as a basis for process redesign and management in public bureaucracies.

The model of process redesign is relatively straightforward. The first step is to identify the critical task or set of tasks of the organization (what should be done) and then identify a progressive manager who will build a network, or capable staff, to implement the tasks (how it should be done). The key to this approach is to build a network around a progressive manager and ensure that the task and the network do not exceed the span of control of this individual. This approach accords with how public bureaucracies in Africa function.[5]

The reality of strengthening organizational capacity through process redesign is more complex. Process redesign is rarely done in Africa because it requires a fundamental assessment of what an organization does and how it does it. Many public organizations do not fare well under such scrutiny because they have ill-defined objectives and poorly designed strategies for achieving them. For many public bureaucracies, the principal task is to provide employment. Moreover, process redesign requires bypassing the formal structure or hierarchy of public bureaucracies and strengthening progressive managers and a network of supporters. Building networks rather than reinforcing organizational hierarchies recognizes the organizational realities that these public bureaucracies are often large, fragmented, poorly managed, and for the most part irrelevant.

Field experience from Kenya suggests how networks and information technology can provide the basis for improved organizational capacity. Even though such networks (pockets of productivity, or islands of excellence) are small, they can lead to dramatic improvements in performance.[6] In Kenya's customs administration, for example, the appointment of an individual in a critical task and the development of a supportive network increased revenue by millions of dollars. In Kenya's agricultural ministries, the appointment of a reforming "saint" in personnel administration reduced fraud substantially and improved complement management.[7]

POOR PROCESS DESIGN: THE PROBLEM OF HIERARCHY IN AFRICAN BUREAUCRACIES

The "what is done" of process design relates to the tasks of the organization. In many African bureaucracies, tasks historically have been assigned to agencies that are no longer appropriate or that are more suited to other agencies or the private sector.

The "how it is done" of process design relates to the way that work is structured. Even when what is done is appropriate, how it is done often is inappropriate. African bureaucracies, like most public bureaucracies elsewhere, are based on the organizing principal of hierarchy, or formal organizational structure. The principal role of hierarchy is to coordinate an organization's interdependencies. Hierarchies achieve coordination by defining standard procedures that govern the behavior of individuals or the premises by which individuals make decisions.[8]

Several arguments have been put forth as to why procedures are so weak in public bureaucracies in Africa. The origins school of thought contends that procedures are weak because they were designed either by colonial administrators or later by expatriate advisors. They are either ritualistically followed or not modified but, in either case, are inappropriate.[9] A related view is that the management systems imported by technical assistance personnel are fundamentally biased and flawed. The "factor proportions" of their management innovations (especially in terms of management capacity) are not congruent with the reality of conditions in Africa.[10]

The cultural school, represented by the work of Robert Price on Ghana, contends that roles are not institutionalized and thus the behavior of administrative staff is not governed by legal rationality, but by social pressures.[11] As such, the bureaucracy is accustomed to pursuing the interest of the individual and his or her social group. Price argues that achieving the Weberian ideal of a legal rational bureaucracy would require a "deviant solidarity" that would ostracize the individual from his or her social group.[12]

A third school views the administration of significant transactions as being principally done by personal intervention rather than procedure.[13] The leadership and in turn the management of the bureaucracy is often highly politicized. Interventionist administration is adopted to meet political demands promptly, to ensure rents, and to ensure response from unresponsive organizations. Interventionist administration erodes procedures.[14]

Weak procedures create weak organizational hierarchies. Although the image is one of centralization, the reality of many African bureaucracies is a subset of competing fiefdoms run by fiat rather than procedure.[15] Instead of being integrated through procedures, public bureaucracies are often fragmented organizations with numerous microhierarchies.[16] The leaders of these microhierarchies either vie amongst themselves for access to senior officials or they languish in isolation. Personal leadership and interventionist administration creates and reinforces fragmented organizational structures determined by the span of control of the senior administrator. "Just-in-reach" organization governs each bureaucracy as well as the subset microhierarchies that compose the bureaucracy.

Given the formidable obstacles that constrain organizational performance, what is an appropriate organizational design for African bureaucracies? This question is not new. A debate about it occurred in the 1970s in East Africa. Influenced by industrial sociology, this debate centered on whether development administration should be based on a mechanical model of organization which fit the Weberian legal rational (bureaucratic hierarchy) approach where procedures prescribe behavior or whether an organic model of organization which had a flatter structure and was less rigid in procedures was needed because development bureaucracies were change agents and change was contingent.[17] One of the most interesting positions in this debate was that of David Leonard. He argued that even though development bureaucracies are change agents, they are still organizations that require the stable implementation of procedures.[18] This belief accords with tenets from organization theory about the goal of organizations to reduce uncertainty.[19]

In 1987, Leonard renewed the debate about organizational performance in bureaucracies in Africa and suggested a methodology for developing an appropriate strategy:

> Our whole search process for management systems for Africa has been fundamentally biased and flawed to date. We have tended to look at those instances in which technical assistance personnel were introducing imported innovations.…These "factor proportions"

are inappropriate to the African environment. Instead we must study the more endogenously based organizational experiments that have a greater chance of being "appropriate technologies" for their environments…what we find will be best analyzed and explained by a combination of universal organizations theory and the sociology of Africa.[20]

Both strains of theory converge on a common issue: the importance of informal organization in coordinating social behavior. Beginning with organization theory, there is a growing body of literature that demonstrates the role of informal organization in compensating for the failures of formal organization or hierarchy.[21] From the sociology of Africa, the underpinning of these societies is the corporate group that stresses group loyalty rather than individual independence.[22] The link between the two strands of theory is collective organization by informal means. To analyze how work is organized, a more recent strand of organization theory is used—process design.[23]

Process Redesign in African Bureaucracies

Process design is how work is structured in an organization. The process perspective focuses on how work is done rather than what the output or product of work should be. Work in organizations is often designed around reporting relations that are vertically structured rather than around work flows that should be laterally structured for efficiency.[24] The process view assumes that most of the inefficiencies of work are caused by the fragmentation of tasks created by the functional and vertical design of organizations. Fragmentation disrupts work flows and creates unnecessary operational handoffs—complex organizational processes required to produce an output—and unnecessary demands on management. Process design views organizations horizontally in terms of work flows rather than vertically in terms of reporting relationships. Process design seeks to eliminate fragmentation of work flow and maximize efficiency through "one-stop service" that integrates as many tasks as possible with a single individual. Phenomenal efficiency gains can be achieved through process redesign, but it requires the careful orchestration of three enablers that maximize the individual's productivity: information technology, flat and innovative organizational structure, and creative human resource management.[25] Process design seeks to unleash the productivity of the individual by assembling the enablers of individual productivity. It differs from the conventional and top-down view of productivity that focuses on organizational productivity and sees individual productivity as residual.

The reform of process design can be done in two ways: process improvement and innovation.[26] Process improvement is incremental reform of existing processes that is done within the scope of existing functions. Process innovation is radical change that introduces new processes across functions. Process innovation is commonly called "reengineering" and it is arguably the dominant management strategy of the decade for both private and public sectors.[27] One of the principal publicists of reengineering, Michael Hammer, defines reengineering as "The fundamental rethinking and *radical redesign* of business *processes* to bring about *dramatic* improvements in performance."[28]

The objective of reengineering for both the private and public sector is to reap dramatic rather that incremental improvements in performance in terms of multiples of efficiency. Multiple efficiency gains are achieved by enabling the individual, principally with information technology that is supported by organizational structures and personnel management, to allow his or her full use of the technology.

Process Design in African Public Bureaucracies

Procedures are compromised in Africa because of factors related to their origins, the cultural milieu, and the politicization of their leaders and managers. Work has little formal structure and often the structure that exists is driven by formal rather than instrumental rationality. The process perspective assumes that work is highly structured and that it can be diagnosed and then redesigned with a concomitant reform of the organizational structure. Process design in public bureaucracies in Africa must cope with procedures that are at once fragmented, incomplete, inaccurate, compromised, and ignored. Goran Hyden observed that "organizational relations bear little resemblance to a chain of command; it is more like a chain letter—the information never returns to the sender."[29]

Table 6-1 compares process redesign in more developed and African countries. The principal objective of process design, the elimination of the fragmentation of work, is required in both environments. What differs is that fragmentation in Africa creates handoffs and handouts. Both practices need to be curtailed. Procedures are often exces-

TABLE 6-1

Comparison of Process Redesign in Developed and African Countries

	Process Redesign in Developed Countries	Process Redesign in African Countries
Objective	Eliminate fragmentation	Eliminate fragmentation
Source	Handoffs	Handoffs
		Handouts
Objective		Completeness
Source		Fragmentation
		Resource constraints
Objective		Accountability
Source		Weak control
Means	Expand across functional boundaries	Compress cross-functional transactions into a network
	Process integration through the individual	Process integration through the network team
		Establish parallel manual and computer processes

sively long-linked in Africa because authorization steps provide opportunities for rents. In addition to eliminating fragmentation, process redesign in Africa needs to address the problems of completeness and accountability. Completeness is needed to ensure that
processes are efficiently and accurately implemented. Accountability
is needed to limit corruption.

Process redesign differs between African and more developed
countries. In developed countries, the objective is to integrate processes by *expanding* across functional boundaries and integrating
principally through the individual. In Africa, process redesign is
achieved by *compressing* cross-functional transactions within a
microhierarchy or network subset of the bureaucracy and integrating through a network or team. Transactions have to be compressed
within a network rather than expanded cross-functionally because
organizational management is limited to the span of personal rather
than procedural control. Integration of process occurs principally
under the auspices of the network organization, not the individual,
because staff have limited skills, need close supervision, and are not
empowered. Finally, process redesign should promote accountabil-

ity. In Africa this can be done by developing parallel (e.g., manual and computer) systems that provide accountability.

Information Technology as an Enabler of Process Redesign

Information technology is, along with organizational structure and human resources, one of the three enablers of process reform. Information technology should enable but not drive process reform, and it should not be the prime enabler. Considerable improvement in organizational capacity can be achieved through process reforms that do not use information technology, especially through less ambitious process improvement. The inertia that prevails in large-scale organizations, especially in developing countries, often hampers process improvement. It often requires a large-scale and publicized reform to move government to change, either in terms of process improvement or innovation.

Although not a necessary and sufficient means of redesigning processes, microcomputers have proved to be especially suited in enabling process redesign in public bureaucracies in Africa. Information technology promotes the three essential tasks of process design: integration, completeness, and accountability. According to Zuboff:

> [M]anagers harness information technology to…accomplish one or more of three interdependent operational objectives—to increase the *continuity* (functional integration, enhanced automaticity, rapid response), *control* (precision, accuracy, predictability, consistency, certainty) and *comprehensibility* (visibility, analysis, synthesis).[30]

Continuity and control promote integration, completeness, and accountability. A process can be greatly simplified and integrated by using a program that requires only a few steps. Completeness is promoted by the data processing cycle, which provides a structure and discipline to work while the technology promotes monitoring to ensure that transactions are complete. Accountability is promoted by creating parallel manual and computer systems that provide extensive audit trails. Experience from Kenya indicates that one of the first benefits of computerization is the strengthening of the manual system, which often remains for some time the principal referent system.[31] Instead of process redesign, what occurs is parallel process renovation.

The manual system is replicated for the most part by the computer system, which is used in turn to renovate the manual system. Although production may not be accelerated, accountability is promoted.

Parallel process renovation demonstrates that considerable improvement can be achieved with limited redesign of processes. There is, however, considerable debate among system developers in Africa about whether computers should be used to replicate existing systems or create wholly new designs. Replication is less demanding on management and may be more appropriate as a first stage of reform. Process innovation may then follow as a second stage once the organization has adjusted to the technology.

The third benefit of information technology, comprehension, is far harder to reap because it first requires well-functioning databases and then managers who see the value of mining them by using a staff skilled at extraction and analysis.[32] The literature on process design does not stress the comprehension or data analysis role of information technology but rather focuses on the computerization of management data and the elimination of functional inefficiencies.[33]

Considerable evidence from Kenya affirms that information technology promotes the three tasks of process redesign: integration, completeness, and accountability.[34] However, it is important to ask if technology is appropriate. The sustainability of information technology should not be viewed in isolation from the sustainability of any government resource. Unfortunately, such a broad perspective is often not adopted. African governments are afflicted with an inability to cover recurrent costs.[35] Viewed broadly, they cannot afford information technology but they also cannot afford their other resources. One problem with information technology is that it tends to be overused rather than selectively applied to key activities. In terms of skill levels, the technology is entirely appropriate. Staff with only rudimentary education are able to use computers.[36] Thus, information technology is both appropriate and sustainable. How can this enabler be best organized to promote process redesign?

PROCESS REDESIGN: NETWORKS ARE MORE EFFECTIVE THAN HIERARCHIES IN AFRICAN BUREAUCRACIES

Network Organizations Defined

African bureaucracies are often decomposed into subsets or microhierarchies.[37] The microhierarchy organization reflects the limitations of management by personal rather than procedural control. Microhierarchies are principally informal and small-scale "just-in-reach" organizations defined by the span of control of their leaders.

Here, I elaborate on the microhierarchy concept and use the term *network organization*.[38] Microhierarchies are networks. The term network is used because, both in theory and in practice, it can link beyond the formal agency subset (the microhierarchy), thus promoting a "process" or lateral organization of work.

A network organization, "is a social network that is *integrated* across formal boundaries [and] interpersonal ties of any type are formed without respect to formal groups or categories."[39] All organizations are networks because they have social relations that define behavior. Networks are difficult to describe precisely because they often transcend formal internal and external organizational boundaries.

A network organization is a set of social relations, so one useful way to view it is in terms of the obligations between its members. Carol Heimer's research has found that networks arise out of the need to manage particularistic rules neglected by the universalistic rules of organizational hierarchies.

> [T]hose who contend that organizations are (and should be) governed by universalistic rules are wrong because life in organizations and networks necessarily entails obligations to concrete others that can be met responsibly only by adopting a particularistic orientation.[40]

Heimer's analysis is not a justification for compromising universalistic rules, but it does remind us of the reality of organizational life that "only by helping friends can anyone ever do business."[41] Small-scale networks (microhierarchies) exist in African public bureaucracies because management is personal, rather than procedural. Small-scale networks are uniquely suited to manage the legitimate (and illegitimate) particularistic demands of employees and clients. The small scale of the networks allows for the intensive management needed by particularistic rules.

> [I]n comparison to universalistic rules, particularistic rules are more complex (they have to take account of more variations), more difficult to formulate (someone has to decide which variations are important enough to be explicitly covered by the rule), more difficult to administer (someone will have to determine which rule applies, and the rules typically have to be treated as guidelines or rules of

thumb rather than laws), and more difficult to evaluate (partly because one must evaluate relationships rather than individuals).[42]

Small-scale network organizations can address the deficiencies of large-scale hierarchies and can cope with the particularistic demands of traditional society. The network form would appear to meet Leonard's recommendation that management forms in Africa combine universalistic organization theory with the sociology of Africa.

The Role of Networks

Networks fit the reality of organizational life in public bureaucracies in Africa. Networks or microhierarchies are created by the fragmentation of large-scale public bureaucracies that is caused by personal rather than procedural management and the pursuit of rents rather than legal rational authority.

Small-scale networks can manage the "higher costs" of particularism compared to universalism: "Particularism is an expensive virtue compared with universalism because it requires tracking individuals rather than categories and requires long relationships [and] extensive record keeping."[43] The capacity to manage particularism is not a necessary and sufficient condition to contain rents. Networks can both promote and control rents.

Networks fit the reality of how work is done not only in Africa but also in developed countries as well. Critical tasks are often done through team-based organization.[44] The literature on quality management stresses the virtue of cross-functional teams and the literature on process reform stresses the need for teams.[45] There is a growing literature on how to design team-based organizations.[46]

Networks are well suited to the contingent task environment of development bureaucracies as well as the contingent internal relations found in weak public bureaucracies. Baker notes, "As a flexible and self-adapting organization, it is well suited to unique customized projects, close customer and supplier involvement in the production process, and complex and turbulent environments."[47]

The role of networks or informal structures in promoting process reform is reviewed later. Here we consider the role of networks in compensating for the failure of formal structure to provide organizational coordination. Organization theory has often neglected the role of informal structures in compensating for the failure or ineffectiveness of formal structures to coordinate. Organization theory has principally focused on the role of informal structure in integrating the individual into the organization rather than its instrumental role in coordination.[48]

Donald Chisholm's work on the coordinating role of informal structures is instructive and is based on the problem of coordinating multiorganizational public systems rather than a single organization.[49] Chisholm's thesis has four arguments. First, following the work of Herbert Simon, organizational interdependencies are often overstated and thus the need for coordination either through formal or informal means is overestimated, and in any case, there are severe limits to rationally ordering collective behavior.[50] Second, there is a strong tendency to overuse formal structures for coordination without recognizing the cost and inefficiencies of such structures. Third, many coordination problems can be solved with informal structures that are more adaptive, problem-oriented, and robust than formal mechanisms. Fourth, organizational arrangements should be designed such that the formal and informal structures coordinate noncontingent and contingent tasks respectively. Chisholm concludes:

> Using smaller formal hierarchies to handle those problems sufficiently simple and known to be categorized as well structured, and informal mechanisms to coordinate where interdependence arises among them—ill-structured problems [is] an appropriate if radical proposal, given prevailing trends in public administration.[51]

In proposing an organizational design for public bureaucracies in Africa, a central question to consider is the type and intensity of interdependencies that such organizations have to manage. A second question is the respective roles of formal and informal structure in providing that coordination.

Viewing public bureaucracies in Africa as a collection of loosely coupled informal organizations suggests that coordination (within and between the microhierarchies and within and between organizations) should be promoted where necessary, principally by informal rather than formal means.

Another step in understanding public bureaucracies in Africa is to determine the interdependencies that require coordination. Following Simon's "empty world thesis," we agree that interdependencies are overestimated in African bureaucracies. African bureaucracies are often truly empty because they are bloated and serve principally as vehicles for employment. Many of the departments and their staff are irrelevant and need not be coordinated. The superfluous layers of organization hinder the coordination of critical tasks. Not only are formal structures inherently weak in coordinating public bureaucracies in Africa, they often address irrelevant tasks. Capacity-building strategies that seek to strengthen formal structures often waste valuable resources on irrelevant organizational mechanisms because they coordinate irrelevant tasks.

There are severe limits to the scale of formally coordinated organizations in Africa. Large-scale systems, however, can be created by coordinating several small-scale organizations primarily through informal means, as Chisholm's study of a public transit system illustrates. In principal then, a large-scale complex task can be effectively coordinated within the public sector in Africa. Informal coordination in Africa is pervasive and in many instances is very sophisticated. Though not a perfect substitute for formal structure, and although informal structures often have a negative effect on public organizations, they can also be a positive force and an extremely effective means of coordination.

Several caveats should be observed. First, the multiorganizational environment of the microhierarchies in African bureaucracies is very different from the multiorganizational environment in more developed countries. In Chisholm's study of transit systems in California, hierarchy*was* an option for multiorganizational coordination, albeit a more expensive and less effective one.[52] Hierarchy is *not* an option for African bureaucracies. It is simply not effective.

The Role of Networks in Managing Information Technology

Networks are the organizational design of choice for managing information technology-based work.[53] Networks can focus management resources on the individual and the team, the principal sources of productivity. Though small in scale, the network promotes the full utilization of the technology. By being small in scale, the technology is introduced on an appropriate scale. Finally, information technology facilitates the transfer of information within the organization, thus flattening the organization and further supporting the small-scale lateral structure of networks.

The Role of Networks in Managing Process Reform

Process reform in African bureaucracies is likely to be less radical in scope but still as significant in impact as process reengineering in bureaucracies in developing countries. The level of performance is so low that process improvement will produce dramatic results. The scope of reform is limited because of the limited scope of the networks. Thus the process reform task is to compress cross-functional processes within the scope of networks. Information technology allows small-scale networks to leverage their productivity dramatically and compress broad cross-functional processes.

Networks are well designed to promote process reform. They are small, management intensive, capable of managing contingencies, and focus on the individual and the team. Most important, networks are able to bridge the organizational contradiction of moving from vertical to horizontal work flows in process reform. Networks and teams are critical to process reform precisely because they are not bound by vertical reporting structures and they provide a transitional organization. Networks can bypass fragmented authority structures as well as superfluous vertical structures and promote a more lateral and efficient work flow. In short, networks provide an organizational vehicle for changing from vertical to horizontal work flows as well as a strategy for bypassing hierarchy.

Networks in Action: A Case from Kenya

Network organizations are key organizational designs needed to promote process reform in public bureaucracies. An excellent example of this thesis comes from Kenya and the efforts to reform the complement system used to manage personnel in the agricultural-sector line ministries.[54] For nearly three years, a technical assistance team worked within the formal hierarchy of the ministry to assist in the reform of the system. After three years, the reform had achieved very little. With the arrival of a progressive senior staff member, the progress of the reform dramatically improved. He built a small network of committed and supportive staff and created a parallel system of data processing of personnel records. The network was within the formal hierarchy but acted on its own and with reference to the network leader. The network was kept small to ensure close management and to ensure that the system was not compromised by unsupportive staff. In less than one year, the network had built an effective system, had installed the system, and had used the system to renovate the manual system and reduce the rents being produced.

Conclusions

The principal leader in an ambitious large-scale public reengineering reform recently remarked that the central problem hampering the reform was the lack of teamwork. Process reform requires rethinking organizational relationships and rationalizing them where possible. In theory, large-scale public bureaucracies are built to promote vertical authority structures to promote the autonomy and accountability of the individual office. In practice, these vertical structures promote handoffs and handouts. By reinforcing the personal interests for maintaining these vertical structures, budgets also promote fragmentation.

Public bureaucracies in Africa are not alone in facing the difficult challenge of process reform. Globally, bureaucracies confront the challenge of building horizontal work flows in vertically structured organizations. The solution is teamwork and the organizational vehicle is the network. For Africa, organizational weaknesses are a strength. Because vertical structures are weak, they facilitate horizontal networks.

Two observations emerge about capacity building in public bureaucracies in Africa. First, these organizations are not unitary hierarchies, but a multi-organizational system composed of informally coordinated microhierarchies or networks. Second, process reform can be achieved without significantly changing the basic organization (the microhierarchy). The implications of these two observations are that capacity building in terms of large-scale structural reform is very hard to achieve, but more importantly, it is not needed for achieving dramatic productivity gains. The key to building capacity in public bureaucracies in Africa is to build networks within and between hierarchies and not to build hierarchies.

Notes

1   David Osborne and Ted Gaebler, *Reinventing Government: How the Entrepreneurial Spirit Is Transforming the Public Sector* (Plume: New York, 1993), 258.

2   David K. Leonard, "The Political Realities of African Management," *World Development* 15 (1987): 908.

3   Robert M. Price, *Society and Bureaucracy in Contemporary Ghana* (Berkeley: University of California Press, 1975); Goran Hyden, *No Shortcuts to*

Progress: African Development Management in Perspective (London: Heinemann, 1983); and David K. Leonard, *African Successes: Four Public Managers of Kenyan Rural Development* (Berkeley: University of California Press, 1991).

4   Jon Moris, "The Transferability of Western Management Concepts and Programs: An East African Perspective," in W. D. Laurence Stifel, Joseph E. Black and James S. Coleman, eds., *Education and Training for Public Sector Management in Developing Countries* (New York: The Rockefeller Foundation, 1977); Leonard, "The Political Realities."

5   Stephen B. Peterson, "Saints, Demons, Wizards and Systems: Why Information Technology Reforms Fail or Underperform in Public Bureaucracies in Africa," *HIID Development Discussion Paper 486*, (Cambridge: Harvard Institute for International Development, May 1994).

6   On the concept of pockets of productivity see Stephen B. Peterson, "Institutionalizing Microcomputers in Developing Bureaucracies: Theory and Practice from Kenya," *Information Technology for Development* 5 (September 1990): 277–326.

7   Stephen B. Peterson, Charles Kinyeki, Joseph Mutai, and Charles Ndungu, "Computerizing Personnel Information Systems: Lessons From Kenya," *International Journal of Public Administration* 20, 10 (October 1997).

8   On standardization see James D. Thompson, *Organizations in Action: Social Science Basis of Administration Theory* (New York: McGraw-Hill, 1967), 65. On establishing decision premises see Herbert Simon, *Administrative Behavior*, 2nd ed. (New York: The Free Press, 1957), Chapter 3.

9   Jon Moris, "Managerial Structures and Plan Implementation in Colonial and Modern Agricultural Extension: A Comparison of Cotton and Tea Programmes in Central Kenya," in D. K. Leonard, ed., *Rural Administration in Kenya* (Nairobi: East African Literature Bureau, 1973), 124.

10   Leonard, "The Political Realities," 908.

11   Price argues that "the corporate nature of social organization in traditional African societies, and the related but more general gemeinschaft orientation toward social interaction that predominates in such systems, do not provide cultural legitimacy for the compartmentalization of personal and official roles." *Society and Bureaucracy*, 206.

12   Price, *Society and Bureaucracy*, 215.

13   Leonard, *African Successes*; Peterson, "Saints, Demons."

14   A further reason for interventionist administration is a lack of depth of management. Procedures assume that an adequate level of supervision

exists. Public bureaucracies in Africa often lack adequate depth of management to ensure that the procedures are properly and promptly applied.

15 Hyden, *No Shortcuts*, 144–147; Robert Klitgaard, *Adjusting to Reality: Beyond State versus Market in Economic Development* (San Francisco: International Center for Economic Growth Press, 1991), 87–89.

16 Hyden, *No Shortcuts*, 146–147; Moris, "Transferability," 79.

17 Tom Burns and G. M. Stalker, *The Management of Innovation* (London: Tavistock Publications, 1961).

18 David K. Leonard, *Reaching the Peasant Farmer: Organization Theory and Practice in Kenya* (Chicago: The University of Chicago Press), 219.

19 Simon, *Administrative Behavior*, and Thompson, *Organizations in Action*.

20 Leonard, "The Political Realities," 907.

21 Donald Chisholm, *Coordination Without Hierarchy: Informal Structures in Multiorganizational Systems* (Berkeley: University of California Press, 1989).

22 P. C. Lloyd, *Africa in Social Change* (Baltimore: Penguin Books, 1967), 30; cited in Price, *Society and Bureaucracy*, 26.

23 Thomas H. Davenport, *Process Innovation: Reengineering Work Through Information Technology* (Boston: Harvard Business School Press, 1993).

24 Davenport, *Process Innovation*, 8; Michael Hammer, *The Reengineering Revolution: A Handbook* (New York: HarperBusiness, 1995), 4–5.

25 Davenport, *Process Innovation*, 16–18.

26 Davenport, *Process Innovation*, 5–16.

27 On reengineering, see Michael Hammer and James Champy, *Reengineering the Corporation* (New York: HarperBusiness, 1993); Hammer, *The Reengineering Revolution*; Davenport, *Process Innovation*; and James Champy, *Reengineering Management: The Mandate for New Leadership* (New York: HarperBusiness, 1995). For an example of public sector reengineering in developing countries, see the Presidential Committee on Streamlining the Bureaucracy, Department of Budget and Management, *Reengineering the Bureaucracy for Better Governance: Principles and Parameters* (Manila: Government of the Philippines, August 1995).

28 Hammer, *The Reengineering Revolution*, 3.

29 Hyden, *No Shortcuts*, 147.

30 Shoshana Zuboff, "Automate/Informate: The Two Faces of Intelligent Technology," *Organizational Dynamics* 14 (Autumn 1985): 7, author's emphasis.

31 Peterson, Kinyeki, Mutai, and Ndungu, "Computerizing Personnel Information Systems."

32 Stephen B. Peterson, "From Processing to Analyzing: Intensifying the Use of Microcomputers in Development Bureaucracies," *Public Administration and Development* 11 (September–October 1991): 491–510.

33 Zuboff stresses the importance of informating rather than simply automating in reaping the full value of an information technology investment. See Zuboff, "Automate/Informate," 10.

34 On computerizing budgets, see Clay Wescott, "Microcomputers for Improved Budgeting by the Kenya Government," *HIID Development Discussion Paper 227* (Cambridge: Harvard Institute for International Development, 1986); on computerizing accounts see Thomas Pinckney, John Cohen, and David Leonard, "Microcomputers and Financial Management in Development Ministries: Experience from Kenya," *Agricultural Administration* 14 (1983): 151–167; Stephen Peterson, Charles Kinyeki, Joseph Mutai, and Charles Ndungu, "Computerizing Accounting Systems in Development Bureaucracies: Lessons from Kenya," *HIID Development Discussion Paper 500* (Cambridge: Harvard Institute for International Development, January 1995).

35 Stephen B. Peterson, "Improving Recurrent Cost Financing of Development Bureaucracies," in Naomi Caiden, ed., *Public Financial Administration in Developing Countries* (Greenwich, CT: JAI Press, Inc., 1995).

36 Stephen B. Peterson, "Microcomputer Training for the Government of Kenya: The Case of the Kenya Institute of Administration," *Information Technology for Development* 5 (December 1990): 292–307.

37 Moris, "The Transferability," 79.

38 The microhierarchy concept as used in development administration in Africa appears to have originated in the work of Jean-Claude Garcia-Zamor. Garcia-Zamor used the concept to distinguish two broad objectives of bureaucrats in a bureaucracy—the policrats who sought major policy change and the technocrats who sought incremental improvements in implementation. Zamor did not elaborate on the organizational dimensions. See Jean-Claude Garcia-Zamor, "Micro-Bureaucracies and Development Administration," *International Review of Administrative Sciences* 29 (1973): 417–423.

39 Wayne E. Baker, "The Network Organization in Theory and Practice" in Nitin Nohria and Robert G. Eccles, eds., *Networks and Organizations: Structure, Form and Action* (Boston: Harvard Business School Press, 1992).

40 Carol A. Heimer, "Doing Your Job and Helping Your Friends: Universalistic Norms about Obligations to Particular Others in Networks" in Nitin

Nohria and Robert G. Eccles, eds., *Networks and Organizations: Structure, Form, and Action* (Boston: Harvard Business School Press, 1992), 144.

41 Heimer, "Doing Your Job," 143.

42 Heimer, "Doing Your Job," 148–149.

43 Heimer, "Doing Your Job," 145.

44 Frederick P. Brooks, *The Mythical Man-Month: Essays in Software Engineering* (Reading, MA: Addison-Wesley, 1975), 32.

45 On the role of teams in quality management, see Edwards W. Deming, *Out of Crisis* (Cambridge: Center for Advanced Engineering Study, Massachusetts Institute of Technology, 1986); and Joseph Juran, *Juran on Leadership for Quality* (New York: Free Press, 1989). For the role of teams in process innovation, see Hammer and Champy, *Reengineering the Corporation*; and Robert Kanter, *The Change Masters* (New York: Simon and Schuster, 1983).

46 Susan A. Mohrman, Susan G. Cohen, and Allan M. Mohrman, *Designing Team-Based Organizations: New Forms of Knowledge Work* (San Francisco: Jossey-Bass, Inc., 1995).

47 Baker, "The Network Organization," 422.

48 Chisholm, *Coordination*, 20–28.

49 Chisholm was studying the San Francisco Bay Area Public Transit System.

50 Herbert Simon, *Reason in Human Affairs* (Palo Alto: Stanford University Press, 1984).

51 Chisholm, *Coordination*, 200.

52 Chisholm, *Coordination*, 200–202.

53 Mohrman, Cohen, and Mohrman, *Designing Team-Based Organizations*; Jay Galbraith, *Competing with Flexible Lateral Organizations*, 2nd edition (Reading, MA: Addison-Wesley, 1994).

54 Peterson, Kinyeki, Mutai, and Ndungu, "Computerizing Personnel Information Systems."

7 POLICY RESEARCH INSTITUTES IN DEVELOPING COUNTRIES

Charles N. Myers

Policy research institutes—autonomous of government yet influential on policy—are an important innovation in capacity building in developing countries. When successful, these institutes improve policy, build capacity elsewhere in government and the private sector, and inform and improve debate about development policy.

Successful establishment of such institutes is not an easy task. Maintaining their viability, influence, quality, and intellectual zest over the longer term is harder still. Two successful examples are the Thailand Development Research Institute (TDRI) in Bangkok and the Social Policy Analysis Unit (UDAPSO) in La Paz, Bolivia. The two cases are used to analyze how policy research institutes are established and sustained, and how they fit and affect broader capacity building along the five analytic dimensions proposed by Hilderbrand and Grindle in Chapter 2.

The crux of the argument is that establishment of policy research institutes is most likely when there are widely perceived changes in the action environment; that such institutes require and produce innovations in organizational structure, management, hiring, promotion, pay, and staff development; and that to be influential and build networks, their relationship to government must be right, their quality high, and a balance must be maintained between response to short-term requests and conduct of a program of long-term research.

In sum, successful policy research institutes contribute to capacity building not only by improving policy and dialogue about development, but also by testing new organizational structures and incentives and setting higher standards of quality, agility, and responsiveness. All of these, of course, are characteristics of capable states.

The term *policy research institutes* is broad and could be understood to cover organizations serving, for example, particular political parties, ideologies, points of view, private industries, or labor unions. Here, the term is used more specifically to cover organizations that have many or most of the following characteristics:

- Independence or autonomy from any particular political party, government, or ideological point of view.

- Commitment to neutrality and objectivity with the goal of informing policy choice, not advocating particular choices.

- Commitment to the highest possible quality of staff, research, publications, and dissemination.

- A policy focus responsive to the agenda of policy makers but based on programs of long-term research.

- Special attention in research to medium- and longer-term issues, some of which may not be on the current agenda of government, but all of which are important for future economic and social development.

- Consensus building with government and the private sector on development policy.

- Cooperation with institutions abroad.

TDRI and UDAPSO shared many of these characteristics. In some ways, however, they were also as different as their locations. The major differences between TDRI in 1992 and UDAPSO in 1995 are presented in Table 7-1.

TDRI in 1992 was a large institute, with research programs on macroeconomic policy, sectoral economics, international trade, natural resources and the environment, science and technology, and human resources and social development. This chapter draws on the

Comparison of Thailand Development Research Institute (TDRI) and the
Bolivian Social Policy Analysis Unit (UDAPSO)

	TDRI	UDAPSO
Date of Founding	1984	1992
Legal Status	Private foundation	Autonomous government agency
Leadership	President and board of directors	Executive director
Research Programs	Full range of development policy	Social policy only
Research Directors	6	1
Senior Research Fellows	16	0
Researchers	9	16
Research Assistants	34	7
Annual Recurrent Budget (in millions of US$)	4.0	0.7

experience of TDRI from 1984 to 1992. UDAPSO in 1995 was a much
smaller institute, with research activities on poverty, education, employment, housing, health, and nutrition. This chapter draws on the
experience of UDAPSO from 1992 to 1995, but with more emphasis
on the last two years. The earlier years of UDAPSO are very well presented and analyzed by Manuel E. Contreras in Chapter 8.

Though the differences were many, there were important simi-
larities in how the two institutions were established, their relationships to government, the nature of their research programs, their attention to staff development and incentives, and the role of
international cooperation, challenges to long-term viability, and contributions to broader capacity building in Thailand and Bolivia.

GETTING STARTED

The initiation of TDRI and UDAPSO—and perhaps of most such
institutes—required the coincidence of four conditions: recognition
of need, a strong leading proponent in government, availability of
core funding, and an affirmative act of government.

Recognition of need was first. In the late 1970s, leading technocrats in the Thai government faced a rapidly changing action environment and the changes were easy to recognize. There was the second oil shock, a recession, a growing budget deficit, a need for structural adjustment, and an incipient change from import substitution to export-led growth. The government's planning agency realized that it had neither the time nor the quality of staff to do medium- to longer-term research on Thai development, or even to respond effectively to short-term issues of increasing complexity as the environment changed. There was a perception that the obvious answers weren't right and the right answers weren't obvious. A high-quality research institute of some kind was needed. As Manuel Contreras recounts in his case study of UDAPSO in the next chapter, there was a similar perception in Bolivia when the social consequences of the 1985 to 1987 economic adjustment became clear and the need for policy research on social issues was recognized.

The second condition was—in the poetic language of Thai politics—a "godfather with a big network." In Thailand, that role was played by Dr. Snoh Unakul, a former governor of the Bank of Thailand and at the time director of the Thai planning agency. Unakul was a man of impeccable reputation and graceful determination. He knew the history and importance of the Korea Development Institute and he wanted to establish something like it in Thailand. He promoted the idea. He pursued funding options. He recruited additional godfathers to the cause. Indeed, when TDRI was finally established in 1984, there was a godfather for each of the new institute's research programs. As Manuel Contreras recounts, much the same role in the establishment of UDAPSO was played by Samuel Doria Medina, minister of planning from 1991 to 1993.

The willingness of an external funder—the Canadian International Development Agency (CIDA) in Thailand, and USAID in Bolivia—to provide core funding came next. In both instances the donors' willingness was attributable in part to their trust in Dr. Snoh and Minister Medina respectively, and in part to a desire to have a major impact on policy. The core funding provided the promise of initial institutional continuity, of salary levels sufficient to attract and retain quality staff, and of some degree of autonomy from day-to-day political pressures and change. Core funding by external donors can, of course, have other less favorable consequences. These are taken up later in the chapter.

Final steps in the initiation of TDRI and UDAPSO involved affirmative acts of government. Recognition of need, a powerful godfather, and availability of core funding can create an institution. If other politicians and technocrats are hostile or even indifferent, however, the new institution may have little impact on policy. In Thailand, establishment of TDRI, a private foundation with special legal status, required an act of the Thai parliament. In Bolivia, establishment of UDAPSO, a decentralized autonomous agency of government, required a government decree specifying its legal status, including the right to pursue and receive grants and contracts on its own. In effect, government was partner to the initiation of both.

In practice, these steps are not linear. They are iterative until a consensus in support of a new institution is formed. The process took more than six years in Thailand and three years in Bolivia. The process might not always involve the three somewhat separate parties: technocrats, external funders, and politicians. In the establishment of the Korea Development Institute, for example, recognition of need, the godfather role, core funding, affirmative establishment (and protection from day-to-day political pressures) came from a single source, the office of the president. In this, as in other aspects of development, South Korea is perhaps a special case.

Relationship to Government

Relationship to government is a critical issue for policy research institutes. If they are too close to government, they may be co-opted, compromised, perceived to be committed to the party in power, and not survive the next government change. If they are too far from government, they may be ignored no matter how good their work.

Thus, there is a fine line: close enough to be influential and useful to government, far enough to be objective and to be able to anticipate issues and to be perceived as such.

What matters are the characteristics of the relationship, not the specific legal forms it may take. TDRI is a private foundation; UDAPSO is a government agency. In legal structure terms, TDRI risked being too far from government and UDAPSO, too close. Neither suffered from its particular legal structure, however.

TDRI was close enough to government because it had senior government technocrats and influential leaders of the private sector on its board of directors. At the operational level, it involved middle-level government technocrats on ad hoc research teams for particular projects. These teams set the agenda, planned and participated in the work, and authored and disseminated the results. Participation in ad hoc policy research project teams provided technocrats with "hands-on" training in policy research and gave them a strong sense of ownership of the results. This connection helped focus the agenda, improve the research, and build networks, and increased the likelihood that policy recommendations would be implemented. In 1995, such a pattern was beginning to emerge in Bolivia.

TDRI also became seen by government as an arbiter of data quality on contentious development policy issues. It served as "honest broker" and "neutral site" for resolution of policy disagreements on critical issues—for example, whether to construct a new hydroelectric project or fertilizer factory—and for building consensus on development policy. This function was seen as useful by government. By 1995 such a pattern—but more informal and based on the executive director's personal network—was beginning to emerge in Bolivia.

UDAPSO's directors strongly defended the autonomy of the institution in order to ensure that it did not become too close to government, or even be absorbed by the Bolivian Ministry of Human Development, which it served. The arguments used in support of autonomy included the need for a different salary scale to attract quality staff, the need to focus on more than just short-term issues, and the need for neutrality and objectivity. The force of these arguments was augmented by the financial support it had obtained from a variety of sources. This support would have been jeopardized if objectivity had been seen to be compromised. It would have ended if UDAPSO had been absorbed by the Ministry of Human Development.

Between 1984 and 1993, TDRI survived cabinet and party changes, a military coup, two interim governments, and the restoration of civilian rule. It remained close to succeeding governments by changes in its board of directors and continued involvement of government technocrats on ad hoc project committees. As governments changed, some TDRI researchers, because of their informal networks, became more influential, others less so. The overall influence of the institution remained high throughout, however. Similarly, in 1994, UDAPSO survived a change in government and party. A new executive director was appointed by the new government. There was little change in the research program, only an amplification of effort and staff. There also was continued, even enhanced, influence on policy.

Both institutions were protected in part by reputation—by the quality and usefulness of past work. Both were protected by informal networks of contacts with influential individuals in government and society at large. Most important, both were able to maintain or reestablish influence on policy by doing first-rate work on problems perceived as important by all political actors. This result was mainly attributable to strong leadership in both institutes and the characteristics of their research programs.

RESEARCH PROGRAMS

The research programs of both institutions had three characteristics in common which were important not only for maintaining influence with government but also for building reputation and institutional and intellectual capital. These characteristics were responsive to the short-term needs of government, long-term research, and anticipation of policy issues that would be important in the future.

Fire Fighting

A policy institute that is unresponsive to the short-term needs of policy makers—unwilling or unable to help with "fire fighting"—will obviously not be influential for long. TDRI responded to government requests to help on issues as diverse as recommendations for renegotiation of a voluntary export restraint (VER) on cassava exports with the European Community (EC), analysis of the impact of a value-added tax (VAT), forecasts of future regional domestic product, and policy options for increasing enrollment in secondary schools. UDAPSO responded to government requests as diverse as help in negotiation of university budgets, evaluation of a proposed policy of free health care for children under five, design of an earnings survey, and evaluation of the revenue assumptions and overall adequacy of a major education reform. Moreover, both institutes understood that in their fire-fighting role, they needed to do high-quality work.[1]

Long-Term Research

Both organizations responded effectively to the immediate needs of government because of the nature of their programs of long-term research. In its first year, TDRI developed five-year research plans for each of the areas in which it would work; these plans reflected the initial core funding of TDRI for five years. At UDAPSO, the process was less formal and the time horizon shorter because the initial core funding was for three years.

In both cases, the idea was to design and initiate programs of in-depth research that were both complimentary and cumulative. They were to be complimentary in the sense that each would use inputs from others and each would produce outputs that were potential inputs to others and to subsequent work. The programs were to be cumulative in the sense that they would increase understanding of underlying behavior, whether of the economy as a whole (e.g., the macroeconomic research program at TDRI) or of labor markets and poverty (e.g., the employment and poverty research programs at UDAPSO).

The research program of UDAPSO was complimented by a program of longitudinal monitoring of government initiatives in the social sector. These evaluations included Bolivia's Social Investment Fund and a World Bank-funded project of early childhood interventions designed to reduce malnutrition, promote cognitive and physical development, enhance future success in school, and allow mothers to participate more fully in the labor market. Some of these evaluations were designed to create longitudinal or pooled time-series data sets of great value for research.

Both TDRI and UDAPSO further complimented their research programs by the creation of institutional databases used by both researchers and government. Both were among the first in their countries to make use of geographical information systems (GIS) for research and for communication of research results.

A basic premise of policy research institutes similar to TDRI and UDAPSO is that good work on policy cannot be done without the underlying programs of research. First-rate work on policy depends on first-rate research on the development issues involved. Even policy work that is responsive to the short-term needs of government draws on this research.

To take the specific examples given above, TDRI was able to respond to the request for help in renegotiation of the VER on cassava exports to the EC because of its program of research on agriculture and rural development, including analysis of cassava production in Northeast Thailand and of the recipients of cassava rents. Similarly, the institute was able to respond to requests for analysis of the impact of a VAT and for forecasts of future regional domestic product because it had developed and regularly updated a sophisticated CGE model of the Thai economy. It was also able to respond to requests for policy options for increasing enrollment in secondary schools because of its program of research on education, which included analysis of the private costs of education and household patterns of demand.

UDAPSO was able to respond to the request for help in negotiation of university budgets because of its research on the efficiency of higher education and the efficiency effects of existing funding mechanisms. It was able to respond to the request for evaluation of a proposed policy of free health care for children under five because of its research on demand for health services and simulations of the effects of price changes on the use of health services. The organization was able to help in the design of an earnings survey because of its program of research on labor markets. It also was able to respond to the request for evaluation of the revenue assumptions and the overall adequacy of the education reform because of its program of research on education. This research included analysis of costs, education markets, demand, and the role of private providers.

In these examples (and others too numerous to describe) there is an element of demand creation. As policy makers became aware of the longer-term research, they asked for short-term help on the same issues. Good work on short-term concerns also created demand for policy options for the longer term on the same issues. Both elements of demand creation increase perception of the usefulness and legitimacy of a policy research institute.

Anticipation

A final characteristic of the research programs was anticipation of problems that were not among the current concerns of policy makers but that were likely to be among them in the future. If the institution guessed right, it was ready with the research and policy options when the problem became important to policy makers.

TDRI, for example, undertook research on natural resources and the environment, science and technology, secondary education, subsidies of health services, and the acquired immunodeficiency syndrome (AIDS) before any of these issues was of concern to policy makers. In each case, policy makers subsequently asked for policy advice. Among the bets that UDAPSO made were work on rural labor markets; work on health care demand, national health accounts, and costing of a basic package of health services in anticipation of a future health reform; and work on middle education, even though at the time education reform (rightly) concentrated on basic education.

There was an element of luck in these choices, but it wasn't only luck. Prescient leadership in the institutes, suggestions from government technocrats concerned about issues not receiving enough attention, and suggestions from external advisors based on the experience of other countries were also involved. Some choices were easy and obvious, as, for example, AIDS in Thailand and health reform in Bolivia.

Overall, the research programs of these policy research institutes represented much of their intellectual and institutional capital. That capital had to be maintained and enhanced if good and improving work on policy options was to continue. That, in turn, depended mainly on the quality of leadership and staff.

STAFF AND STAFF DEVELOPMENT

At their inception, the two research institutes faced very different national endowments in the number of senior and junior researchers—mainly economists in both cases—with strong training and experience who were potentially available as leaders and staff. Thailand has a history of high investment in human capital with a long tradition (and donor support) of overseas graduate study, including Ph.D.s in economics. The main human resource development issues for TDRI therefore were related to incentives and optimal utilization. Its initial salary scale was equal to pay in the private sector. This compensation was high enough to attract back to Thailand first-rate economists working in institutions such as the World Bank and the International Food Policy Research Institute.

Bolivia had lower investment and relatively fewer internationally trained first-rate economists. Moreover, UDAPSO's initial salary scale was less competitive than TDRI's. It was higher than the regular government scale, but lower than private sector pay and some project-funded government positions. Among the many human resource development issues for UDAPSO, then, were finding talented people, attracting and retaining them, training and upgrading, and coping with turnover.

The three presidents of TDRI and the two directors of UDAPSO since inception had doctoral-level training. There the similarity between the two institutes ends, however. At TDRI, directors of research programs, research fellows, and most researchers had Ph.D.s. At UDAPSO, the senior researchers had at most master's degrees and most of the rest of the research staff had only bachelor's degrees. Most research assistants at TDRI had master's degrees; research assistants at UDAPSO had bachelor's-level training and many had not yet completed the thesis required for their professional degree.

Internal research teams at TDRI typically consisted of a team leader (often the research program director), several research fellows, researchers, and research assistants. The research assistants did the data processing and some data analysis but relatively little writing. Research teams at UDAPSO typically consisted of one or two researchers and one or two research assistants. As in TDRI, the research assistants did data processing and analysis, but at UDAPSO they also helped with writing, sometimes co-authoring working papers and in some instances writing working papers on their own.

POLICY RESEARCH INSTITUTES AS GRADUATE SCHOOLS

Both institutes hired the best graduates each year as entry-level research assistants. For these new researchers a policy research institute is in a sense a "graduate school." Newly hired staff use what they have learned rather than decapitalize in jobs that make no use of their training. This was a potential problem in both countries, but particularly in Bolivia. Often the best work economists do in their career is their theses. The jobs available for most make little or no use of their training. Even those in university teaching have to moonlight in consulting or take second jobs to supplement their incomes—leaving little time and few opportunities for serious research that would build their skills. For UDAPSO, the new graduates were in this sense better prospects than graduates from earlier years who had lost their skills. Indeed, recruiting of first-rate middle-level researchers was particularly difficult. Searches for five middle-level staff in 1994 took more than six months and numerous re-advertisements to identify appropriate candidates. It would, of course, be nearly fatal to the cohesion of a research institute if entry-level staff were uniformly technically better and more productive than the senior staff for whom they work.

Not only did new researchers in TDRI and UDAPSO use and solidify skills they learned in university, they also learned new techniques from the more senior staff and in formal training programs offered in-house. For example, at TDRI use of CGE models were important for skill development, and at UDAPSO, use of discrete dependent-variable techniques were similarly useful for skill building. This pattern built human capital in both UDAPSO and TDRI. Not surprisingly, it also built aspirations for further graduate study—for Ph.D.s in Thailand, and for completion of undergraduate theses, master's, and Ph.D. programs in Bolivia.

The attraction of further study was more serious for UDAPSO than for TDRI. Middle- and senior-level researchers at TDRI already had final degrees. Research assistants came and went, and there was also a greater available supply of them in Thailand. UDAPSO depended much more on its junior staff as well as its researchers, many of whom wanted to pursue advanced degrees. Although this interest in further study was good for Bolivia, it led to much higher levels of turnover in UDAPSO than in TDRI.

INCENTIVES AND UTILIZATION

TDRI started with more talent and the prospect of less turnover than UDAPSO. These were important advantages but not guarantees of success. The structure of TDRI devolved authority and responsibility to the directors of its six research programs. Research directors had considerable autonomy in the conceptualization, conduct, staffing, and dissemination of their research programs and projects. They were expected to be entrepreneurial in building and financing their research. They were responsible to the president of TDRI for the quality of all the work in their programs.

Clearly the research directors had strong incentives to seek out the best possible staff, to upgrade their skills when necessary, and to engage them in research projects that made optimal use of their talents. Internal staff were supplemented in most programs by university faculty who were selected by the research directors. The faculty members worked at TDRI on sabbaticals and leaves of absence, or on a part-time basis. TDRI was able to attract some of the best university faculty to its research and some stayed on. All interacted with internal staff and all learned from one another. By 1995 this pattern had not yet developed at UDAPSO.

The research directors, in turn, could offer numerous incentives to staff and invited faculty to excel, including participation in authorship, visibility at national conferences, prominence in the media, international travel for regional conferences, leadership of research projects, and the opportunity to work and co-author papers with international experts who worked at TDRI under various programs of international cooperation. The research directors also reviewed the performance of staff and recommended promotions and salary increases for their staff to the president of TDRI.

Placing so much responsibility and discretion in the hands of the research directors created the potential for abuse. Some researchers did leave TDRI because they felt that a research director had not sufficiently credited their work or increased their level of responsibility. Some also felt that university faculty were given better assignments and more prominence.

There was a trade-off here. Staffing decisions and incentives were decentralized to minimize the institutionalization of seniority and sinecure and to maintain a strong emphasis on performance and quality, but the cost of this structure was the potential for abuse. One researcher said—perhaps correctly—that she got less opportunity and visibility because she didn't play golf and the research director did. Nevertheless, from the vantage point of 1995, the benefits appear significantly to have outweighed the costs. This issue is taken up again in the final section of this chapter.

UDAPSO started with a smaller potential pool of talent and a less competitive salary structure than TDRI, but it had one advantage in recruiting and keeping staff that TDRI quickly lost: the absence of other alternatives for potential staff to do serious research. For young economists in Bolivia interested in learning and doing high-quality research on social sector issues, UDAPSO was pretty much the only game in town. Like TDRI, though, it functioned in part as a "graduate school." This too was understood and appreciated by potential new staff. Both the absence of alternatives and the chance to learn offset UDAPSO's lack of competitiveness in salaries with the private sector. Only one offer of a new staff position at UDAPSO in 1994 was rejected because of higher pay in the private sector.

Given the comparatively lower levels of formal education, the main staff development activity at UDAPSO was training. The training took several forms, including short courses abroad, seminars in Bolivia, organized training within UDAPSO, and informal training provided in research teams.

With help from international cooperation, UDAPSO staff were sent abroad for periods of up to three months; for example, to a summer program on health policy and planning at the Harvard School of Public Health. Other staff were sent to short courses and workshops (e.g., on databases and information systems) offered in Bolivia. Formal training was also offered in UDAPSO. For example, there was introductory and advanced training in the use of discrete dependent-variable techniques (LOGIT and PROBIT) for new and middle-level staff, all of whose formal training stopped at ordinary least squares. This program was offered three times at the introductory level and twice at the advanced level to reinforce skills and to train new staff hired because of turnover. Another example was a two-week workshop on the use of GIS, including installation and training in the use of hardware and software and in the use of the technique in databases and information systems, and for research and presentation of research results.

At UDAPSO as at TDRI, informal training of staff took place in research teams. Leaders of research projects were responsible to the director of UDAPSO for the quality and timely completion of their work. Quality was assessed by the director with the input of international experts working at the institute with support from international cooperation. The leader(s) of projects had the same incentives as TDRI research directors to provide as much upgrading on the job as possible. The incentives were strong enough that project leaders provided repeated training of young staff hired because of turnover. If most project leaders—the mid-level researchers—at UDAPSO had left for advanced graduate study, or other activities, the outlook would have been dire.

The saving grace was the continuity of some of the more senior people in UDAPSO with their incentives to train new staff in order to maintain the quality of their research programs, and UDAPSO's ability, sometimes after months of search, to hire new people at this level.

Although training and incentives are part of human resource development in both institutions, initial staff endowments and aspirations created different patterns. The risk at TDRI was that lesser-quality staff might want to stay too long, and would resent incentives that rewarded more productive staff. The risk at UDAPSO was that the better-quality staff would want to go on for advanced study precisely because UDAPSO trained them and gave them the opportunity to write, publish, and be influential as relatively junior staff. UDAPSO needed to continue to cope successfully with turnover. It was likely to be part of its environment for some time to come.

TDRI's success in doing high-quality research and policy work was not a surprise, given the quality of its research directors and staff.

UDAPSO's ability to do good research and policy work was a special credit to its leadership and relatively young staff. For poor countries with few highly trained researchers, UDAPSO may be a particularly hopeful example.

International Cooperation

International cooperation at TDRI and UDAPSO took two forms. The first was financial support. Both received core funding from international donors. Both received program-level and project-level support. For example, TDRI received USAID funding for the macroeconomic program, and UDAPSO had support from the World Bank for poverty research and Swedish funding for five permanent positions through the Bolivian civil service program.

The second kind of international cooperation was collaboration between policy research institutes. Both TDRI and UDAPSO had close working relationships with the Harvard Institute for International Development (HIID); in both cases the relationship with HIID was supported by USAID. These relationships had many common characteristics and patterns of evolution, and some differences consistent with the differences between TDRI and UDAPSO.

Ideally, international collaboration between policy research institutes should be long-term, engage the interest and commitment of senior professionals in both institutions, involve work on a series of policy research projects, and result in co-authored publications. During the nearly eight years of work with TDRI and in the relationship with UDAPSO, the available budget for the HIID relationship was used primarily to support close working relationships between a relatively small number of expatriate researchers and TDRI/UDAPSO leadership and staff. Short-term, one-time consultants were sent to TDRI and UDAPSO when needed and requested, but they were the exceptions. The normal pattern was one of expatriate commitment of long duration, involving many return visits to work on institutional development or particular programs of research, or both. This arrangement was cost-effective and met the needs of both partners for institutional and research capacity development at TDRI and UDAPSO, and for co-authored publications and learning about development at HIID. About half of the consultants were from Harvard. In addition, the available budget was used to support sustained periods of residence—of one to three months—by some of these individuals, particularly at TDRI. This pattern was also cost-effective.

Another common characteristic involved exchanges in both directions. UDAPSO staff participated in training programs at Harvard. HIID hosted a visiting fellow from TDRI for a year in Cambridge. Both UDAPSO and TDRI hosted graduate students from Harvard and elsewhere. These students were working on theses or other projects that fit the research priorities of the institution.

There is a predictable evolution in patterns of collaboration with new research institutes over time. The initial objective is to help build institutional and staff capacity. At the beginning of the relationships, TDRI and UDAPSO were at an early stage of development, with limited personnel, and they needed to recruit additional first-rate researchers, formulate research plans, set priorities, ensure quality control, and obtain research funding. Correspondingly, much of HIID's work with these institutes at the beginning—but also continuing in subsequent years—was on these activities. This involvement was followed at both the institutional and research program levels by advice and assistance on promoting collaboration among research programs areas (particularly at TDRI) and on organization of research activities. There was advice and assistance on staffing, planning, funding, and proposal preparation. There was also help in the creation of information systems and publications programs.

The main difference between the patterns at UDAPSO and TDRI was in training. HIID played a much more active role in the training of staff at UDAPSO than at TDRI, including the formal training course in LOGIT and PROBIT; the workshop in the use of GIS hardware and software; an intensive seminar on higher-education planning, research, and accreditation; and a workshop on estimation with census data of local infant mortality rates.

As the relationships matured, as the institutions become stronger and better staffed, the emphasis shifted to collaborative research. Indeed, all of the activities described so far could be seen as intermediate steps, necessary for the conduct of quality research on important issues of Thai and Bolivian development—research with policy implications to enhance, inform, and improve policy choice. This is also the type of international cooperation and technical assistance between U.S. universities and developing countries which is likely to continue for the foreseeable future.[2]

From the first year onward, the relationships focused more and more on a series of research projects, co-authored policy papers, and publications on critical issues of development. At TDRI, HIID helped initiate and collaborate on research on macroeconomic policy, natural resources and environment, industry and trade, science and technology, and human resources and social development. Work at UDAPSO included research papers on rural labor markets, middle education, and poverty.

The structure of the relationship changed with the activity. In both relationships, there were resident advisors in the first year and a half, when the prime focus was on institutional development. At TDRI, this pattern evolved into one of continued work on research and policy analysis by the small core group of expatriate researchers who were identified and paired with local researchers in the initial eighteen months. The same evolution was expected at UDAPSO, although resident positions were expected to continue for three more years.

Over time, other international collaboration occurred at both TDRI and UDAPSO. CIDA financed relationships between TDRI and Canadian universities. The UN, through the Economic Commission for Latin America and the Caribbean (ECLAC), provided experts and other help to UDAPSO. This diversification in international relationships is natural and desirable because no single institutional partner has a monopoly on experience, talent, or commitment.

Long-Term Viability

Policy research institutes can make a difference. They are also potentially fragile institutions that may not survive over the long term. Perhaps the most critical question about policy research institutes of the kind considered in this chapter is whether and how they can survive and prosper, retain high-quality staff, produce quality work, and maintain influence on policy over the long term.

There are three general threats to survival and quality: finance, political change, and institutional stupor or self-satisfaction. Some lessons for the future of UDAPSO (and other institutes at UDAPSO's stage of development) can be found in TDRI's history of dealing with these issues for more than a decade.

Finance

Both institutions started with core support from foreign donors. There is the danger that the availability of core support will lull an institution into total dependence on it with no preparation for the day when, sooner or later, the support will end. This did not happen at TDRI because the Canadian support covered administration and overhead but only a portion of the research. Support had to be found for other research programs and research projects and it was, initially from other international donors (e.g., USAID, UNDP, United Nations Environment Programme [UNEP], United Nations Fund for Population Activities [UNFPA]), and later from national sources. Building an endowment was pursued from the second year onward as a way eventually to replace the core support from the Canadians.

The general evolution of support for policy research institutes is from initial dependence on a single foreign donor, to support from other donors, to eventual support by local private and public sectors. The policy research institute must play an energetic role through the quality and dissemination of its work to create demand, to develop "markets" for policy research among other foreign donors, in government, and among other local funders. By 1992, TDRI was receiving funding from more than one hundred sources, many of them domestic.

UDAPSO's second director, who took office in April 1994, was immediately doubtful that USAID's support would continue beyond a few more years at best, and certainly not indefinitely. He initiated strong efforts to diversify funding sources. Support was obtained from UNICEF, the World Bank, the International Labour Organisation (ILO), and the Bolivian Civil Service program (for five staff positions). By the beginning of 1995, dependence on the USAID funding had been reduced to less then 50 percent.

The advantage of this pattern—of the incentives created by the financial imperative—is that both institutions had to meet a market test. They had to deliver quality work responsive to client concerns. The disadvantages are that client concerns may not always coincide with broader development priorities, and the financial imperative may harm longer-term research programs that are the institutional capital that enables a policy institute to respond well to shorter-term requests. If the financial situation is precarious, the danger is overresponsiveness to the market to such an extent that the institution becomes more a consulting firm than a policy research institute.

Avoiding these problems depends on the quality and continuity of leadership, and on creating incentives that balance rewards for quality research with rewards for success in funding it. TDRI and UDAPSO had excellent leadership, but neither found quite the right balance of incentives. Both also had trouble saying "no" to projects with inadequate funding or time to permit quality work, or both.

In the longer run, some source of core support for at least administration and overhead needs to be found. It would be better if some core support for research activities not currently fashionable with funders in the market could be found as well. The rest of the research and policy work will—and should be—subject to the market test. At TDRI, some of this support came from an endowment and some came from application of an overhead rate to direct research costs. At UDAPSO, an overhead rate was under consideration in 1995, but other sources of core support for the longer term were still uncertain.

All this effort is not simply to ensure financial viability. It is to reassure the best staff that there are prospects of continuity in research programs and employment. It is also to keep the salary scale as competitive as possible with the private sector and other options that may attract staff away from the institute. Partially because of the success of Thai development, TDRI's salary scale, even with upward adjustments, became less competitive than it had been in the beginning. Early signs of this problem were the hiring away of research assistants with strong computer skills. Later, TDRI lost senior researchers to the private sector and various government agencies whose salary scales had gone up rapidly. UDAPSO's salary scale in 1995 was likewise less competitive than it had been in 1992. Up to 1995, the comparative absence of other serious research opportunities for staff had limited the consequences of declining competitiveness. Unless UDAPSO could increase salaries, though, it would face losses in addition to the turnover of staff for graduate study.

A persisting danger is that a policy institute may, with effort, survive and prosper in financial terms and still gradually lose its best staff. This loss jeopardizes future quality and, in the long run, financial support itself. The implication of this threat is that priority must be given to spending available resources to retain the best quality staff, even at the cost of more modest offices and equipment, fewer administrative staff, fewer cars and drivers, less discretionary travel, and other perks.

Political Change

Policy research institutes are also threatened by political change. This is a direct threat to a government agency such as UDAPSO and an indirect threat to a private institute such as TDRI. New leadership may associate the institutes with the previous government and reject them. Political change may be associated with big disagreements about development policy. A research institute may be seen to be on the "wrong side" of the policy issues, compared to competitors such as universities or other research centers. There may be little or no understanding of the value of the institutes. In this case, "demand creation" and market development must begin all over again.

There is, of course, no guarantee that a research center will survive political change. Based on the experience of TDRI, however, the best options seem to be those described in the section on relationship to government: maintaining neutrality and objectivity, serving as a neutral site for building of consensus on controversial policy decisions, continued work on problems that a new government will come to see as important, response to short-term needs and requests, building of support and informal networks by involvement of middle-level technocrats and leading academics in research programs, and—at the board-of-director level—maintaining contact and support among influential people in government and out. TDRI was so successful at this last level that ministers and other cabinet-level appointees from among its board, senior leadership, and staff were recruited into successive governments. The same pattern was seen at the Korea Development Institute.

Institutional Stupor

There is, finally, the danger that a research institute will become self-satisfied and complacent and drift into a kind of institutional stupor. This danger may be greatest when financial viability is ensured, political change is benign, and staff have many years of tenure. The energy and verve that characterize a new institution, the hiring of new staff, and the struggles for influence and survival can disappear. Productivity—if not quality—can drop. Research and policy recommendations can become predictable rather than innovative or challenging. The institution continues, but its importance and influence decrease. There were some protections against this complacency at TDRI. Some were internal and some came from changes in the external environment. UDAPSO in 1995 was too young to worry about these problems, and with its level of turnover, atrophy seemed very far away indeed.

The incentives systems at TDRI have already been described. The risks of abuse and favoritism by the research directors were seen as worth the incentives for quality and productivity. The induced turnover of less qualified and less productive staff and the hiring of new staff to replace them helped to keep the research programs fresh. So did the involvement of the best university faculty and technocrats in the research. Continued international cooperation with researchers from abroad served the same purpose. Complacency at TDRI was also reduced by the emergence of competing research centers of good quality and with good connections. These centers included a new institute for work on science and technology and a new institute to work on natural resources and the environment.

As in international cooperation, the emergence of competing research centers is—as a nation develops—inevitable and desirable. No single policy research center can have a permanent monopoly on new thinking, quality research, or the right answers or points of view. It was undoubtedly time for diversification, specialization, and competition of ideas in Thailand. In 1995 it was probably too soon—given the scarcity of highly trained researchers—in Bolivia.

Conclusions

There are several lessons about the potential contribution of institutes like TDRI and UDAPSO to capacity building in developing societies. Such institutes serve a special purpose and are more likely to be established when there are big changes in the action environment—particularly new demands on government and few good ideas on how to meet the demands. The most obvious contribution of a policy research institute is to supply fresh ideas based on quality research. The less obvious contributions to capacity building, though, may in the long run be more important.

Such institutes can promote the use of data and evidence in place of ideology, intuition, or political whim. They can set new standards of quality and responsiveness in place of mediocrity, indifference, or sloth. They can be models of hiring and promotion based on performance, productivity, and staff development in place of favoritism, nepotism, seniority, or sinecure. They can promote a market test of institutions and ideas in place of inertia and self-perpetuation. They

can promote reasoned debate about development in place of confrontation. They can be a mechanism for accessing and understanding policy research expertise and experience in other countries in place
of ignorance or xenophobia. They can help build networks in government and the broader society in place of barriers, jealousies, and
turf. The networks, in turn, can build commitment, interest, and the
number of stakeholders in all these innovations.

In short, policy research institutes can improve policy and debate
about development. They can also be pioneers and models and can
help diffuse innovations in capacity building—innovations that include many of the characteristics of capable states.

Certainly, the cases of TDRI and UDAPSO show that the establishment of policy research institutes is hard and that there are many
threats to viability and quality along the way. Creating and sustaining such institutes takes persistence, effort, and luck. Given a bit of
luck, however, the persistence and effort may very well be worth it.

Notes

1   See Dwight H. Perkins, "Technical Assistance in the University Context,"
    in Perkins, et al., eds., *Assisting Development in a Changing World: The
    Harvard Institute for International Development (1980–1995)* (Cambridge:
    Harvard Institute for International Development, 1997).

2   Perkins, "Technical Assistance," 1995.

8 Capacity Building in the Bolivian Social Policy Analysis Unit

Reflections of a Practitioner

Manuel E. Contreras

The importance of capacity building for development is firmly stressed in academic, multilateral, and government circles. Despite growing academic interest in developing analytical frameworks and analyzing case studies on this topic, and the efforts of donor organizations to address issues of improving the performance of the public sector in developing countries through capacity-building projects, there is a great level of dissatisfaction with the results.[1] Moreover, because there is a growing perception that building research capacity in developing countries is necessary to "solve problems of development as they arise," and that strengthening indigenous capacity to carry out applied and strategic research is crucial to development, there is greater need to examine how this process is being carried out in developing countries.[2]

Bolivia's experience with the Social Policy Analysis Unit (UDAPSO) shows that it is possible to improve the public sector's analytic capacity to formulate social policy, provided that at least the four following conditions are met:

■ Adequate political support and concrete mission and focus for such an institution

■ Strong management and leadership at the head

■ Favorable external and internal incentives to hire and maintain the best people available

■ Access to financial resources and first-class technical assistance.

Moreover, UDAPSO's experience illuminates the complexities of developing a policy research institution to improve policy analysis and formulation in a developing country with a low human capital base and a weak social sector research tradition. It illustrates issues of managing and developing research institutions under four interdependent dimensions: strategic management; collaborative institutional arrangements; internal management, administration, and supervision; and research operations. The case confirms Moses N. Kiggundu's view that "it is the acquisition, retention and effective utilization of this *skills mix* operating within a *scientifically driven value system* that makes for effective research institutions."[3]

This chapter reflects on my work in setting up and running UDAPSO in the Bolivian government between 1992 and 1994. It endeavors to provide academics with an account of a capacity-building experience—from conceptualization to implementation—from the point of view of the practitioner. I share with policy makers the lessons learned that can now be distilled with the benefit of short-term hindsight. In the process, I highlight the wider impact and externalities that capacity-building projects have, particularly in personnel development and in the local research community.

Although the literature on policy research institutes in developed countries is growing, it is still sparse.[4] In developing countries, there has been no systematic study of the evolution of these institutions.[5] One of the objectives of this chapter is to make this process systematic in order to contribute to comparative studies such as the one presented by Charles N. Myers in Chapter 7. He compares UDAPSO with the Thailand Development Research Institute (TDRI). This comparative analysis is increasingly pertinent given the growing awareness of the importance of information and analysis in social policy making, and the recognition that "'social policy brokers'…help to develop shared meaning and to build consensus on the formulation and implementation of social policy…and have begun to play an interesting role in the development of integrated social policy agendas."[6]

The creation of UDAPSO in 1992 marked a transition in the way the Bolivian government proposed to address social development. It was a move away from the short-term project approach—as embodied in the Emergency Social Fund (ESF) (1985–1990) and its successor, the Social Investment Fund (SIF) (1990–the present)—toward a long-term local capacity-building approach that recognized the need to develop domestic capacity in problem identification and policy formulation within the public sector.[7] Its creation was a "distinctive development in public enquiry" on the social sectors and the start of multidisciplinary policy-oriented research.[8]

The Paz Zamora administration's (1989–1993) desire to institutionalize social policy research and analysis and strengthen its policy formulation capacity came from its decision that social policy was going to be the main priority in its last two years in office. The economy was stabilized, there were positive macroeconomic indicators, and there was modest economic growth. There was consensus among the main political parties, opinion makers, and policy makers that the challenge ahead was to increase growth rates, and investment in human capital was key in achieving this. This decision was expounded in the promulgation of the Social Strategy in September 1991 that defined the government's priorities in the social sectors and established the guidelines for action. Human capital development was the strategy's cornerstone, along with efforts to improve the efficiency of social expenditures, and to target social interventions toward the poor. The Ministry of Planning and Coordination, the senior ministry in Bolivia, set up UDAPSO based on the successful UDAPE model (Economic Policy Analysis Unit, the economic think tank established with USAID support in 1984).

UDAPE gathered, analyzed, and disseminated data on macroeconomic issues. With the assistance of the Harvard Institute for International Development (HIID) beginning in 1987, it monitored the macroeconomic indicators of the country and developed analytical skills in general equilibrium models and sophisticated economic analysis that enabled it to be a key player in negotiations with the IMF. Indeed, with macroeconomic stability, "UDAPE became the watchdog of the nation's economy."[9] By 1990, UDAPE had done important sector work with various line ministries. Within this context, it developed the social strategy document. To a large degree, the government created UDAPSO to further pursue and implement this strategy. UDAPSO followed closely the internal organization of UDAPE and was also directly dependent on the minister of planning. The fact that both institutions were in the same ministry and had regular and direct contact with the minister facilitated close coordination between them.

The chapter is organized in six sections. I first highlight the favorable external environment. Then I analyze the institutional impact of UDAPSO's creation and its organizational structure and management style. Having set the external and internal characteristics of the institution, I proceed to analyze UDAPSO's effects on those who worked there, on the external environment, and on the government. I describe human resource development, the technical and analytical work that made up its research contribution, and finally its influence in policy formulation and implementation. The chapter ends with a brief set of conclusions and the main lessons learned. Throughout, I seek to relate my experience to the issues raised by Moses N. Kiggundu on the interrelationship of management skills and internal value system necessary to run a successful research institution.

External Environment

The development of UDAPSO in 1992 must be seen in the context of a series of favorable external conditions. At the macro level, there was a strong perception in top government circles and in public opinion that an explicit social policy was necessary. On the one hand, the government realized it had to show more actions and results in the social sector, both to maintain popular support for its economic reform program and to ensure success in the general elections in 1993. Simultaneously, there was a genuine belief among the more enlightened members of the government and key policy makers that it was necessary to move along the reform process and concentrate on human development to make the adjustment process more viable and to contribute to sustained economic growth. Moreover, multilateral and bilateral international aid agencies were also proposing that once countries stabilized their economies, it was imperative that they address social development in a climate of structural reform. Thus, any move toward that end was well received, and the creation of UDAPSO gave rise to positive expectations and was supported by the donor community, the press, and institutions such as the German-funded Instituto Latinamericano de Investigaciones Sociales (ILDIS), which had established itself as a nonpartisan discussion forum in 1985. Similarly, key World Bank staff associated with Bolivia were interested in UDAPSO from the start and helped in every way possible by providing access to documents, financing research assistance, and advocating the work UDAPSO was doing.

There was a well-founded perception that information on Bolivia's social sector was sparse and that, despite the existence of household surveys since 1989, there was inadequate social policy analysis. Bolivian universities were not strong in policy-oriented research and there was very little analytical work in the different social sector ministries. There were mostly sector reports that were general diagnostics with anecdotal narrative characteristics. Possible exceptions were the studies on population and reproductive health carried out by the population unit (UPP) of the Ministry of Planning. The National Statistics Institute (INE) also carried out some studies, but these did not have wide dissemination. Most studies using household survey data were carried out by external consultants.

Equally important was the strong commitment to UDAPSO shown by Samuel Doria Medina, the minister of planning. He had led the formulation of the Social Strategy, which emphasized the need for a pragmatic social policy think tank. The minister's strong personal commitment was compounded by his trust and support of me as director. Although Doria Medina and I had not worked together before, we shared a common academic background in postgraduate studies in the London School of Economics and a belief that good ideas and political support were needed to get social policy going in Bolivia. Thus, I was given a virtual free hand in running UDAPSO and all the political support I needed to get things done, from trivial administrative pursuits to critical backing in front of other ministries and a strong endorsement in the eyes of the donor community. The minister had a clear understanding that a technical analysis unit was required, and he therefore did not interfere at all in the appointment of technical staff, which was my sole responsibility as director.

The Ministry of Planning's endorsement was key for obtaining donor support such as USAID's financing for operations. Initially, however, UDAPSO started as a unit of UDAPE with a staff of six and benefitted from that unit's financial, infrastructure, and human resource base. The close relationship to UDAPE also helped the new social policy unit develop a keen sense of the overall macroeconomic constraints when analyzing social policy alternatives. Once the assistance contract with USAID was signed, UDAPSO was able to expand to twelve analysts and acquire adequate physical and office infrastructure. Early on, it counted on a good set of computers and the appropriate software, access to recent publications and journal literature, and the possibility of participating in national and international seminars. I was fully aware that it was essential to keep abreast of the current literature and make the most of all training opportunities to qualify our staff if we were to develop into a quality research center. The contract with USAID was key to providing the unit with long-term high-quality technical assistance through a contract with HIID.

This group of favorable external factors had a positive influence on the institutional development of UDAPSO, which took on innovative organizational characteristics.

INSTITUTIONAL AND ORGANIZATIONAL INNOVATION

UDAPSO's work originally concentrated on analysis in the areas of education, health, poverty and income distribution, micro-enterprise development issues, gender studies, and the tracking of social sector expenditures. In the second year, gender and micro-enterprise development studies were abandoned, in the first case, because another government unit took charge, and in the second because there was not sufficient government interest in this area. Instead, rural development and employment analyses were introduced, in part as a response to greater government interest in these issues.

UDAPSO adopted three broad strategic orientations: convocation-centered, "seeking to bring people together to explore issues and exchange views"; information-centered, "generating information primarily for publications"; and consociational, that is, a balance between convocation and information activities.[10] It therefore had a wide span of influence on the way social issues were addressed in the government after its creation.

First, with the creation of UDAPSO, social sector policy issues became concentrated within a single institution of the Ministry of Planning, which until then had been mainly concerned with economic development. This allowed the unit to become a center for the discussions of social policy. Nongovernmental organizations (NGOs) and the donor community could participate in policy dialogues with UDAPSO on social policy and refer to it when needed, instead of having to speak with each and every one of the specific sectors.

Second, because UDAPSO established an analysis unit in the public sector with a cadre of senior and junior specialists, the line ministries and institutions gradually began to require its services in a variety of instances. The Junta Nacional de Solidaridad y Acción Social (Junta), in charge of homeless children, the elderly, and women, was the first institution to demand the unit's help. It first requested help in developing project proposals and then—under World Bank auspices—in the design of an evaluation of the impact of a Child Health Care and Nutrition Program (PIDI). This example illustrates well the importance of having a sound technical unit in the public sector, not involved on the operational side, that could serve as an external evaluator using data collected by another public institution, the INE. Other ministries were slower in accepting UDAPSO's existence. The Ministry of Health, for example, required a few years of gradual collaboration in specific tasks—such as the joint preparation of Bolivia's report to the Pan American Health Organization—before they realized that the organization had health economists and could play an important role in health reform, particularly in health finance and cost-effectiveness studies.

Admittedly, UDAPSO's acceptance by the sector ministries was slow, largely because they considered it competition. Suddenly, a new public institution from the Ministry of Planning was working in social policy issues and developing policy proposals and—what was worse—economists and other social scientists were speaking of health issues (without being doctors) and on education (without being teachers). Once the analysis unit proved itself in the field, however, the sectors saw that they could benefit from working with it, and collaborative relations developed.

A major challenge that UDAPSO faced at the outset was the reorganization and strengthening of the Education Reform Task Force (ETARE). ETARE was created six months before the new unit was established in the Ministry of Planning and had produced no visible results. It worked with a very low profile and its leadership was not deemed appropriate for the task at hand—designing the education reform program and building consensus for its proposal. At the request of the minister of planning, I assumed the task of finding a new director and helping this director to restart ETARE and to focus the design of the education reform to fit in better within the Social Strategy. Although UDAPSO formally assumed oversight of ETARE for a few months, it was more of a personal endeavor to provide the education task force with the necessary technical, administrative, and moral support until it gained its own momentum and new personality. Some UDAPSO analysts did, however, participate in ETARE projects, particularly those involving the financing of the education reform proposal. Thus, ETARE had the principal role in assisting the Ministry of Planning to move forward education policy analyses, except for higher education.

The formation of UDAPSO also had institutional repercussions on a variety of private institutions, as well as on the international aid agencies. In UDAPSO, the government now had an institution that was technically competent, that had the backing of the minister of planning, and that could coordinate projects involving many public sector agencies and multidisciplinary studies. Thus, it was involved in the design of an integrated system of social statistics (together with INE, all the sectors, and agencies such as UNICEF), and in developing a multidisciplinary and multisectoral action plan. A good example of its policy coordination was the preparation of the social sector papers for the Consultative Group in 1992. UDAPSO staff prepared the minister of planning's presentation and the director delivered a prospective paper that highlighted the social policy challenges facing Bolivia. The paper was well received by the donor community.[11] This example illustrates the trust that the unit enjoyed from the minister of planning, and the role it played in setting policy in such an international forum. It also reflects positively on the competence achieved by the institution in rising to the occasion.

Similarly, NGOs and other social actors could engage in a policy dialogue with UDAPSO and know that they were dealing with a semi-autonomous, technical unit of the most powerful ministry in the government. To the extent that it was done at all, this was a role that previously had been carried out by some department of the Ministry of Planning by temporary national consultants. With the unit's creation, such assignments could be carried out on a regular basis by a permanent institution, organically set in the public sector.

A case in point was the production of the poverty map based on the national census of 1992. The previous poverty map had been created in 1988 through a UNDP project by national consultants working in the Ministry of Planning for that specific task, under the leadership of a foreign consultant. In contrast, the poverty map produced by UDAPSO was an interinstitutional effort of the UPP of the Ministry of Planning, the INE, and UDAPE. Although a foreign consultant helped develop the methodology, it was a public sector effort and the first major project to utilize the census data in a comprehensive manner. The poverty map was useful for both public and private agencies, as well as for the donor community. It was used by the PIDI program to identify the neighborhoods where the child-care centers were going to be located, and by the secretary of rural development when it had to select the eighty provinces where it was going to concentrate its development strategy. By 1995, it had been updated and published three times, and the experience gained in this effort had remained within the public sector. The map can be updated and improved, or more detailed and specific studies carried out at the request of policy makers because the capacity of the public sector has been developed. Currently, UDAPSO is developing social statistics and poverty data at the municipal level to address the demands arising from the new Popular Participation Law that creates a municipal structure to administer health and education infrastructure.

Multi-institutional work provided the opportunity to build important operational collaborative alliances both within the public sector and with other actors and helped UDAPSO gain a prominent place among the various stakeholders and actors in the Bolivian social policy arena.[12] Indeed, building these relationships was a central part of my responsibility. In this process, having well-respected senior analysts in the staff was an important asset.

The development of a single technical unit in the public sector dedicated to studying and analyzing social issues was, in itself, an important institutional innovation. The government now had a research center that could be tapped for information, data analysis, and advice. Similarly, the donor community saw in UDAPSO a serious technical institution to consult and visit in order to obtain data or studies or to discuss policy issues. NGOs and the academic community were also able to benefit from its publications or invite its officials to seminars or meetings where social science research was being discussed. Suddenly the government was producing social research and participating in an ample and diverse policy dialogue with many institutional and social actors. To a certain degree, this was possible thanks to the type of people UDAPSO recruited, who brought with them their personal networks, and the nonbureaucratic and technical management style that allowed for individual initiative within the institution. These characteristics differentiated the unit from other public institutions and developed because it did not have political staff.

Organizational Structure

UDAPSO's organizational structure was well suited for the formation of good analysts, which was top priority, given that human capital was UDAPSO's prime asset.

The unit was directly responsible to the minister of planning. We had close contact with the minister and met for one formal two-hour meeting per week, together with both his undersecretaries and the directors of INE and UDAPE. UDAPSO was organized in three departments composed of senior and junior analysts. The management style was team-based: we were "a small number of people with complementary skills...committed to a common purpose, performance goals, and approach for which [we held ourselves] mutually accountable."[13] It had a flexible formal structure and was fundamentally based on the formation of task forces for specific endeavors. These groups were formed by a senior analyst with a few junior analysts, although sometimes more experienced junior analysts were asked to lead task forces. The general focus was product-driven and the staff was steered toward meeting deadlines and presenting specific products (reports, analyses, or papers) rather than toward a timely and constant presence in the office. Contrary to the norm in most public institutions (including UDAPE), there was no entry and exit book to record and control staff working hours. The working environment was results-oriented and employees were judged and rewarded according to their performance, not according to their compliance with time schedules.

Therefore, the incentive structure was founded on working papers presented, task force leadership roles, and peer evaluation. At the annual salary review, senior analysts evaluated all the staff and their recommendations were then discussed with the director. Thus, by broadening job definitions, increasing personal discretion, and developing a merit-oriented process of staff selection, task assignment, and evaluation, UDAPSO was able to develop an "aura of mission." This is similar to what Hilderbrand and Grindle, and Tendler and Freedheim, discovered about the effect of nonmonetary incentives on performance in other developing countries.[14] In UDAPSO's case, this sense of mission was further enhanced by the influence the staff perceived we had on key government officials and the political support we enjoyed.

Much of this sense of mission was possible because we were able to establish a homogeneous group of young motivated professionals, who shared a series of common characteristics such as age (between

25 and 40 years, with most in their thirties), education (all from private and foreign universities), training (most were economists), and a strong sense that what we were doing was important.[15] Women were well represented on the staff.

The salary structure was higher than in most public sector institutions, but by no means was it the highest-paying organization. Salaries at UDAPE and at many projects with time-specific contracts in the Ministry of Planning were higher. So, salary was not the main incentive for working in UDAPSO. One important incentive was being able to work on macro issues pertaining to the social sector. Many of the more experienced staff had worked in specific areas such as micro-enterprise development, health, or nonformal education project evaluation, but had never been able to assess other areas or their particular area of expertise from a countrywide and policy perspective. For junior staff, there was the added incentive of training in specific analytic techniques, of working in multidisciplinary teams, and of improving their writing skills. Another incentive was the possibility of keeping up on recent literature and interacting with good external consultants.

Staff recruitment, with a few exceptions, was done through informal channels. In a country such as Bolivia, with a small population and few good professionals, it proved best to hire people on personal recommendations. For specific technical positions that required a mixture of technical competence and interpersonal skills to become team players in an institution that was just starting and could not rely strictly on rigid terms of reference, I recruited the first group of staff from men and women who had worked with me before or who were recommended by acquaintances. They composed the core group of senior analysts. The second group of economists was hired after a more formal screening process but still through the recommendation of personnel already working at UDAPSO or UDAPE. Only one main analyst was hired through an advertisement in the newspaper. Staff turnover was low and working relations were good. There was healthy competition among the staff both on technical expertise and on what came to be the "dominant" view of social policy. This view centered on a targeted, poverty alleviation approach with a strong emphasis on human resource development as a cornerstone, the need to develop policy within the context of a market economy, and a vehement belief that efficiency in the social sectors was as important as equity. We developed a strong sense of commitment and mutual accountability for the work we did, both of which are key elements for developing a high-performance team.[16]

My experience corroborates the model put forward by Kiggundu regarding the importance of strategic management. As director, my main responsibility was to provide internal leadership and manage the external interfaces with our clients, stakeholders, and potential threats. In this process, I strove to create UDAPSO's character and mission, "giving it the image, values and uniqueness that distinguishes it from others."[17] Among the relationships developed to pursue this goal was the key strategic collaborative agreement with HIID.

The organizational development of UDAPSO was influenced by the relationship with HIID. Initially, this relationship developed from former ties between HIID and UDAPE and the personal relationship of the director with HIID staff. Once UDAPSO had a separate contract with HIID, a resident advisor played a key role in a series of issues.

The role of HIID was crucial for the way the policy analysis unit developed from the start. At the outset, my friendship and professional links with Ricardo Godoy helped establish a relationship of mutual trust and respect. The association with Harvard that HIID brought was a source of prestige among other institutions in Bolivia and gave pride and inspired the staff. HIID was an excellent source of consultants and of up-to-date and pertinent publications. It was our window to the complex web of institutional interdependencies to which a research institution should be linked. Additionally, HIID support was very important for me as director because its staff provided a select group of people with diverse experiences to discuss ideas and evaluate the evolution of technical work. Senior consultants and the resident advisor supplied much-needed guidance in prioritizing the research agenda and focusing the work toward a more policy-relevant perspective.

Foreign consultants were necessary for at least three reasons. First, they trained staff in particular skills and transferred expertise and knowledge through the various assignments. Second, they advised on best practice and gave recommendations on how to pursue future work or how best to interpret results. Third, they served as a "quality control" mechanism and gave the individual analysts and especially the director—who was not an expert on econometrics—advice on the quality of the work and the relevance of the research pursued. As a result, working with quality foreign consultants was an important incentive for the staff.

The scarcity of highly qualified professionals in Bolivia, especially in analytical studies dealing with the social sectors, suggests that foreign consultants will continue to be needed, probably less so for transferring skills and techniques, but definitely for advising and for providing quality control. Foreign consultants have a great advantage in being able to draw on their comparative experience and to provide an "external" nonpartisan and therefore possibly more objective point of view. Moreover, senior consultants with strong academic backgrounds serve as role models for analysts and researchers. This is particularly important in a society with weak universities and research institutions, where there are few such role models.

HUMAN RESOURCE DEVELOPMENT

Personnel training was an important aspect of UDAPSO's activities and probably one of its most significant and self-sustaining contributions to the evolution of social policy analysis in Bolivia. Specific efforts were made to provide formal training by setting up seminars and workshops in Bolivia and by sending analysts abroad to participate in training activities. In-house training seminars in handling large data sets and using statistical software, in basic and intermediate statistics and econometrics, and in specific analytical tools, such as discrete dependent-variable techniques (LOGIT/PROBIT) were key in preparing analysts for future work on household surveys.

Similarly, training abroad in more general areas such as poverty measurement, education planning, and health projects (at Harvard) allowed junior analysts to gain the skills and confidence to assume greater responsibilities in their respective teams and even become senior analysts. Both in-house training and courses abroad proved to be of great use and were a significant stimulus to staff. In both cases, analysts became acquainted with and worked with the most up-to-date literature. Study tours also played a role in training staff. They provided the opportunity to learn by seeing other experiences. A particularly useful example was the tour that education analysts took before the unit had to negotiate the university budget for the second time; they went to Chile to learn how the higher-education system was organized and what role the Ministry of Education played.

There was also implicit on-the-job training by having staff work as counterparts to consultants and encouraging their participation in multidisciplinary teams within and outside UDAPSO, as members of multi-institutional working groups in the public sector. This training exposed analysts to new theoretical and conceptual issues, and caused them to interact with a wide array of real-life problems in the social sectors and with line ministries, which were our main clients. Ex-UDAPSO staff stressed that working in multidisciplinary teams was one of the positive aspects of their work. For example, senior sociologists had never worked in such close contact with economists before, and, also, for most young economists, it was the first time they worked with sociologists, urban planners, physicians, and pedagogues. In both cases there were positive interactions.

One aspect of UDAPSO's activities that was not sufficiently stressed was fieldwork. As in most technocratic research institutions, academic knowledge was valued more than empirical know-how. Although fieldwork was encouraged, there was a greater emphasis on desk work, and therefore, for example, junior analysts working on extreme poverty in the department of Potosí (based on census data) had never been to the department and had never experienced the harsh human characteristics of poverty there. Similarly, the higher-education task force in charge of negotiating with public universities had been trained in private universities and abroad, and therefore had no firsthand experience of public higher-education in Bolivia. Eventually, however, staff members were encouraged to visit the institutions and projects under analysis and fieldwork was valued more. At times, analysts were sent on field trips that improved their understanding of the problem as they became aware of the local importance of universities in the different cities of the interior. In part, these were shortcomings of the small numbers and the youth of the staff. Senior analysts did have ample field experience that compensated to some degree for the shortcomings of junior analysts.

Staff training and the good reception of the new type of social research started by UDAPSO had positive externalities on the whole spectrum of social policy dialogue and practice in Bolivia. In the words of Rodney Pereira, a senior analyst of UDAPE, the "status" of social policy was improved. According to an ex-UDAPSO analyst, currently pursuing a Ph.D. in economics at Berkeley, "UDAPSO showed [him] why economics is important…also in areas where people are the main concern." A clear indication of this improvement was the interest in social policy issues that it generated in economics students at the Catholic University of Bolivia. In the mid-1990s, eight thesis projects were being pursued in many aspects of social policy, several of which were under the guidance of UDAPSO trained staff. The first thesis on health economics using a LOGIT model was defended by a current UDAPSO analyst who, in turn, supervised another thesis on health economics.

As in the case of Thailand reported by Charles N. Myers, Bolivia's social policy unit proved to be a "second graduate school" even for those analysts with graduate training. Working in UDAPSO not only taught them new skills, but developed policy-relevant multi-disciplinary training not generally found in graduate schools.

RESEARCH CONTRIBUTION

UDAPSO's research agenda was set broadly by the Social Strategy, which established the priority of human capital development, poverty alleviation, and a more efficient use of financial resources. Thus, UDAPSO had a long-term research plan in these areas, but also had to respond to specific demands on short notice from the Ministry of Planning.

UDAPSO brought together a small but important group of researchers who, probably for the first time, looked into the household, demand side of social issues in Bolivia from a quantitative and analytical perspective. Although urban household surveys had been carried out for many years, very little research was done with this information in Bolivia. What work had been carried out was mostly on the employment module and had been pursued by international aid agency personnel or private consultants.[18] UDAPSO was the first government institution that was able to obtain a complete data set from the INE—thanks in part to collaboration from the minister of planning and the directors of INE—and that had the necessary hardware, software, and technical assistance to work on this data, and more importantly, to serve as an outlet for its final product. This contribution was best illustrated in the studies on poverty and higher education. In both instances, the Ministry of Planning was provided with up-to-date quantitative information that enabled it to make its case in the public policy debate. In higher education, it gave the media hard data that allowed for a better public discussion of relevant issues.

UDAPSO also carried out innovative research using the only available rural household (USAID-funded) survey of the department of Cochabamba. UDAPSO presented the results in a local ILDIS policy discussion forum in Cochabamba with positive comments. The unit was a strong advocate for having a countrywide rural household survey and showed the benefits of using this type of data for policy analysis, but was unable to get its proposal accepted by INE. As of 1995, Bolivia had only urban household surveys.

The extensive use of household survey data enabled UDAPSO staff to provide INE personnel with feedback on the structure of the questionnaires and the data, and so it was able to influence the data collection process to make it more appropriate for the policy analyst, thus ensuring greater and better use of the information. Household survey data were appreciated more after our studies showed the usefulness of this type of information for social policy issues.

UDAPSO's work on household surveys started a new trend in applied research in Bolivia and introduced characteristics of empirical and quantitative techniques that were new to a research tradition based mainly on qualitative papers. Another important contribution was the start of a greater policy orientation in the research. Albeit still at an initial stage, this emphasis was new to the way reports were written in the public sector and the way research was carried out in private and public institutions, which strongly emphasized diagnosis. Considering its mandate to formulate policy, this orientation was stressed and it did force analysts to think through the policy relevance of their research from the outset and helped develop a greater analytical capacity in the staff. This contribution must be seen in a context where university training in policy analysis was totally lacking.[19]

UDAPSO working papers were well received among other public sector institutions such as line ministries, ETARE, and research NGOs, as well as in multilateral and bilateral institutions. Although working papers were not subject to external peer review, they were discussed internally before they were copied and distributed. They were cited in studies by the World Bank, Economic Commission for Latin America and the Caribbean (ECLAC), ILO, and the Swiss, U.S., and Netherlands government cooperation agencies in Bolivia. The unit's research was also well received and stood out in the reports on the state of social science research in Bolivia commissioned by the Netherlands Technical Cooperation Agency. Indeed, its poverty work, based on income distribution in urban areas, received a strong backing in the Consultative Group in 1993, and the Netherlands delegation said that they would continue to support "the excellent analytical work of institutions such as UDAPSO on poverty."[20] Research dissemination was also an important part of UDAPSO's networking; this also allowed the unit to develop additional strategic collaborative alliances with multilateral organizations to pursue joint research projects. The quality of its research publications extended beyond the local academic environment and the international development community. Two publications—one on economic growth and urban poverty, and another on higher education—were favorably reviewed in international academic journals.[21] Working papers should still be submitted to formal external peer review by sector specialists, and UDAPSO staff should be encouraged to publish their findings in international journals.

Strengthening research capacity requires academic leadership, the ability to build on previous studies, and the ability to count on a stable corps of analysts. In the words of Frits Wils, "research is a highly demanding activity, and one which is difficult to master. It requires thematic and methodological expertise, independent judgment, creativity and the capacity to question what one finds."[22] Moreover, research in an institution like UDAPSO is always competing against "fire-fighting" activities that range from analyzing a specific project or budget for tomorrow or writing "position papers," to drafting speeches for the minister on a wide array of social sector topics. Striking the right balance between satisfying such random and short-term needs and defining strategic research lines that will provide important policy recommendations in the future is crucial for a successful policy analysis unit. This equilibrium implies saying no to some requests, and establishing clear research priorities, "with relevant research questions and…understand[ing] how these might be addressed using systematic analytic techniques."[23] It also requires being able to draw policy implications from research; this was probably the most difficult task I faced in UDAPSO, and one for which I had no formal training.

Although the use of research findings for policy formulation was not widespread, the most successful example was no doubt the data acquisition and analysis carried out in the field of higher education. In this case, the findings served the policy makers, and also helped raise public awareness of the inefficiency and inequity of public universities. This outcome was only possible, however, when staff were willing to translate some results and policy recommendations into readable newspaper articles and were prepared to participate in public debates on these issues.[24] In other words, highly technical academic working papers were not enough for widespread public dissemination, but provided the base for preparing such interventions.

POLICY FORMULATION

Institutional innovation, staff training, policy research documents, and HIID assistance were all supposed to enable UDAPSO to accomplish its mission: to formulate policy and provide government with concrete guidelines to implement it. I will evaluate how well UDAPSO achieved this important objective in the cases of gender studies, higher education, and micro-enterprise policy. First, however, I must stress that the time period in question—just over two years—is undoubtedly very short to be able to perceive long-term impact. However, there were important advances in this field, which is in its infant stage in Latin America.[25]

Staff training and the research papers produced were important initial investments for providing policy advice. They must be seen as crucial start-up costs, particularly considering the inexistence of qualified senior personnel, the young age of most analysts, and the innovative nature of many of the jobs pursued. In part, this view helps to counter criticisms made about the academic nature of UDAPSO's work.

On the advice of Charles N. Myers of HIID, and following the example of the TDRI, UDAPSO concentrated on one major project a year. It chose to carry out a study of the situation of women in Bolivia during its first year. The topic was chosen for a variety of reasons. First, I had become aware of the importance of women in development projects in the SIF, where I became acquainted with Sonia Montaño and her work on this topic. Second, I was conscious that the issue of women in development (WID) was a high priority in the development and policy debate. The topic therefore had the support of the donor community and could be easily funded. More importantly, there had been much work on the subject already in Bolivia, mainly by the NGO community. Third, the situation of women and their key role in development was explicitly mentioned and prioritized in the Social Strategy. Thus, there was the interest of high-level political leaders and policy makers, there were financial and human resources, the topic was in line with the national priorities, and there was a senior analyst in UDAPSO who had experience with WID issues and could therefore coordinate the project.

I received the support of the minister of planning and advice that proved crucial. He suggested I contact the sister of the president, who was president of the Junta, and who had been working on WID issues and believed she had the responsibility for improving the situation of women in the government. After a few meetings, we worked out a project with several thematic participatory workshops. It was easy to obtain the funding. The governments of Canada and the Netherlands, UNICEF, and UNDP funded the project. As the study progressed, we all became more aware of its importance, and thanks to the support of Rosario Paz Zamora, the results of the study were presented to the president of the republic and all his cabinet, with important press coverage. A week later, the program that the study recommended was presented in the Consultative Group in Paris, and a few months later what became known as the Program for Women was formally started in the Junta, under the leadership of Sonia Montaño, with funding from the Swedish government. The program was to implement the legal recommendations of our study. This program became an undersecretariat in the Secretariat of Gender, Ethnic, and Generational Affairs in the Ministry of Human Development.

Although many studies on the situation of women in Bolivia had been carried out under the auspices of NGOs, and UDAPSO's study built on this work, our involvement provided gender studies with an institutional legitimacy. The support of Rosario Paz Zamora opened many doors. Working closely with the Junta allowed UDAPSO to build its credibility and its services were required for many other issues dealing with its work.

The second major contribution of the analysis unit in policy formulation was in higher-education. This experience illustrates the importance of going beyond research, and including deliberation, persuasion, and advocacy in order to develop policy formulation and help its implementation.[26] Traditionally, the higher-education budget was based on historical trends. Under pressure from the universities, the higher-education budget had increased by 44 percent in nominal terms between 1990 and 1991. This situation required attention in light of the government's efforts to devote greater resources to primary education—which was the priority sector of the social strategy—and to comply with agreements with the World Bank, which was funding the task force in charge of education reform. The minister of planning took it upon himself to become involved in the university budget negotiations. To carry out this political decision, he asked UDAPSO to develop a strategy and supply guidelines to distribute the university budget among the nine public universities.

UDAPSO's first proposal was to stop all negotiations with the universities until they provided the necessary information to analyze their academic and financial situation. Until then, only financial issues had been discussed between the government and the public universities, and negotiations usually took place in the Ministry of Finance. Once UDAPSO drew up a list of academic, administrative, and financial data that universities should submit, and they grudgingly complied, it became obvious there was no department in the Ministry of Planning which could assume responsibility for evaluating the data received and lead the negotiations. The same was true for the Ministry of Education, which the minister of planning did not trust because of its institutional weakness. So, the policy analysis unit ended up reviewing the data and proposing a negotiation strategy with each university. Originally, it was the minister of planning who was going to carry out the negotiations, but his overextended agenda gradually shifted the responsibility for the initial round of negotiations to us. Suddenly, UDAPSO's director and his staff became the coordinator and technical counterpart of negotiations between the Ministry of Planning and the public universities.

Analyzing the data from the public universities and presenting it in working papers, publications, and a variety of charts and graphs enabled UDAPSO to show the internal inefficiencies of the universities, pointing out that there was an inappropriate use of funds rather than a scarcity of resources. These data and analyses were mostly used by the minister in the negotiations and in his contact with the press, which reproduced some of the more alarming figures. Thus, the unit started to get public exposure. After a round of strenuous negotiations, the final budget figures for the nine universities were increased by 17 percent.

The following year, the unit prepared a strategy to be able to have differentiated budget increases tied to performance criteria. In view of the expertise gained the year before, a more careful scheme was started which built on the research papers produced. Not only was there greater proficiency in data collection and analysis, but the staff assigned to the higher-education task force had also gained ability in negotiation and knew more about the internal workings of the different universities. Moreover, this time round, UDAPSO was aware that a more aggressive public relations profile was necessary. So, based on a UDAPSO publication that analyzed the internal and external inefficiencies of public universities, a series of articles were written by its staff in reply to criticisms of the publication. The debate lasted three months with articles being written every weekend. This debate was probably a first in the Bolivian press and has subsequently been referred to as "the most far reaching and appealing public debate of the last two decades," by a well-respected higher-education analyst.[27] Moreover, in La Paz and Santa Cruz I participated in three television debates on higher education, and at the universities of La Paz and Oruro I debated on higher-education issues. As a result, the government was able to sign performance contracts with each of the public universities that provided for an initial 10 percent increase in their budgets, with a premium based on specific reforms that provided additional resources of up to 8 percent. This was a significant breakthrough in government-public university relations in Bolivia.

In addition to the concrete budgetary results and the papers written on issues of higher-education, UDAPSO decided that the second-year "project" was going to be higher-education. So it organized an international conference in Cochabamba, where international scholars and consultants presented papers on higher-education finance, efficiency, administration, and private universities. The conference was well received by both public and private universities, and provided an academic forum in which many of the issues raised in the heat of the budgetary negotiations could be discussed in a more reflective manner. Again, probably for the first time, the government was addressing issues of equity and efficiency in higher-education technically, and was starting a policy dialogue with public and private universities. The publication that resulted from this meeting was well received by the international academic community.[28]

The public exposure UDAPSO received and the diffusion its policy advice and studies got in the media allowed it to be identified as the unit within the government that specialized in higher education, and the one that could and should provide policy guidelines for university reform. This is arguably the best tribute to the social policy formulation role played by the unit in this area. The need to address higher-education issues on a permanent and institutionalized basis was so clearly made by its experience with the public universities that an undersecretariat for higher-education in the Ministry for Human Development was established.

UDAPSO's experience with higher-education policy illustrates the importance of producing good papers, while also being willing to assume a more operative role—such as actually negotiating. With hindsight, the risk was worth taking because it allowed UDAPSO to learn from the process and have immediate and significant policy impact. It portrays well the importance of process in policy formulation and confirms Majone's point that, "objective analysis, unassisted by advocacy and persuasion, is seldom sufficient to achieve a major policy breakthrough…[t]o be effective, then, an analyst must often be an advocate."[29] As in gender studies, to be successful, political support from somebody important in the executive was crucial.

The third case illustrates this point well. Considering the priorities set out in the Social Strategy and the experience of a senior analyst in the micro-enterprise sector, this topic was a major area of research in UDAPSO's first year. The ILO Programa Regional de Empleo en América Latina y el Caribe (PREALC) regional project, which supplied the resources for the study, was also important. Thus, we hired two external consultants and developed a strategy paper for developing micro-enterprises. A series of workshops was sponsored to present the results, which received favorable comments from both the micro-enterprise associations and NGOs working in the sector. In this area, however, no government counterpart or agency had requested the study or become involved in its design and elaboration. As a result, the study had no immediate policy impact. It was literally shelved during the Paz Zamora administration. In the succeeding administration, however, the secretary of industry formulated a strategy for the micro-enterprise sector which contained most of the recommendations made by the UDAPSO study two years earlier. This case illustrates the importance of having an interested and invested "client" for the research done. When such a client does not exist, policy recommendations fall on barren ground.

CONCLUSIONS

The creation of UDAPSO developed the government's capacity to analyze and formulate public policy. From this viewpoint, in Hilderbrand and Grindle's words, it was an effective organization. Good examples of this effectiveness were the initiatives in gender studies and in higher education that set out policy and encouraged its implementation. The policy recommendations had concrete repercussions in the behavior of the government.

UDAPSO also had important institutional, personnel development, and research impacts. It managed to concentrate all policy issues in the social sector and become a competent technical counterpart for both public and private institutions. Once the initial fears were overcome and the unit had proved itself, it provided technical help to public sector institutions. It also proved capable of coordinating certain actions in the social sector.

In personnel development, in the two and a half years under review, UDAPSO trained a small cadre of young economists in analytical techniques to work on social sector issues from a new perspective, household demand characteristics. Senior analysts were exposed to this type of outlook on the social sector and were able to learn from economists, as well as teach them based on their own experience and professional skills. All analysts benefitted from working in multidisciplinary teams. The quality of the staff training is borne out by the successful careers of analysts once they left the institution. Some became directors in public agencies and NGOs and others pursued academic careers, from developing postgraduate courses in Bolivia to becoming doctoral students in economics in U.S. universities. This type of effect is the most sustainable because the individuals trained will continue to interact with other people and to have an impact in their workplaces. A good illustration of this indirect influence is the effect they have already had in the economics department of Bolivia's Catholic University. Admittedly, this effect was also a result of the type and quality of the research pursued.

UDAPSO's research was innovative and influenced the way social policy research continued to be carried out. It introduced a more empirical and analytical approach, and encouraged more quantitative analysis that made social policy research more rigorous. In sum, UDAPSO made research in social policy attractive and "respectable" even for economists. This effect is very important, although it was not expected when the institution was being conceived. Such an outcome occurred because an intelligent group of men and women were given the means (material and otherwise) to pursue research in collaboration with established researchers in the field. Thus, a sort of graduate seminar was developed. In a country without good graduate studies, these externalities must be evaluated favorably.

What was the role of HIID and foreign consultants in all this? Perhaps the best test to gauge their value (added) is to ask if all the positive points raised above could have been achieved without them. The answer is a definite no, at least not in the short period of two and a half years. HIID's counsel helped determine the general research focus and was then key in providing good scholar/practitioners as advisors who helped train the staff and served as external evaluators of the quality of the work done. Advisors also helped redirect the emphasis of the research when necessary. If UDAPSO had had a resident advisor earlier than it did, it probably would have had a better structured research agenda and, with hindsight, I can envisage a better ranking of priorities and greater effectiveness in reviewing certain working papers that I did not have adequate skills or experience to improve further.

At another level, the association with HIID gave staff an added incentive when they worked as counterparts to external consultants and knew that much was expected of them. Similarly, the possibility of going to Cambridge was always an additional stimulus. The association with HIID and the "quality control" function that it performed was crucial in adding legitimacy to UDAPSO's work, especially in the eyes of other public institutions; this was so in the proposal to evaluate the PIDI.

Although UDAPSO was a spin-off of UDAPE, the necessity of this type of institution permeated other sectors of government. The Paz Zamora administration created a think tank in the Ministry of Labor, and the next administration set up two think tanks, the Unidad de Análisis de Política Exterior (UDAPEX) in the Ministry of Foreign Affairs to analyze foreign policy and advise the minister on economic integration issues, and the Unidad de Apoyo a la Educación Superior (UDAES) in the Ministry of Human Development to study higher-education issues such as accreditation and to work on a proposal to reform public universities. Although this proliferation of analysis units may seem premature and it may be argued that given Bolivia's scarce resource base, it is best to have a single strong institution, more units can lead to a decentralization of capacity building in policy analysis and policy formulation. Indeed, developing analysis units has been identified by scholars as a central component of the so-called second-generation reforms.[30]

UDAPSO helped the Bolivian government solve short- and medium-term policy issues. The competence and credibility that the unit developed allowed the government to engage in a more technical policy dialogue with different social actors in Bolivia and with the international community. Moreover, in a relatively short time span, it provided a focused long-term view of social policy and helped create an ideology of social policy in Bolivia. This contribution is in line with the characterization of policy research institutions that are not supposed to "create new knowledge, but rather to articulate a vision of the world."[31]

What explains UDAPSO's success? There are important demand and supply considerations. From the demand side, there was a need for this type of institution. At the government level, there was a political commitment toward social development and the need to formulate policy. Creating a social policy analysis unit allowed the government to comply with its own agenda and to show multilateral organizations that it was mainstream. Agencies such as the World Bank and bilateral donors, on the other hand, also had a demand for data gathering, analysis, and project evaluations that could now be carried out by a technical government organization and not by ad hoc consultants. Moreover, there was a growing demand for the type of research that UDAPSO was doing in all development agencies.

From the supply side, there was an adequate institutional framework in which UDAPSO could fit in the Ministry of Planning. Moreover, the ministry already had experience in lodging UDAPE, and therefore the risks and costs of setting up the social analysis unit were considerably lower because of this prior experience. Indeed, UDAPSO reproduced the UDAPE model in terms of its main donor (USAID) and in working with HIID. USAID was also familiar with working with a policy analysis unit and was sensitive to developing its management potential and supportive of the personnel training emphasis. HIID, on the other hand, had expertise elsewhere and in Bolivia and was able to provide sound technical assistance. A good rapport developed between UDAPSO and HIID staff and consultants. Finally, the unit was able to attract a small group of young, well-trained analysts, train them further, and reinsert them in an institution with a strong sense of mission and a results-oriented set of values. Developing a strong esprit de corps is a key ingredient for the successful start-up of any organization. UDAPSO's experience confirms that in research institutions it is fundamental to have a strong strategic management capacity and leadership from the person in charge of the institution.

What remains to be seen is how sustainable UDAPSO is. Its heavy reliance on a single major donor and a single major client is probably its main risk for long-term sustainability. The strategy of diversifying its financial resource base will no doubt reduce this risk. Joint research projects were started with multilateral and bilateral agencies with that purpose in mind. If the quality of the work is adequate, it will not be difficult for UDAPSO to pursue this strategy further. Another source of threat to long-term stability is the changing nature of the Bolivian public sector and the politicization of the institution. This threat can be reduced somewhat by diversifying the client base and strengthening the internal structure of the institution and its relationship to the various dependencies of the Ministry of Human Development. Ultimately, however, maintaining the skills mix and the value system will enable UDAPSO to survive.

From this experience there are five lessons. First, for a policy research institute to be effective it must be within the government structure and answer to the highest authority in the area (in Bolivia, the minister of human development). It must be above line ministries or secretaries, although it should work with them and not around them. More effort should be devoted to constructing healthy relationships with all clients in the public sector. UDAPSO concentrated too much on its main client and was too closely associated with the minister of planning and became liable to the passions of party politics. When the Sanchez de Lozada administration took office it initially mistrusted UDAPSO, despite having been ratified by the new minister of human development. To a degree, the initial favorable external environment, which helped UDAPSO develop, changed. Building a wider variety of clients, on the other hand, is key to policy implementation. Policy proposals without a client who is a partner in the policy formulation will not be carried out, and thus will have no influence on policy. The research agenda will be influenced by government policy, but the ultimate decision should be with the director or an external board of trustees. This idea was discussed in UDAPSO, but was never implemented.

Second, there is a trade-off between becoming too closely involved with one particular minister and participating directly in negotiations with social actors, and remaining strictly as an advisory body to the government at large. The first option yields quick policy results, but can inadvertently alienate certain sectors and may lead to difficulties in institutional sustainability where there are political changes in the public sector. If we look back on UDAPE's experience, certain ministers relied on the institution more than others. Less intensive use need not necessarily mean that the institution is not performing well. These periods can be used to build up basic research and train staff. In 1994, when the Bolivian public sector was being restructured and the Ministry of Planning was eliminated, UDAPSO found it difficult to relocate to the Ministry of Human Development and, to an extent, to rebuild its credibility with the new authorities and regain a prominent place in the government.

Third, the institution should clearly define its research agenda and strive for the highest quality research. This point is well addressed by Charles N. Myers in Chapter 7. Having one major project per year is a good idea to focus research activity, but other research areas should also be identified and pursued. In its first two years, UDAPSO sometimes spread its resources too thin.

High-quality research requires leadership at the director level, and access to resources that permit a think tank to hire the best people available and obtain quality technical assistance. It is important to set a policy-relevant research agenda from the start and to find an adequate mix between "fire-fighting" activities and necessary basic analytic research. There should be a clear demand for practical papers and policy proposals. Policy-relevant research must be useful for line ministries, secretaries, local governments, and municipalities. Research dissemination and advocacy of the policy proposals is vital. Public relations is important: once research results become available, a greater effort should be made to disseminate the findings at all levels—policy makers, academics, and the public. The institutions should synthesize government thinking on social policy and be a reference point. The technical and apolitical nature of the institution should be stressed.

Fourth, although initial funding for UDAPSO came from external donors, this is not sustainable in the long run. Thus, the institution should be able to develop proposals to obtain external funds and the government should provide for local resources to replace external ones. Active participation in fund-raising and competitive bidding should be encouraged.

Fifth, people make institutions. Hiring and working conditions should be attractive and the work environment should be task oriented, problem solving, and product driven. Building analytic capacity is a slow and costly process, and policy research centers like UDAPSO have great potential to train people, who become its main asset. There must therefore be a clear policy to train and to promote individuals so that they stay in the institutions and help upgrade the human resource base.

NOTES

1   Arthur A. Goldsmith, "Institutions and Planned Socioeconomic Change: Four Approaches," *Public Administration Review* 52, 6 (1992): 582–587; John M. Cohen, "Building Sustainable Public Sector Managerial, Professional, and Technical Capacity: A Framework for Analysis and Intervention," *HIID Development Discussion Paper 473* (Cambridge: Harvard Institute for International Development, 1993); and Mary E. Hilderbrand and Merilee S. Grindle, "Building Sustainable Capacity: Challenges for the Public Sector" (paper prepared for the United Nations Development Programme, 1994).

2   Frits Wils, *Building Up and Strengthening Research Capacity in Southern Countries* (The Hague: RAWOO, 1995), 8.

3   Moses N. Kiggundu, "Managing Research Institutions in Developing Countries: Test of a Model," *Public Administration and Development* 14 (1994): 201–222. Quote from p. 206, emphasis in the original.

4   James A. Smithe, *The Idea Brokers: Think Tanks and the Rise of the New Policy Elite* (New York: The Free Press, 1991) for the United States; Lindquist, "Think Tanks or Clubs? Assessing the Influence and Roles of Canadian Policy Institutes," *Canadian Public Administration* 36, 4, (1993): 547–579 for Canada; and Alan Jarman and Alexander Kouzmin, "Public Sector Think Tanks in Inter-Agency Policy-Making: Designing Enhanced Government Capacity," *Canadian Public Administration* 36, 4, (1993): 499–529 for Australia.

5   A possible exception is Daniel Levy, *Building the Third Sector: Latin America's Private Research Centers, and Nonprofit Development* (Pittsburgh, PA: University of Pittsburgh Press, 1996).

6   Fay Durrant, "Role of Information in Social Policymaking: Latin America and the Caribbean," in Daniel Morales-Gómez and Marrio Torres A., eds., *Social Policy in a Global Society* (Ottawa: IDRC, 1995), 176.

7   These experiences have been documented and analyzed by the actors themselves and World Bank staff. See Gerardo Avila, Fernando Campero, and Jorge Patiño, *Un puente sobre la crisis. El Fondo Social de Emergencia* (La Paz: Fondo de Inversión Social, 1992) and Steve Jorgensen, Margaret Grosh, and Mark Schacter, *Bolivia's Answer to Poverty, Economic Crisis, and Adjustment*, World Bank Regional and Sectoral Studies (Washington, DC: The World Bank, 1992).

8   Lindquist, "Think Tanks or Clubs?"

9   On UDAPE's development, see Ricardo Godoy and Manuel E. Contreras, "Bolivia," *HIID Conference History Volume*, forthcoming.

10 Lindquist, "Think Tanks or Clubs?" 556–558.

11 Manuel E. Contreras, "Social Policy Challenges for the Next Decade" (paper presented at the Consultative Group Meeting for Bolivia, Paris, October 1992). The main issues raised were later reproduced in Bolivia in Nico van Niekerk, "La economía va cada vez mejor, pero que pasa con la gente? deuda o beneficio social," in *Políticas sociales y ajuste estructural. Bolivia 1985–1993* (La Paz: CID-COTESU-MCTH, 1993).

12 I follow Kiggundu, "Managing Research Institutions," on this point.

13 Jon R. Katzenbach and Douglas K. Smith, *The Wisdom of Teams: Creating the High-Performance Organization* (New York: Harper Collins, 1994), 45.

14 Hilderbrand and Grindle, "Building Sustainable Capacity," and Judith Tendler and Sara Freedheim, "Trust in a Rent-Seeking World: Health and Government Transformed in Northeast Brazil," *World Development* 22, 12, (1994):1771–1791.

15 These characteristics were also found to be important in the evaluation of the high level of performance in the ESF, see Avila, et al., *Un puente sobre la crísis* and Jorgensen, et al., *Bolivia's Answer to Poverty*.

16 Katzenbach and Smith, *The Wisdom of Teams*, 65–67; 109–111.

17 Kiggundu, "Managing Research Institutions," 203–204.

18 A good example is the study of the impact of the ESF on employment, based on household survey data. See John Newman, Steen Jorgensen, and Menno Pradhan, "How Did Workers Benefit from Bolivia's Emergency Social Fund?" *The World Bank Economic Review* 5, 2, (1991): 367–393. In Bolivia, the private research Centro de Estudios Laborales (CEDLA) uses the employment module and the private consultant firm CIESS-Econometrica is probably the main user of the social data sets.

19 In 1995 a master's program in public administration and public policy was started in the Universidad Católica Boliviana with HIID assistance. Some scholars expect schools of policy research to "do for the management of public affairs what business schools have done for the private sector." C. Juma and N. Clark, "Policy research in sub-Saharan Africa: an exploration," *Public Administration and Development* (May 1995), 135.

20 Netherlands Delegation, "Statement of the Netherlands Delegation," Bolivia Consultative Group, December 9–11, 1993 (mimeo).

21 Miguel Urquiola S., *Participando en el crecimiento. Expansión económica, distribución del ingreso y probreza en el area urbana de Bolivia: 1989–1992 y proyecciones* (La Paz: UDAPSO, 1994) was reviewed in the *Journal of Latin American Studies* 27 (February 1995) by Rhys Jenkins. *Desafíos de la educación superior* (La Paz: UDAPSO, 1994) was reviewed in *Comparative Education Review* 39, 2 (May 1995) by Daniel Levy.

22 Wils, *Building Up and Strengthening Research Capacity*, 11.

23 Lorraine Blank, Margaret E. Grosh, and Pauline Knight, "Building Analytic Capacity in Conjunction with LSMS Surveys: The Jamaican Story," unpublished manuscript (Washington, DC: The World Bank, 1995).

24 See, for example, Manuel E. Contreras, "Educación Superior: Contra el pacto de la mediocridad," *Momento Político (Presencia)* Año III, 15 (July 9, 1993): 6–7 (with Miguel Urquiola S.); "La Educación Superior en Bolivia: Un desafío por asumir," *Ventana (La Razon)* Año III, 10 (30 May 1993): 8–9; and "Universidad que no publica, universidad que no investiga," *Presencia* (February 15, 1993).

25 Carol Weiss, "The Many Meanings of Research Utilization," *Public Administration Review* (1979): 426–431. For a brief analysis of the situation of social sciences and policy making in Latin America, see José Joaquín Brunner, "Investigación social y decisiones políticas," *Sociedad* 3 (November 1993): 31–43.

26 See Giandomenico Majone, "Policy Analysis and Public Deliberation," in Robert B. Reich, ed., *The Power of Public Ideas* (Cambridge: Harvard University Press, 1988), 156–178.

27 Gustavo Rodríguez Ostria, "Políticas públicas y modernización de la universidad boliviana," in Fundación Milenio, *Diálogos de Milenio, no.15, Educación Superior en Bolivia* (La Paz, April 12, 1995).

28 See note 21.

29 Majone, "Policy Analysis and Public Deliberation," 175.

30 Merilee Grindle, "Las reformas de segunda generación: Hacia la construcción de un estado capaz" (transcript of lecture presented at the Universidad Católica Boliviana, La Paz, June 23, 1995).

31 L. Dubozinkis, from Lindquist, "Think Tanks or Clubs?" 552.

9 BUILDING RESEARCH CAPACITY IN THE NONGOVERNMENTAL ORGANIZATION SECTOR

Martha A. Chen

Currently there is unprecedented interest among donor and intergovernmental agencies in the role of nongovernmental organizations (NGOs) in international development. In these circles, NGOs are widely recognized as an institutionalized response to unsolved problems and are called on to play expanding roles in development at local, national, and international levels. Many NGOs have proved innovative and effective at the project level in providing humanitarian assistance, health and education services, credit and micro-enterprise projects, and more. Increasingly, some NGOs have begun to play significant roles beyond projects in influencing national policies and programs and in shaping the international development agenda. Although no panacea, NGOs have demonstrated an ability to complement the functions of governments, mobilize the participation of citizenry, and experiment with new approaches to development.

As one aspect of their changing roles and increased visibility, NGOs are more frequently involved in research and advocacy as well as (or instead of) projects. This chapter explores the following set of interrelated questions: Why do NGOs need research capacity? What types of research capacity do they need? How is this research capacity being built? What are some of the problems associated with building

NGO research capacity? The thesis of this chapter is that there are several generic as well as NGO-specific constraints to building research capacity. Conventional methods of building research capacity and conventional methods and theories of social science research need to be reexamined. To illustrate these arguments, the chapter describes an ongoing collaborative effort by the Harvard Institute for International Development's (HIID's) program on nongovernmental organizations to help build gender research capacity in one of the world's largest and best-known NGOs, the Bangladesh Rural Advancement Committee (BRAC).

Despite their increased roles and visibility, NGOs are commonly thought to suffer from four sets of weaknesses: limited technical capacity, limited scale, limited strategic capacity, and limited managerial capacity. First, NGOs are thought to have limited technical capacity for complex projects because of their small size and budgets, limited numbers of staff, and modest pay scales, which often fail to attract those people with advanced technical and professional skills. Second, they are thought to have a limited ability to "scale up" successful projects because of the short-term nature of their interventions, their dependence on short-term project-tied funds, and their inadequate attention in project planning to sustainability questions. Third, NGOs are thought to have limited strategic perspective and linkages with other important actors because of their primary (often exclusive) focus on micro-level and locality-specific interventions and because of their widely shared value system, which leads many of them to underrate the ability and intentions of other types of institutions. Finally, they are thought to have limited managerial and organizational capabilities because they often lack the necessary skills and because of their value system, they tend to equate effective administration with inflexible bureaucracy.[1]

Whereas the vast majority of NGOs share one or more of these common weaknesses, this characterization of the sector is no longer adequate. To begin with, it is based on the assumption that most, if not all, NGOs are engaged in running local projects. Increasingly, many are engaged in research and advocacy in addition to (or instead of) running projects. Moreover, many operate at the national and international levels in addition to (or instead of) the local level. In fact, many NGOs are achieving scale through leveraged policy impacts rather than through expanded program coverage and many have developed the strategic and analytical capacity to negotiate effectively for policy reform at the national and international levels. For example, the Self-Employed Women's Association (SEWA) in India engages in field operations at the local level, policy advising at the national level, and policy advocacy at the international level to promote the recognition and protection of self-employed women workers.[2]

The common characterization of NGOs does not fit a set of "older" NGOs that are known to have achieved specialized technical capacity, scale, strategic linkages, or managerial capabilities in their work. Indeed, many of these older organizations are being called on to provide technical training to government officials and to help strengthen the management and administration of government programs. However, these older organizations—many of which have received worldwide recognition—now are addressing some new variations on the common NGO weaknesses. These variations include the fact that their modest pay scales and uncertain career paths make it difficult for them to retain staff who have received advanced technical and professional training at their expense; the fact that donor funding is still tied to short-term projects that often undermine (or preclude) their own plans for long-term sustainability; and the fact that their values dictate a complex blending of professionalism and bureaucracy with participatory, flexible, and responsive processes.

For example, by 1995, BRAC ran 25,000 primary schools and a health program that promoted rehydration therapy to treat diarrheal diseases in all villages of Bangladesh. Given their world-renowned technical and managerial capacity, BRAC was asked by the government of Bangladesh to help improve the government's primary health program by strengthening its primary health centers and increasing levels of vaccination coverage and contraceptive use.

An additional reason that many NGOs no longer suffer from a common set of weaknesses is that they face a new set of constraints associated with the highly uncertain environment in which they work. Given the pace of change and the nature of crises in the world, NGOs are being called on to play an expanding role in a highly uncharted institutional context in which there are few rules, regulations, or even precedents.[3] They are increasingly called on to provide humanitarian assistance not only across national borders but also in the midst of conflict. In providing humanitarian assistance in Somalia, Cambodia, Rwanda, and Bosnia, for example, they are being asked to help resolve conflicts and promote peace. At the national level, NGOs are increasingly called upon not just to supplement government services but to provide basic services that are no longer provided by the state. In countries in which the government has virtually collapsed, NGOs are called on to play a wide variety of public roles.

Given this fast-changing and increasingly complex environment, capacity building in the NGO sector has to be as multidimensional as capacity building in the public sector. It must strengthen their human resource and organizational capacity, and build task networks within the sector and among the NGO, public, and private sectors; and the institutional environment in which they operate. Most NGOs seek to develop their staff—their human resources—through a variety of training opportunities: technical and managerial, short-term and longer-term, in-service and formal. As they mature and become more professional, they seek to improve their management systems— their organizational structures—by improving staff recruitment and personnel policies, by restructuring job descriptions and authority structures, by improving communication within and among NGOs, and by introducing monitoring and information systems. They seek to build coalitions and networks with other such organizations or with organizations in the public and private sectors around certain issues or tasks. Given the expanding scope and nature of their operations, NGOs around the world also are lobbying for legal protection and political space and are debating alternative mechanisms for accountability and regulation. They are seeking, that is, to strengthen the institutional context of the sector.

In many contexts, NGOs seek policy analysis, social science, and advocacy skills as well as technical and managerial skills. Thus, a relatively new and less common area of NGO capacity building—one that bridges human resource and organizational capacity building— is the capacity of NGOs to do research. The research capacity needs of those exclusively engaged in research or advocacy are quite distinct from those engaged in running projects as well as research or advocacy. This chapter focuses on the latter group, those engaged primarily in operational activities but which, time-to-time or issue-by-issue, engage in research or advocacy.[4] Building the human resource capacity of these NGOs to carry out research that is relevant and meaningful to their work can serve to strengthen their organizational capacity for strategic planning, program design, policy analysis, and advocacy.

NGOs tend to have a great deal of accumulated information and experience and they are often uniquely positioned to accumulate information and experience from unusual perspectives—at the slum or village level, from the perspective of disadvantaged social groups, or during emergencies and conflicts. Many have come to realize, though, that their information and experience is valuable only to the extent that it can be interpreted and put to use. They seek to use the information and experience available to them in one or more of the following ways: to learn from their own experience; to inform others of their experience; and to influence policies. To use their information and experience in these ways, they have recognized a need to develop their capacity to do research.

Building Research Capacity

Building the capacity to do research is a relatively new area of NGO capacity building.[5] Experience to date suggests that different research skills, frameworks, and methodologies are required depending on the use to which the research will be applied.

Improving Their Practice

Most NGOs seek to develop their capacity for analyzing, reflecting on, and learning from their own experience in order to improve the effectiveness of their work. They do this frequently, for example, to solve specific problems or develop future strategies. To undertake research that can provide better guidance and direction to their own programs, NGOs need training in relevant social analysis, evaluation methods, and policy analysis. They also need relevant, applied, multidisciplinary conceptual frameworks and methods with which to analyze all stages of the development process—from diagnosing needs and constraints to selecting (and hypothesizing the likely impacts of) inputs and interventions; from tracing processes of implementation, response, and change to assessing obstacles and resistance, making midterm corrections, and measuring and evaluating outcomes and impact.

To illustrate, BRAC established its research division to look at the actual impact of its programs on the lives of women (and their families) in order to improve its policies and programs. Over the years, BRAC asked the research division to investigate the effect of its rural banking and enterprise-promotion activities on women's workload and nutritional status, the demands of participating in its various programs on women's time, the sustainability of the village-level organizations of women it helped organize and develop, and more.

Informing Development Practice

Many NGOs seek to develop their analysis and documentation skills in order to disseminate and exchange their knowledge of socio-economic realities, their perspective on development issues, and the general lessons drawn from their own experience. To undertake research that can promote better exchange and dissemination of their knowledge and experience, they need training in policy analysis, project analysis and appraisal, and documentation (e.g., case writing). They also need exposure to relevant development theories and debates within which to locate their comparative experience.

BRAC developed several effective programs for women that, if properly analyzed and documented, could be used to inform development practice. Several of these programs were being documented in the mid-1990s, including two of its economic programs for women (poultry rearing and silk production) as well as its reproductive health program for women.

Influencing Development Policies

Some NGOs seek to influence sectoral, national, and international policies based on their field-level data and information, their experience with innovative practices and policies, and their capacity to speak from a unique vantage point that lies in the credible middle ground between local grassroots perspectives and national or international policy perspectives. To undertake research that can influence development policies, NGOs need training in data collection and policy analysis as well as knowledge of development theories and debates, specific policy issues, and the political process that generates these policies. They also need training in how to package and present their research for effective advocacy.

Constraints

Over the years, BRAC lobbied for changes in certain government policies, including the import and pricing policy for cotton and silk yarn and the licensing policy for rice mills. In lobbying for changes in these policies, BRAC staff would have benefitted from improved policy analysis and advocacy skills.

Other case studies in this volume analyze several generic constraints to building capacity that are common to most research organizations. The NGO experience reflected in this chapter suggests that they find it particularly difficult to overcome these common constraints and also face constraints to building research capacity that are specific to NGOs.

As described in the other cases, generic constraints to building research capacity include several human resource and organizational constraints. In terms of human resource development, given the technical or specialized nature of their work, research organizations need to be able to find and attract well-qualified researchers. The ability to find and attract qualified researchers depends partly on the available pool of researchers and partly on the competitiveness of the salary scale offered by the hiring organization. In his case study of policy research institutions in Bolivia and Thailand, Charles N. Myers reports in Chapter 7 that the available pool of qualified researchers was far larger in Thailand than in Bolivia, but that the policy research institutes in both countries had to train and upgrade their staff. The next challenge is to retain good staff. Precisely because of the technical or specialized skills of their staff, research organizations find it particularly difficult to retain staff. Myers, as well as James A. Trostle, Johannes U. Sommerfeld, and Jonathon L. Simon (Chapter 3), found that research organizations in developing countries suffer high turnover of staff because qualified researchers can find jobs with foreign agencies relatively easily.

In terms of organizational constraints, Myers also raises the issue of the goals or "mission" of the research organizations themselves. He notes that the policy research institutes have to balance three types of policy research often without clear guidelines but with competing claims as to the relative importance of each: short-term research, longer-term research, and anticipatory research. Other organizational constraints identified in the case studies include financial management problems and weak incentive systems.

In terms of institutional environment, Myers describes the important relationship of policy research institutions, whether autonomous or semi-autonomous, to government and policy makers. The inherent dilemma that policy research institutes face, he argues, is between becoming too close to government to be seen as objective and nonpartisan, and becoming too distant from government to be heard and to be influential. Trostle, Sommerfeld, and Simon similarly describe the relationship of research organizations to donor agencies and list several constraints related to donor financing, including the donor's need to spend large amounts of funds quickly and the research organization's need to sustain donor interest.

Turning to the training and technical assistance for research capacity building, the other case study writers point to several weaknesses, including limited local technical support following specialized training and the short-term and one-time nature of most technical assistance. A range of technical assistance arrangements are possible, from short-term, one-time consultants to longer-term, multiple-visit consultants to resident advisors.

Another critical constraint to building research capacity is the lack of an intellectual framework that is appropriate to the type of research required. This constraint can arise either when the research organization remains unclear as to what theories, hypotheses, or questions should govern its research or when there are no theories that are relevant and appropriate to its needs.

In undertaking research, NGOs face particularly severe human resource constraints in that they are often less able (or less willing) to develop their human resources, to put the necessary incentive systems in place to retain staff, or to adopt organizational norms and systems. Even if they are willing and able to do so, they find it difficult to retain research staff who, once trained, are often offered better-paying positions or more secure career paths by other organizations.

Further, operational NGOs that decide to engage in research face particularly severe organizational constraints, especially if their top management or policy makers are so preoccupied with the operational side of their work that they are not able to focus on the research side. One common—and critical—organizational constraint is goal uncertainty. That is, NGOs can be unclear as to why (or for whom) they are doing research. A second constraint is goal overload. That is, competing goals and demands placed on the research unit as a whole can translate into competing pressures and demands on research staff time. A third organizational constraint is data overload. That is, the pressure to undertake competing studies can generate large amounts of data that are not fully or properly analyzed. The research staff of operational NGOs are often caught between competing demands from the organization itself for research geared to internal learning as well as research geared to external dissemination or policy influencing, for short-term project analysis research as well as for longer-term policy analysis research.

In terms of communication and linkages, researchers in operational NGOs are expected to communicate with two audiences, the internal audience of program managers and policy makers and the external audience of policy makers and development practitioners. However, they often find that it is difficult to communicate with either audience. The internal audience is often wary of their research, because findings reflect on the efficiency and effectiveness of their programs. The external audience is often skeptical of their research, especially if the findings are not adequately analyzed and written up.

NGOs that undertake research—unlike standard research organizations—face intellectual constraints specific to the context and the way in which they work. Particularly if they want to learn from their experience or inform development practice, research needs to be action-oriented and multidisciplinary. NGOs that undertake research are more likely to focus on the development process (on the implementation and impact of interventions) than on specific development issues. To identify relevant applied frameworks and methods, they often have to draw on many academic disciplines, including the management, legal, and natural sciences as well as the social sciences. Analyzing practical experience involves understanding the management and technical aspects of specific interventions as well as the social, economic, and political context of these interventions.

In short, NGOs require scholar-practitioners who can analyze program and policy interventions in the context of relevant social science frameworks. With this challenge in mind, HIID's program on nongovernmental organizations engaged in a collaborative effort with one of the world's largest and best-known NGOs to help build the capacity of its research staff to do gender research.

Building Gender Research Capacity: A Case Study

BRAC is one of the largest and best-known NGOs in the world. Established in 1973, by 1995 BRAC had more than 12,000 staff members working in more than 30,000 villages providing health, education, credit, organizational, and other services to low-income households. Given its scale and effectiveness, BRAC is well known for its strong management capacity, its technical expertise, its strategic perspective, and its ability to learn from its mistakes.

BRAC's development activities are concentrated in three main program divisions: rural banking and development; health; and education. Another division that provides support services to these programs offers assistance in training, management development, construction, and logistics. BRAC's research division provides research and policy analysis services to the individual program divisions and to the organization as a whole. The overall management structure is very flat: all division heads report directly to the executive director and there are few intermediate levels between top management and field implementation. In all of the programs, the field management units are kept quite small.[6]

BRAC established its research and evaluation division in 1975. The initial mandate of the division was to provide a critical understanding of socio-economic processes at the village level. Its first set of studies investigated the distribution of resources within several villages. The findings of this work convinced BRAC of the need to target its programs to the poorest households. Over the years, as its major programs became well established, the research division was increasingly asked to provide operational feedback on the implementation and impact of the organization's programs by carrying out preproject appraisal and baseline studies, undertaking midproject diagnostic studies, and monitoring and evaluating programs.[7]

Since 1975, BRAC's research division has developed into one of the largest among operational NGOs that have the primary purpose of program interventions rather than research or advocacy. In 1995, it had more than one hundred researchers: roughly forty-five of them in the head office and sixty-five in various field locations. To keep up with this growth in numbers, the research division made considerable investment in developing research capacity: through formal training, in-service field training, and research collaborations.[8] The division also joined other institutions in collaborative research, generally centering around a specific research project. Until the collaboration with the United Nation's Development Fund for Women (UNIFEM) and HIID's NGO program, none of these collaborations focused exclusively on gender research.

Under the structure in effect in the mid-1990s, the research division had two units: a health unit and a socio-economic unit, which addressed problems and issues raised by programs such as the credit-enterprise and education programs. The research activities fell under several thematic areas around which working groups were formed:

population and health and nutrition; socio-economic development; and education and training.

Between 1975 and 1995, BRAC's research division produced well over 250 reports. Study findings were disseminated not only through reports but also through seminars and workshops. Some BRAC research findings—particularly on health and education—were also published in a wide range of international journals. To ensure that the findings from these research studies were accessible to BRAC headquarters and field-based staff, various feedback mechanisms were put in place. The division organized monthly meetings between research staff and senior program managers, and research staff regularly attended meetings of field-level program staff. In addition, research outputs were translated into Bangla and research findings were disseminated to relevant field staff. Relevant program staff regularly reviewed research proposals also.

As an NGO concerned with empowerment and poverty alleviation among the masses of Bangladesh's poorest households, BRAC had a long-term interest and involvement in working with and for rural women who often represent the poorest of the poor, and who play a critical role in lifting their families and communities out of poverty. Thus, a significant proportion of BRAC's programming work was targeted at rural women and girls. Seventy percent of places in BRAC-run primary schools were allocated to female students. Women were encouraged to attend functional education, human development, and occupational skills development courses, and special women's programs were implemented; they reached a high proportion of women within all of BRAC's rural development activities.

In numerical terms, this determined concentration on girl's and women's involvement had positive results. Hundreds of thousands of girls from the poorest families maintained regular attendance at BRAC schools. Nearly a million women from the poorest families were members of BRAC-organized village groups. They attended courses and they received credit and other inputs from BRAC.

As impressive as these figures may be, BRAC, as a questioning and learning organization, sought additional ways to improve its outreach and performance. One manifestation of this effort was the concern with looking beyond statistics on women's participation to question the actual impact of this participation on their lives and the lives of their families. Early on, this concern focused on women's perspectives on BRAC programs, including which program components women preferred, how best to make these programs operational, and how well these programs were running. Later, this concern focused more on whether these programs were having the intended impact on women's lives and whether BRAC's programs addressed only the material condition of women's lives or also the socially defined position of women relative to men in Bangladesh rural society.

BRAC's research division had to incorporate these changing concerns into its research activities. Of the more than 250 research reports, about 10 percent dealt exclusively with issues relating to women's development. Many other reports disaggregated data by gender. However, very few provided a gender analysis of the findings; that is, very few examined socially defined gender roles and relationships. As a result, BRAC decided to strengthen its capacity to undertake gender analysis.

Between 1992 and 1995, at the invitation of BRAC, HIID's program on NGOs was involved in a collaborative effort to build capacity to undertake gender research. This capacity-building experience encompassed strategic planning, technical assistance, collaborative research, and training. In July 1992, at the request of BRAC's founder-director, UNIFEM sent a two-person team to Bangladesh to explore options to strengthen its capacity to undertake gender research. The members of that team were a senior staff person from UNIFEM and the director of HIID's program, both gender specialists. They carried out a strategic review and planning exercise with BRAC's research staff. During that exercise, the staff were encouraged to assess the current situation and to draw implications for the future regarding gender research at BRAC. They were asked to consider the priority audience for research, priority research topics, relevant theories, frameworks, and methods, and the packaging and utilization of research. On the basis of their strategic review, the consultants made several recommendations regarding development of capacity to meet these needs, including training in gender analysis for the research staff, collaborative research on the impact of its programs on women's lives, and establishment of a Gender Resource Center at BRAC.[9]

Technical assistance and collaborative research focused on how to assess the impact of BRAC's interventions on women and their families. In 1992, the organization extended its rural development program to one hundred villages of an area of Bangladesh where an international health research organization, the International Centre for Diarrhoeal Disease Research, Bangladesh (ICDDR,B) had been involved in demographic surveillance and health interventions since the early 1960s. The rich database on health and demographic indicators monitored by ICDDR,B was expected to prove a unique opportunity to investigate possible linkages between socioeconomic development and changes in the well-being of the rural poor, especially of women and children, and to study the mechanisms through which this impact happens. To this end, a research collaboration between BRAC and the ICDDR,B was established.

In June 1993, BRAC and ICDDR,B held a methods workshop at Harvard University. They convened an interdisciplinary group of academics and practitioners to brainstorm about conceptual and methodological issues involved in the study. During the workshop, it became clear that most of the academic experts were skilled at measuring impact, but had limited exposure to program interventions and processes. Based on her experience with BRAC and other NGO programs, the director of HIID's program was asked to present a conceptual model that could be used to track the process of change as women participated in economic, health, and education programs, and the dimensions of their lives in which women experience change.

At the conclusion of the workshop, BRAC asked HIID's program director and a researcher from the Bangladesh Institute of Development Studies (BIDS) to design a research project to assess the impact of BRAC's programs on women's lives based on this conceptual model. The model was designed to monitor the impact of development interventions and to investigate the pathways through which women experience change.

In this model, there were four hypothesized pathways to change in women's lives: material, cognitive, perceptual, and relational. Material pathways refer to changes in women's access to and control over material resources. Cognitive pathways are changes in the levels of women's knowledge and skills as well as their awareness of the wider environment in which they live. Perceptual pathways refer to changes in women's self-perceptions as well as changes in the perception of women by others. Finally, relational pathways refer to changes in women's contractual agreements and bargaining power in their transactions or relationships with others. In this model, these pathways of change can be experienced by women as individuals, by women in relation to other agents in their lives, and by those other agents themselves. These agents include other members of the BRAC-organized, village-level women's groups, members of their immediate and extended family, members of their own or their husband's kinship group, other members of the village community in which they live, local village elite, local government officials, local agents in various economic markets, or others. Table 9-1 presents this model in schematic form and can be used to track the process of change in women's lives.[10]

This model was used to design a pilot study by BRAC researchers which generated a set of measurable indicators of change in women's lives. These indicators and other insights from that study were then used to inform discussions of BRAC's future policies and to inform the large collaborative research project between BRAC and the ICDDR,B.[11]

HIID's NGO program was also involved with BRAC in two collaborative research projects. One project focused on sectoral approaches to promoting enterprises of low-income women, and the other dealt with alternative forms of organizing women for economic empowerment. In the first project, HIID collaborated with several NGOs, including BRAC, to produce eight case studies of sectoral projects for women, a co-authored monograph considering lessons from the eight cases, and a training program based on the lessons learned.[12] The sectoral approach to promoting the enterprises of low-income women called for recognizing women's work within selected sectors of the economy, diagnosing the constraints faced by women within given sectors, and helping women address these sector-specific constraints. BRAC's poultry rearing program for women was chosen to illustrate a sectoral strategy that involves upgrading women's traditional skills and building the necessary infrastructure and services to promote a sector that has been overlooked by government. The organization's silk production program for women was chosen to illustrate a sectoral strategy that involves training women in new skills and building the necessary infrastructure and services to develop a new sector.[13]

In the second collaborative research project, ten Southern Asian NGOs, including BRAC, documented their experience in organizing low-income women for economic empowerment with a particular focus on different forms of local organizations such as trade unions, cooperatives, peer lending groups, and village organizations. BRAC was asked to document its experience in organizing more than 25,000 village organizations of women.[14] HIID's program director served as a member of the research advisory team to the project and helped run the research design workshop.

TABLE 9-1
Pathways of Change

Unit of Change	Material	Cognitive	Perceptual	Relational
Self	Credit	Nonformal education	Increased self-esteem	—
Women's Group	Credit	Nonformal education	Increased solidarity	—
Immediate Family	Assets	—	Greater respect for women	Increased bargaining power for women
Extended Family	—	—	Greater respect for women	Increased bargaining power for women
Kinship Group	—	—	Greater respect for women	Increased bargaining power for women
Community	—	—	Greater respect for women	Increased bargaining power for women
Elite	—	—	Greater respect for women	Increased bargaining power for women
Officials	—	—	Greater respect for women	Increased bargaining power for women
Market Agents	—	—	Greater respect for women	Increased bargaining power for women
Others	—	—	Greater respect for women	Increased bargaining power for women

In January 1995, the director was asked to head a midterm review of the BRAC-ICDDR,B collaborative research project. The other members of the review team included a Bangladeshi economist, a Harvard public health specialist, and a U.S. medical anthropologist. The terms of reference for the mid-term review called for an assessment of the research framework and methodologies as well as progress to date. Among other recommendations, the review team concluded that the research framework needed to reflect a better understanding of the sequence and content of BRAC's interventions in support of low-income women, the changes in women's lives that are expected to occur, and the hypothesized linkages between these changes and changes in the health and well-being of women and their families.

Another dimension of the collaboration between HIID and BRAC was training. In January 1995, at the request of BRAC, HIID ran a training program on gender research for the research staff. The objectives of the training workshop were to build capacity among researchers to undertake gender analysis of program impacts and to review past and current gender research. The training syllabus included a brief history of feminist thought, a discussion of gender analysis in various social sciences, the application of relevant gender and social analysis frameworks to the Bangladesh context, and a gender "audit" of selected BRAC research studies. In addition to HIID's NGO program director, the training faculty included four BRAC researchers and trainers, two Bangladeshi feminist scholars, and a gender awareness trainer from India. The workshop was attended by twenty BRAC researchers, four of its trainers, and two of its program staff. One of the clear lessons from the workshop was the need to develop a common analytical framework for analyzing the linkages between social institutions, economic classes, and gender roles and relationships in rural Bangladesh.[15]

Constraints to Building Gender Research Capacity

Common Constraints in Building Research Capacity

Between 1975 and 1995, BRAC encountered two internal and two external sets of constraints to building its research capacity. The internal constraints, deriving from limitations related to human and organizational resources, are described in the other case studies in this volume that focus on research capacity building. The external constraints, which are not discussed in other chapters, can be classified as intellectual constraints, associated with formal academic training and the social sciences, and technical assistance or capacity builder constraints, associated with the external advisors to and collaborators with BRAC's research division.

In terms of human resource constraints, BRAC found it particularly difficult to find, attract, and retain researchers. To begin with, the researchers they were able to attract often had received poor-quality or inappropriate training. Although more than half of the core research staff held higher degrees from foreign universities, the disciplinary boundaries or technical nature of their education often limited their ability to carry out the cross-disciplinary research required. Secondly, because BRAC offered relatively low salaries and an uncertain career path, many of the researchers, particularly the better trained, soon moved on.[16] Of the core research team in 1995, almost half had worked with BRAC for less than two years and less than 20 percent had been there for more than five years.

In terms of organizational constraints, the research division suffered from competing demands on its time, an uncertain research agenda, and poor communication with the operational programs. The pressures of competing demands from program staff and from partner institutions limited the research division's ability to prioritize between research projects, develop an overall research agenda, devise individual work plans (much less career paths), and allow adequate time for the analysis of research findings. Another problem was limited time for, and a general wariness toward, communication between researchers, policy makers, and program planners within BRAC.[17] The combined effect of these organizational constraints was that the research done by the division often remained underanalyzed and underutilized.

In terms of intellectual constraints, BRAC found that the standard social science training its research staff received did not necessarily prepare them for the kind of research needed. First, such training often limits the capacity of researchers to "see" what a given discipline does not teach them to recognize or to "see" what falls in the gaps between disciplines. For example, standard economics focuses on income-generating or so-called productive work to the relative neglect of income-conserving activities. In Bangladesh, this means that the fuel, fodder, and water collection and the postharvest processing activities of women often remain unrecognized or undervalued by economists. Second, training in social science theory often leaves the researcher unable to analyze or anticipate the complexities of real-life situations. For example, standard anthropology focuses more on social rules and norms than on social practice. In Bangladesh, the numbers of women living on their own without the support or maintenance that extended families are assumed to provide often remain underestimated by anthropologists. Moreover, the disciplinary boundaries of individual researchers lead to a limited ability to develop a common, cross-disciplinary framework of analysis. Fourth, training in social science methods does not necessarily equip the researcher to determine the appropriateness or limitations of various methods for different research frameworks or issues. Finally, of course, training at foreign universities seldom includes a focus on the political economy of rural Bangladesh.

In terms of capacity-building constraints, BRAC faced problems in identifying appropriate research advisors or research collaborators.[18] In a somewhat ad hoc fashion, its research division contracted advisors for specific research projects with arrangements involving short-term, one-time consultants to longer-term, multiple-visit advisors to one or two resident advisors. Also, over the two decades, BRAC established partnerships with more than a dozen research institutions (mostly foreign) that provided training to its researchers or engaged in collaborative research with them, or did both. Despite the benefits to BRAC from these partnerships, their number and variety placed competing demands on its research time. Moreover, because most of these partnerships centered on particular research projects using specific research frameworks and methods, the collaborations focused more on completing the research projects than on building research capacity. Moreover, because some of the collaborators were not familiar with Bangladeshi rural society or with BRAC's programs and because some of them offered training in research methods without an overarching research framework, some of the collaborations proved distracting or confusing to the organization's own research agenda.

Constraints Specific to Gender Research

In the course of their collaboration, in addition to the more common constraints described above, BRAC and HIID encountered two sets of constraints specific to building the capacity to do gender research. The first was the need to neutralize gender research by distinguishing it from gender awareness training; the second was the need to integrate gender analysis in all of BRAC's research.

Neutralizing Gender Analysis. BRAC engaged a team of gender trainers to sensitize its staff to gender dynamics between men and women within the organization. In strengthening the capacity of BRAC researchers to undertake gender analysis, HIID's NGO program director had to draw the real but often blurred distinction between gender analysis and gender awareness training. This distinction has at least three dimensions (Table 9-2). First, gender analysis needs to focus on the external environment, on gender roles and relationships in the villages where BRAC works. In contrast, gender awareness training focuses on gender roles and relationships within BRAC itself. Second, gender analysis, while based on the assumption that the roles and relationships of men and women are socially determined, seeks to explore the specific content of these roles and the specific dynamics of gender relationships in different contexts. Gender awareness training, in contrast, seeks to raise awareness of gender roles and relationships as they are seen to operate within BRAC. Third, gender analysis looks at how the interrelated hierarchies of gender and class operate to determine gender roles and relationships in rural Bangladesh. Gender awareness training focuses primarily on the gender hierarchy.

Integrating Gender Analysis. HIID's NGO program director had to emphasize that gender analysis or research should not be seen as a separate exercise from other research. Indeed, gender should be seen as a critical variable without which all research at BRAC would be underinformed. However, gender cannot be integrated as an essential analytical variable unless there is a common analytical framework within which to integrate it. Because BRAC researchers had been

TABLE 9-2

Distinguishing Gender Analysis from Gender Awareness Training

Key Variables	Gender Awareness	Gender Analysis
Unit of Analysis	Bangladesh Rural Advancement Committee	Village
Purpose	Raise awareness of gender dynamics	Analyze gender dynamics
Underlying Assumption	Gender hierarchy	Gender and class hierarchies

trained in distinct disciplines—most commonly, economics, medicine, and demography—they did not share a common analytical understanding of village realities in Bangladesh. For instance, there was no common understanding of the dominant socio-economic institutions in Bangladeshi villages. These institutions included marriage, kinship, patron-client relationships, economic classes, political factions, social networks, the local judiciary, and markets. There was even less commonality of understanding about how these institutions interacted to determine gender roles and relationships and, thereby, to condition women's lives.

A discussion of markets at the gender research training workshop illustrates this problem. BRAC economists reported that labor, credit, and produce markets operated as free, open, and competitive markets. BRAC anthropologists replied that these markets were governed by kinship rules and patron preferences as to who gets hired, who is given a loan at what rates of interest, and who sells or buys what and where. The BRAC gender researchers added that women were further constrained from competing on an equal footing with men in the labor, credit, and produce markets because of marriage and kinship rules that dictate where women could go and what they could do. This encounter helped BRAC's researchers reassess their assumptions about how markets operate and why gender analysis is useful. It also highlighted the need to develop a common analytical framework for analyzing the linkages between social institutions, economic classes, market institutions, and gender roles and relationships in rural Bangladesh.

CONCLUSIONS

As this case illustrates, building the capacity of NGOs to do research requires identifying relevant types of research, appropriate analytical frameworks, and appropriate capacity builders. The particular kind of research required by operational NGOs is distinct from mainstream academic research. To provide useful preproject assessment, midproject diagnosis, and postproject evaluation to organizational policy makers and program staff, researchers need to combine the skills of policy analysts, management and implementation specialists, technical specialists, and social scientists (to understand village dynamics). In addition, to analyze effectively the combined effect of various programs, researchers need to combine these multidisciplinary skills under a common analytical framework.

The analytical frameworks appropriate to operational NGOs are applied frameworks that combine an understanding of development policies and practice with an understanding of socio-economic realities. More specifically, researchers require two types of common analytical frameworks, one for diagnosing village dynamics, and the other for assessing program objectives and impact. The first framework—a social relations framework—would be used for analyzing the linkages and interplay between social institutions, economic classes, household types, and gender roles and relationships. Such a framework should be developed by researchers building on the conceptual categories of existing social relations frameworks—such as that used in gender-awareness training at the Institute of Development Studies (IDS) at the University of Sussex—but matching them to the concrete reality of local life in developing countries.

The IDS framework outlines five distinct but interrelated dimensions of social relationships within local institutions that are significant to the analysis of social inequality in general and gender inequality in particular: rules, activities, resources, people, and power. These are defined, in brief, as how things get done (rules); what is done (activities); what is used, what is produced (resources); who is in, who is out, who does what (people); and who decides, whose interests are served (power).[19] To develop an appropriate social relations framework, researchers should explore these dimensions within important local institutions such as marriage and kinship systems, patron-client relationships, economic classes, social networks, political factions, the local judiciary, and local markets. The common analytical framework so developed could then be used not only by researchers but also by program staff and planners. If developed and used in this way, such a framework could promote a common basis of analysis and a common language of discourse.

The second framework—a program assessment framework—would be used for assessing the objectives and impact of different components of NGO programs. It should also be developed by research staff building on a useful framework from the field of gender planning: the practical needs-strategic interests framework. This framework draws a distinction between the practical needs of women which derive from the specific material conditions under which they live and work and the strategic interests of women that derive from the structure and nature of their relationship with men.[20] To develop an appropriate program assessment framework, researchers should apply this framework to the concrete reality of women's lives. The program assessment framework could be used to frame the objectives of NGO programs, to test hypotheses regarding change in women's lives, and to assess the impact of programs on women and their families. The program assessment framework, like the social relations framework, could then be used to promote within an NGO a common framework of analysis and a common language of discourse on its programs.

To address these intellectual constraints and challenges, operational NGOs require a particular "breed" of capacity builders to help develop a special "brand" of research. These capacity builders are scholar-practitioners who can analyze program and policy interventions in the context of relevant social science frameworks. Unfortunately, many academic researchers have only limited exposure to program interventions and processes and many development practitioners have only limited familiarity with research theories and methods. As we have seen, however, BRAC was able to identify a few scholar-practitioners to help build its research capacity.

Building the capacity of NGOs to carry out research that is relevant and meaningful to their work can strengthen their capacity for policy analysis, strategic planning, and program design. Just as important, building capacity to carry out research that effectively analyzes and documents their experience can disseminate important lessons from the NGO sector.

BRAC's research served this second purpose in two ways. First, some of its programs had an impact beyond the organization because of the research they carried out. Most notably, BRAC's research on its oral rehydration program had a significant impact on national as well as international approaches to oral rehydration therapy. Second, some research qua research had an impact beyond BRAC. The methodology for assessing the effect of its primary schools on children, for example, was used by both governmental organizations and NGOs in Bangladesh, Pakistan, and Nepal.[21] Nevertheless, some of BRAC's experience, particularly with low-income women, might have had a greater impact if more focused gender research had been undertaken and if existing gender-related research had been better analyzed and more widely disseminated.

Notes

1   See David Brown and David Korten, "Understanding Voluntary Organizations: Guidelines for Donors," *World Bank Working Papers 258*, Country Economics Department (Washington, DC: The World Bank, 1989).

2   At the local level, SEWA provides education, health, financial, marketing, and other services to women workers and organizes them to resist exploitation and demand higher prices and wages. At the national level, SEWA has raised the visibility of women workers in different trades and services through research and documentation and has advised the government of India on appropriate policies and programs in support of women workers. At the international level, SEWA has raised the visibility of home-based workers, drafted an international convention to recognize and protect such workers, and lobbied for the convention to be ratified by the International Labour Organisation and the International Confederation of Free Trade Unions. SEWA has consciously and consistently used the more positive term "self-employed" to define the large sector of women who work in what is usually referred to by the more negative terms "informal" or "unorganized" sector of the Indian economy.

3   In their framework for analyzing capacity building in the public sector, Grindle and Hilderbrand identify the institutional environment as an important dimension of capacity that facilitates or constrains the performance of the public sector. In their view, this dimension of capacity includes laws and regulations, financial and budgetary support, policies and reform programs, assigned responsibilities, structures of authority, and informal power relations. Each of these features is seen as two-edged: as important for effective functioning yet liable to lead to inflexibility and rigidity. For the NGO sector as opposed to the public sector, there is a greater risk of these features being absent than of being constraining.

4   For the rest of this chapter, the term NGO is used to refer to this second group of NGOs.

5   Efforts to build NGO research capacity are relatively undocumented and undertheorized as well. There are at least two growing bodies of literature that deal with research by the NGO sector: the literature on participatory rural appraisal (Robert Chambers, "Shortcut Methods for Gathering Social Information for Rural Development Projects" in M. M. Cernea, *Putting People First: Sociological Variables in Rural Development* [New York: Oxford University Press, 1985]), and the literature on action learning (D. Kolb, *Experiential Learning: Experience as the Source of Learning and Development* [Englewood Cliffs, NJ: Prentice Hall, 1984]; R. W. Revans, *The Origins and Growth of Action Learning* [Bromley, Kent, UK: Chartwell-Bratt, 1982], and P. Senge, *The Fifth Discipline: The Art and Practice of the Learning Organization* [New York: Doubleday, 1990]). The first refers to a

particular research method that is becoming popular largely with NGOs and the second refers to a particular organizational theory about learning from action and experience. (This theory is also called action research, organizational learning, and learning systems, and it was originally developed in regard to the public and private sectors but is being extended to the NGO sector). Neither deals directly with the capacity of NGOs to carry out social science or policy analysis. For this reason, this chapter draws heavily on HIID's own experience and that of the NGOs it works with rather than on these bodies of literature.

6   BRAC top management includes heads of other support services (accounts, publication, government relations) as well as heads of BRAC's retail stores (which market Bangladeshi handicraft) and BRAC's commercial ventures (a printing press, a cold storage plant, and three garment factories). Refer to Catherine H. Lovell, *Breaking the Cycle of Poverty: The BRAC Strategy* (Hartford, CT: Kumarian Press, 1992).

7   All of these are what Myers refers to as short-term research needs.

8   Senior researchers who have served at least five years with BRAC and who have demonstrated the requisite skills and interest are encouraged to pursue a doctoral degree. Younger researchers who have served at least three years with BRAC and who demonstrate the requisite skills and interest are encouraged to pursue a master's degree.

9   As envisioned, the resource center would foster external linkages with ongoing debates and research strategies in the field, increase information flows, repackage research findings to diverse audiences, and provide access to valuable secondary sources on information not sufficiently available in Bangladesh [Marilyn Carr and Martha A. Chen, "Establishment of a WID/Gender Research Programme in BRAC" (report of UNIFEM Mission, 1992)]. In November 1994, at the request of BRAC, UNIFEM sent two consultants to assist BRAC in drawing up plans for such a gender information and resource center. BRAC hopes to put systems in place for such a center now that its new headquarters building is complete.

10   This table or matrix can be used to track the process of change through a sequence of pathway-agent interactions (by numbering the boxes of the matrix in the sequence in which change is reported to occur). Refer to Martha A. Chen and Simeen Mahmud, "Assessing Change in Women's Lives," concept paper for the BRAC-ICDDR,B Collaborative Resource project, 1993.

11   At the end of the methods workshop, another HIID researcher and researchers at the Harvard School of Public Health were asked to write a similar conceptual paper on the impact of socioeconomic interventions on health and well-being.

12 See Martha A. Chen, ed., *Beyond Credit: Promoting the Enterprises of Low Income Women* (New York and Ottawa: UNIFEM and Aga Khan Foundation Canada, 1996).

13 Other sectoral strategies include linking women to existing infrastructure; shifting women to new markets or tasks; introducing new technologies for women; and organizing women to resist exploitation in the marketplace.

14 As of mid-1995, BRAC had organized more than one million women (and 150,000 men) into more than 25,000 village organizations.

15 See Martha A. Chen, "Gender Research Training Workshop, BRAC, January 1995," report of a training workshop.

16 Trostle and Simon, "Building Applied Health Research Capacity in Less-Developed Countries: Problems Encountered by the ADDR Project," *Social Science and Medicine* 35, 11 (1992): 1383, list low salaries and uncertain career paths as two of the constraints to building applied health research capacity in less-developed countries.

17 Trostle and Simon ("Building," 1382) list "poor communication among researchers, policy makers, and program planners" as one of the constraints to building applied-health research capacity in less-developed countries. They refer to the problems research institutions face in sharing information with ministries of health and other implementing agencies. In the BRAC case, this constraint refers to poor communication between researchers, policy makers, and program planners *within* an implementing agency: both because of time constraints and because the BRAC researchers are being asked to assess and evaluate BRAC programs (which creates a somewhat ambivalent relationship between BRAC researchers and BRAC program staff).

18 For a discussion of the frustrations and failures inherent in capacity building in the public sector, refer to Part III of this volume.

19 Naila Kabeer, *Reversed Realities: Gender Hierarchies in Development Thought* (London: Verso, 1994), 281–282.

20 Caroline Moser, "Gender Planning in the Third World: Meeting Practical and Strategic Gender Needs," *World Development,* 17, 11 (1989): 1799.

21 BRAC researchers developed this research instrument called "Assessment of Basic Competencies (ABC)" in collaboration with many governmental and nongovernmental organizations.

Part II

Strategies for Capacity Building

Reforming Institutions

10 SUCCESSFUL ECONOMIC DEVELOPMENT AND HETEROGENEITY OF GOVERNMENTAL FORM ON AMERICAN INDIAN RESERVATIONS

Stephen E. Cornell and Joseph P. Kalt

Research and teaching on the foundations of economic development are arguably in the midst of a transition—from "institutions matter" to "where do institutions come from?" The change in focus is more than an intellectual fad. It arises from both the successes and the frustrations of the field.

Hard theoretical and empirical research, as well as recent world events, continue to drive home the point that the formal and informal institutions by which people govern themselves hold the necessary, if not sufficient, keys to the wealth of nations. From the kind of theoretically informed search for generalizable paradigms represented by North, Ostrom, Putnam, Olson, and Bates, to concrete case studies and everyday reports from the World Bank, to the "natural" experiments such as East/West Germany and North/South Korea, a central lesson of the post-World War II period seems to be that institutions and the policies that flow from them determine at least whether a society is able to move close to the production possibility frontier defined by its resources, or will be consigned to poverty far off the frontier.[1]

The almost cliché advice of economists to the effect that economic development "requires getting price signals right and creating a climate that allows businesses to respond to those signals in ways that increase the returns to investment" has been vindicated as a general matter.[2] But "getting prices right" (i.e., establishing and sustaining markets) and creating an environment that channels rent-seeking into productive endeavors requires a whole panoply of formal and informal social institutions that set down the "rules of the game." Formal institutions range from courts and constitutions to laws and regulations. Informal institutions range from norms regarding whether it is proper to vote to standards of on-the-job behavior. Getting prices and incentives "right" requires getting institutions "right."

North has captured the basic story:

- *Specialization* is productive, apparently reflecting diseconomies of scope in (at least) human capacities.

- Successful specialization requires a certain amount of *coordination* (so that an appropriate mix of desired goods and services is produced within a group) and *exchange* (so that members of a group are not stuck solely with the particular item they produce).

- Coordination and exchange require *enforceable and stable rules* of allocation and dispute resolution.

- Rules of allocation and dispute resolution require *third-party enforcement* by parties restricted in their ability to wield enforcement powers for self-aggrandizing rent-seeking.[3]

Foundations of the New Social Contract Theory

The ability to create a list like the foregoing oversimplifies the challenge of economic development. In point of fact, there cannot be much of the world that has not been exposed to some version of the "get prices and institutions right" advice. Yet, in society A the advice takes hold, and in society B it does not. More generally, notwithstanding the change in political and market affairs occasioned by the collapse of the Soviet Union, it is hard to argue that there are invisible handlike forces compelling convergence of political and economic systems on an optimum—at least not at a rate sufficient to make convergence a more interesting topic than the diversity of systems that seems to predominate.

The challenging problem for human beings that is embedded in the new institutionalist description of the foundations of economic development (and social success, more generally) is that the rules of the game, and the institutions through which those rules are devised, implemented, and enforced, are Samuelsonian shared public goods. As such, their creation and maintenance present self-interested individuals with prisoners' dilemmas, rife with defection and free-riding opportunities. Ordinary, self-interested rationality by utility-maximizing humans gives the invisible hand fits under such conditions, and the provision of mutually beneficial rules of the game and associated institutions, much less their optimal provision, is problematic in the extreme. How have many groups of humans succeeded in getting out, and staying out, of the Hobbesian world?

The classic solution to the large numbers problem of providing the costly-to-exclude public good is disinterested third-party enforcement—a party that can discipline free-riding defectors.[4] This solution is what we teach undergraduates in economics, often as if it is a positive theory of the state, under the category of "public goods as a form of market failure and the efficiency-enhancing role of government." If government itself, however, is a public good, how do people organize themselves to produce it? As Putnam puts it:

> Part of the difficulty is that coercive enforcement is expensive….The more basic problem, however, is that impartial enforcement is itself a public good, subject to the same basic dilemma that it aims to solve. For third-party enforcement to work, the third party must itself be trustworthy, but what power could ensure that the sovereign would not 'defect'? 'Put simply, if the state has coercive force, then those who run the state will use that force in their own interest at the expense of the rest of society.'[5]

Of course, people do create institutions of collective action, including governments; and "defecting," rent-seeking sovereigns are common, but not universal. Again, though, from Putnam:

> How and why are formal institutions that help surmount collective action problems actually provided? It would seem that the participants themselves cannot create the institution, for the same reason that they need it in the first place, and an impartial "lawgiver" is as problematical as an impartial Hobbesian sovereign.[6]

As we have written elsewhere, we cannot, for example, write a contract (i.e., a constitution) to abide by our constitution without falling into an infinite regress of such contracts. Formal mechanisms of social control and organization should archetypically be subject to free riding, as ruling cliques whittle away at the constitution, otherwise well-meaning citizens wait for their neighbors to bear the costs of policing such usurpers, and scofflaws cheat on their taxes and run traffic lights.[7]

This, the Hobbesian conundrum, is leading scholars from many social science disciplines (and even evolutionary biology) to conclude by deduction that the formal mechanisms and institutions via which humans organize processes of specialization, exchange, and third-party enforcement and dispute resolution must be founded on some form of extraconstitutional cooperative agreement—a social contract—that glues individuals together. The economist's perspective in these inquiries is perhaps best represented by Douglass North's *Institutions, Institutional Change and Economic Performance*, which aggressively confronts—but admittedly fails to answer—the question of how the state as the coercive third-party (i.e., non-rent-seeking) enforcer of society-wide systems of contracts, rules, and property rights could ever be constrained solely to the third-party role in a world peopled by wealth-maximizing, free-riding individual actors.[8] North is led to search for foundational shared "mental models" and "ideologies."[9] In Robert Putnam's *Making Democracy Work* (Putnam, 1992), the political scientist finds that "social capital"—embracing networks of reciprocity, trust, cultural norms, and the like—generated 700 to 800 years ago through civic associations is the dominant factor explaining the disparate social and economic development conditions found across the various regions of present-day Italy.[10]

The rational choice movement in sociology, as represented by James Coleman's *Foundations of Social Theory* and Jon Elster's *The Cement of Society*, is setting about to provide an understanding of the mechanisms by which a culture's shared norms of behavior and perception shape and constrain economic man—perhaps yielding the "sociology of knowledge" and "soft" solutions of our "sociologically minded brethren" that economists and political scientists have begun to call for.[11] From the historian's perspective, Basil Davidson's *The Black Man's Burden: Africa and the Curse of the Nation-State* drives home the conclusion that differential success in postcolonial Africa is directly related to the structural concordance or incongruence of the nation-state systems left behind by the colonial powers with the historical political cultures of the diverse multitude of native societies.[12]

Finally, evolutionary approaches, per Axelrod's *The Evolution of Cooperation*, are also relevant to the discussion and solution of problems of competition and cooperation.[13] Game theoretical models of narrowly self-interested actors produce primarily nonexistent conclusions in the large-number context, and social scientists are forced to come to grips with the fact that they are studying a *social* animal.[14] Leading evolutionary scholars are turning to models in which humans are the animal that preeminently solved the problems of cooperation and defection with mixtures of the reasoning, language, and the interpersonally triggered private emotional rewards and penalties of a truly social being, i.e., a being with capacities for "social sentiments" of self-righteousness and guilt, belonging and loneliness, love and hate, loyalty and disaffection.[15] A society's culture—its positive descriptions of the actual and the possible and its norms of personal and social propriety—structures perceived opportunity sets and gives specific content (i.e., tastes) to rational individuals' hard-wired capacities for "utility." The foundations of a social contract are in these cultural descriptions and norms, particularly norms of social interaction and political legitimacy. The form and change over time in a social contract is best understood as determined by a process of highly path-dependent *cultural* evolution, rather than the choice-theoretical invisible hand of economics.[16]

EVIDENCE FROM AMERICAN INDIAN NATIONS

Interesting and useful lessons on economic development are now emerging from a somewhat unusual context—American Indian reservations in the United States. Since the early 1970s, American Indian tribes on reservations in the United States have been accorded a high degree of political sovereignty.[17] Tribal governments now have the power to legislate, regulate, and adjudicate public policy on their respective reservations. On most reservations, tribes are self-governed under constitutional democracies. The resulting governments entail tribal legislatures, courts, police, taxation, business and environmental regulatory authority, provision of public services, and provision and maintenance of infrastructure.

At present, American Indian citizens on the nation's more than 300 reservations are the poorest minority in the United States. Reservations are commonly characterized by severe unemployment and attendant social and economic symptoms of poverty. Notwithstanding these generalizations, however, a handful of Indian nations have broken ranks and embarked on paths of sustained economic development with the dawn of the era of self-determination in the early 1970s. Previous research has indicated that such factors as resource endowments and human capital stocks explain very little of the differential economic success now apparent among tribes. Rather, the relatively successful tribes over the last two decades are marked by creation of stable political institutions that are relatively effective at implementing public decisions and inhibiting rent-seeking. Moreover, effective political institutions are consistently marked by a congruence between their form and powers, on the one hand, and the form and powers of prereservation 19th-century tribal government, on the other hand.[18]

Although it seems clear that institutions "matter" crucially to the economic development of reservations, our previous research indicates that there is a very wide variety of institutional and constitutional forms among even the group of successful reservations. This chapter hypothesizes that this variety reflects a process of "same problems, different solutions." The "problems" include establishment of a rule of law, adoption of public policies of relatively free trade with the non-Indian economy, and maintenance of a substantial degree of political stability. The "solutions" consist of the institutional designs adopted and implemented by tribal governments, including their judicial, legislative, and executive institutions.

In this study, we examine the nature of the problem-solving capacities of these institutions among many tribes. Particular attention is paid to two economically successful and developing (nongaming) reservations: the Flathead Reservation of Montana and Cochiti Pueblo in New Mexico. The former is characterized by a highly developed parliamentary democracy, whereas the latter operates under a traditional theocracy and no written constitution. Are they facing the same problems, but finding different solutions?

SOCIAL CONTRACT THEORY AND INSTITUTIONAL DIVERSITY IN INDIAN COUNTRY

Our research to date has focused on explaining the relative successes and failures in economic development in Indian Country over the last two decades. Holding constant tribes' resource and human capital endowments, within the group of tribes who have the same governmental system, there are sharp divergences in economic performance. We find that, with resources and governmental form held constant, differential performance across tribes is consistent with differences in the cultural legitimacy of the tribal government. In particular, the twentieth-century governments of most tribes were created for them by the U.S. government. For some, the U.S.-designed tribal governmental form matched the indigenous (and hence presumably culturally based) prereservation political system relatively well. For others, the cultural match was very poor. The former kinds of tribes are outperforming the latter markedly. Yet there are also notable cases within the group of identifiably successful tribes among which governmental form differs dramatically—from democracy to theocracy. At the very least, this difference suggests that one size does not fit all tribes. Why is this?

The new social contract theory would hypothesize that heterogeneity of governmental form among successful societies means that such societies are solving a common set of problems—shutting down unproductive rent-seeking and holding the government to the third-party enforcer role—with *effective* institutions of self-government. Cultural heterogeneity among such tribes, however, arguably makes the form of government that "works" for each tribe (because it is both effective and *legitimate*) different by imparting differential patterns to the match between cultural attributes and workable form.[19] Are these hypotheses borne out?

A Framework for Linking Culture to Institutions

The new social contract theory is plagued by problems of interdisciplinary communication. In particular, concepts of "social capital," "norms," and "political culture" can seem excessively vague. We have argued elsewhere that to be productive of economic progress and social health, the formal institutions of government that undergird processes of savings and investment, specialization and exchange, and rights enforcement and dispute resolution must pass tests of both *effectiveness* and *legitimacy*.[20]

At a minimum, effective governance requires mechanisms for shutting down nonproductive rent-seeking that consumes investment. These mechanisms entail not only the obvious function of maintaining law and order, but also the function of limiting the use of governmental mechanisms for purposes of wasteful rent-seeking via aggrandizing rules, regulations, and policies. The latter test of effectiveness is a version of the third-party enforcement problem, and effective institutions entail devices for limiting the power of the individuals in control of the apparatus of government at any particular time. Without devices that are effective in this way, property rights (public or private) are insecure, and processes of both savings and investment and specialization and exchange are thwarted. Such devices are perhaps most commonly recognized in their formal, written-down manifestations: constitutional separations of power, checks and balances, constitutional or legal enumeration of rights, development of judicial precedents, and the like. Surely, however, a society's formal governance institutions do not have to be written down to exist and function; they may be embedded in oral and ceremonial traditions, symbolic structures, and norms—that is, in culture. Indeed, such are the foundations of highly developed formal institutions ranging from English common law to the prereservation governments of many American Indian tribes.

Let us be more concrete about "culture." Many attributes of culture—say, clothing styles and artistic expression—carry no implications as to workable institutional forms. The new social contract theory implies that effective institutions of governance—because of their collective-goods attributes and because they ultimately involve the wielding of political power—require concordance with a society's norms of political propriety along at least four primary dimensions:

- *Structure of authority*, or the division of powers and responsibilities across such tasks as dispute resolution (judicial affairs), enforcement (coercion and policing), law and rule making (legislative affairs), administration and implementation of public initiatives and investments (executive and bureaucratic functions), and external political, economic, and military affairs (international relations).

- *Scope of authority*, or the range of powers and responsibilities wielded by the government over the foregoing areas of authority. For example, do the society's informal norms support or abhor governmental ownership of businesses? Is it seen to be the proper role of government to enforce contracts?

- *Location of authority*, or the level of social organization—family, local community, tribe—in which political power and responsibility are properly vested, according to a society's norms.

■ *Source of authority*, or the mechanisms by which individuals who assume governmental roles and control over means of coercion acquire *legitimate* authority, and the actions that violate norms of legitimacy.

When political culture—as described by these four normative dimensions—supports institutions as legitimate, the private rewards and penalties of the "social sentiments" are triggered by the social networks within which individuals are embedded in ways that inhibit free riding and defection vis-à-vis those institutions.[21] Numerous examples from fieldwork in Indian Country illustrate the "policing" role of culturally founded legitimacy. If the central government of the Oglala Sioux tribe of the Pine Ridge (South Dakota) Reservation tries to follow the example of many tribes and launch tribally owned businesses, but Sioux political culture locates *legitimate* allegiance to authority at the subtribal level of the reservation's districts, the first time a crisis in such a business's finances or management arises, support for the enterprise withers, free riders are not constrained in consuming available rents, and the enterprise collapses after one round of funding from some federal program. Or, if the formal role of a tribe's chief executive is as negotiator of external agreements with outside joint venture investors, and this role is not supported by cultural norms because extant norms prescribe *shared* senior leadership, e.g., the new manufacturing plant landed with the national automobile company by the tribal chairwoman flounders in mediocrity as other tribal politicians and citizens fail to support the collective effort needed to make it work. Or, archetypically, when the chairwoman opposes the effort by another leader to have that other leader's nephew appointed shift foreman at the auto assembly plant, no patriotic "triggering" speeches for the authority of the office of the chair are made, the chairwoman's support evaporates, a political crisis ensues, the chairwoman is impeached, and the joint-venture partner pulls out. Destructive rent-seeking can take numerous forms small and large when governance institutions are not legitimate.

On the other hand, there are no guarantees that culturally legitimate institutions will be effective, or that effective forms will be evolved. A society might well find itself with institutions that are firmly grounded on extant cultural norms, but confronting an environment that renders those institutions ineffective. To borrow a common example from the American Indian context, a tribe historically dependent on unownable migrating wildlife for economic sustenance may have had no reason to have developed a culturally sanctioned law of contract backed by a culturally sanctioned, politically independent judicial system. In the environment confronted in the late twentieth century, however, a tribal government lacking such institutions is likely to be particularly ineffective.[22] Although further discussion is beyond the scope of this study, the evolutionary (as opposed to invisible hand) mechanisms of cultural change suggest that the implied pressure for cultural and institutional adaptation (i.e., leading to formation of effective contract law and judicial systems) are relatively slow acting and provide no clean theory of equilibrium convergence.[23]

Most contemporary tribal governments were accorded effective powers of substantive self-government at approximately the same time twenty years ago. Over the twenty-year period since the resurgence of tribal self-rule, and starting from a relatively homogeneous base of poverty and dependence on federal and state funds and systems, the economic performance of tribes has spread out. To what extent can cross-sectional differences in performance be explained by differences in the effectiveness and legitimacy of tribes' self-governance systems?

The particular history of the formal institutions by which contemporary American Indian reservations are governed today provides hard-to-find "torque" on research questions of this kind. Because tribal constitutions were effectively imposed on tribes in most cases (and changes in those constitutions were and are often made subject to control by an outside power through U.S. Secretary of the Interior approval), and tribes demonstrably differ a great deal in their present and historic sociopolitical cultures, the Indian context affords the possibility of observing mismatches between "social contracts" and formal institutions. The public goods theory of such institutions directly yields the hypothesis—testable because of the torque of the Indian setting—that a mismatch between the underlying social contract and the formal institutions of a self-governing society should hamper institutional legitimacy and lead those formal institutions to perform relatively poorly. Moreover, because we have tribes with the same formal institutions (derived from the Indian Reorganization Act [IRA] of 1934), but with different sociopolitical cultural settings (contracts), the Indian context provides some prospect of isolating social contracts as undergirding determinants of social success. This prospect is further assisted by the fact that American Indian societies are relatively homogeneous within tribes when compared to, say, the United States as a whole, but remarkably heterogeneous across tribes. Later in the chapter, this divergence is used as a basis for trying to understand the effectiveness of vastly different governmental forms.

BACKGROUND ON ECONOMICS AND POLICY IN INDIAN COUNTRY

The resurgence of Indian self-rule is most directly the result of a series of federal legal decisions over the last two decades and the Indian Self-Determination and Education Assistance Act of 1975. Indian nations now generally have rights of self-government exceeding a U.S. state's, with the ability to establish their own courts, police, legislatures, bureaucracies, business and environmental codes, tax systems, civil and criminal procedures, and most of the other functions of sovereign polities.[24]

Most of these nations operate under constitutions that were drafted by the U. S. Government in the 1930s, pursuant to the IRA of 1934. IRA constitutions were modeled after business or social club boards of directors. They typically provide for:

- A representative tribal council of (commonly) seven to twenty members with legislative powers.

- A tribal chairperson or president selected in parliamentary fashion by the council or in U.S. executive fashion by direct popular election.

- Little or no provision for judicial institutions or functions.

- Little enumeration of powers of the various parts of the tribal government, and

- A requirement that the U.S. Secretary of the Interior approve of any changes in the tribal constitution.

Even tribes without IRA constitutions often had their constitutions drafted by others (e.g., at the time of a treaty), and non-IRA constitutions often follow the foregoing structure.[25]

As a general matter, American Indian reservations are quite poor communities. Reservation unemployment is typically around 45 percent (even without adjusting for the not surprisingly large discouraged worker effects on officially defined U.S. Bureau of Labor Statistics unemployment). Average social conditions are correspondingly unsatisfactory, with rates of social pathologies (e.g., suicide, crime) far above the rates for the United States as a whole.

Such "average" images of struggling and underdeveloped economies mask diversity in reservation performance (Table 10-1). Some reservations appear to be almost pure transfers-and-grants economies with little on-reservation economic productive activity and most employment in social service sectors. The Pine Ridge Reservation in South Dakota, for example, is the poorest community in the United States, according to the U.S. census. At Northern Cheyenne in Montana, the tribe reports that approximately 95 percent of all reservation income is derived from federal and state programs, with the remaining small amount of income coming from on-reservation agricultural production. At the neighboring Crow Reservation, on paper the tribe is one of the wealthiest societies in the world as a result of extremely rich endowments of coal and agricultural lands, with measured per capita wealth exceeding $3 million as of 1988; yet the effective rate of income generation off of this wealth amounts to an annual rate of return of approximately 0.01 percent.[26] As at many reservations, Crow unemployment adjusted for discouraged workers is in the range of 80 to 90 percent.

In contrast, some reservations have been booming economically and rapidly progressing in terms of social conditions. This fact holds even outside of the much-publicized cases of successful gaming tribes (which have been able to capitalize on their sovereignty and capture niches in the gambling market). The Flathead Reservation in Montana, for example, is the site of a healthy private sector economy based on agriculture and tourism, with real incomes growing and unemployment quite low for rural Montana. With a different strategy of tribal ownership of enterprises, the Mississippi Choctaw have made the tribe the fourth or fifth largest employer in the state of Mississippi, and the traffic flow at morning rush hour is onto the reservation as thousands of non-Indians commute to work at the tribe's automobile subassembly plant, its industrial park, its greeting card factory, its shopping centers, and its tribally run schools and other social service organizations. The White Mountain Apaches in Arizona have followed a similar organizational strategy to build a natural resource-based economy that is the economic base for Indians and non-Indians in its region. With a tribal membership of 12,500, the White Mountain Apaches operate tribal enterprises with revenues of $80 to $100 million per year, including a major logging and saw-mill industry, a ski resort, the premier for-fee sport hunting business in the United States, and an aerospace manufacturing subcontractor. At Cochiti Pueblo in New Mexico, the tribe owns an upscale retirement community, operates one of the nation's top twenty-five public golf courses, and manages tourism on a large recreational lake.

EXPLAINING CROSS-TRIBE DIFFERENCES IN PERFORMANCE

With tribes operating in a common policy environment vis-à-vis federal and state authorities, and with all tribes being turned loose to pursue self-government in approximately the same way at approximately the same time, what explains the fairly sharp differences in their economic performance? The answers to this question of the origin of the wealth of Indian nations are, of course, multilayered and incomplete. We believe the evidence is strong, however, at several layers of inquiry.

First, it is clear that formal institutions matter in precisely the "get the institutions right" sense. In previous research, we have reported cross-sectional analyses of the sixty-seven largest tribes (populations over seven hundred) for which data on economic performance and plausible explanatory variables are available.[27] These analyses indicate with quite strong degrees of statistical confidence that, holding constant variables suggested by neoclassic growth theory (including human capital endowments, natural resource endowments, marketplace opportunities, and the like), constitutional forms add significantly to the explanation of cross-tribe differences in economic performance. The relevant results are shown in Table 10-2, which reports the *ceteris paribus* contribution to the level of tribal employment of alternative formal governmental institutions. Over the sample, the combination of a directly elected chief executive and an independent judiciary adds the most to tribal economic performance—raising employment almost 20 (19.9) percentage points relative to a tribe governed by an "Athenian" democracy with no independent judiciary. The latter is the poorest performing type of formal government in Indian Country. "Athenian" democracies (known as general councils in Indian Country) provide no separation of powers or other organizational constraints on rent-seeking through the political arena. They also make every voting-age member of the tribe a member of the

TABLE 10-1

Economic Performance and Institutional Forms on American Indian Reservations

Reservation	Change in Income 1977–1989 (%)	1989 BLS Employment[a] (%)	Employment Related to Fitted Expectation[b] (%)	Governmental Form[c]	Independent Judiciary	Cultural "Match"[d]
Flathead	16	83	+11	Parliamentary	Yes	Yes
White Mountain Apache	12	89	+23	Executive	No	Yes
Cochiti Pueblo	10	96	+20	Theocracy	?	Yes
Mescalero Apache	9	80–90	+33	Executive	No	Yes
Muckleshoot	6	74	+5	Parliamentary	No	Yes
Pine Ridge Sioux	–1	50	–20	Executive	No	No
San Carlos Apache	–7	49	–15	Executive	No	No
Rosebud Sioux	–10	10	–38	Executive	Yes	No
Hualapai	–11	26	–18	Executive	No	No
Yakima	–12	39	–1	Athenian	Yes	No
Crow	–12	33	–7	Athenian	No	No
Northern Cheyenne	–15	52	–4	Executive	No	No
All Reservations	–1	55	—	—	—	—

T A B L E   1 0 - 1
Economic Performance and Institutional Forms on American Indian Reservations (continued)

Sources: U.S. Census, 1990; Bureau of Indian Affairs, U.S. Department of the Interior, *Indian Service Population and Labor Force Estimates*, various issues.

[a] BLS employment is 100 percent minus the BLS unemployment rate (with the latter measuring the percent of the workforce actually looking for employment and not finding it).

[b] Employment related to fitted expectation represents the difference between actual employment levels and the employment levels predicted by a model of sixty-seven reservations, controlling for reservation governmental form, local economic conditions in surrounding counties, human and resource capital endowments, and on-reservation property rights structures. This model is presented and estimated in Cornell, S., and J. Kalt, "Where's the Glue? Institutional Bases of American Indian Economic Development," project report series (Cambridge: Harvard Project on American Indian Economic Development, John F. Kennedy School of Government, Harvard University, 1991).

[c] Parliamentary refers to governments in which the tribal chief executive is selected by the representative tribal council. Executive refers to governments in which the tribal chief executive is directly elected by the tribe's reservation citizens. Theocracy indicates that the tribal religious leader(s) appoints the key tribal authorities and establishes central tribal policies. "Athenian" refers to democratic decision-making authority being vested in a tribal council in which all adult members of the tribe serve on the tribal council.

[d] Cultural match refers to possible congruence between historical self-selected governmental form and modern (largely imposed) governmental form (see text and Cornell and Kalt, "Where Does Economic Development Really Come From? Constitutional Rule Among the Contemporary Sioux and Apache," *Economic Inquiry* 33 [July 1995]).

TABLE 10-2

Contributions of Alternative Governmental Forms to Reservation
Employment Levels[a]

	General Council (Athenian) (%)	Parliamentary System (%)	Independent Chief Executive (%)
No independent judiciary	—	10.8	14.9
Independent judiciary	5.0	15.8	19.9

[a] Contributions at mean sample values, as determined by the model estimated over sixty-seven tribes in Cornell and Kalt (1991). The effects of resource endowments and adjacent non-reservation economic conditions, human capital (education and labor force experience), and degrees of mixed jurisdiction re: on-reservation property rights due to allotment history are held constant. Contributions are measured relative to a reservation with a general council form of government, with no independent judiciary. All effects shown are statistically significant at the 90 percent level and above.

Source: Cornell, S., and J. Kalt, "Where's the Glue? Institutional Bases of American Indian Economic Development," project report series (Cambridge: Harvard Project on American Indian Economic Development, John F. Kennedy School of Government, Harvard University, 1991).

tribal council. In so doing, they turn the political arena into a tragedy of the commons for rent-seeking political factions and individuals.[28]

At a second layer of inquiry, we believe the evidence is compelling that there is, indeed, a social contract that undergirds successful formal institutions of self-government and, thereby, social and economic success at the level of Indian nations. The foregoing description of the contributions of various types of formal governmental structures does not explain all of the variation in the performance of cross-reservation economies. As shown in Table 10-1, tribes differ sharply in economic performance (the first and second columns of figures), and such differences persist when performance is measured (conceptually) as distance from the production possibility frontier defined over resource endowments and governmental form (column three of Table 10-1). In particular, holding constant production possibility frontiers (as given by resource endowments, etc.) *and* holding constant governmental form, there remain sharp differences in tribal economic performance. For example, the White Mountain Apache and the Pine Ridge Sioux have had very similar IRA governments with strong chief executives and no independent judiciaries since the 1930s. Yet as shown in Table 10-1, the Apaches are performing more than 20 percentage points (in terms of employment) higher than would be predicted by neoclassic growth theory mediated by the new institutionalism, and the Sioux are performing 20 percentage points more poorly than predicted (column 3, Table 10-1).

We hypothesize that such differences arise as a result of mismatches between indigenous tribal sociopolitical norms regarding the location, scope, source, and structure of political authority, on the one hand, and the (imposed) formal institutions of tribal government on the other.[29] It is relatively easy to document the immediate (commonly in the mid- to late 1800s) prereservation governmental systems of many tribes. As self-governing societies that had passed the test of environmental adoption to that point in time, such systems were embedded in the indigenous, diverse cultures of tribes. In some cases, the basic structure of the modern government accords well with the historic structure; in other cases, the mismatch is stark. Thus, for example, the quite successful Cochiti Pueblo has never given up its traditional theocracy and has no written constitution. Cochiti shows a "match" in Table 10-1. On the other hand, the modern Crow Government of undifferentiated Athenian democracy bears little or no resemblance to the hierarchical and two-branch governmental structure of prereservation Crow society. Crow is a "no match."

Applying pseudoregression Boolean procedures to the sample of twelve tribes for which data on current and prior governmental systems are obtainable and which are shown in Table 10-1 permits testing as to whether a "match" between the current governmental system and the indigenous political culture adds significantly to our ability to explain and predict the relative economic performance of tribes.[30] Our tests indicate that economic success (defined either as the ability to sustain growth in the present period of self-determination or as the ability to simply sustain more than a transfers-and-grants economy) is undergirded by a set of jointly necessary and sufficient conditions. These conditions are summarized in Box 10-1. The new social contract theory and the new institutionalism, with additional confirmation from extensive fieldwork, imply that items 2 (limits to political power) and 3 (a match between governmental forms and cultural norms) reflect the requirements of effective and legitimate government. They make specialization and exchange (item 1) and productive use of tribal resources (item 4) feasible.

The evidence derived from contemporary American Indian reservations supports the conclusions that: (1) economic and social success require "getting institutions right" in the way that we indicated in the first section; (2) formal institutions of social control and organiza-

> **BOX 10-1**
>
> Necessary and Sufficient Conditions for Economic Development Observed on American Indian Reservations
>
> - *Specialization and Exchange*: A willingness to specialize and engage in trade with the broader off-reservation economy.[a]
> - *Limits to Power*: A formal non-Athenian governmental structure that provides some mechanism of confining the government to the third-party enforcer role and shuts down rent-seeking.
> - *Cultural Legitimacy*: A match between cultural norms governing political affairs and the present formal governmental institutions.
> - *Resources*: A nontrivial stock of at least one resource (e.g., human capital, natural resources).
>
>   a The designation of a tribe as willing to engage in specialization and exchange is based on the fact that many tribes demonstrate hostility to "international" trade with the off-reservation economy in the form of refusals to import nonmember skilled labor, explicit policies of "self-sufficiency," and closure of various markets (such as recreational tourism). Such insularity is invariably associated with lack of economic development.
>
> Source: Cornell, S. and J. Kalt, "Where's the Glue? Institutional Bases of American Indian Economic Development," project report series, (Cambridge: Harvard Project on American Indian Economic Development, John F. Kennedy School of Government, Harvard University, 1991).

tion are shared public goods for which no meta-enforcer exists to shut down defections and free riding; and (3) successful formal institutions of governance are founded on an informal, shared system of coordinating norms and conventions that we can call a social contract. Yet inspection of Table 10-1 raises further questions. In particular, what are the formal institutions of governance that "work"? Even within the group of relatively successful tribes that appear at the top of Table 10-1, we see heterogeneity in governmental form. The theocracy at Cochiti Pueblo, in particular, stands out relative to the constitutional democracies of the other economically prospering tribes. How is it that effective and legitimate governmental forms span such a range?

Cochiti and Flathead: Same Problems, Different Solutions

The Confederated Salish and Kootenai tribes of the Flathead Reservation and the Keres people of Cochiti Pueblo are among the most economically successful American Indian societies in the current era of self-determination (Table 10-1). Accepting the previously described framework, the Flathead and Cochiti nations must be meeting the conditions set forth in Box 10-1. Both tribes are notably willing to specialize and engage in "international" trade (i.e., item 1 in Box 10-1), and both have adequate (but not spectacular) resource bases on which to build economies (item 4).

The stark difference between Flathead and Cochiti is found in their forms of government. The Flathead Reservation is organized under a highly articulated and sophisticated parliamentary democracy as provided by its amended 1935 IRA constitution. This government is structured as if drawn from a high school civics text on good government. The Cochiti, on the other hand, avoided the IRA constitutions and, instead, are organized under a theocracy that has operated continuously for centuries. Its structure, powers, and procedures are unwritten. Democracy is absent; a theocrat known as the *cacique* appoints tribal officials and functionaries.

In what follows, we attempt to dissect how the different governments of Flathead and Cochiti can both prove to be so effective and legitimate. In some ways, the government at Flathead, with its strong separations of powers and rule-of-law principles, is too easy to diagnose within the new institutionalist framework. However, substantial additions to our understanding of the elements of effective and legitimate government are promised by investigation of Cochiti.

The image of a highly traditional, nondemocratic theocrat ruling over a society readily calls to mind problems of corrupting power, despotic rent-seeking, and the like. Yet the new institutionalism and the new social contract theory would predict from Cochiti's economic success that Cochiti's government, in fact, operates under norms and (albeit, unwritten) culturally founded rules that limit the theocracy to the role of third-party enforcer and shut down wasteful rent-seeking. This is the key hypothesis to be tested here. Our research strategy is to dissect the actual mechanisms and principles by which Cochiti government operates. If we do not find the rules and procedures that solve the rent-seeking and third-party enforcer problems, the new institutionalism and new social contract theory are not supported. As we write this, of course, we know the results. Going in, however, we did not. This fact increases the power of the findings, although we recognize that Cochiti represents a single case.[31]

Current Economic and Social Conditions at Flathead and Cochiti

Flathead

Tables 10-3 and 10-4 summarize current economic and social conditions at Flathead and Cochiti. The Flathead Reservation consists of approximately 1.2 million acres in western Montana. It is governed by the Confederated Salish and Kootenai tribes, and has its origin in the Hellgate Treaty of 1855. This treaty was designed to consolidate three groups onto a single reservation—the Flatheads, the Pend d'Oreilles, and the Kootenais. The Pend d'Oreilles and Flatheads are Salish peoples whose languages are closely related but whose cultures and histories differ to some degree, whereas the Kootenais are a non-Salish people who speak a very different language, mutually unintelligible with Salish.[32] The Pend d'Oreilles and Flatheads also had a long history of alliance and cooperation, often hunting buffalo together on the plains east of the Rockies. The Kootenais, scattered in several bands ranging northwest of the Flatheads and Pend d'Oreilles into Idaho and British Columbia, had once been enemies of the Salish, but some time before contact with Europeans, Kootenai bands in western Montana made peace, and occasionally joined the Pend d'Oreilles for hunting and common defense against the Blackfeet.[33]

Following the Hellgate Treaty, U.S. authorities treated the three tribes as a single political unit. They originally appointed a Flathead chief as head chief of the new confederation, although it does not appear that either the Pend d'Oreilles or the Kootenais recognized the authority of this position. The Kootenais in particular remained aloof, living in a separate cluster of settlements on the reservation. To this day, many Kootenais continue to congregate and live at some distance from the Salish.[34]

The Flathead Reservation is largely rural, with substantial agricultural and forest resources. Its boundaries encompass a sizeable portion of Flathead Lake, which has become a major recreational and summer home site. In recent years, the reservation has seen significant economic growth, especially in the small-business sector of services and retail sales largely related to agriculture and tourism. Individual tribal members and firms run by tribal members also participate in logging, construction, and farming. The tribal government has attempted to own and operate many enterprises in recent years, including an electronics assembly facility and a small sawmill. These efforts have consistently been unsuccessful. Overall, however, the Flathead Reservation has fared relatively well in the era of self-determination. Its income growth and improvement in employment from the mid-1980s to the mid-1990s are among the most impressive in Indian Country. As of the 1990 U.S. census, Flathead per capita income exceeded the national average for reservations by more than 40 percent. While the rest of Indian Country experienced a decline in real income and a rise in unemployment rates over the period since the peak in federal spending on Indian affairs in 1977, both income and employment improved substantially at Flathead (Table 10-3).

A relatively large share, 48 percent, of the tribal workforce works for federal, state, or tribal governments (Table 10-4). In part, this fact reflects the importance of the forestry sector at Flathead; the commercial forest resources are publicly owned by the tribe and the managers and specialists in forestry are recorded as governmental employees. The share of employment in the public sector also reflects the tribe's building up of its own governmental capacity in order to

TABLE 10-3

Social and Economic Conditions on Flathead and Cochiti Reservations

	Flathead (Salish/Kootenai)	Cochiti Pueblo	All Tribes
Reservation Population, 1990	21,061	1,400	808,100
Reservation Indian Population, 1990	7,667	936	437,800
Indian Unemployment, 1990	17%	4%	45%
Change in Unemployment, 1979–1990	down 11%	down 26%	up 14%
Indian Per Capita Income, 1990	$6,428	$5,828	$4,478
Change in Income, 1977–1989	up 16%	up 10%	down 1%
Indian Median Household Income, 1990	$14,898	$18,036	$12,459
Indian Family Poverty Rate, 1990	32%	27%	47%
Indian High School Graduates, 1990	32%	34%	31%
Speak Native Language	14%	61%	52%
Speak Little/No English	3%	21%	23%

Sources: U.S. Census, 1990; U.S. Dept. of the Interior, Bureau of Indian Affairs, *Indian Service Population and Labor Force Estimates*, selected volumes.

TABLE 10-4

The Structure of the Flathead and Cochiti Economies

Sector of Employment	Flathead (%)	Cochiti (%)	All Tribes (%)
Private	52	62	54
Government	48	38	46
Managerial/Professional	22	34	18
Sales/Administration	21	31	25
Services	18	11	22
Agriculture/Forestry	10	1	5
High-Skill Manufacturing	13	9	13
Low-Skill Manufacturing/ Construction	16	14	18

Source: U.S. Census, 1990.

take over functions otherwise filled by the U.S. Bureau of Indian Affairs and other public agencies.

Tribal members are a minority on the Flathead Reservation (Table 10-3) because of a history of "allotment" under which tribal lands were transferred into individual Indian and eventually non-Indian hands in the first part of the 1900s. There is also a high degree of intermarriage between tribal members and nonmembers, both non-Indians and Indians from other tribes. Until 1960, enrollment as a tribal member required only one-sixteenth Salish or Kootenai ancestry. Since 1960, this criterion has been set at one-fourth ancestry. Improved economic conditions in recent years seem to be accompanied by some resurgence of traditionalism in civic and religious affairs. Nevertheless, the civic culture of Flathead appears to be relatively far removed from its prereservation roots when compared to most other reservations. One objective indicator of this distancing is the retention of native language. As indicated in Table 10-3, there are virtually no exclusively native speakers at Flathead; and only 14 percent of tribal members are fluent in the native language, compared to an average of 52 percent nationally.

Cochiti

With per capita income more than 30 percent higher than the national average for reservation Indians, median household income approximately 45 percent higher than the national average for reser-

vations, and unemployment at only 4 percent, Cochiti Pueblo represents one of the most economically successful tribes in the country
(Tables 10-1 and 10-3). As with Flathead, income growth and improving unemployment rates indicate that the Cochiti has been among
the leading tribes in the country when it comes to taking advantage
of its powers of self-government in the era of self-determination in
Indian affairs.

The Cochiti Reservation consists of approximately 26,000 acres
and is located on the Rio Grande River approximately fifty miles north
of Albuquerque, New Mexico. The Cochiti tribe is one of several
Keresan-speaking Pueblo tribes that historically resided in New
Mexico. These Keres and other Puebloan tribes bore the brunt of the
Spanish colonization of what is now New Mexico; that colonization
began in the mid-sixteenth century. Through rounds of subjugation,
enslavement, revolt, appeasement, and accommodation, the Pueblo
tribes (including Cochiti) typically revealed an adaptive strategy that
was a complicated mixture of taking certain matters (such as religious ceremonies) underground while absorbing and adopting other
dimensions of Spanish (and eventually American) culture and economic systems.[35]

By the mid-1990s, the reservation economy at Cochiti was based
largely on tourism and recreation. As previously noted, the tribe owns
a town. The town of Cochiti has a population of approximately six
hundred. It is a growing, incorporated retirement community based
on land originally leased from the tribe and catering to the market
created by the temperate climate and mystique of New Mexico.
Through the Cochiti Community Development Corporation and
other tribally owned enterprises and agencies, the Cochiti tribe provides public services and infrastructure to the town, including an array of city services, swim and tennis facilities, a premier golf course,
and marina facilities on Cochiti Lake. The latter two services draw
from the wider public as well, especially the populations of Albuquerque, Los Alamos, and Santa Fe. Cochiti Lake is the product of an
Army Corp of Engineers project completed in 1975. Following
completion, seepage under the dam virtually destroyed the
reservation's prime agricultural land. As indicated in Table 10-4, agricultural employment is virtually nonexistent at Cochiti today. Instead, employment is concentrated in white-collar managerial and
professional positions, sales and administration (particularly in the
commercial sector), services, and construction.

Cochiti's economic system is embedded in a highly conservative culture. Religious affairs as well as subtribal social groupings and fraternal organizations are kept extremely private in accord with long-standing Puebloan practices. Norms of personal deportment and behavior are strong, and education is highly valued. Among adults over twenty-five years of age, more than 40 percent have some college education or higher. The comparable figure for reservation adults nationwide is less than 25 percent. Cultural continuity and homogeneity are high, as suggested by the 61 percent native language retention (Table 10-3).

Flathead and Cochiti Solutions to the Problems of the Wealth of Nations

There must certainly be many layers to explaining the relative economic success of the Flathead and Cochiti Reservations since the start of the era of self-determination. Sustained economic development involves bringing many pieces together, from technical capacities to the social contract. We have argued here, however, that the latter is foundational in the sense of necessary and sufficient conditions. The kinds of results summarized above lead to the nested hypothesis that Flathead and Cochiti are satisfying the conditions set forth in Box 10-1. From Box 10-1's list, we now discuss the role of resources, specialization and exchange, limits to power, and cultural legitimacy in the Flathead and Cochiti context.

Resources

A strong version of the economics of comparative advantage might predict that resource endowments affect the *level* of economic development, but not *whether* economic development can take place in a society. If nothing else, any society has labor resources that might be leveraged into productive action. Yet in Indian Country there are many places where virtually no productive activity that is not transfer-dependent takes place. At reservations such as Crow, Northern Cheyenne, and Pine Ridge, unemployment pushes to 90 percent and higher, and what employment does exist is largely in federally supported programs serving the needs of the rest of the unemployed population.

Reservations such as Crow are well endowed with natural resources.[36] The absence of substantial productive economic activity at Crow implies that a large resource endowment is not a sufficient condition for development to take hold. At the same time, however, the tribes that have been able to launch and sustain productive economies in samples such as that shown in Table 10-1 all have nontrivial resource endowments in the form of natural resources or human capital. Thus, a substantial resource base of some sort is a necessary ingredient for reservation development.

Both Flathead and Cochiti have substantial, but not overwhelming, resource bases on which to build their economies. For Flathead, the combination of good agricultural land, harvestable forest resources, and tourist attractions provides the foundation. Cochiti has capitalized on recreational tourism opportunities and the New Mexico climate and mystique. In neither case, however, are the tribes uniquely endowed relative to neighboring Indian and non-Indian settings. Relative to many other tribes that have comparable resource endowments but have not been able to sustain economic activity, Flathead and Cochiti have capitalized on their resources through specialization and "international" exchange.

Specialization and Exchange

The people of both Flathead and Cochiti are best characterized as "free traders." With comparative advantages in tourism, recreation, and retirement and vacation settings, contrary policies of economic insularity would be particularly counterproductive. Notwithstanding this implication, many tribes with similar opportunities demonstrate hostility to "international" trade with the off-reservation economy. This hostility takes the form of, for example, refusals to import nonmember skilled labor, explicit policies of "self-sufficiency" that manifest themselves as rejection of business or capital from outsiders, and closure of various markets that involve extensive interaction with nonmembers (such as recreational tourism). Insularity in these forms is associated with lack of economic development.[37]

The Flathead and Cochiti show mercantilist tendencies in only one significant area. The Cochiti are quite unreceptive to importation of high-skilled (especially managerial) non-Cochiti labor, because of the strong linkages that exist between culturally legitimate sources of authority, such as the authority to boss others around in a workplace, and Cochiti religious culture. That the Cochiti apparently can move forward economically without extensive reliance on non-Cochiti managers and professionals may reflect a surprising abundance of high-skilled Cochiti managerial labor. Not only does the tribe have a level of indigenous college-and-above education that is high relative to other tribes, but there is also evidence that the Cochiti export such labor. That is, the Cochiti managerial pool contains many individuals who have been or are employed in managerial and professional positions in, for example, Albuquerque.

For both the Flathead and Cochiti, interaction and trade with outsiders have long and consistent histories. Salish proclivities for marriage outside the tribe appear to antedate the coming of the Europeans, and the tribe was apparently highly adaptive to such events as the importation of the horse, new technology, and the appearance of new neighbors.[38] The Puebloan peoples, meanwhile, absorbed the blow of Spanish invasion and colonization and emerged with distinct cultural identities that reflected both continuity and adaptation. Even more tellingly, the pueblos of New Mexico were major trading centers along the lines of a modern-day Rotterdam even prior to the coming of the Europeans.[39] Today, culturally sanctioned forms of interaction and exchange are manifested in Flathead's opening of a major resort on the banks of Flathead Lake and the Cochiti owning a town populated by non-Indian retirees. In fact, the town of Cochiti was started in the 1960s under a lease from the tribe by the Hunt brothers (of silver, oil, and professional sports team fame). When these original lessees went bankrupt with the oil and silver market collapses of the early and mid-1980s, the Cochiti took back the lease. They debated internally whether to push the town to disband (potentially leaving the tribe in possession of a huge stock of fine homes). They decided, however, to stay in the retirement community business.

Culturally Legitimate Limits to Power

The final two categories from Box 10-1 are best addressed in tandem. Especially in the case of the Cochiti tribes, the continuity and community acceptance of theocratic government make its cultural legitimacy self-evident. The interesting questions concern whether and how this government is limited to the role of a third-party dispute resolver, rather than being a vehicle for wasteful rent-seeking. Flathead solves these problems with textbook democracy formalized in the 1930s. Where, if at all, does the legitimacy of this system come from? We turn first to a description of Flathead government.

Flathead. The Confederated Salish and Kootenai tribes of the Flathead Reservation were the first Indians to adopt an IRA constitution (in 1934). The resulting government at Flathead is a classic three-branch parliamentary system. The key governing and lawmaking body is the tribal council. It consists of ten members elected at-large with reservation district residency requirements. Council members serve staggered four-year terms. The tribe instituted primary elections in 1981 with the intention of encouraging majority coalescence around elected representatives.[40]

The chief executive of the Flathead Government is the tribal chairman. The chairman is selected in parliamentary fashion by the tribal council (rather than through direct election by the citizens). The chairman serves two-year terms and acts as spokesperson for the council. A tribal executive director reports to the chairman and oversees eight divisions covering approximately forty programs and several tribal enterprises. This executive branch is subject to a civil service system that governs appointment, advancement, compensation, discipline, and dismissal among professionals within the Flathead Government.

The Flathead Government is widely known for its well-developed and independent judicial system. The system includes a tribal police force managed by the tribe under a block grant system that permits a tribe to contract to itself services that might otherwise be performed by, for instance, the U.S. Bureau of Indian Affairs. An office of attorney general serves as chief prosecutor for the tribe, and the office is fully staffed by professionals who might be found in any U.S. state government. A tribal court system serves as primary adjudicator of civil and criminal matters. The appointment and removal of judges is governed by tribal ordinances that delineate criteria and proscribe interference in judicial affairs by the tribal council. Finally, in an important innovation designed to provide for the rule of law and to eliminate political tampering, the Flathead participate in an intertribal "supreme" court. This court is a cooperative effort of several Montana and Wyoming tribes. It has the power to hear appeals from the Flathead court. Its judges are drawn from the participating tribes and its rules promote judicial fairness by, for example, providing that a judge may not sit on a case from his or her own tribe.

Several elements of the Flathead governing system reveal its explicit checks-and-balances structure. Many less economically successful tribes, for example, struggle with problems of politicization of (i.e., rent-seeking through) the tribal court system. Both the frequency of examples from the field and the quantitative results demonstrate the deleterious effect this politicization has on economic development.[41] Particularly in an economy founded in large part on private businesses, as at Flathead, a stable and nonpolitical court system that can fairly adjudicate and enforce contracts is critical.[42] Interestingly, key components of the Flathead judicial system, such as participation in the intertribal appeal system, are not embedded in the tribe's constitution. Instead, they emanate from council ordinances that might be thought subject to easy and frequent change. Interested parties at Flathead, however, report that (paraphrasing) "constitutions and ordinances can both be changed, but we've built up a tradition around here that says our courts should be independent."

The current Flathead Government is the product of considerable reform over the years. Lopach, Brown, and Clow report that until roughly the mid-1970s the dominant force on the reservation was the Bureau of Indian Affairs superintendent.[43] At that time, however, a group of leaders emerged who are credited with wise reforms that promoted separations and limitations of power and the isolated tribal government in the role of disinterested third-party enforcer. Prior to 1984, for example, the executive bureaucratic functions of the tribe's government were organized under a committee system reporting directly to council members with vested interests.[44] The creation of an executive director reporting to the tribal chairman provided insulation of executive functions from the key tribal politicians. Such separation of politics from the day-to-day operations of a tribe is as rare as economic success in Indian Country.[45] The result of separation and limitations of power at Flathead is a notably professional and non-rent-seeking government.

One interesting puzzle in Flathead government is its parliamentary structure vis-à-vis the tribal chairman. Prereservation Flathead society was governed by a strong chief-executive system in which a single head chief appears to have been endowed with extensive powers of lawmaking, adjudication, and even law enforcement.[46] Based on criteria of cultural "match," it might be expected that the Flatheads would not see a relatively weak parliamentary chief executive, lacking the independent political power base of direct election and serving at the behest of the elected council, as legitimate. On the other hand, imposition of a single powerful chief executive on the amalgamation of Flatheads, Pend d'Oreilles, and Kootenais on the Flathead reservation would please the Flatheads but lack *shared* legitimacy. We can speculate that a parliamentary system that does not focus power in a single strong chief executive, but that instead disperses power across factions creates a government with more shared cultural legitimacy on an amalgam reservation. Further investigation of such reservations—of which there are many—would be needed to test this speculation.

Cochiti. Three aspects of contemporary Cochiti political organization are especially remarkable. First, as Lange notes, "In governing, Cochiti officers are guided by no written laws, or a constitution.…Instead, problems are met by the officers and council by means of innumerable 'regulations,' comprising a body of common law. This body of unwritten, yet efficacious, law is both rigid and flexible, as the situation demands.…"[47] Second, while the formal structure of Cochiti governance is recorded only in the work of researchers and has no formal constitutional basis, it is elaborate, stable, and, judging at least from the recent record of economic development, unusually successful. Third, Cochiti governance is theocratic, operating under the ultimate control of the religious leaders of the pueblo.

Not only can the contemporary governance of Cochiti be characterized this way; historical Cochiti governance can be as well.

The Medicine Societies. In the 1920s Goldfrank wrote, "the religious societies are at present the most important factor in Cochiti culture."[48] In the 1940s and 1950s, these societies, which Lange calls medicine societies, retained central importance.[49] There were three such societies through most of this century: Flint, Giant, and Shikame. The major functions of these societies had to do with three things: curing disease, ceremonial retreats or fasts to bring rain, and the selection of pueblo officers.[50]

This last function is the key relationship in the system of Cochiti governance. Traditionally, and until very recently, the senior shamans or heads of the three medicine societies appointed the six major officers who managed daily pueblo affairs. The head of the Flint Society—who is also the *cacique*—selected the war captain and lieutenant war captain. The head of the Giant Society selected the governor and lieutenant governor, and the head of the Shikame Society selected the fiscale and lieutenant fiscale.[51] In a given year, the senior officers were selected from one of the two "kivas"—either Turquoise or Pumpkin—into which the pueblo is divided, while the lieutenants were selected from the other. The following year, when a new set of officers was appointed, the kiva links were reversed, thereby maintaining a balance, over time, between the two "sides" of the pueblo.[52] The separations of power and impediments to rent-seeking are clear in this structure.

By the 1950s, there had been a noticeable decline in the prestige and, to some degree, the significance of the medicine societies. Lange attributes this decline to education, increased Cochiti contacts with the outside world, and other factors, and found it most apparent in certain of "the overt aspects of their functions," such as curing and weather control.[53] Yet their significance in tribal governance and, through it, in social control remained, owing to their continued power over the appointment of officers. Even this importance, however, has been changing in more recent years. The decline in prestige and significance of the medicine societies has been accompanied by a decline in numbers. In 1960, the headman and last surviving member of the Giant Society died. With this, the *cacique*, headman of the Flint Society, took over the naming of governors as well as war captains.[54]

The Cacique. The *cacique* is the chief religious leader of the pueblo, the keeper of Cochiti traditions and supervisor of religious life, a man of great knowledge, and the highest-status individual in the community. In 1927, Goldfrank wrote: "The Keres Indian name for *cacique* is *cteamurni hotcheni*, leader-chief. He spends much of his time in prayer, fasting, and retreats. He does not enter into any of the economic activities of the pueblo."[55] The prayer and fasting are on behalf of all the people, for the *cacique* is ultimately responsible for the spiritual and physical well-being of the entire community. Among the various names for him is *yaya*, "mother," for he is viewed as the mother of his people. Father Noel Dumarest, pastor to Cochiti and other pueblos from 1894 to 1900, describes the limits to power that constrained the *cacique:* "He can enter into no social entanglements, he is a man of peace. *Therefore he is relieved of all executive functions.* He neither denounces nor punishes. He gives advice and counsels harmony."[56] Once a man has become *cacique*, he may no longer serve on the council of *principales*, the pueblos' secular deliberative body. He does not attend council meetings unless asked for specific information. As one Cochiti told Lange, it "isn't right for the *cacique* to hear arguments or sarcasm."[57]

Although the *cacique* is uninvolved in the daily, secular affairs of the community, he is at the center of its theocratic political structure, for it is the *cacique* who traditionally appointed the war captains each year and, more recently, appoints the governors as well. As for the *cacique* himself, alone among the various official positions within the pueblo, he is appointed for life. Appointment is by his predecessor. When the present *cacique* is dying, he appoints his successor, with the primary constraint being that the appointee must be a member of the Flint Society and, typically, a shaman of long training and experience.

On the other hand, his own power is not unlimited. "Traditionally," writes Lange, the *cacique* "could be, and was, brought to trial by the war captains in response to charges of negligence or wrongdoing. The *cacique* could, on decision of the council of principales, be punished, deposed, or even executed."[58] It remains part of the war captains' job "to call the *cacique* to task if he is failing in his ceremonial duties."[59] Within the last few years, the pueblo declared a *cacique* senile and removed him from office. In such cases, where a *cacique* leaves office without naming a successor, the war captains (the war captain and his lieutenant) select the new *cacique*.

Officers. Day-to-day Cochiti affairs are in the hands of six officers: the war captain and his lieutenant, the governor and his lieutenant, and the fiscale and his lieutenant. The functions of these various executives were—and remain—quite different. Traditionally, the war captains, appointed by the head of the Flint Society, who is also the *cacique*, were responsible for deciding the location of the village and they led the village in resisting attack. In addition, then and now, they supervised the ceremonial life of the community and were responsible for the preservation of tribal lore. Those who divulged tribal secrets were punished by the war captains.[60]

The governor and lieutenant governor, traditionally appointed by the head of the Giant Society, and more recently by the *cacique*, have responsibility for civil affairs and in particular for relations with the world outside the pueblo. These positions may be relatively recent innovations, perhaps introduced by the Spanish, as external affairs became increasingly complex and as outsiders either sought analogues to their own secular governing individuals or tried to bypass the religious structures of Cochiti governance.[61] Today, outsiders are referred to the governor, and most of the economic affairs of the pueblo go through him and the council of principales. He also organizes the labor in the community, and has the power to punish those who do not comply with his instructions. According to Lange, the governor makes decisions largely on precedent; if no precedent exists, he may refer the decision to the council, or turn to his fellow officers or the council for advice.[62]

The other two officers in the Cochiti system are the fiscale and the lieutenant fiscale, traditionally appointed by the head of the Shikame Society. Their primary duties have to do with the physical structure and operation of the church.[63] Dumarest argues that they, like the governors, may be a Spanish innovation—the institutionalization of the old position of servant to the village priests.[64] The fiscales appear to carry less prestige and influence than the war captains and the governors.

Both historically and today, all of these officers are appointed each December to one-year terms. On rare occasions, a particularly effective officer might be retained for a second year, in which case the entire slate of officers is retained. However, because service is both burdensome and without compensation, after two years in office incumbents are relieved so that they can recover economically.[65] All are men; none may belong to a medicine society.

The Council of Principales. The principales are all those who have served in one of the six major offices of the tribe, plus those who are currently serving. These people constitute the council. Membership is for life, barring misconduct, which apparently is rare. Goldfrank argues:

> It is difficult to state just how much power rests with the principales....They are essentially a body of consultants, the governor bringing various civil matters before them such as land renting and at times punishments and fines. They are informed by the war captain when a person seeks adoption by one of the clans or when a witch is to be tried. However, their sanction is of great importance, since they are honored members of the community, and it is doubtful whether the governor or war captain would act in direct opposition to their expressed will.[66]

Our own fieldwork suggests that this is still the case. Council and officers appear to turn to each other for advice or, in some cases, for decisions. Council decision making pursues consensus but settles for strong majorities; when the council is more or less evenly divided on an issue, it turns to the six officers, "who act as a sort of higher council, or ad hoc committee."[67] Similarly, both the governors and the war captains often look to the council for advice, and may even defer to it for a decision. In our own experience, when it comes to major decisions in secular, civil affairs, the governor typically looks to the council for guidance.

Law and Order. Judicial and enforcement functions at Cochiti appear to follow a pattern readily apparent in political organization: a separation of religious and secular affairs, with the governor as judge and enforcer in the secular realm, and the war captains in the religious realm. For example, as ownership of property developed in the late nineteenth and early twentieth centuries, a body of unwritten law grew up having to do with trespass, theft, and other offenses. Cases involving these crimes came largely to the governor for disposition.[68] At the same time, law enforcement often involves a wider circle, with each of the principals turning for advice or assistance to a different group of knowledgeable men. "The council actively participates in the secular phases, less openly in the ceremonial, their places being taken by the medicine men, headed by the *cacique*...."[69]

For example, accusations in the secular realm are presented to the governor. He reviews the case and makes a decision based on precedent. If he cannot reach a decision, he turns to his lieutenant and other members of the council. They assemble, question witnesses as well as the accuser and accused, and eventually make a decision, which is announced by the governor.

Summary

At least within the documented record, there is remarkable temporal continuity in Cochiti political organization. That organization draws a clear separation between secular and sacred affairs—yet, through the appointment process, also bridges them. It concentrates a great deal of power in the theocrat—yet, through the power of the war captains and the injunction against direct involvement in secular affairs, also constrains him. The theocracy at Cochiti is remarkably crisp and formal in its constitutional constraints on the use of political power for rent-seeking purposes, and in the checks and balances that hold the government to a third-party role.

Conclusions

As Merilee S. Grindle suggests in Chapter 1, the issue for economic development is not too much state versus too little state, but the presence or absence of a capable state. Following North and others, we have argued that this is fundamentally a matter of the design of governing institutions. We see institutional capability as having more than one dimension, however, and we hypothesize that economic development requires effective and legitimate government. "Effective" here has referred to government in its role as the enforcer of the rules of the game by which the successful society channels its resources and energy into productive endeavors. Fulfillment of this role requires that wasteful rent-seeking be shut down, and that the instrument of government be confined to the role of a disinterested third-party enforcer of the rules of the game. Effective government must also be legitimate, though. That is, as a society's preeminent public good, its authority must be supported by culturally embedded norms that regulate free riding and defections.

American Indian tribes on U.S. reservations, like developing nations around the world, are now struggling with the problems of sovereign self-government. A few tribes have begun to emerge from a pattern of underdevelopment and poverty. These tribes are solving the problems of getting institutions right. However, because tribes differ so much culturally one from the other, the formal governmental structures that are legitimate for one tribe may not be so for another. As a result, tribes with the same governmental form perform differently in the development arena; these differences can be explained by differences in the underlying social contract regarding the norms of legitimate authority. In some cases, such as the Flathead in Montana and Cochiti Pueblo in New Mexico, tribes operate under drastically different political systems—from democracy to theocracy—but perform well economically. The evidence reviewed here indicates that differences in the cultural norms of legitimacy that make up a society's social contract make it necessary to use different governmental structures to solve the common problems of sustaining economic development.

Notes

We are indebted to Tanya Kean, Manley Begay, Karl Eschbach, Miriam Jorgensen, Jonathan Taylor, Tawhid Ali, the numerous Kennedy School master's thesis writers who have engaged in extensive fieldwork, and, most especially, the participating tribes in the Harvard project. This publication was made possible through support provided by the U.S. Agency for International Development under Cooperative Agreement No. DHR-0015-A-00-0031-00 to the Center of Institutional Reform and the Informal Sector (IRIS) and administered by the Office of Economic and Institutional Reform, Center for Economic Growth, Bureau for Global Programs, Field Support and Research.

1   See Douglass C. North, *Structure and Change in Economic History* (New York: Norton, 1981); Douglass C. North, *Institutions, Institutional Change, and Economic Performance* (Cambridge: Cambridge University Press, 1990); also, Robert D. Putnam, *Making Democracy Work: Civic Traditions in Modern Italy* (Princeton, NJ: Princeton University Press, 1992); Mancur

Olson, *The Rise and Decline of Nations* (New Haven: Yale University Press, 1982), and Robert Bates, "Contra Contractarianism: Some Reflections on the New Institutionalism," *Politics and Society* 16 (1988): 387–401. In addition, see World Bank, *Adjustment in Africa: Reform, Results, and the Road Ahead* (New York: Oxford University Press, 1994), and World Bank, *World Development Report 1991: The Challenge of Development* (New York: Oxford University Press, 1991); also Grindle and Hilderbrand, Chapter 2 of this volume.

2   World Bank, *Adjustment in Africa*, 61.

3   North, *Institutions*, and many others.

4   Thomas Hobbes, *Leviathan: The matter, forme, and power of a common wealth, ecclesiastical and civil* (London: Printed for Andrew Crooke, 1651).

5   North, *Institutions*, quoted in Putnam's, *Making Democracy Work*, 165.

6   Putnam, *Making Democracy Work*, 166.

7   Stephen Cornell and Joseph P. Kalt, "Culture and Institutions as Public Goods: American Indian Economic Development as a Problem of Collective Action," in Terry L. Anderson, ed., *Property Rights and Indian Economies*, (Lanham, MD: Rowman and Littlefield Publishers, Inc., 1992), 33.

8   North, *Institutions*.

9   North, *Structure and Change in Economic History*; Douglass C. North, "Ideology and Political/Economic Institutions," *Cato Journal* (Spring/Summer, 1988), 15–28; and North, *Institutions*, and Arthur T. Denzau and Douglass C. North, "Shared Mental Models: Ideologies and Institutions," Center for the Study of Political Economy (unpublished) March 3, 1993.

10 Putnam, *Making Democracy Work*. See also Bates, "Contra-Contractarianism: Some Reflections on the New Institutionalism."

11 James Coleman, *Foundations of Social Theory* (Cambridge: Harvard University Press, 1990); Jon Elster, *The Cement of Society* (Cambridge: Cambridge University Press, 1989); North, "Ideology and Political/Economic Institutions," and Bates, "Contra-Contractarianism."

12 Basil Davidson, *The Black Man's Burden: Africa and the Curse of the Nation-State* (New York: New York Times Books, 1992).

13 Robert M. Axelrod, *The Evolution of Cooperation* (New York: Basic Books, 1984).

14 Ken Binmore, *Game Theory and the Social Contract: Playing Fair* (Cambridge: MIT Press, 1994).

15 See especially Jerome Barkow, Leda Cosmides, and John Tooby, eds., *The Adapted Mind* (New York: Oxford University Press, 1992); Cosmides and

Tooby, "Evolutionary Psychology and the Generation of Culture, Part II: A Computational Theory of Social Exchange," *Ethnology and Sociobiology* 10 (1989); also William F. Allman, *The Stone Age Present* (New York: Simon and Schuster, 1994) and Robert H. Frank, *Passions Within Reason* (New York: W.W. Norton & Co., 1988).

16 Just to make this sensitive point clear, this framework for understanding the origins and evolution of different social contracts does not involve reference to genetic or racial differences across social groups. It is, instead, founded on a theory of *cultural* evolution. Moreover, as detailed here and in prior research, the cases of highly successful American Indian societies demonstrate that there is no meaningful version of a stereotyping generalization of Indian culture as "backward" or otherwise impeding of economic development. Similarly, there is no evidence to support a stereotyping of Indian culture as uniformly "progressive." Notwithstanding both benevolent and malevolent stereotyping, and just as with other societies, there is no single American Indian "culture;" there is only cultural—and social contract—heterogeneity. See also Robert Boyd and Peter J. Richerson, *Culture and the Evolutionary Process* (Chicago: University of Chicago Press, 1985); William H. Durham, *Coevolution: Genes, Culture and Human Diversity* (Palo Alto, CA: Stanford University Press, 1991); Stephen Cornell and Joseph P. Kalt, "Cultural Evolution and Constitutional Public Choice," in J. Long, ed., *Uncertainty and Economic Evolution: Essays in Honor of Armen Alchian*, (London: Routledge Press, forthcoming).

17 The language of discourse in American Indian affairs differs markedly from that used in international economic development, particularly as related to native peoples. Among U.S. native peoples on reservations, terms such as "American Indian," "tribe," and nation are generally the terms of preference. Out of respect for the overwhelming support and assistance of the tribes participating in our fieldwork, we employ such terms in our research and writing.

18 See, e.g., Stephen Cornell and Joseph P. Kalt, "Reloading the Dice: Improving the Chances for Economic Development on American Indian Reservations," in Stephen Cornell and Joseph P. Kalt, eds., *What Can Tribes Do? Strategies and Institutions in American Indian Economic Development* (Los Angeles: University of California Press, 1992); Cornell and Kalt, "Where Does Economic Development Really Come From? Constitutional Rule Among the Contemporary Sioux and Apache," *Economic Inquiry* 33 (July 1995); and "Where's the Glue? Institutional Bases of American Indian Economic Development," project report series, Harvard Project on American Indian Economic Development, Kennedy School of Government, Harvard University, Cambridge, 1991.

19 See Stephen B. Peterson, Chapter 6 this volume, who argues that one of the problems frequently encountered in African public administration is

a mismatch between the hierarchical organizational forms and processes ubiquitous in African (and non-African) governance (and favored by formal organization theory) and the network form more compatible with how African societies actually work.

20 Cornell and Kalt, "Reloading the Dice"; Cornell and Kalt, "Where Does Economic Development Really Come From?"

21 Formally, institutional legitimacy is the ability of the institutions to trigger supportive social sentiments. Presumably, in a path-dependent setting, legitimacy increases with a track record of effectiveness (see Seymour Martin Lipset, *Political Man: The Social Bases of Politics* [New York: Anchor Press, 1963]). Such a track record supports positive norms of the feasible. As North's focus on shared "ideologies" (with their normative overtones) suggests, legitimacy also requires concordance with normative norms concerning the right, proper and moral. In both cases, norms of political culture may evolve through "pre-adaption;" i.e., norms regarding sources of proper political power may originate in religious affairs, and be melded by "natural selection" into political institutions when preexisting institutions are subjected to environmental stress (Cornell and Kalt, "Cultural Evolution").

22 In fact, we review statistical evidence of precisely this consequence later on.

23 Cornell and Kalt, "Cultural Evolution."

24 Although the boundaries between tribal sovereignty and federal and state authority are contentious and somewhat unstable, the key elements are that tribes are subject to U.S. civil rights laws (including the Bill of Rights), tribes and tribally owned enterprises (but not private Indian enterprises or individuals) are free of nontribal taxation, state governments have very little regulatory authority on reservations, and congressionally mandated federal regulatory authority is often subject to lax enforcement. See Stephen Cornell and Joseph P. Kalt, "The Redefinition of Property Rights in American Indian Reservations: A Comparative Analysis of Native American Economic Development," in Lynma H. Legters and Fremont J. Lyden, eds., *American Indian Policy and Economic Development* (Westport, CT: Greenwood Press, 1994).

25 In the introductory chapter, Merilee S. Grindle suggests that the chapters in this volume for the most part take up cases in which decisions about *what* governments should be responsible for have already been made via political processes, and that the focus, therefore, is primarily on *how* governments carry out their responsibilities. In Indian Country, however, the peculiar history of imposed government means that *both* the what and the how of government often are at issue, with many Indian nations just beginning to engage these questions.

26 Stephen Cornell and Joseph P. Kalt, "Culture and Institutions as Public Goods: American Indian Economic Development as a Problem of Collective Action," in Terry L. Anderson, ed., *Property Rights and Indian Economies* (Lanham, MD: Rowman and Littlefield Publishers, Inc., 1992).

27 Cornell and Kalt, "Where's the Glue?"

28 Cornell and Kalt, "Culture and Institutions," and "Where's the Glue?"

29 Cornell and Kalt, "Where Does Economic Development Really Come From?" and "Where's the Glue?"

30 Charles C. Ragin, *The Comparative Method* (Berkeley: University of California Press, 1987).

31 The epistemologic standing of this kind of "make a prediction and throw open the curtain a single time" methodology is problematic. As Gould has documented at length in the case of Charles Darwin, the ability of a theory to predict what lies behind a single curtain in a world of multiple possible outcomes does provide scientific knowledge. See, for example, S. J. Gould, *Hen's Teeth and Horse's Toes* (New York: W.W. Norton & Co., 1983), especially Chapter 9.

32 Stuart A. Chalfant, "Aboriginal Territories of the Flathead, Pend d'Oreille and Kutenai Indians of Western Montana," in David A. Horr, ed., *Interior Salish and Eastern Washington Indians*, vol. II (New York: Garland Press, 1974) 25–116; Olga Weydemeyer Johnson, *Flathead and Kootenay: The Rivers, the Tribes and the Region's Traders* (Glendale, CA: The Arthur H. Clark Company, 1969).

33 Chalfant, "Aboriginal Territories."

34 John Fahey, *The Flathead Indians* (Norman, OK: University of Oklahoma Press, 1974); Ronald L. Trosper, "Native American Boundary Maintenance: the Flathead Indian Reservation, Montana, 1860–1970," *Ethnicity* 3, no. 3 (September 1976): 256–274.

35 Charles H. Lange, "Cochiti Pueblo," in Alfonso Ortiz, ed., *Handbook of North American Indians* (Washington, DC: Smithsonian Institution, 1979), 366–378; Esther Schiff Goldfrank, *The Social and Ceremonial Organization of Cochiti*, Memoirs of the American Anthropological Association no. 33 (Menasha, WI: American Anthropological Association, 1927); Albert H. Schroeder, "Rio Grande Ethnohistory," in Alfonso Ortiz, ed., *New Perspectives on the Pueblos* (Albuquerque, NM: University of New Mexico Press, 1972), 42–70.

36 Not to mention human capital. Crow high-school graduation rates, for example, significantly exceed the national reservation average.

37 See also Cornell and Kalt, "The Redefinition of Property Rights," and "Where's the Glue?"

38 James J. Lopach, Margery Hunter Brown, and Richmond L. Clow, *Tribal Government Today: Politics on Montana Indian Reservations* (Boulder, CO: Westview Press, 1990); Chalfant, "Aboriginal Territories of the Flathead."

39 Edward P. Dozier, *The Pueblo Indians of North America* (Norman, OK: University of Oklahoma Press, 1970).

40 Lopach, Brown, and Clow, *Tribal Government Today.*

41 Cornell and Kalt, "The Redefinition of Property Rights."

42 Cornell and Kalt, "The Redefinition of Property Rights."

43 Lopach, Brown, and Clow, *Tribal Government Today.*

44 Lopach, Brown, and Clow, *Tribal Government Today.*

45 Cornell and Kalt, "The Redefinition of Property Rights."

46 Harry Holbert Turney-High, *The Flathead Indians of Montana*, Memoirs of the American Anthropological Association No. 48 (Menasha, WI: American Anthropological Association, 1937); Peter Ronan, *History of the Flathead Indians* (Minneapolis: Ross & Haines, 1890).

47 Charles H. Lange, *Cochiti: A New Mexico Pueblo, Past and Present* (Albuquerque, NM: University of New Mexico Press, 1990 [1959]), 191.

48 Goldfrank, *The Social and Ceremonial Organization of Cochiti*, 25.

49 Lange, *Cochiti: A New Mexico Pueblo.*

50 Leslie A. White, "A Comparative Study of Keresan Medicine Societies," *Proceedings of the 23rd International Congress of Americanists, 1928,* New York (1930):604–619, cited in Lange, *Cochiti: A New Mexico Pueblo.*

51 Goldfrank, *The Social and Ceremonial Organization of Cochiti*; Lange, *Cochiti: A New Mexico Pueblo.*

52 Some system of alteration appears to have operated over most of the nineteenth and early twentieth centuries (see Goldfrank, *The Social and Ceremonial Organization of Cochiti*). The system was lost for a time in the 1920s; from 1920 to 1946, all but two yearly governors came from the Turquoise kiva, leading to great dissension within the tribe. Since 1947, Cochiti has returned to yearly alteration in the kiva membership of senior officers (see Lange, *Cochiti: A New Mexico Pueblo*).

53 Lange, *Cochiti: A New Mexico Pueblo.*

54 Lange, *Cochiti: A New Mexico Pueblo*, 252.

55 Goldfrank, *The Social and Ceremonial Organization of Cochiti*, 40.

56 Noel Dumarest, *Notes on Cochiti, New Mexico*, Memoirs of the American Anthropological Association 6, 3 (Menasha, WI: American Anthropological Association, 1919), 197, emphasis added.

57 Lange, *Cochiti: A New Mexico Pueblo*, 252.

58 Lange, "Cochiti Pueblo," 373.

59 Lange, *Cochiti: A New Mexico Pueblo*, 200.

60 Lange, *Cochiti: A New Mexico Pueblo.*

61 Lange, *Cochiti: A New Mexico Pueblo.*

62 Lange, *Cochiti: A New Mexico Pueblo.*

63 Lange, *Cochiti: A New Mexico Pueblo.*

64 Dumarest, "Notes on Cochiti."

65 Goldfrank, *The Social and Ceremonial Organization of Cochiti*; Lange, *Cochiti: A New Mexico Pueblo.*

66 Goldfrank, *The Social and Ceremonial Organization of Cochiti*, 27; see also Lange, *Cochiti: A New Mexico Pueblo.*

67 Lange, *Cochiti: A New Mexico Pueblo*, 215.

68 Goldfrank, *The Social and Ceremonial Organization of Cochiti.*

69 Lange, *Cochiti: A New Mexico Pueblo*, 220.

11 ESTABLISHING FISCAL DISCIPLINE

THE CASH BUDGET IN ZAMBIA

Bruce R. Bolnick

Before price inflation can feasibly be phased out, and before the capital market is opened for free borrowing and lending, the first and most obvious need is to balance the central government's finances.

—*Ronald McKinnon*[1]

Fiscal discipline is widely regarded as the foundation for successful stabilization in developing countries. Yet the literature offers few clues about *how* to build the institutional capacity needed "to balance the central government's finances" in a high–inflation country where fiscal mismanagement has become the established practice. A survey of the literature on macroeconomic reforms by Michael Roemer and Steven Radelet, for example, makes no mention of institutional impediments to prudent fiscal policy.[2] Likewise, Dornbusch's checklist of budget reforms neglects the institutional and organizational problems relating to budget management.[3] Selowsky points out this gap in the analysis and notes that "unless governments support the fiscal adjustment with appropriate institutional reform and coordination, the adjustment will not be perceived as sustainable…."[4] In the political economy literature, Grindle and Thomas have emphasized that the implementation process determines the sustainability of reforms.[5] Krueger takes us closer to the heart of the matter by noting that "establishing bureaucratic machinery and mechanisms…to carry out desired policies is not as simple as had been assumed."[6] Still, one is hard pressed to find a direct response to the challenge posed by Nellis, who wrote, "The next and most crucial step…is to specify precise operational methods and tools by which to improve performance in institutions."[7]

This chapter responds to this challenge to the policy literature by examining the mechanism adopted in Zambia in 1993 to restore fiscal discipline.[8] The key institutional innovation was the introduction of a cash constraint on government spending. The cash budget embodied a pledge that no expenditure would be financed by borrowing from the Bank of Zambia—that is, the government would no longer resort to printing money to cover expenses. Issuing new rules, however, does not ensure compliance. Supported organizational changes were needed to put the rules into effect. To this end, the Ministry of Finance and the Bank of Zambia created a joint committee to monitor fiscal and monetary conditions on a daily basis. The cash-budget mechanism provided the government with the capacity to curb fiscal deficits and prevent fiscal impulses from undermining monetary management, despite severe cash constraints for most of the first year. Equally important, the cash budget helped implant a *perception* that the fiscal regime was coming under control. The effort to enforce fiscal discipline paid off in lower inflation starting six months after the cash budget went into operation. Of course, progress toward stabilization was not costless; the treasury's strict cash diet led to severe cuts in real government operations, which were not handled efficiently. These problems need to be understood in order to gain a balanced picture of the reforms.

In broad terms, Zambia's decision to adopt the cash budget exemplifies what Bates calls a "surrendering of sovereignty," to limit executive discretion.[9] Bates views development policy as a multiperiod game between government executives and private players. The former choose between stabilizing policies and "defection" for opportunistic gains; the latter choose simply whether or not to invest. When the private players perceive a high risk of defection by policy makers, they withhold investment, leading to a low-level equilibrium trap. To escape this prisoner's dilemma outcome, policy makers can "seek means of tying their own hands" by instituting reforms that constrain their ability to defect.

In terms of Bates' model, the cash budget mechanism in Zambia was introduced to serve as a constraint that would prevent inflationary financing of government expenditures by the central bank. Many countries, of course, have institutional rules that serve the same purpose.[10] What sets Zambia's experience apart is that the key economic organs of government had lost the capacity to manage macroeconomic policy effectively during two decades of economic decline. Thus, capacity building was a core requirement of Zambia's economic stabilization program.

The main thread of this chapter is a description of the steps taken to implement the cash budget, along with a description of the effects of the new system. It explores how a key change in the rules of the game contributed critically to the stabilization program; how these rules were institutionalized into the daily routine of macroeconomic management; how the system gained legitimacy through strong support from top echelons of government and through adaptations that helped it to survive recurrent budget crises; and finally, how the system bred side effects that affected the subsequent dynamics of reform.

The chapter also touches on several technical points that are worth highlighting:

■ The decision to introduce the cash budget emerged from a process that conforms to the state-interests crisis model as described by Grindle and Thomas.[11]

■ Although not universally applicable, the simple fiscal rule that was adopted for the cash budget is appropriate for situations characterized by sharply accelerating inflation and a lack of public confidence in policy management.

■ The cash budget required a measure of flexibility; a brittle system would have shattered quickly under the strains of the adjustment process.

■ Perhaps most important, implementing fiscal control was complicated by poor revenue performance; yet the expenditure constraints served to focus attention on the need for reforms on the revenue side of the budget.

The next two sections provide background information on the context for Zambia's policy reforms and on the macroeconomic principles underlying the cash budget rules, respectively. The core of the chapter is a description of how the cash budget was introduced, how it was designed, and how the government established an effective monitoring system for tracking the treasury's cash position and resolving problems as they arose. This description is followed by an evaluation of the system's effectiveness as a tool for fiscal control, and an elaboration of some notable side effects. The chapter concludes with a summary and assessment, including comments on the replicability of Zambia's approach.

ZAMBIA'S BUDGET PRIOR TO 1993

During the 1980s, government budget deficits in Zambia averaged 10.3 percent of gross domestic product (GDP).[12] In 1991, the Movement for Multiparty Democracy (MMD) was voted into office on a platform of stabilization and reform. By this time, the financing of fiscal deficits in Zambia had led to an external debt that ranked as one of the largest in the world (per capita), along with triple-digit inflation.[13] The new government set out to implement a wide range of reforms, and curing inflation was a top priority. By the second half of 1992, some progress had been made in reducing the budget gap. Nonetheless, inflation accelerated because of continued rapid growth of the money supply, combined with near doubling of velocity.[14] The latter statistic signaled waning public confidence in the MMD's ability to manage the reform program. Strong action was needed to avert a potential collapse into hyperinflation.

The MMD budget for 1992 sought to reduce the fiscal deficit to 1.9 percent of GDP, compared to 7.4 percent of GDP in 1991. The target for M2 growth was 30 percent, compared to 98 percent the previous year.[15] Unfortunately, fiscal policy was bedeviled by the effects of a severe drought. Drought-related expenditures exceeded kwacha revenues from dispensing emergency supplies of grain. Nonetheless, the deficit for 1992 was only slightly over target, at 2.2 percent of estimated GDP.[16] The denominator here, however, was greatly inflated because prices rose by 191 percent in 1992 (December to December) on money-supply growth of 99 percent.

The problem was not just the drought. On the contrary, the new government found that it lacked the capacity for effective macroeconomic management. During the last decade of Kenneth Kaunda's government, real wages for civil servants had eroded so severely that morale in the civil service was poor, control systems had lapsed, and a lack of professionalism pervaded the key organizations.

A few examples suffice to demonstrate the scope of the problem. The Bank of Zambia had not produced audited accounts since 1988; its accounting system was plagued with human and computer errors. Monthly reports on reserve money and net credit to government were subject to adjustments that sometimes exceeded 10 percent of the budget for the full year. Similar problems beset economic statistics produced by the central statistical office. At the Ministry of Finance, no one regularly reconciled internal reports on fundings and revenues with accounting records from the Bank of Zambia. No useful statistics were available on obligations incurred by operating ministries. Monthly budget records did not include domestic interest expenses, which were simply met by the Bank of Zambia through printing money. No one was aware that the commercial banks used for transferring tax revenues from field collection points were routinely holding the funds for six weeks. The budget office tried strenuously to restrain expenditure during 1992, but it lacked the capacity for effective control, particularly as high inflation transformed the approved budget into a work of fiction.

In his 1993 budget address, the minister of finance emphasized these problems:

> Although Government departments were advised to be prudent, they always knew that additional expenditures would be funded by supplementary appropriations. If revenues were adequate to cover this expenditure, well and good; if not, the difference was financed through the central bank or additional borrowing abroad.... Although we intended otherwise last year, we were unable to break out of this pattern. When the Government ran short of money it turned to the central bank…That approach simply cannot continue.[17]

The minister went on to state that the government was introducing a cash-budget system for 1993 to regain control of fiscal operations. By ending the entrenched practice of funding expenditures regardless of the funds available, the cash budget became a key instrument in the implementation of Zambia's stabilization program.

The actual decision on the cash budget conformed to the state-interests model described by Grindle and Thomas.[18] This model suggests that policy elites assume a leadership role, with prominent support from technical advisors in shaping decisions, particularly during crisis, when stakes are high and international pressures are strong. Krueger also observes that a crisis deals the technocrats a strong hand by "weakening normal political resistances."[19]

In the present case, the major players were the minister and the permanent secretary of finance, the budget director, and technical advisors (including expatriates, who first identified the cash budget as one possible option), with pressure from the International Monetary Fund (IMF). The decision to adopt the cash budget was not widely discussed and it came rather late in the budget process. In fact, there was no mention of the cash budget in drafts of the budget address prepared in mid-December 1992. Yet by the end of that month, meetings were called to put the plan into action. This was the first time most bureaucrats in the Ministry of Finance heard about the cash budget. Their general reaction was support for the concept of not printing money to pay bills, but deep skepticism about the feasibility of adhering to a cash constraint.[20] This skepticism might have condemned the effort to failure, had top-echelon officials not responded strongly to reports from the monitoring committee on problems with the system.

PRIMER ON THE MACROECONOMICS OF THE CASH BUDGET

The literature on fiscal policy provides justifications for a government to "print money," to a limited extent, as a source of finance.[21] The main point, expounded initially by Phelps, is that government can minimize the deadweight loss from raising finance by setting the welfare cost of the inflation tax, at the margin, equal to the efficiency loss from other tax instruments.[22] If the demand for real money balances is inelastic, this rule warrants a substantial amount of inflationary financing. Even with a zero-inflation target there is room for the government to pay bills by "printing money," to the extent that the demand for real money balances is growing. To this extent, an increase in the money supply generates no inflation.[23] It is not always valid, then, to equate prudent fiscal management with zero borrowing from the central bank. Indeed, many Zambians questioned the advisability of adopting such an exceptional control mechanism. Critics pointed out that many governments routinely spend more than they raise in revenue. The answer to such critics, in McKinnon's words, is that "deficit-prone" developing countries "have used up any credibility that some of them may once have had…." As a consequence, McKinnon concludes that "strict budget balance" is the foundation for a successful adjustment program.[24]

Thus, moderate deficits are compatible with macroeconomic stability in countries where saving rates are ample, the demand for real-money balances is growing, financial markets are deep enough to absorb government debt without an extreme increase in interest rates, and the public has confidence that government will prevent the situation from spinning out of control. The same norms do *not* apply to countries with triple-digit inflation, weak expenditure controls, low saving rates, falling demand for domestic real-money balances, shallow financial markets, a collapsing economy, and a crisis of confidence in government's ability to keep its fiscal house in order. Under such circumstances, strict discipline is instrumental for gaining the credibility needed for stabilization.[25] Also, where the fiscal organization lacks effective *operational* controls, a clear-cut rule—no funding if there is no money in the bank—is easier to invoke than a rule that sanctions unfunded expenditures in some discretionary circumstances.

One secret of success among Asia's "tigers," old and new, is consistent application of conservative fiscal and monetary policies.[26] Singapore, for example, forswears borrowing from the monetary authority. Indonesia's disinflation in the 1960s was based on a balanced budget rule that precluded domestic borrowing by the treasury.[27] Bolivia "eliminated its flow budget deficit" in 1985 to bring hyperinflation under control.[28] Argentina, likewise, passed a law in 1991 stipulating that the central bank could issue peso reserve money only to the extent that it was backed by foreign-exchange reserves.[29] Such precedents were invoked in order to gain support for the decision to adopt cash-budget procedures in Zambia.

The purpose of the cash budget was to stop inflation. The linkages here operate through monetary effects of fiscal transactions. At the most basic level, high inflation is unquestionably fueled by rapid growth of the money supply (say, M2). In turn, rapid growth of M2 can be traced to excessive injections of reserve money (RM), and fiscal transactions are primary determinants of changes in RM.[30] To understand how the rules of the cash budget were linked to reserve money, consider the following effects of government transactions at the Bank of Zambia:

- When line ministries make payments from their accounts at the Bank of Zambia, there is a corresponding *injection* of RM into the economy.

- When tax revenues or proceeds from the recovery of government-financed crop loans are deposited to the Bank of Zambia, there is a corresponding *withdrawal* of RM.

■ When the treasury honors maturing treasury bills (held outside the bank of Zambia), the payment *injects* RM; similarly, when the treasury receives payment for newly tendered T-bills, there is a corresponding *withdrawal* of RM.

■ Transfers between government accounts at the Bank of Zambia, as well as transfers between the government and the Bank of Zambia, have no direct impact on RM in circulation.

■ When the treasury purchases foreign exchange from the Bank of Zambia to pay foreign debt service, kwacha balances are transferred from a treasury account at the Bank of Zambia to an account in the name of the Bank of Zambia itself; the transfer has no direct effect on RM. There may be an indirect effect if the Bank of Zambia would otherwise have sold the foreign exchange, withdrawing kwacha from circulation. Then the treasury transaction precludes a withdrawal of RM and the net effect is a higher level of RM in circulation.

■ When the Bank of Zambia credits the treasury with the kwacha counterpart to an inflow of donor funds, the transfer of kwacha from to the treasury has no effect on RM. If the treasury spends the kwacha domestically, however, then there is a corresponding *injection* of RM. If the Bank of Zambia sells the donor-sourced foreign exchange to the market in exchange for kwacha, then the net effect on RM is neutral.

■ A loan or overdraft facility to the treasury from the Bank of Zambia takes the form of an account transfer that has no immediate effect on RM. When the treasury spends such funds domestically, there is an *injection* of RM into the economy.

In general, kwacha flows from the domestic economy to a government account at the Bank of Zambia withdraw reserve money from circulation, whereas kwacha outflows to the domestic economy inject reserve money into circulation. These technicalities relating fiscal transactions to reserve money dictated the design of the cash budget.

Of course, treasury transactions are not the sole source of changes in reserve money. Others include: purchases and sales of foreign exchange by the Bank of Zambia, loans and loan recoveries by the central bank, and other Bank of Zambia receipts and expenditures. Such transactions are called "quasi-fiscal" if they are undertaken by the central bank in lieu of budget expenditures.[31] Bringing such quasi-fiscal transactions under control proved to be of great importance to the eventual success of the stabilization effort in Zambia. This does not alter the fact, however, that the Bank of Zambia could not effectively control the growth of reserve money without careful management of treasury transactions.

Introduction of the Cash Budget

To stop the treasury from "printing money" to meet its obligations, the permanent secretary at the Ministry of Finance issued a standing instruction to the Bank of Zambia stating that funding requests from the treasury should not be honored, and debit transactions should not be posted to a treasury account, unless the treasury had sufficient cash in the bank to cover the expenses. The instruction defined "cash in the bank" as a net credit balance in the treasury's "composite position," which consisted of the consolidated balance in specified accounts.[32] In essence, cash outflows on behalf of the treasury could not exceed cash inflows. The treasury was enjoined from borrowing from the Bank of Zambia or running a net overdraft for the year at the bank, with exceptions. This rule still permitted a deficit at any point in the budget year if cash were raised in advance by borrowing from entities outside the central bank, by selling treasury bills, for example.

The Ministry of Finance further instructed the Bank of Zambia to apply a similar cash constraint to each line-ministry account. No payment on behalf of a line ministry could be posted without funds in its account to cover the debit. Thus, line ministries were denied overdraft facilities, even if this meant that the Bank of Zambia had to return government checks to third parties because of insufficient funds.

These rules were a major departure from past practices in Zambia, which had been reckless in terms of expanding reserve money. The new rules also represented a major departure from normal practices in most other countries, where budgetary transactions routinely take place without regard to *daily* cash balances. In a country with a well-run budget system, imposing a daily cash constraint could actually hamper the timely release of fundings and the orderly provision of public services.

The rules for the cash budget were established by a written instruction from the Ministry of Finance, so they could be amended or overridden by subsequent instructions. Alterations did occur from time to time. The surprising thing—in view of the extreme budget exigencies that ensued—is that breaches were limited in frequency and magnitude. Why such restraint? I see four explanations.

First, the foundations for the cash budget were sturdier than the letter of instruction by itself. The policy was endorsed by the cabinet, trumpeted publicly in the budget address, and approved by the national assembly as part of the budget program. Although it was left to the Ministry of Finance to determine the exact rules, major departures could not be introduced at whim.

Second, even critics of the harsh new fiscal constraints, inside and outside of the government, generally agreed that the government needed to stop "printing money" as a default source of funds whenever payments fell due. This consensus was the product of bitter lessons learned over the previous decade of stabilization failures. In 1993, the need for restraint was felt more keenly than ever because the economy was teetering on the edge of hyperinflation.

Third, the new government was consciously engaged in a struggle for credibility. The stakes were high because credibility was a key to reviving the economy and sustaining donor support. By pre-announcing the cash budget as a foundation of stabilization policy, the government created a situation in which it could not violate the rules without incurring a heavy cost economically and politically. Unlike the previous government, the MMD claimed legitimacy on the basis of its promise to bring democratic freedoms and economic reforms.

Finally, the budget office found that it was convenient (usually) to adhere to the cash rule in order to cope with the constant barrage of pressures to spend. "Yes, but there is no money" became an effective control device, especially when combined with the slippery-slope argument: if we violate the rule for your ministry, how can we then deny extra funds for other ministries?

In short, the heart of the reform was not the change in rules, per se, but the political *commitment* to the cash budget and the organizational innovations that were put in place to *implement* the cash-budget rules. It is tempting to say that the system would have been more credible and more effective had the constraints been written into law rather than being promulgated by an administrative directive. In view of Zambia's weak record of law enforcement, however, encoding the rule in a statute would hardly have improved its credibility.[33] For with or without a formal statute, the credibility game could only be won by consistent implementation of the fiscal controls.

Flexibility in the Rules

A pure cash rule would preclude any injection of reserve money attributable to fiscal transactions. It would encompass all payouts by the Bank of Zambia on behalf of the government; it would disregard all transfers between government accounts at the central bank; it would treat matching debits and credits to different government accounts as a wash; and it would prohibit bridge financing by the Bank of Zambia. A pure rule of this sort would have been too brittle to withstand the pressures created by the austerity program, and also more difficult to control. Zambia's cash budget modified these strict conditions to provide a measure of resiliency to the system, without undermining the essential controls over fiscal injections of reserve money. For present purposes, three such modifications are worth noting.

First, the cash-budget instructions allowed the Bank of Zambia to provide a "cash cushion" to the treasury each January because most government accounts were zeroed out at the end of each budget year, eliminating carryover balances. Yet basic government operations in January could not be delayed until sufficient revenue collections for the new year reached the Bank of Zambia. The cash cushion facilitated the orderly release of basic budget fundings in mid-January. In principle, this start-up fund should have been matched at year-end by unused cash balances. In fact, the arrangement called for the government to repay the loan at an earlier target date. The cash cushion did not create a bulge in reserve money. Its impact on reserve money was offset by the absence of spending by line ministries from carryover balances during the first two weeks of the year.

Second, the Bank of Zambia was authorized under the cash-budget rules, starting in 1994, to insulate domestic fundings from the effects of poorly synchronized external cash flows. Budget activities in 1993 were often handcuffed by external debt-service obligations that were unmatched by timely inflows of donor funds. Such uncovered debits reduced the treasury's composite position to the point of blocking ordinary fundings, despite a substantial credit balance in the treasury's main budget account. Thus, transitory net outflows for foreign debt service precluded the use of domestic revenues for funding government operations.

The insulating mechanism introduced in 1994 took the form of a contingent instruction to the Bank of Zambia, to provide a bridge loan to cover the kwacha cost of foreign exchange for essential debt-service payments, *if* prior donor inflows were insufficient to cover the expense.[34] Repayment of any such bridge loan then had first claim on subsequent balance-of-payments support. This device enabled the treasury to honor essential debt-service obligations without depleting the cash needed for other budgetary operations.

How did this device affect reserve money? The bridge loan itself is an internal kwacha transfer at the central bank, which has no direct effect on reserve money. When the treasury uses such funds to purchase foreign exchange from the Bank of Zambia, there is a reverse transfer, which also has no direct effect on reserve money. There may be an indirect effect if the Bank of Zambia would otherwise have sold the foreign exchange to the market to withdraw reserve money from circulation. If the foreign exchange is held at the central bank anyway, the net effect on reserve money is nil and the bridge loan did not compromise the macroeconomic objectives.

When donor funds arrived *before* the scheduled date for an essential debt-service payment, the Bank of Zambia was instructed to hold the kwacha counterpart funds in a suspense account rather than promptly crediting the treasury. The arrival of donor funds at the central bank does not withdraw reserve money from circulation; so crediting the treasury with the extra cash would invite a net fiscal injection of reserve money—precisely what the cash budget was meant to prevent. Instead, the kwacha counterpart funds were credited to the treasury only as the funds were needed to honor an external debt-service obligation. Then, the Bank of Zambia posted a kwacha credit to the respective donor account on behalf of the treasury, while debiting the external debt-service account to cover the cost of the foreign exchange. This arrangement leaves unchanged both the treasury's composite balance and reserve money. If the donor-supplied foreign exchange were sold to the market, then a corresponding kwacha amount could be credited to the treasury to support domestic expenditures. Under the IMF program for 1994, such kwacha funds were earmarked for domestic debt-service obligations. When the Bank of Zambia sells donor-sourced foreign exchange to the market and the treasury uses the kwacha proceeds to redeem treasury bills, the result is neutral with respect to reserve money.

A third modification to strict cash budgeting dealt with *domestic* debt service. Each week the government had to honor maturing securities plus interest payments on outstanding bonds. The cash-budget rules could not hamper these constitutional obligations—not to mention the fact that a default would have spoiled the government's credibility. Debits for domestic debt service occasionally pushed the treasury's composite balance into the red, particularly when revenues were running well below target. On such occasions, the payout was permitted despite violating the cash-budget constraint. Other fundings, however, were then halted until a positive net balance was restored by revenue inflows. The technicalities outlined here illustrate how the system was made more flexible, without greatly compromising the objective of ending fiscal infusions of reserve money.

Monitoring and Control

In Zambia, as elsewhere, it is one thing to announce a policy and draft an instruction, and quite another matter to carry it out. How was the cash budget put into operation?

The decision to implement the cash basis was made in December 1992, effective for 1993. This radical change in the budget rules required major adjustments in many of the reporting systems, over a time frame of just a few weeks. Key units were instructed to develop *daily* reports for delivery to a newly formed monitoring committee comprised of officials and advisors from the Ministry of Finance and the Bank of Zambia. The Joint Data Monitoring Committee (JDMC) was charged with ensuring effective implementation of the cash-based budget; proper management of reserve money; and overall adherence of macroeconomic policy to program targets. The committee was assigned to meet daily to scrutinize fiscal and monetary data, analyze near-term prospects, identify substantive problems, discuss alternative solutions, and recommend appropriate remedies.[35] The committee submitted weekly written reports to the minister, the governor, an interministerial technical group on economic policy, and other top officials. Thus, critical issues were promptly reported to the top economic policy makers via the JDMC.

The most pressing initial task was to improve the data reports. Virtually all of the data reaching the JDMC proved to be unreliable and inconsistent at first, including Bank of Zambia accounting records. Over several months, the data steadily improved as problems were identified by the committee and fixed by the responsible organizational units. For monitoring the cash budget, the key reports included: (1) a daily summary of the treasury's cash position showing balances for major government accounts as well as the composite position, as defined in the letter of instruction from the Ministry of

Finance; (2) daily inquiry statements showing transactions in the major accounts; (3) reports from the Ministry of Finance on daily tax collections and funding approvals; and (4) a report on daily balances for all ministries and agencies. The Bank of Zambia provided daily reports on reserve money, along with less frequent reports on net banking-system claims on government and reports on treasury-bill transactions.[36] Later, the Bank of Zambia added reports on exchange rates, net international reserves, and sources and uses of foreign exchange.

The appendix presents a simplified version of the main table used for monitoring the cash budget. By reviewing these account statistics and other data reports on a daily basis, the JDMC could identify deviations from the cash budget, anticipate forthcoming cash problems, and recommend remedial actions. In the course of this work, the committee emerged as an active inside lobby promoting sound macroeconomic policy management.

MACROECONOMIC EFFECTS OF THE CASH BUDGET

With the strong support from top officers at the Ministry of Finance and the Bank of Zambia, the JDMC was reasonably effective as an instrument for implementing the cash budget. Outright breaches were uncommon and quickly spotted when they did occur. Figures 11-1 through 11-4 provide a quantitative picture of the outcome for the first year of the system's operation. Overall, the figures show that the cash budget provided the government with the capacity to curb fiscal deficits and prevent fiscal impulses from undermining monetary management, despite severe cash constraints for most of the year and several breaches of the rules. The effort to establish fiscal discipline paid off in lower inflation beginning six months after the cash budget went into operation.

Figure 11-1 shows that the government ran a primary cash surplus of K24 billion in 1993 in the treasury's main account.[37] This was a complete turnaround from past behavior. The previous year the main account ended with a *debit* balance equivalent to K69 billion at 1993 prices. The treasury's composite balance was positive most of the year, with the exception of a temporary shortfall at the end of May and a more serious breach at year-end. The cash deficit in May arose from a string of weeks when the treasury-bill tender failed to raise enough new cash to cover redemptions. On top of this, the bud-

FIGURE   11-1

Cash Balances, 1993

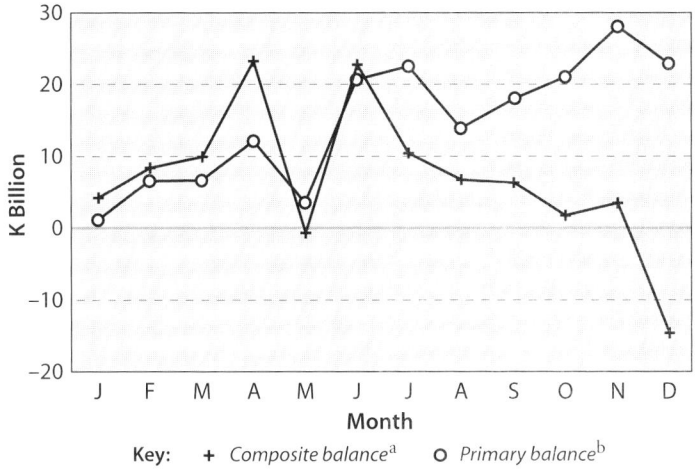

Key: + *Composite balance*[a]   o *Primary balance*[b]

[a]   The composite balance excludes temporary "excess" balances in donor-funds accounts.

[b]   The primary balance is proxied here by the balance in the treasury main account.

Source: Bank of Zambia, Ministry of Finance, and author's calculations.

get office engaged in a minor spending spree in response to a backlog of political pressures, after squeezing hard to achieve the IMF benchmarks for the end of April. Even so, this violation of the cash budget was more apparent than real. The slight negative balance was more than offset by net inflows from earlier T-bill sales, which had been buried in an account outside the composite balance (on the recommendation of the committee) for just this eventuality. In addition, line ministries were carrying large cash balances at the time. Hence, there was no net injection of reserve money from fiscal operations for the year to that date.

The more serious breach of the cash budget occurred in December. The root of the problem—a large shortfall in real revenues—is visible in Figure 11-2. By July, the treasury faced a cumulative revenue shortfall of 30 percent compared to the corresponding date for the previous budget year. The effect of poor tax collections was compounded by poor recovery of crop loans and delays in the disbursement of aid inflows. In the face of these revenue shortfalls, the cash constraint cast into sharp focus the problem of balancing competing claims for fiscal resources. A perpetual atmosphere of crisis sur-

FIGURE 11-2

Real Revenue, 1993

1992 Performance = 1.00[a]

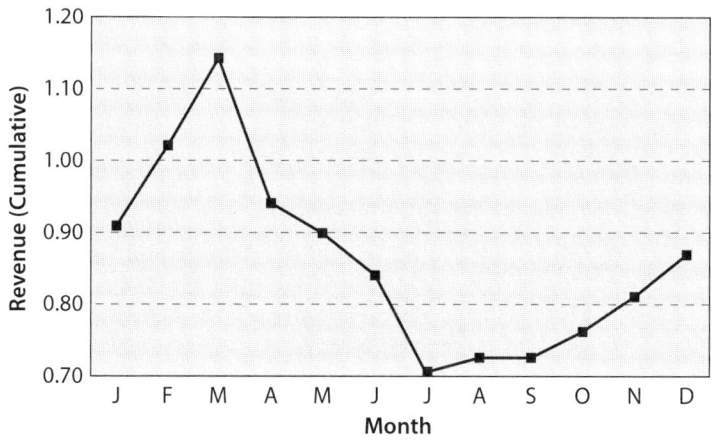

[a] The value below (above) 1.0 indicates that revenues to date are less (more) than corresponding revenues for 1992, after adjusting for CPI-inflation.

Source: Bank of Zambia, Ministry of Finance, and author's calculations.

rounded meetings of the JDMC and the budget office. The fiscal tri-
age necessitated by the cash budget won few friends, but it played a
vital role in averting inflationary responses. Two examples will provide a sense of the stresses confronting the treasury in 1993 and the
role of the cash budget in constraining the outcomes.

Crop Financing

The 1993 budget allotted K20 billion for maize marketing and crop
financing in the third and fourth quarters. When the time arrived,
there was not enough cash in the bank to meet the expense. In addition, plans to devolve more marketing responsibilities to private traders fell short of expectations because of the prevalence of extremely
high interest rates and an unstable exchange rate. By September, a
political crisis was at hand and a compromise was needed to prevent
a collapse of the cash budget. At the behest of the president, the Bank
of Zambia lent the treasury K5 billion—which no one expected to be
repaid. Another payout of K17 billion was deferred by issuing promissory notes to farmers at full market interest rates, redeemable the
following February. This device was terribly unpopular and widely

ridiculed, but it prevented a huge surge in reserve money just when inflation was starting visibly to fall. It also allowed the treasury to accommodate the payoff in the 1994 budget. On balance, the cash budget rules were bent by K5 billion, but the system averted a far greater loss of monetary control.

Civil Service Wages

The contract with the civil service union expired in April 1993. As negotiations for a new contract dragged on through midyear, inflation remained stubbornly high, partly because of price reforms and partly because of delays in gaining control of the nonbudgetary sources of reserve-money growth. The twelve-month inflation rate reached 226 percent in June 1993. With such figures in view, the union sought a wage increase in the range of 200 to 300 percent, backdated to April. Government negotiators (who themselves would be affected by the settlement) prepared a counteroffer that would have raised monthly wage costs by nearly 80 percent. At this point, the Ministry of Finance intervened by invoking the cash-budget constraint and arguing that the pending settlement would leave everyone worse off by fueling inflation. The president accepted the argument and delivered a televised speech to the nation on wage policy in July. The speech included this pertinent passage:

> With the introduction of the cash-based budget in January, we have achieved the discipline required to keep the budget under control….[T]he alternative of printing money to satisfy additional demands is a destructive path which has been tried, failed, and rejected.[38]

Ultimately, the wage settlement was scaled back to 50 percent, effective in August rather than April. This cut the budget cost for 1993 by nearly two-thirds. Unhappily, no measures were put in place to generate additional revenues before January 1994, so even the reduced wage settlement seriously depleted the government's cash position. Indeed, revenues continued to decline because of poor tax administration, tight money, and a concurrent appreciation of the kwacha, which diminished the base for trade taxes. Accentuating the cash squeeze, large net payouts were required to redeem domestic debt after mid-November, because the sale of new treasury bills did not cover maturing bills. Under the circumstances, adhering to the cash budget required draconian cuts in nonwage fundings. The treasury could not sustain the required degree of restraint. In an attempt to fund essential services without opening a floodgate in December, the Ministry of Finance instructed the Bank of Zambia to permit a net debit on the composite balance up to the amount of credit balances held by line ministries. After eleven months of operating under rigid restraint, the budget office took advantage of this latitude, leading to a year-end composite debit of K14 billion. By this time, however, inflation had already declined to a low plateau and the demand for kwacha money balances had begun to revive. In any case, the cash constraint was back in place on January 1 as a central element of the 1994 budget.

A major objective of the cash budget plan was to prevent fiscal decisions from causing rapid growth of reserve money. Figure 11-3 shows that treasury transactions actually generated a net withdrawal of reserve money until December. Contrary to expectations, this fiscal fix did not immediately stem the rapid growth of reserve money (though it certainly helped to prevent an even worse outcome). By early March, the stock of reserve money was above target by 25 percent. The JDMC identified the source of the problem as foreign-exchange operations of the central bank, which were not yet being monitored carefully. It took several weeks to confirm this conclusion

FIGURE 11-3
Monetary Impact Cumulative Change, 1993

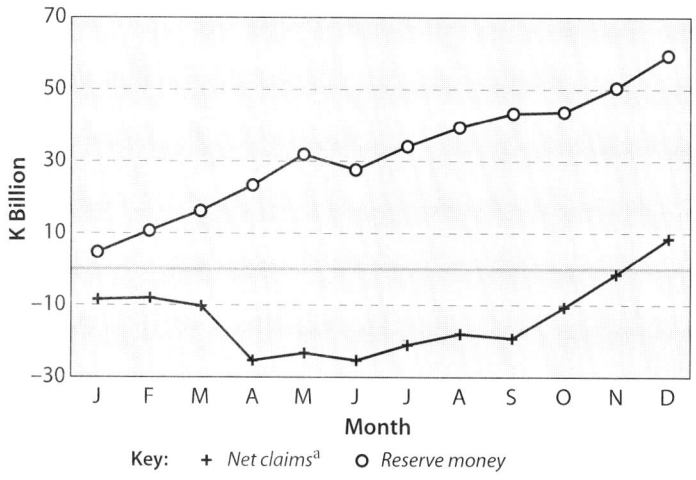

Key: **+** Net claims[a]   **O** Reserve money

[a] Net claims data exclude commercial bank current account balances at BOZ.

Source: Bank of Zambia, Ministry of Finance, and author's calculations.

and several more weeks to implement remedial action, involving a major change in energy-pricing policy. Because of initial inattention to quasi-fiscal transactions of the central bank, the expected macroeconomic benefits accruing from the cash budget were delayed five months.

By June, however, reserve money was under control. Figure 11-3 shows clearly the break in the trend after May. By August the inflation trend also broke. This is shown in Figure 11-4, which compares the twelve-month inflation trend to a moving average of two-month inflation rates (annualized). After peaking at nearly 400 percent, inflation declined precipitously in August. Thereafter, despite short-term ups and downs, the twelve-month inflation trend declined quickly and steadily.[39] By September 1994, twelve-month inflation was below 30 percent for the first time in more than a decade. Inflation for the last six months of 1994 was 22 percent (annualized). Without the cash budget, the stabilization program would not have held together through 1993 and 1994.

FIGURE 11-4
Inflation 1993–1994
2-Month versus 12-Month Trend[a]

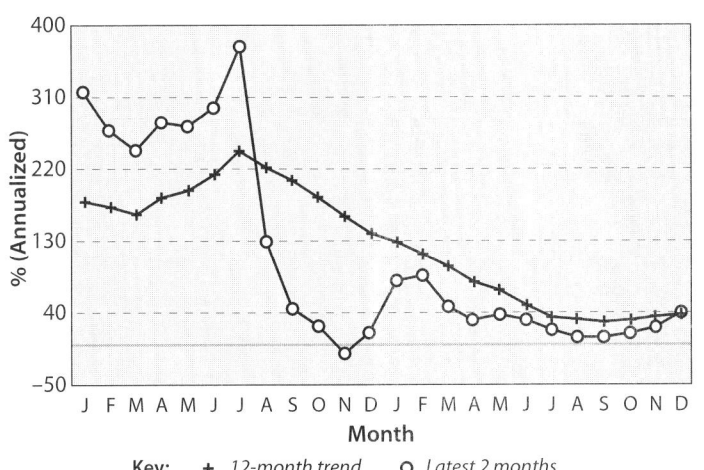

Key: + *12-month trend*   O *Latest 2 months*

---

[a]   Two-month averages are used to smooth the series.

Source: Bank of Zambia, Ministry of Finance, and author's calculations.

Side Effects

Policy actions and rules, like medicines, have to be judged in terms of their side effects as well as their direct effects. Although the cash budget was a success in terms of its intended macroeconomic impact, it also produced significant side effects that should be understood as important elements of the reform process. The side effects were both negative and positive.

Induced Budget Disorders

Disorderly budget practices were well entrenched in Zambia before the cash budget came along, but imposition of tight fiscal constraints enhanced the incentive for line ministries to take advantage of procedural slack and to play tactical games with budget priorities. The main procedural problem was a lack of control over commitments. Line ministries were prone to sidestep financial controls by obtaining supplies on credit and then submitting the bills as arrears at year-end. The treasury expected the cash budget to exacerbate this problem in 1993; estimates made at the end of the year indicated that arrears nearly doubled in real terms in 1993 compared to 1992. Fully covered, the carryover of bills from 1993 would have cost 6 percent of primary domestic expenditures in the 1994 budget. In fact, the 1994 budget provided cover for less than half the arrears; the remainder had to be absorbed by the line ministries out of new fundings or by suppliers, who would learn the hard way that cash-short government departments were no longer reliable customers. Improved control over commitments became a high priority for a later round of budget reforms in 1995.

The Ministry of Finance itself found a creative way to sidestep the cash controls. On several occasions the ministry met obligations by issuing special, off-tender treasury bills. This device entailed no immediate call on cash balances, but the interest charges magnified the expense once the bills matured. Also, special-issue bills worsened net claims on government, which was a key benchmark indicator for the IMF program. As a result, this costly practice was widely condemned by donors and advisors, but episodes persisted.

Another bureaucratic response to budget cuts, familiar everywhere, was to starve essentials in order to bolster the case for more funding. Many line ministries seemed to pursue this tactic when faced with the cash-budget constraints. Thus, police lacked funds for fieldwork even though their ministry officials found money for travel. Likewise, diplomatic personnel went unpaid while their ministry spent large sums to refurbish consulate offices and purchase a building in an expensive overseas capital. By creating deficiencies in essential expenditures, this behavior may have been a deliberate effort to get the government to back away from the cash budget or it may simply have been symptomatic of careless practices that had been covered previously by printing money. Either way, the misplaced priorities reflected badly on the government's management of required cutbacks.

The cash budget created other problems with expenditure management, in terms of budget office procedures. Previously, the budget office reviewed fundings once per month at a single meeting, where all requirements were reviewed. After the cash budget was imposed, fundings tended to trickle out as revenues reached the Bank of Zambia. Operating ministries perceived that they could pressure the budget office for emergency funds any time of the month and stand a chance of getting their money from the next day's revenues. The budget office had to deal with a steady flow of urgent spending requests, without seeing the whole range of requirements and revenue flows for the month. Management resolve could have coped with this trickle funding, but in practice, the payroll had to be delayed occasionally when ad hoc fundings depleted the treasury's cash balance. Improved revenue flows improved the situation in 1995.

Ceilings Become Floors

A second adverse side effect stemmed from the simplicity of the cash rule. Repeated emphasis on cash in the bank becomes a drawback when the cash flow improves, because it creates an expectation that any available monies can be spent. Under Zambia's stabilization program, the constraint on spending for any month was *the lesser* of the amount of cash in the bank or the flow-target set in the program. Once officials became conditioned to the cash constraint, they tended to forget about the program constraint. In effect, some players came to regard the cash flow as an unconditional floor on expenditure, rather than a conditional ceiling. In the second quarter of 1993, for example, the program called for a surplus so that the treasury could accumulate cash balances to cover deficits programmed for later in the year. The calendar asymmetry stemmed from normal seasonal patterns in expenditure, particularly for agriculture and capital projects. Yet information that there was cash in the bank became a tool for politicians to press for more funding. Similar problems arose in 1994 when revenues improved following the establishment of the Zambia Revenue Authority (ZRA).

Spotlight on Revenue

Other side effects were actually beneficial to the reform process. Perhaps the most important beneficial side effect was that the cash budget focused attention on revenue problems, which had previously been neglected. An early outcome of the monitoring system was the observation that reported revenue collections were uncorrelated with revenues reaching the Bank of Zambia. This observation prompted an examination of data for the previous year, which revealed that customs revenue totaling nearly 10 percent of the budget for the year did not reach the Bank of Zambia during the budget year. An audit showed that the gap was caused partly by reporting errors, but mostly by transit lags. In the absence of monitoring by the treasury, the commercial banks had grown accustomed to holding government revenues for roughly six weeks on average. Once this was known, new arrangements were negotiated, cutting the average transit time to about six days.

The main revenue problem, though, was collection performance itself. As the cash budget created a succession of budget crises, attitudes toward tax administration took an abrupt turn. It was obvious that major changes were needed in the tax organizations and in budget support for tax administration. Creation of a new revenue authority to professionalize tax administration became a clarion call for the 1994 budget. During the transition to the ZRA, tax collections deteriorated because the tax collectors worried about their jobs and their bosses assumed lame-duck attitudes. Soon after the ZRA became operational, however, the declining revenue trend strongly reversed.

In addition to sparking active concern with tax revenues, the cash budget also underscored the importance of obtaining timely disbursements of funds from donors. The JDMC found that many disbursement problems lay squarely in Zambia's court. For example, disbursements were often delayed for lack of timely documentation, such as shipping papers or audit reports. Other large sums remained undisbursed for months because of insufficient compliance with conditionality requirements. Some compliance problems were simple matters of inattention, though others were rooted more deeply in political controversy.[40] Once these problems were identified, steps were taken to implement forward-looking procedures to improve performance.

Spotlight on Data

Another beneficial side effect was that the monitoring system created a demand for accurate daily statistics and a timely process for identifying errors and discrepancies. Monitoring meetings centered on examining daily reports and comparing information from different sources. Data problems were found at nearly every meeting, ranging from simple data-entry mistakes in the bank accounts (e.g., a debit of K3.5 *million* instead of billion) to budget office errors in failing to record the reversal of certain fundings. Constant scrutiny provided an impetus for Ministry of Finance and Bank of Zambia officers to improve their reporting on fiscal and monetary transactions. Many of the improvements were slow to take root. For example, more than a year after the monitoring committee was formed, it was still very difficult to obtain consistent figures for basic statistics such as budget fundings for the year to date. Even so, the monitoring process cast a steady spotlight on such data problems, making them hard to ignore.

Krueger observed that reforms set in motion endogenous responses that determine the sustainability of the reforms.[41] Although she was referring to political-economy responses, her statement applies equally to processes within government. In this regard, the side effects triggered by the cash budget were integral elements in the dynamics of reform. Many of the problems highlighted by the cash budget, such as unfunded procurements, became agenda items for subsequent reforms. Likewise, the cash budget cast an intense spotlight on critical problems of revenue administration and management information systems, leading to permanent changes in procedures and even organizations. Another side effect, the problem of trickle funding, had quite a different implication: however well a strict cash constraint served to rein in a budget system that was out of control, it may not be a sound rule for orderly expenditure management under more normal conditions. To the extent that the cash budget succeeds in promoting stabilization, it may outlive its purpose.

CONCLUSIONS

Countries that attempt to adjust following a period of long-term decline may be hampered by a lack of capacity to implement macroeconomic reforms. Therefore, it is worth taking a close look to see how reforms have been implemented in countries that have been through the process. The case in point is the stabilization program undertaken in Zambia in the early 1990s, and in particular the use of a cash budget as an institutional constraint to establish fiscal discipline. After two decades of deteriorating economic conditions, the government of Zambia found that its key economic organizations were poorly equipped to administer sound fiscal and monetary policies. To stabilize the economy, the government first had to establish the capacity to control expenditures and strengthen coordination between fiscal and monetary management. By compelling the treasury to live within its means, the cash-budget system proved to be an effective compass for guiding fiscal policy through troubled terrain. Within six months, inflation fell to the lowest level in a decade and remained so, with ups and downs, through 1994.

The World Bank defined capacity building to include three distinct elements: (1) improving the quality of human resources, including capabilities of the "technocratic elite"; (2) restructuring organizations to be more effective; and (3) providing political leadership to nurture weak institutions.[42] All three elements were essential in the implementation of fiscal reforms in Zambia. The critical institutional innovation was imposition of a cash constraint on government expenditures.[43] This restrictive change in the rules was supported by a key organizational innovation in the form of a joint committee of officials from the Ministry of Finance and the Bank of Zambia, charged with monitoring the cash budget and other macroeconomic statistics on a daily basis. The committee operations provided an effective training forum through open discussions about data problems, reporting systems, operating procedures, cash-flow management, IMF program requirements, and budget conflicts. In the process, the committee became a strong lobby for prudent macroeconomic management. It also generated pressures for personnel in various operating units to improve the quality of their work. The third element of capacity building—political leadership—was equally vital. Without strong and active support from top echelons at the Ministry of Finance and the Bank of Zambia, the monitoring committee would have been ineffectual and the new system of fiscal controls would have reverted quickly to business as usual.

Among the main technical points of this chapter, I would highlight the following:

■ With the economy on the verge of hyperinflation, the minister of finance was accorded wide latitude to define macroeconomic policies for bringing inflation under control. These conditions enabled the minister and his technocrats to impose fiscal discipline, in the form of the cash budget, without a prior political struggle.

■ The cash-budget rules sanctioned pragmatic compromises that gave the system flexibility without seriously jeopardizing the macroeconomic objectives.

■ Because of revenue deficiencies, the cash budget created an extraordinary contraction of real expenditure, which was not well managed. The fiscal adjustment would have been far more orderly if revenue reforms had been implemented earlier.

Looking ahead, will the cash-budget system be sustained in Zambia? After a rocky first year, the system became more routine in 1994, aided by reforms to tax administration and by smoother flows of donor support.[44] In 1995, the government reiterated its commitment to "the discipline of the cash budget."[45] It is debatable, though, whether the cash budget should be a permanent feature of the fiscal landscape. There are two reasons to view this as a transitory system required during the initial phases of establishing fiscal discipline. First, the cash constraint implies a target of zero-seigniorage financing for government; this may be essential for an economy that has suffered a long period of mismanagement, but it is tighter than needed under normal economic conditions. As a corollary, in more normal times the phasing of budget outlays should not be dictated by the daily cash flow to the treasury. Second, convening a large joint committee to scrutinize daily statistics is a costly way to manage macroeconomic policy. The system is quite effective, and probably essential, during the early phases of adjustment, but in the long run there should evolve a more cost-efficient system for data interchange and monitoring of fiscal and monetary positions.

Finally, one may ask whether other countries can emulate Zambia's use of the cash budget to establish fiscal discipline. Since Zambia itself benefitted from knowing about experiences in other countries like Indonesia and Bolivia, there is every reason to suppose that Zambia's experience can be instructive in other contexts. Informal reports suggest that other countries in the region have been giving serious consideration to emulating Zambia's budget control system. If so, then this chapter may serve a purpose in providing ideas about how to proceed, as well as insights into the problems that may be encountered along the way.

TABLE 11-1
Treasury Position (Millions of Kwacha)

Date	Treasury Blocked Account a/c 293 (a)	Treasury Account a/c 999 (b)	Loans & Investments Transact. a/c 063 (c)	Loans & Investments T-bills a/c 066 (d)	Loans & Investments Bonds a/c 039 (e)	GRZ[a] Main Account a/c 099 (f)	Line-Ministry Balances (g)	Other Operating Balances (h)	GRZ Donor Funds (i)	Treasury Composite Balance (j)	GRZ Overall Position (k)	BOZ[b] T-bill Holding (l)	Bridging Loans to Gov't. (m)
31/12/92	-11,279	0	-53,063	32,319	70	-24,001	115,121	4,570	48,238	0	9,888	91	0
30/06/93	13,273	-48,045	-37,506	1,201	785	20,439	11,486	6,891	103,430	40,112	79,950	886	0
31/07/93	7,875	-48,045	-39,655	70	1,344	22,575	14,236	7,033	74,503	10,600	44,062	2,946	0
31/08/93	5,000	-48,045	-51,185	2,810	1,276	13,769	13,672	7,536	88,400	6,833	38,606	587	0
30/09/93	5,000	-48,051	-61,957	968	1,097	18,146	14,488	6,967	96,508	6,525	39,405	295	0
31/10/93	0	-48,051	-65,175	4,582	1,687	21,266	14,607	7,317	97,142	2,100	30,858	260	0
30/11/93	0	-48,051	-67,504	8,466	1,496	28,226	9,933	6,972	98,303	3,817	26,487	1,341	-4,162
31/12/93	1,685	-48,051	-68,818	12,301	2,129	23,044	11,726	6,959	90,093	-14,092	12,950	255	-20
31/01/94	-13,395	-101,787	-3,467	1,027	-503	5,799	14,409	6,825	100,713	11,264	16,470	530	-20
28/02/94	-16,567	-104,087	-21,685	6,153	-1,328	5,891	11,785	6,416	113,270	9,995	5,515	292	0
31/03/94	-16,567	-107,652	-37,618	1,850	-1,295	10,667	18,321	6,485	130,179	11,477	10,175	1,533	0
March 28	-19,586	-104,144	-34,800	288	-997	9,827	14,784	6,502	124,727	6,738	2,676	1,852	0
29	-16,567	-104,144	-37,798	1,850	-996	9,496	14,898	6,502	128,482	8,729	7,801	1,618	0
30	-16,567	-104,145	-40,906	1,850	-1,034	6,428	20,645	6,487	132,216	6,248	11,051	1,560	0
31	-16,567	-107,652	-37,618	1,850	-1,295	10,667	18,321	6,485	130,179	11,477	10,175	1,533	0
April 5	-16,567	-107,488	-37,482	1,625	-1,641	12,504	16,986	6,515	130,165	12,866	10,432	1,859	0
6	-11,567	-104,238	-41,097	1,550	-1,631	9,458	16,370	6,488	130,219	6,194	11,335	1,634	0
7	-11,567	-107,257	-38,351	1,550	-1,627	10,560	15,671	6,379	130,720	10,545	11,721	1,586	0
8	-11,567	-107,257	-38,355	1,550	-1,821	10,912	14,863	6,375	130,974	10,954	11,312	2,428	0

TABLE 11-1

Treasury Position (Millions of Kwacha) (continued)

Date	Treasury Blocked Account a/c 293 (a)	Treasury Account a/c 999 (b)	Loans & Investments Transact. a/c 063 (c)	Loans & Investments T-bills a/c 066 (d)	Loans & Investments Bonds a/c 039 (e)	GRZ Main Account a/c 099 (f)	Line-Ministry Balances (g)	Other Operating Balances (h)	GRZ Donor Funds (i)	Treasury Composite Balance (j)	GRZ Overall Position (k)	BOZ T-bill Holding (l)	Bridging Loans to Gov't. (m)
April (cont'd)													
11	-11,567	-107,257	-38,491	3,255	-1,803	11,733	13,546	6,487	131,528	7,405	6,571	2,945	0
12	-11,567	-107,257	-38,491	2,632	-1,802	13,171	14,662	6,484	131,528	9,467	9,708	4,460	0
13	-11,567	-107,257	-38,431	2,632	-1,811	14,657	13,712	6,480	138,578	18,053	17,365	4,381	0
14	-11,567	-107,257	-44,734	2,632	-1,823	16,163	13,010	6,407	138,602	13,269	11,774	4,358	0
15	-11,567	-107,257	-40,840	2,632	-1,809	12,784	15,914	6,323	138,602	13,799	15,173	4,257	0
18	-11,567	-107,257	-40,840	8,092	-1,800	14,709	14,188	6,381	138,646	10,317	9,976	2,863	0
19	-11,567	-107,257	-42,912	6,092	-1,786	16,241	9,315	6,392	142,808	15,953	10,748	2,789	0
20	-11,567	-107,257	-47,176	6,092	-1,755	17,292	12,954	6,400	142,808	12,771	11,212	2,725	0
21	-11,567	-107,257	-60,167	6,092	-1,748	18,156	12,440	6,396	145,272	3,116	1,039	2,743	0
22	-11,567	-107,257	-62,283	6,092	-1,732	7,255	21,399	6,385	149,030	-6,129	746	2,670	0
23	-11,567	-107,257	-62,283	6,092	-1,732	7,255	21,700	6,386	155,822	663	7,836	2,670	0

Source: Research Department, Bank of Zambia.
a GRZ = Government of the Republic of Zambia.
b BOZ = Bank of Zambia

Appendix: Monitoring the Treasury's Cash Balances

Appendix Table 11-1 shows a simplified version of the treasury position table reflecting the situation reported on April 25, 1994. This table contains thirteen columns of time-series data for various account balances and sums of account balances (in units of millions of kwacha). The data cover balances as of end-December 1992, month-end figures for June 1993 through March 1994, and daily balances for the nineteen most recent business days. This appendix explains the contents of the table.

Column (a): Treasury Blocked Account a/c 293. Account 293 was the source of the cash cushion of K13,395 million that the Bank of Zambia (BOZ) provided to the government (GRZ) in January (see text). A further debit of K3,172 billion reflected a loan in mid-February to facilitate the smooth handling of maturing promissory notes. Repayments by GRZ appear as credit entries. The activity on March 29 reversed a posting error spotted by the JDMC. One function of the monitoring committee was to spot and correct such posting errors, which were not infrequent.

Column (b): Treasury a/c 999. When GRZ accounts are zeroed at the end of each budget year, outstanding balances are transferred to "x" accounts. A/c 999 showed the aggregate of these "x" accounts. Activity after end-December, 1993, reflected the posting of such transfers, corrections of posting errors, and the clearing of treasury checks that were outstanding or in the process of collection at year-end. The latter represented cash outlays in 1994; hence, they entered the 1994 budget program as an adjustment for computing the balance on a cash basis.

Column (c): Loans and Investments a/c 063. This account mainly captured activity relating to foreign debt-service payments; less frequently, the account handled domestic payments for crop financing, fertilizer expenditures, and capital payments to parastatals. Table 11-1 shows a debit balance of K62,283.3 million on April 23. Debits for domestic payments were generally matched by credits transferred from the main account. Debits for foreign debt-service payments were usually matched by kwacha credits to donor-fund accounts; they were the counterpart to inflows of balance-of-payments support. When donor funds were not sufficient, then debt-service debits to a/c 063 could be covered by temporary bridge loans (see text). The debit balance in a/c 063 was offset by credits to various donor accounts, so this balance did not constrain the composite balance for the treasury. Thus, foreign debt service did not encumber domestic budget operations unless errors were made in covering the debits. An example of such an error can be seen on April 23, when debits for debt service were not properly covered by credits to the donor-fund accounts. The error reduced the composite balance by K4.6 billion, artificially constraining treasury operations.

Column (d): Loans and Investments a/c 066. This was the "T-bill" account, where proceeds from T-bill sales were credited and payments for redemptions were debited. Fundings for domestic debt service took the form of transfers to this account from the main account. The declining balance between April 15 and April 18 reflected the fact that proceeds from selling new T-bills at the weekly tender fell short of the amount needed to redeem maturing bills. Such net payouts from a/c 066, however, depleted the treasury's cash balance.

Column (e): Loans and Investments Bonds a/c 039. This account registered bond transactions: credits from new bond sales and debits covering payments of interest and principal.

Column (f): Treasury Main a/c 099. Domestic revenues were deposited to a/c 099 and budget fundings were debited here, for transfer to operational accounts. The cash budget constrained new fundings to the lower of the balance in this main account or the composite position.

Column (g): Line-Ministry Balances. These were the aggregate working balances in line-ministry accounts. The cash-budget process deemed funds to have been spent once transferred to line ministries. Thus, balances in column (g) were excluded from the treasury composite position. Reserve money was unaffected as long as funds remained in line-ministry accounts, so this balance had to be treated separately in tabulating budget outcomes for the financial program.

Column (h): Other Operating Balances. Some budget fundings went to special accounts for purposes such as revolving loan funds or project grants. Column (h) showed the combined balance in such accounts, including sums carried over from prior years. (Unlike most accounts, these were not zeroed at year-end; hence, the *change* in this balance since December 31 represented net transactions during the budget year.) For the cash budget, these balances were treated like line-ministry balances.

Column (i): GRZ Donor Funds. Credits represented the counterpart to foreign exchange received from donors, including project and balance-of-payments support. Donor-fund accounts were not zeroed at year-end; hence, the balance shown here included the carry-forward from prior years. The increment after end-December indicated the amounts credited to GRZ during the budget year. As noted in the text, kwacha counterpart funds were not credited to GRZ immediately on receipt of donor support. BOZ held such funds in suspense accounts until the foreign exchange could be put to use, mainly for external debt service. In this case the kwacha credits to donor accounts offset debits to a/c 063, leaving the composite position and reserve money unaffected. Such deposits to the donor accounts ought to have been transferred to a/c 063 to clear that debit balance. The transfer was rarely made, however, because of restrictions that donors placed on the use of the counterpart funds. These restrictions created an administrative burden that had no substantive effect because the funds were fungible. For example, if a donor insisted on using counterpart funds for social-sector programs, then the budget office could fund K1 billion for social-sector programs using domestic revenues; transfer K1 billion of funds from the donor account to the main account to recompense the treasury for this social-sector expenditure; and transfer the K1 billion so received from the main account to a/c 063 to cover the cost of debt-service payments.

Donor foreign exchange also could be sold to the market, at which time the kwacha proceeds would be credited to GRZ's donor-fund account. This type of transaction improved the treasury's composite position and relaxed the overall cash constraint. Such extra funds were earmarked primarily to cover domestic debt service costs as debited to a/c 066. This combination of transactions was neutral with respect to the composite position and reserve money, since the kwacha inflow from the sale of foreign exchange matched the outflow for domestic debt service. In this manner, donor support in excess of the amount required for external debt-service payments could be used to reduce domestic debt.

Column (j): Treasury Composite Balance. This was the key measure of cash in the bank under the cash-budget rules. The composite position was the algebraic sum of balances in accounts 039, 063, 066, and 099, plus the *net change* in donor-fund balances since the beginning of the year. Column (j) captured all of the main inflows to the treasury—domestic revenue, sale of treasury securities, recovery of loans and advances, and donor support—and all of the main outflows, including fundings to the line ministries.

Consider the decline in the column (j) balance from April 15 to April 18. This reflected: a net debit to a/c 066 due to a shortfall in the rollover of treasury bills; a net credit to a/c 099 for revenues reaching BOZ; a net credit to a/c 039 for receipts from bond sales; and a net credit to the donor-fund accounts reflecting the kwacha counterpart to donor foreign exchange that was sold to the market. This illustrates how the composite position incorporated the net effect of changes in all of the basic treasury accounts.

Column (k): GRZ Overall Position. This column shows the government's overall net balance at BOZ, including amounts like the line-ministry balances that are left out of the composite position for the cash budget. This balance is equal in magnitude and opposite in sign to BOZ net claims on government.

Column (l): BOZ T-bill Holding. BOZ acquired T-bills primarily through rediscounts, which arose when a T-bill holder (generally a commercial bank) redeemed bills before maturity. A penalty discount rate was charged by BOZ to discourage such transactions. When BOZ rediscounts T-bills, it injects reserve money into the banking system. From time to time, BOZ also acquired T-bills under special arrangements to clear other treasury obligations.

Column (m): Bridging Loans to Gov't. As explained in the text, the cash budget incorporated an arrangement for bridging loans from BOZ to cushion the operating budget from the effects of honoring essential external debt-service obligations, when donor inflows were temporarily insufficient. Column (m) showed the outstanding balance on such bridge loans. Most of the time, this balance was zero.

Notes

1   Ronald McKinnon, *The Order of Economic Liberalization* (Baltimore: Johns Hopkins University Press, 1991), 4.

2   Michael Roemer and Steven Radelet, "Macroeconomic Reform in Developing Countries," in Dwight Perkins and M. Roemer, eds., *Reforming Economic Systems in Developing Countries* (Cambridge: Harvard Institute for International Development, 1991).

3   Rudiger Dornbusch, "Policies to Move from Stabilization to Growth," *Proceedings of the World Bank Annual Conference on Development Economics* (1990): 19–48.

4   Marcelo Selowsky, "Comment on Dornbusch," *Proceedings of the World Bank Annual Conference on Development Economics* (1990): 54.

5   Merilee Grindle and John Thomas, "Policymakers, Policy Choices, and Policy Outcomes: The Political Economy of Reform in Developing Countries," in Dwight Perkins and Michael Roemer, eds., *Reforming Economic Systems in Developing Countries* (Cambridge: Harvard Institute for International Development, 1991).

6   Anne Krueger, *Political Economy of Policy Reform in Developing Countries* (Cambridge: MIT Press, 1993).

7   John Nellis, "Comment on Van Arkadie," *Proceedings of the World Bank Annual Conference on Development Economics* (1989): 179.

8   The adjustment program also entailed financial programming, tax reform, decontrol of prices, liberalization of the financial markets, and parastatal reform, including (slow) privatization.

9   Robert H. Bates, "Institutions as Investments," *HIID Development Discussion Paper 527* (Cambridge: Harvard Institute for International Development, May 1996).

10 Carlo Cottarelli, "Limiting Central Bank Credit to the Government: Theory and Practice," *Occasional Paper 110* (Washington, DC: International Monetary Fund, 1993).

11 Grindle and Thomas, "Policymakers," 1991.

12 Source: World Bank, *Zambia: Prospects for Sustainable and Equitable Growth* (Washington, DC: World Bank, Report 11570-ZA, 1993).

13 For more detailed information on macroeconomic management under the Kaunda government, see Young and Loxley, *Zambia: An Assessment of Zambia's Structural Adjustment Experience* (Ottawa: North-South Institute, 1990), Lewis and McPherson, *Improving Exchange Rate Management in Sub-Saharan Africa* (Cambridge: Harvard Institute for International Development, 1994), and Bolnick, *The Macroeconomic Framework for the Budget Program in Zambia* (Boston: Northeastern University [processed], 1994.) Parente and Prescott ("Changes in the Wealth of Nations." *Quarterly Review*, Federal Reserve Bank of Minneapolis [1993]: 3–16.) place Zambia in a tie with Mozambique at the top of the list of "development disasters" for the period 1960–1985, based on a sample of 102 countries. Page ("The East Asian Miracle: Four Lessons for Development Policy," in S. Fischer and J. Rotemberg, eds., *NBER Macroeconomics Annual 1994*,

[Cambridge: MIT Press, 1994], 219–268) shows Zambia as an extreme negative outlier in his graph of growth-equity performance.

14 For details on the financial market developments during the adjustment process, see Bolnick (1995).

15 Source: Republic of Zambia (1992, 1993) and Bank of Zambia (various dates).

16 Minister of finance, *budget address* (Lusaka: Republic of Zambia, 1993).

17 Minister of finance, *budget address* (Lusaka: Republic of Zambia, 1993).

18 Grindle and Thomas, "Policymakers," 1991.

19 Krueger, *Political Economy*, 125.

20 The most trenchant criticism was that controlling payouts from BOZ left a glaring loophole insofar as ministries could still procure supplies, sign contracts and otherwise commit to expenditures in excess of program targets.

21 See Dornbusch and Fischer, "Moderate Inflation," *World Bank Economic Review* 7, 1 (1993): 1–44. Vegh, "Government Spending and Inflationary Finance: A Public Finance Approach," *IMF Staff Papers* 36, 3 (1989): 657–677; Cooper, "Economic Stabilization in Developing Countries" (San Francisco: *ICEG Occasional Paper* 14, ISC Press, 1991); and Adams, *The Fiscal Costs of Premature Financial Liberalization: Some Evidence from Zambia* (Oxford: Centre for the Study of African Economies [processed], 1994). The latter paper equates zero treasury borrowing from the central bank with zero growth in reserve money. This is incorrect. The zero borrowing condition means that *the government* refrains from using seigniorage financing, but reserve money can still expand via other central bank transactions. In effect, seigniorage is channeled to the financial system instead of the fiscal system.

22 Edmund S. Phelps, "Inflation in the Theory of Public Finance," *Swedish Journal of Economics* 75, 1 (1973): 67–82.

23 Anand and van Wijnbergen, ("Inflation and the Financing of Government Expenditure," *World Bank Economic Review* 3, 1 [1989]: 17–38) neatly distinguish between the inflation tax = inflation × real money balances, and real seigniorage = growth in real money balances. Also see Richard B. Goode, *Government Finance in Developing Countries* (Washington, DC: Brookings Institution, 1984) for a clear explanation.

24 McKinnon, *The Order of Economic Liberalization*, 5.

25 Blanchard and Fischer, *Lectures on Macroeconomics* (Cambridge: MIT Press, 1989) Chapter 11, present a formal model in which zero inflation is the "reputational" equilibrium.

26 See Page, "The East Asian Miracle: Four Lessons for Development Policy," in *NBER Macroeconomics Annual 1994*, S. Fischer and J. Rotemberg, eds., (Cambridge: MIT Press, 1994): 219–268. A simple test can be obtained using data from the IMF (*International Financial Statistics Yearbook* [Washington, DC: IMF, 1994]). Examining Monetary Authority data for Claims on Central Government (line 12a) and Central Government Deposits (line 16d), one finds virtually zero use of seigniorage during the 1980s by central governments in Singapore, Korea, Thailand, Malaysia, and Indonesia. After 1985, the same picture emerges for Bolivia and Israel, and in Argentina after 1990.

27 Anwar Nasution, *Financial Institutions and Policies in Indonesia* (Singapore: Institute of Southeast Asian Studies, 1983).

28 Jeffrey Sachs, "The Bolivian Hyperinflation and Stabilization," *American Economic Review* 77, 2 (May 1987): 279–283.

29 Jonathan Friedland, "Argentine Economy Minister Reassures Fed Official of Currency's Stability," *Wall Street Journal* (December 29, 1994): A6.

30 This is so because changes in RM are large relative to variations in money multiplier (M2/RM). For example, in Zambia the money multiplier fell just 6 percent between December 1992 and December 1993, while reserve money grew by 138 percent.

31 Blejer and Cheasty, ("The Measurement of Fiscal Deficits: Analytical and Methodological Issues." *Journal of Economic Literature* XXIX, 4, [1991]: 1644–1678), and Anand and van Wijnbergen "Inflation and the Financing of Governemnt Expenditure," among others, emphasize the importance of using an inclusive measure of fiscal transactions.

32 See the appendix for details.

33 Cottarelli, "Limiting Central Bank Credit to the Government." Cottarelli points out that institutional constraints on central bank lending to government can be circumvented or removed even when written into law.

34 The standing instruction set a cap on this bridge financing, but the cap was not a binding constraint.

35 A year later, the meetings were reduced to three per week. All JDMC meetings were held at BOZ, which caused frequent problems with attendance by officers from the Ministry of Finance.

36 BOZ also started at this time to develop a system for daily monitoring of sources of movement in reserve money; it proved quite difficult during the first year to reconcile the source's data with actual movements in reserve money, because BOZ was not producing regular balance sheets or monetary survey reports.

37 The *primary* balance is defined as the difference between current revenues and *non-interest* expenses. This measure of fiscal balance is frequently used to gauge policy adjustments.

38 See Chiluba, *State of the Economy and Wage Policy* (Lusaka: Republic of Zambia, 1994).

39 Two main causes of the ups and downs were extreme movements in the exchange rate after inflation declined and real interest rates turned positive in August, and normal seasonal variations in food prices.

40 Another factor impairing the flow of donor support was the declaration of a state of emergency in March 1993, after discovery of an opposition-party plot to cause civil disturbances to undermine the government. Later in the year, donors held up disbursements and pledges over allegations that certain ministers were involved in drug trafficking. Problems of this sort were obviously beyond the purview of the JDMC.

41 Krueger, *Political Economy*, 1993.

42 World Bank, *Sub-Saharan Africa: From Crisis to Sustainable Growth* (Washington, DC: 1989), 54.

43 Following North, (*Institutions, Institutional Change and Economic Performance* [Cambridge: Cambridge University Press, 1990]) the term *institutions* refers to the rules of the game, whereas *organizations* are comprised of the teams and players.

44 Preliminary figures for 1994 show a primary domestic surplus (cash basis) of K75 billion, or 3.3 percent of GDP, up 85 percent in real terms from 1993. Adding interest expenses left the overall domestic balance with a deficit of K27 billion that was matched by net foreign assistance. Even so, M2 grew 70 percent, primarily because of foreign-exchange transactions. The inflation rate for 1994 (December to December) was 35 percent, compared to 138 percent in 1993 and 191 percent in 1992.

45 Minister of finance, *budget address* (Lusaka: Republic of Zambia, 1995).

12 Capacity Building in the Context of the Kenya Tax Modernization Program

Graham Glenday

Kenya began implementing a tax reform program in 1986. This reform program took more formal and substantial shape in 1990 as the Tax Modernization Program (TMP), a broad-based reform of both tax structures and administration. Such tax reforms are complex and involve large, and typically in the sub-Saharan African context, fairly weak bureaucracies. To meet such a challenge, this chapter argues the importance of a product-oriented approach to capacity building. To achieve significant improvements in the outputs of the tax system, the capacity-building interventions (including changes to the tax policies, administrative systems, human resources, and organizations) have to be implemented in a coordinated and comprehensive fashion. Close attention has to be paid to the pace and sequencing of introducing changes so that the demands of capacity building fit the absorption capacity of the organization, and the innovations gain the benefits of the potential positive interactions among the capacity-building interventions. Tax structure changes may have only limited effects without appropriate administrative reforms, but jointly, structural and administrative changes can have significant reinforcing effects.

The TMP in Kenya is generally regarded as a success story. Although elements of failure and underperformance can be found in the TMP, a successful development effort in the sub-Saharan African region, generally characterized by disappointments in its economic development performance, is worthy of study.[1] This program involved a full range of capacity-building components. As such, it helps elucidate the role of capacity building in tax reform as well as other development projects aimed at strengthening economic management.

This chapter describes the objectives and activities of the TMP and their outcomes through mid-1995. It focuses on the capacity-building aspects of the program. In order to draw some lessons from the Kenyan TMP experience, it will be necessary to develop some analytical framework and concepts. Although this chapter falls more in the area of capacity-building practice, some reference to the theory is necessary. Indeed, this is important, as many of the terms used in capacity building have definitions that vary across analytical disciplines and contexts. Capacity building is viewed narrowly by some as merely increasing the supply of specific types of human capital, whereas others view it more broadly as the development of both the personnel and the institutions to deliver some product or service in a sustainable fashion. Similarly, institutional development is taken by some to refer to the development of formal organizations, whereas others take it to cover both the formal and informal relationships and rules that develop in a civil society that allow the operation of governments and private sector entities.[2] To effectively discuss capacity building in the context of tax reform and modernization, some specific meanings are given to concepts, and a conceptual framework is presented that appears to be useful, at least in dealing with tax reform programs.

CONCEPTUAL FRAMEWORK

Ultimately, we are interested in "successful" capacity building. To judge success requires identification of the purpose or output of capacity building. It is not an end in itself. Input-oriented capacity building tends to become a vehicle to build a "container for a vacuum." No substantial or sustainable output can be expected. Much of the literature struggles to describe or define capacity building. The range of project and program situations is so wide in terms of objectives, scopes, and institutional environments that definitions become very generic and general. As such, definitions of capacity building tend to lose prescriptive and operational value. They also lose any relationship with the standard evaluation criteria of effectiveness and efficiency of any intervention. An input-oriented focus on capacity may judge a project successful, for example, merely because a high volume of training was undertaken. An output-oriented focus, in contrast, would question the effectiveness of the training in promoting the sustained production of the "effects" being sought.

The task of defining capacity building becomes more manageable and useful when a *product-oriented approach* is taken. In the case of a complex program such as tax reform, many intermediate or proximate products are required that collectively produce the high-level or ultimate outputs. The capacity to deliver simple intermediate outputs may require only a single step or process, and as such is amenable to relatively simple design, implementation, and analysis. Ultimately, however, the outputs have to contribute to the goals of the tax reform.

The ultimate or high-level goals of tax reform are well known, but worth restating, because they form the ultimate basis for judging the success of the program. Judgment has to be made in terms of both the short-run outcomes and the capacity built to sustain these outputs in the longer run.[3] The primary purpose of taxation is to raise revenues to fund the production of public goods and services. Several secondary goals determine the quality of this revenue-raising performance. First, revenues should be "buoyant" or "elastic" over time so that government revenues grow at least as fast as the economy in order to keep budget deficits manageable and to avoid economic instability. Second, the burden of the taxes should be equitably or fairly distributed. Third, the tax system should be designed to minimize the efficiency costs of raising the revenues. This design includes minimizing both the allocative efficiency costs arising from the price effects of taxes, and the technical efficiency costs of the resources devoted both to tax administration by the public sector and to tax compliance (or evasion) by the private sector. To be judged successful, a tax reform program should be making sustainable improvements in all or some of these ultimate objectives.[4] Given the scope, size, and complexity of a tax system, interventions to improve the system can be numerous and various. They include "traditional" capacity-building interventions such as training and institutional development. Whether they constitute successful capacity-building interventions will depend on whether they individually or jointly result in improvements in the ultimate objectives.

Capacity-building interventions are often grouped into human resource development, organizational development, and institutional development (defined broadly). To discuss and analyze capacity building in the context of tax reform, however, specific meanings are given to these terms and the role of policy development is added. Essentially, the institutional development of tax systems is divided into two components. One is the development of the extensive mechanistic systems that are involved in tax administration; these systems are implemented by large revenue departments. The other is the development of the broader tax policy structure that both reflects the social institutions of a country and sets the rules of the "tax game"; this structure is the responsibility of the ministry of finance. These groupings are analytically and operationally useful, if not completely independent perspectives.

Human Resource Development

Human resource development includes training in tax policies and procedures for new and existing tax officers. It also includes the development of training schools, programs, and policy. Taxpayer education on tax law, regulations, and compliance procedures also forms a component of human resource development. Taxes are largely collected by voluntary compliance through self-assessment and tax payment systems. The taxpayer therefore is as important a player in a tax system as the formal tax administration.

Systems Development

Tax administration involves extensive information systems to assess, collect, audit, monitor, and forecast tax revenues in addition to the budget, finance, personnel, and other administrative systems required to manage a large bureaucracy. In a modern tax system, computer-based information technology is extensively employed to implement many of these systems. Again, tax systems extend beyond the boundaries of revenue departments to include the taxpayers as well.

Organizational Development

The focus of organizational development is on organizational reform. Traditionally in most countries, tax administration has been implemented under the general civil service rules of the country. These rules have often constrained the management styles and employment conditions that could be used to provide *incentives* for efficient administration. Organizational development is used in the context of tax reform to mean the development of new corporate structures that allow radical changes in management and employment conditions to change the whole *motivational environment* of tax officers. Various types of revenue authority outside of the traditional civil service structure are now being implemented in many countries. Within any corporate environment (traditional civil service or new revenue authority), however, systems changes always require some degree of organizational change as well. Such organizational changes, motivated by new systems, are classified under systems development.

Policy Development

Tax policy development has two major dimensions. One is the development of the tax structures (tax bases, tax rates, and styles of assessment and collection); the other is the development of the capacity to analyze and develop tax policies and the related legislation. The latter obviously involves the three capacity-building components already described. The former is also important for capacity building in tax systems in an indirect manner—tax structures can be supportive of effective and efficient tax administration, or tax structures can provide incentives for noncompliance and corruption. This strong interaction between tax policy and administration also makes the timing and sequencing of introducing new tax policy important if it is to be well administered. In other words, policy implementation has to be preceded or accompanied by capacity development. Tax administration gives the *de facto* expression to *de jure* tax policy. At the same time, however, tax policy development is embedded in general economic policy development. Therefore, at its highest levels, tax policy development is located within the ministry of finance.

Types of Capacity-Building Projects

In the context of output-oriented capacity building, a project or program is not designed or evaluated merely in terms of the inclusion or use of these capacity-building components, but rather it is necessary to demonstrate how these components contributed to the objectives of the project or program. Most projects and programs are targeted at improving specific outputs. These are defined as *specific* capacity-building projects or programs, in contrast with *general* capacity-building projects or programs that aim at building up an "enabling environment" or capacity for a wide range of functions. A civil service reform program would be classed as a general capacity-building program in that it aims to improve the structure, conditions of employment, and training policies of the civil service, which would permit improvement in the general functioning of the government. General capacity building is a necessary, but not a sufficient condition to improve output in any specific functional area of the public service. Specific capacity building is still required to obtain specific outputs.[5]

Programs aimed at strengthening economic management, or a subset of economic management such as tax reform, involve complex sets of policies and implementing administrations. Such programs can be designed to be either comprehensive or partial. A comprehensive program consists of a package of interventions. In the context of tax reform, the package consists of changes in tax policy, tax systems (procedures, forms, information technology), and organizations.[6] These changes need to be backed up with analysis and design work, testing, and training. The interactions between the components of the program are important so that the sequencing, timing, pace, scale, and scope of the interventions are taken into account. For example, if the administrative capacity is not in place, then the time and resources have to be provided for its development prior to (or at least to accompany) the introduction of a policy. The interactions and synergies have to be understood. It is often the case that all elements have to function well to achieve the desired output. Partial programs tend to fail if they depend on the existing components already in place to support the new intervention. In the context of tax reform, a new policy often fails for lack of the necessary administrative reform. Value-added tax (VAT) legislation is passed, for example, but the administrative capacity is not sufficiently developed. Alternatively, training may not be effective if it is out of synchronization with the introduction of the policy or procedure it is designed to support, or if the organizational structure is not conducive to absorbing or retaining the trained personnel. A comprehensive and coordinated approach is often required to obtained any noticeable results.[7]

Even where a comprehensive and coordinated approach is planned for a major reform, not all components of a program can be undertaken simultaneously. The need to stage or sequence interventions or components of a program arises either because there is a logical sequence to the implementation or because there are limiting political or capacity-building resource constraints. To illustrate the issue of the logical sequence of interventions, consider the typical role of specific training related to the design and implementation of tax policy or administrative system or procedure.

Step one is the design of the tax policy or procedure, or both. Training can either be embedded in the design stage or immediately follow the design stage. In the former case, training could consist of presentation of the concepts, models, or tools to undertake the design, and creative brainstorming workshops to consider alternative designs. It is especially desirable if the implementers of a new policy or administrative procedure can be involved in its design to enhance understanding and commitment to the reform.

Step two is the implementation of the policy or administrative procedure, or both. Specific training always has to accompany implementation. This training can range from educating the public and administrators about a new policy or procedure to providing specific instruction for the officers administering the new policy or procedure. It may include the standard user training that accompanies the implementation of a new computer system.

Step three is the institutionalization of the training on the new policy or procedure. For the general public, explanatory material may be redrafted. In the case of tax officers, training curriculums and material for new-recruit or refresher training may be amended to incorporate the new policy or procedure. If the new tax policies and procedures are extensive, then a substantial reform of the tax training institution may also be necessary.

The sequencing and time frame of a tax reform is an important consideration in the context of donor or government funding of the reform efforts. The weaker the initial capacity of an administration, the longer and more sustained the interventions need to be. A strong administration may well have the capacity effectively to absorb intermittent short-term advice. Absorb here means both interpret and filter the advice of short-term experts (who may not have had a full opportunity to analyze and understand local conditions) and translate the advice into operational structures, systems, and organizations in the local context. A moderately strong administration may require longer-term and more persistent assistance to develop appropriate policies and implement them. The assistance would be expected to tail off in intensity over time as capacity is built to sustain new structures and systems. If an administration is very weak, however, it may be necessary to start slowly with a lower level of long-term assistance to build up the capacity to absorb a more intense assistance program. For example, moving a program of high-intensity computerization assistance into an organization with little or no computer experience is seldom successful. A slower start-up is required to build up sufficient experience to absorb and manage a more intense and rapid computerization effort. The success of any project to support reform of policies, systems, and organizations depends heavily on an initial assessment of the capacity of the organizations involved. This assessment will determine the style, profile of intensity, and time frame of the technical assistance provided.

Another example of sequencing is the timing of the organizational reforms required to support the implementation of policy and administrative reforms. The urgency of organizational reform is a function of the shortage of the skills required to implement a new tax structure or system. In a very weak administration that is unable to attract or retain staff with strong technical skills, organizational reform is a precondition to tax reform.[8] A weak administration is characterized by an organization that cannot satisfactorily achieve its corporate mission with its current technology given its current management and technical skill levels. An administration of moderate strength is taken to be able to achieve its corporate mission using its current technology, but would have difficulty in dealing with the organizational changes required to adopt new technologies or new missions. In such administrations, organizational reform can be delayed, but sustainability of reforms that involve skill levels higher than the administration has been able to attract and retain ultimately make organizational reform a necessity. It may be necessary, however, to demonstrate the success of new tax structures and systems (perhaps on a pilot or limited scope of application) before support can be gained for radical changes to the organization to allow the general and sustainable implementation of reforms. A strong administration is considered to be an organization that can comfortably achieve its current mission and that has the depth of management skill to handle organizational change. In other words, organizational reform as described in this chapter would be unnecessary for a strong administration to adopt structural or systems reforms.

The scale of a reform is another important consideration in capacity-building strategies for organizations of weak or moderate strength. Should organization-wide strategies be attempted, or should interventions be of more limited scale? In Chapter 6, Peterson advocates the approach of innovating through selected informal or formal micro-hierarchies, networks, or centers of excellence within a large, but weak bureaucracy rather than attempting to reform the overall hierarchy of the bureaucracy. This approach is not generally suitable for tax administrations because these tend to be large organizations with well-developed hierarchical structures and mechanistic systems for assessing, collecting, auditing, and investigating taxes. This "hardwired" approach is required to ensure a high degree of uniformity and fairness in application of tax legislation, and to control corruption and tax evasion. Generally, broad-based, incremental approaches are required to move the whole organization along the tax reform path. Under this approach, a clear vision of the sequence of steps is required to ensure that the overall reform is ultimately achieved. There are functions within a tax system, however, that are more amenable to selective or targeted implementation within a microhierarchy. These functions include in-depth audit, investigation, and policy development where, in the initial stages, centers of excellence can be developed that can be later generalized to the wider organization.

An alternative approach, where a specific function is required that is beyond the capacity of an existing organization, is to contract out the function. The scale of such a function could be large or small. Examples of such functions may range from computerization of administrative systems to tax audits. Where the scale is large and requires the deep involvement of the existing administration, however, as is the case with computerization of a tax administration, timing and sequencing of implementing a contract again become crucial, especially for administrations of weak or moderate strength.

In general, work is contracted out to lower the overall costs of production or improve productivity.[9] In the context of capacity building, however, analysis of contracting out functions needs to go beyond the immediate output improvements. It should also consider the role of the contract in capacity building within the client organization. This assessment would include consideration of whether the contracted function would be repatriated to the organization by contract completion, particularly where the function is a recurrent activity.

The timing of capacity-building interventions is often dependent on the strength and commitment of the leadership.[10] For changes in tax policy and organization, leadership support at the highest political levels is required as fundamental adjustments to political and economic relationships arise both within the society as a whole and within the public sector administration. For more incremental human resource and systems development, it is often sufficient to have support at the departmental management level. Changing economic and political conditions in a country can be expected to vary the strength of leadership support over time. For example, a rapidly rising national debt with attendant high inflation can motivate political leaders to implement revenue-raising tax reforms to regain economic stability even where such policies may hurt otherwise favored interest groups. A tax reform program has to stand ready to take advantage of such opportune circumstances as they arise to implement the more radical structural, systems, or organizational reforms.

In the remainder of this chapter, the capacity-building concepts are illustrated in the context of the TMP in Kenya. First, an overview of the main features and results of the TMP through mid-1995 is provided to motivate the discussion of capacity-building interventions and strategies employed in the TMP. Second, specific examples are drawn from the TMP to illustrate the causes of success or failure of capacity building in light of the conceptual framework.

AN OVERVIEW OF THE TAX MODERNIZATION PROGRAM

The TMP formally commenced in January 1990, although a sequence of tax policy reforms had started with the 1986 budget.[11] The TMP involved reforms in the tax structure and administration (including computerization) in all the major taxes on income, consumption, and international trade. It involved the provision of technical assistance, equipment, and training through projects sponsored by international donor agencies—the African Development Bank, the United Nations Development Programme, U.S. Agency for International Development, and the U.K. Overseas Development Agency— as well as by the Government of Kenya itself. Projects were implemented by a range of institutions. The Harvard Institute for International Development had responsibility for the overall coordination of the TMP, tax policy, development of a tax policy-making capacity, and customs administration. Other institutions provided assistance in income tax and VAT administration and computerization.

At the commencement of the TMP, the responsibilities for tax policy and administration were divided among five departments of the Ministry of Finance. The analysis and development of tax policy and legislation were the responsibility of the Department of Fiscal and Monetary Affairs, and tax administration was divided among four departments— income tax, customs and excise, value added tax, and inland revenue. These four revenue departments employed more than 4,000 officers and support staff, whereas tax policy responsibility was vested in fewer than twenty persons. The Department of Fiscal and Monetary Affairs had responsibility for coordinating the preparation of the national budget, and hence, the tax policy function was embedded in the overall economic and budgetary policy and management function of the Ministry of Finance.

Tax Structure Reform

In general, under the TMP major shifts in the tax structure were achieved. Tax rates were lowered and rate structures were rationalized. At the same time, tax bases were broadened by legislated changes in the tax bases and, more importantly, improved tax administration techniques and capacity also widened the tax net. In addition, tax structures were reformed to support trade liberalization and lower effective protection for domestic industry. Export promotion, capital market development, and a greater reliance on consumption rather than income tax bases to spread the tax burden and encourage investment were also part of the reforms.

The major rate structure changes can be illustrated by the changes in the rates of import duties, VAT, and income tax. The import duty rate structure was rationalized by reducing the number of rate bands from a peak in 1987 to 1988 of twenty-four to six in 1995 to 1996 with the top rate of duty being reduced from 170 percent to 40 percent.[12] The simple average import duty rate declined from a peak of 46 percent in 1989 to 1990 to 21 percent in 1995 to 1996. The VAT tax rate structure was also markedly rationalized, with over 76 percent of goods taxable at the standard rate from 1994 onward compared to below 50 percent in 1990 when the VAT was first introduced. The number of above-standard VAT rates was reduced from twelve to one, and the highest tax rate was brought down from 150 percent to 25 percent. In the income tax, the top individual marginal tax rate was gradually lowered from 65 percent in 1987 to 35 percent effective in 1996. The company tax rate was also brought down from 45 percent in 1989 to 35 percent effective mid-1995, and the differential tax rates for the insurance and mining sector companies were removed.

Tax Administration Reform

A wide range of new administrative techniques were introduced. Only the highlights are covered here. Two major tax-system-wide changes were introduced. The first was the issuing of a personal identification number (PIN) in 1993 to each potential taxpayer. Although the administrative center of the PIN system was in the income tax department, the PIN was used across all revenue departments. The PIN was key to maintaining computerized tax accounts and sharing tax information across revenue departments. The second systemwide change was the restructuring of the revenue departments into a quasi-independent corporation, the Kenya Revenue Authority (KRA), under the Ministry of Finance in mid-1995. This restructuring was done to improve the conditions of employment of revenue officers, the resource base, and organizational flexibility for tax administration. The objectives and structure of this corporation are expanded on later.

The major change in the income tax system was the introduction of self-assessment (as opposed to agency assessment) starting with the 1992 tax year. This change necessitated major reorganizations of staff functions from routine desk assignments to jobs including audit selection and the conduct of audits of various types and levels of intensity. New tax forms had to be designed and introduced. A complete retraining program had to be implemented to back up the self-assessment system. Another major administrative change was in the introduction of installment payments for corporate and other business income in 1990: first, as a single installment payment at the end of the third quarter of a current tax year; by 1992, as a three-installment payment at the end of the second, third, and fourth quarters; and finally, effective in 1996, as a four-installment system. All these innovations in the income tax were supported by training and the gradual expansion of computerization. In the income tax department, computerization expanded from the initial three target functions in 1990 of registration, accounts receivable of income tax, and control of document flows between the department and companies in Nairobi-based districts to include by 1995 all districts, collection receipting, and management information.

In the VAT, the core achievement was the successful implementation of the VAT in 1990 to replace the manufacturing-level sales tax.[13] Following initial design and implementation of the basic VAT systems and initial training, ongoing training in the VAT was undertaken with an emphasis on building control and verification capacity. After 1990, the administration had to cope with a major expansion in the tax base to include most services, and an expansion in the number, size, and scope of activities of the regional VAT offices. Registered taxpayers expanded from less than 4,000 in 1990 to more than

18,000 in 1995. Most importantly, computerization supported a "front-end" VAT collection receipting and defaulter identification system at the point of receipt of monthly VAT returns and payments in the Nairobi headquarters. In addition, a registration system to keep track of active traders, and a VAT accounting system to identify traders in arrears and analyze VAT performance were implemented in the early 1990s. This implementation was followed by an expansion of the system to the district offices outside Nairobi.

In the Customs and Excise Department, four major administrative reforms were implemented.[14] First, rapid release and selective examination procedures were reinstated along with simplification of the import release process. A system of "100 percent examination" had been attempted during the 1980s. The return to selective examination under the TMP allowed resources to be refocused on the core customs activities of valuation, intelligence, and investigation, and reintroduced more transparency and accountability into the import process. Second, the transit control regulations and procedures were markedly tightened. Third, a radical preshipment inspection (PSI) program was introduced to improve import valuation and control, and to assist in the buildup of customs valuation capacity. The PSI arrangement included features of independent computerized documents being supplied rapidly to customs to form minimum valuation bases, and the reconciliation of customs and PSI documents to ensure compliance and accountability of all parties. Fourth, new export promoting programs were introduced. These programs included manufacturing under bond (MUB) for export after 1988, and export processing zones (EPZs) and duty/VAT exemptions for imported inputs in the production of exports and duty-free products for the domestic market (the Export Promotion Programs Office [EPPO] program), both since 1990. These programs demanded the development and implementation of new administration techniques, including, as an interim measure, the contracting out of the verification side of the MUB and EPPO programs.

In summary, the Kenyan tax reform had three distinct periods. The 1986 to 1989 period initiated tax structure changes and an analysis of the potential scope and role of tax reform. The 1990 to 1994 period sustained the momentum of tax structure changes, but added a strong dimension of administrative change, including the beginnings of computerization. It encompassed a broad base of training support covering functions from tax policy analysis to new basic administrative procedures. It also revealed, however, the limitations on the performance of the system arising from inappropriate micro-incentives of the traditional public sector corporate structure, and the only modest strength of the revenue departments. These barriers were partly broken by contracting out of certain key functions such as customs valuation under the preshipment inspection program of imports. Ultimately, however, it became clear that further major organizational reforms were necessary. The third period started in 1995 with the change in the corporate structure of tax administration under the KRA.

CAPACITY-BUILDING SUCCESSES AND FAILURES

Specific Capacity Building: Meeting the Ultimate Goals of Tax Reform

As described earlier, capacity building should be product oriented. Given the major reforms in tax structure and administration just outlined, how well did the TMP do through mid-1995 in meeting the ultimate goals of taxation? It is useful to review the overall impact of the TMP before reviewing the contributions of its specific components and interventions. This type of review keeps the woods separate from the trees; it allows an evaluation of the aggregate impact of all the more or less successful separate interventions.

First, in terms of revenue yields, the TMP was highly successful, as indicated in Table 12-1. Ordinary revenue yields rose in each year of the TMP. After rising gradually from 20.9 percent of gross domestic product (GDP) in 1989 to 1990 to 22.8 percent of GDP in 1992 to 1993, ordinary revenue yields rose sharply in 1993 to 1994 to 27.9 percent of GDP, and were provisionally estimated at 29.9 percent of GDP in 1994 to 1995. The yields beginning in 1993 to 1994 were historical highs for Kenya. They also exceeded the revenue target of tax reform, which was only 24 percent of GDP by 1995.[15] Macroeconomic stabilization demands arose in 1993; these demands required a markedly higher revenue effort than 24 percent of GDP. Fortunately, the combination of all the improvements in the tax system had already built up sufficient capacity by 1993 that the system could respond and meet the higher revenue needs.

Second, the economic efficiency costs of revenue collections were markedly lower as a result of the reforms. Although the specification of an optimal tax system is notoriously difficult in a second-best world, it is usually possible to infer the direction of changes in the efficiency

TABLE 12-1

Tax Revenues as Shares of Gross Domestic Product, Kenya, 1980–1981 to 1994–1995

Fiscal Year	Income Tax (%)	Consumption Taxes (VAT, Excise Duty) (%)	Import Duty (%)	Other Taxes, Fees, and Income (%)	Ordinary Revenues (%)
80/81	7.0	8.5	5.2	3.0	23.8
81/82	6.2	8.0	5.7	2.8	22.7
82/83	6.3	7.3	4.5	3.4	21.6
83/84	6.0	8.0	4.1	3.0	21.4
84/85	6.5	7.6	3.3	3.0	20.9
85/86	6.6	7.3	3.9	3.0	21.5
86/87	6.2	8.1	4.0	2.8	21.6
87/88	6.4	9.1	3.9	2.4	22.0
88/89	6.3	9.0	3.7	3.6	22.9
89/90	6.4	8.4	3.2	2.9	20.9
90/91	6.7	8.9	2.4	3.3	21.3
91/92	7.1	10.0	2.1	3.3	22.6
92/93	6.9	10.6	2.5	2.7	22.8
93/94	10.3	11.3	4.1	2.1	27.9
94/95[a]	10.9	11.0	4.7	3.3	29.9

Sources: Government of Kenya: Economic Surveys, 1981 to 1995; Revenue Estimates, 1982 to 1995.

[a] Gross domestic product estimates for 1994–1995 are provisional.

costs of certain changes in a tax structure. For example, if the same or higher revenues can be collected at lower tax rates (particularly tax rates on international trade), the case for an efficiency gain is strong. Base expansions at the same or lower tax rates in most cases also indicate efficiency gains. The general lowering of top and average tax rates and the rationalization of rates on all major tax bases in combination with higher revenue yields argues that significant economic efficiency gains were achieved. Perhaps the most surprising result was in the area of import duties. Although the simple average duty rate fell over the period from 46 percent in 1989 to 1990 to 26 percent in 1994 to 1995, import duties, after initially falling as a share of revenues to a low of 9.5 percent in 1991 to 1992, rose to 16.1 percent by 1994 to 1995. Similarly, import duties relative to GDP dropped to a low of 2.1 percent in 1991 to 1992 and then reached 4.7 percent of

GDP in 1994 to 1995, as indicated in Table 12-2. The longer-run efficiency of the tax system was also enhanced by shifts in the tax structure to rely more heavily on domestic consumption taxes (VAT and excises) and also remove the double taxation of income from corporate equity investments. These shifts in tax structure favor higher levels of investment and economic growth.

Third, the equity of the tax system was enhanced at least on the horizontal dimension. The expansion of the VAT and income tax bases by legal measures and by tighter administration resulted in a broader base of Kenyans paying tax. Before the PIN system was introduced in 1993, less than 200,000 companies and individuals filed tax returns. By the end of 1994, some 1.6 million PINs had been assigned, which was expected to translate into a rapidly growing number of tax filers. The impact of the tax reforms on vertical equity is less certain. While top income tax rates fell, there were significant expansions in the taxation of employer-provided benefits that largely accrued to high-income earners. The efforts to improve compliance were also largely targeted at high-income persons. For example, the in-depth tax au-

TABLE 12-2

Import Duty Collection Performance in Kenya, 1989–1990 to 1994–1995

Fiscal Year	Import Duties (K£ mil.)	GDP (%)	Import Duties Relative to:		Simple Average Import Duty Rate (%)	Maximum Import Duty Rate (%)	No. of Duty Rate Bands	Home-Use Imports Paying Duties[a] (%)
			Ordinary Revenue (%)	Home-use Imports (%)				
89/90	301.8	3.2	15.4	12.0	46.3	135	11	53
90/91	251.9	2.4	11.1	9.5	44.3	100	15	50
91/92	255.9	2.1	9.5	9.8	37.9	70	12	61
92/93	366.9	2.5	11.2	9.7	35.5	60	10	59
93/94	734.5	4.1	14.8	12.7	37.3	50	8	52[b]
94/95	929.9	4.7	15.6	15.6	26.4	45	7	63

[a] Non-taxpaying imports include duty-free imports (typically about 12% of home-use imports) and duty-exempt imports (imports by diplomatic and aid agencies, charitable donations, imported inputs for the production of exports under export promotion programs, etc.).

[b] The decline in non-taxpaying imports in 1993–1994 is largely explained by the large duty-exempt food imports for refugees and as drought relief. In addition, the export compensation program was terminated in September 1993; this resulted in increased applications for duty-exempt imported raw materials under the EPPO program to produce exports.

dits were primarily targeted at higher-income persons to maximize the tax yields from the added enforcement effort.

Fourth, the stability of revenues was enhanced. The record revenue yields in 1993 through 1995 were achieved in low-growth-rate years of the Kenyan economy. The prospects of revenue yields remaining above the longer-run target of 24 percent of GDP were therefore good. Outside of the taxation of oil products, nearly all tax rates were put on an *ad valorem* basis, which, combined with base broadening measures, increased the responsiveness of tax revenues to economic growth.

Fifth, the tax reform efforts generally were expected to be sustainable. In terms of tax structure reforms, the improvements through 1995 would have to be actively reversed by legislative changes. Policy pronouncements generally indicated a continuation of the structural reforms.[16] In terms of new administration techniques and systems, the gains made through 1995 were expected to be consolidated and strengthened by the formation of the KRA, which would relax constraints on resources, professional personnel, and appropriate work incentives. It was expected that the KRA would be able to retain the officers trained under the TMP. Where systems such as the preshipment inspection of imports were contracted out, these were funded by local charges. The dependence on long-term expatriate advisors was not high. Although these experts played important roles in initiating, coordinating, and guiding the reforms, their numbers were limited to between five and twelve at various times between 1990 and 1995. These numbers were small compared to more than 4,000 employees of the revenue departments and the treasury involved in implementing the TMP.

General Capacity Building

While most of the new policies and administrative techniques demanded specific capacity building to support them, the importance of creating an appropriate enabling environment for tax administration gradually became a core element of the TMP. The objectives of the general capacity building were to increase the operating and maintenance resources of the revenue departments, enable tax administrations to attract and retain skilled and professional staff, and create an organizational environment with incentives structured to improve collection efficiency and decrease revenue leakages from corrupt activities. From 1993 onward, specific budgetary measures were implemented to exempt the revenue departments from across-the-board budget cuts that were repeatedly hitting government ministries over the years in an attempt to meet budget deficit targets. Over the latter half of the 1980s, recurrent expenditures on tax administration remained close to 0.7 percent of revenue collections. From 1990 onward, funding levels started to decline, falling to below 0.6 percent by 1992 to 1993. A target level of 1 percent of estimated revenues was announced in the 1993 budget. Although the announced target funding levels for recurrent expenditures were never reached, increased funds were allocated to the revenue departments and revenue targets were generally exceeded.[17] Prior to these funding increases, budget cuts had left the revenue departments by 1991 to 1992 with only 28 percent of recurrent budgets going to operating and maintenance (O&M) expenditures—a similar, but worse situation compared to other government ministries.[18] Revenue department funding increases starting in 1993 and 1994 combined with pay-scale increases that lagged significantly behind general price inflation resulted in O&M expenditures rising to about 38 percent of recurrent expenditures in 1993 and 1994 and reached 45 percent in 1994 and 1995. Increased O&M expenditures clearly assisted the revenue departments to exceed revenue targets. O&M funds are critical, for example, for the conduct of field audits and investigations that require funds for travel, communications, and document handling. Increased O&M resources, however, still left the problems of an underremunerated staff being unable to maintain the skill levels required to implement a modern tax system, and an inefficient organizational structure. To solve these problems, the KRA Act was passed in May 1995 and became effective in July 1995.[19]

The KRA operated outside of the terms of service of the public service, and outside of the State Corporations Act.[20] The board of the KRA had the degrees of freedom to determine the hiring, firing, and pay policies of the KRA. Within its budget limits it should be able to match private sector wage rates, particularly in key skill areas of management, accounting, auditing, and information technology. The basic budget of the KRA was 1.5 percent of the estimated revenue target for a fiscal year. If the revenue target was exceeded in any quarter, then the KRA received 3 percent of the excess collections as long as the combined funding did not exceed 2 percent of the actual collections in a quarter. The KRA, therefore, had the motivation to design individual and group performance incentive schemes to raise revenue collections. The KRA also had the flexibility to save excess funds in a reserve account to fund future development expenditures. Broadly speaking, the establishment of the KRA allowed a radical redesign of the revenue administration organizations with a focus on the micro-incentives of the tax officials.[21]

Another feature of the overall TMP, and an expected major KRA output, was a strengthening of taxpayer education and service. A share of the increased resources devoted to tax administration was set aside to improve these outputs. The transactions cost of a tax system consists of the combination of the government administrative costs plus the private sector compliance costs. Increased expenditures on taxpayer education and service can decrease the compliance costs. As long as the drop in the compliance costs exceeds the magnitude of the increased administrative expenditures, then the overall economic transaction cost of the tax system decreases. In general, the KRA should have the flexibility and resources to allocate them both to improve compliance and to reduce the total costs of collection.[22]

Leadership

Much of the success of the TMP can be attributed to continuous on-going support from the political leadership of the Ministry of Finance. This support strengthened when Kenya suffered a cutback in aid financing during the two years after November 1991. The aid cutback engendered a realization of the importance of greater fiscal self-reliance. This high-level support allowed radical policy and organizational changes.

Success of administrative reform depended on the support of the top tax officials. The TMP was designed to involve all the heads of the key departments. At this level, much of the variance in performance of the different taxes and components of TMP (such as computerization efforts) relates to the strength and commitment of the departmental leadership. Not surprisingly, the administrative strengths of the individual departments were also highly correlated with the strength of the leadership. The types and successes of the different administrative interventions (including computerization) that were undertaken in the different revenue departments were largely dependent on the strengths of leadership and the organization.[23]

Coordinated and Comprehensive Reforms

The TMP was designed as a comprehensive tax reform program involving reform of all major tax structures and all major components of the tax administration—policy, systems (including computer systems), human resources, and organization. Accordingly, coordination of these efforts was crucial to success. The coordination of tax systems development included: functional coordination (of policy, administration, computerization, and training); interdepartmental coordination (concerning tax data, taxpayer identification, audit and collection activities, and the reallocation of responsibilities among departments); and resource coordination (both aid and government resources).

A relatively simple example of coordination of TMP functional components arose in the first year of the program with the implementation of the installment system in September 1990. Rapid implementation was achieved within three months of the passage of enabling legislation in the June 1990 budget because the income tax administration was given support to design new forms and procedures. In addition, the computerization of the registration of taxpayers had advanced sufficiently far to allow computerized preparation of mailing labels to distribute the installment tax return forms in time for an end-September filing.

A second and more complex example arose with the implementation of the self-assessment system. The policy decision was taken and enabling legislation was prepared in 1991, more than two years ahead of the first self-assessment return being filed at the end of April 1993 for the 1992 tax year. This advance work allowed time for the TMP to assist the income tax department in detailed preparations of forms, information brochures, procedures, internal documents, personnel reorganizations, and training required to initiate a self-assessment program.

A third illustration of coordination of TMP functional components concerned the shift of the special Hotel Accommodation Tax into the VAT as a tax on accommodation, restaurant, and other related services in the 1991 budget. At that time, VAT collection capability was largely concentrated in the major urban areas of Nairobi and Mombasa. The Hotel Accommodation Tax was collected by the Department of Inland Revenue, which had offices in many districts of Kenya. This was the only major tax collected by this department; otherwise its responsibilities focused on monitoring the collection of fees and other miscellaneous revenues by various government agencies. The expansion of the VAT to include accommodation and restaurant services added some 2,000 new taxpayers, widely distributed across Kenya, to the VAT base. Accordingly, following detailed studies of the taxation of accommodation and restaurant services, and of the organization and operations of Inland Revenue, Inland Revenue was merged with the VAT Department to give the VAT the regional reach it needed to handle not only hotels and restaurants across the country, but also the expanding range of regionally dispersed services covered by the VAT. Hence, a relatively simple legislative change had to be accompanied by major organizational changes as well as training for many of the Inland Revenue officers to allow them to contribute to VAT administration.

A fourth illustration of coordination concerned maintaining the relationships between the various indirect taxes. When excise duties were expanded in 1991 to cover imports in addition to domestic production, changes were required in customs entry forms and computer programs, and import duties and the VAT required restructuring. Import duties were reduced to accommodate the excise on imports, and the VAT was set at the standard rate on all excisable goods with corresponding changes in the excise duties to attain the desired total indirect tax rate on consumption of the good. Thus the tax policy unit in the Ministry of Finance had the important role of coordinating amendments in the tax structures.

Pace and Scale of Reforms

Tax reforms such as those undertaken in Kenya are large-scale, complex ventures requiring comprehensive and coordinated strategies to achieve noticeable successes. In the context of organizations of weak to moderate strength, the pace of reform was slowed down to the absorption capacity of the tax administration organizations and the taxpaying public. Broad-based incremental improvements to large administrative systems were implemented. Policy and systems changes were sequenced with human resource and organizational developments. This sequencing put a strong focus on the appropriate time frame within which successful capacity could be built. The Kenyan case provides strong evidence that for the sub-Saharan African countries, a time frame of at least five years is required to obtain significant changes in output and the sustainability of that output. As Table 12-1 illustrates, significant revenue enhancement in Kenya was only achieved after three years of comprehensive and coordinated capacity-building efforts. During the TMP, the donor community identified strong concerns with the general lack of success of capacity building in sub-Saharan Africa. This general concern, coupled with the typical project planning horizon of many donors of only two or three years, made sustaining financial support for the TMP difficult. Aside from the African Development Bank, no other donor was willing to sustain support for more than three or four years. It was only the commitment of the leadership of the Government of Kenya to continuously seek financial support for the TMP that sustained the program for long enough and consistently enough to gain successful capacity building.

A few examples from the TMP can illustrate the reasons for the long time frame required for successful capacity building in tax administration. First, the introduction of self-assessment in the income tax was a major change in administrative strategy. As already described, its implementation required a coordinated sequence of changes to legislation, administrative procedures, training, and public education over a period of some two years to obtain the initial implementation. Subsequently, to obtain an effective and selective in-depth audit system, further training and organizational changes were required, including redesigning much of the income-tax training school program. To obtain sustainability of the program, the implementation of the KRA was undertaken. Clearly this sequence of steps required a planning time frame in excess of the typical two-to-three-year technical assistance project.

A second illustration is drawn from the steps required to implement valuation capacity in customs. Although valuation training can be provided, it is of limited use without easy access to market information. This access requires both information technology and an independent source of market information. Computerization of customs formed a major long-term project that was necessary before development of a valuation system. The preshipment inspection program was used as an interim measure to get access to independent market information and to build a valuation database that could eventually lead to an independent valuation capacity.

A third illustration of the long time required for capacity building comes from tax policy development. The job description of a high-level tax policy advisor normally demands professional graduate training plus approximately five to ten years of experience in public finance, tax legislation, and tax administration matters. The development of in-house capacity requires professional staff with similar capabilities. Such professional skills are also difficult to retain without attractive conditions of employment. In the case of Kenya, no tax policy staff had all the requisite qualifications, whereas some staff had some of the qualifications. Staff retention was also difficult under normal public service employment conditions. Accordingly, a program of professional graduate training was instigated and policy commitments were made to seek employment conditions for tax policy staff in the Ministry of Finance in line with those in the KRA. This staff development program would need to continue in the long term to attain a fully competent in-house capacity in tax policy.

Interaction Between Tax Policy and Administration

The nature of fundamental interaction between tax rates and tax administration requires elaboration to illustrate the importance of the simultaneous reform of both. It is well known that excessively high tax rates can reduce tax collections. First, pure consumption demand decreases with tax-induced price increases. If the price elasticity is sufficiently high, and if the tax rate is increased enough, tax revenues can eventually decrease with a tax rate increase—the so-called Laffer curve effect. Second, the demand response by the formal taxpaying market to higher tax rates is increased by a higher share of the market crossing over to the informal or parallel untaxed markets. Third, higher tax rates induce tax avoidance and evasion behavior within the formal markets. Many such behaviors are observed:

- Business activity gets misreported as a larger share or is conducted as unrecorded cash or barter transactions.

- Businesses split up or appear to be smaller than they are in order to stay under minimum income or turnover limits required for filing tax returns.

- Political or other influences are used to get an official exemption— the value of the exemption increases with the tax rate.

- Tax officials are induced through bribes to accept lower tax payments.

Operating either outside of the formal markets or outside the law generally involves added transaction costs or higher risks of paying penalties, or both. Evasion or avoidance of all or part of high tax rates offsets these added costs for a share of the market. The question then becomes, How effective is merely reducing and rationalizing tax rates at increasing taxpayer compliance? Are reduced tax rates a perfect substitute for stronger administration?

The evidence from the Kenyan experience suggests that the *combination* of stronger tax enforcement activities along with tax rate cuts is very effective. Either measure implemented separately has limited success. Dropping the tax rate will improve the compliance of those already within the tax net—the tax evasion cost versus tax savings trade-off changes in favor of higher compliance as tax rates drop. Bringing in persons who have been operating completely outside of the tax net, however, requires inducements that are stronger than merely a lower tax rate. Consider three examples. First, the total tax rate (import duty, excise duty, plus VAT) on a large passenger car (over 2.5 liters in engine capacity) dropped from more than 700 percent in the mid-1980s to about 150 percent by 1993 to 1994, 140 percent in 1994 to 1995, and 125 percent in 1995 to 1996. In the mid-1980s, no large imported cars paid any duty or taxes. By 1993 to 1994, the share of taxpaying imports had risen to 63 percent of all large car imports by number and 48 percent by value (excluding duty-free imports by diplomats and other similar privileged persons.) With the introduction of the new PSI program in May 1994 in combination with still lower duty and tax rates, 74 percent of large cars by number and 61 percent by value paid duties and taxes.

Second, as already described, the general effectiveness of import duty collections rose significantly as average and top import duty rates were lowered. The improved performance, however, arose from a combination of tax structure and administrative changes. As illustrated in Table 12-2, import duty collections were at a low during the 1990 through 1993 period when measured relative to GDP, total ordinary revenues, or home-use imports. During this period, top and average duty rates were lowered and the number of rate bands was reduced. Lowering the top tax rates reduced the benefits of import duty evasion. Fewer, more uniform duty rates removed options to reclassify imports to lower duty rates. These effects were not yet strong enough, however, to effect compliance significantly. By 1991, however, legal constraints on duty exemptions began to be introduced, and in 1992 the legislative powers of the minister to award discretionary exemptions were removed; this resulted in a rising share of taxpaying imports. Duty collections rose somewhat in 1993 to 1994, but then rose significantly in 1994 to 1995. In part this increase reflected the lowering of the top and average rates and further rate band rationalization, but more importantly, May 1994 marked the introduction of the new PSI program along with tighter import release procedures. These combined effects show up in the duty collections in the top rate band, which includes a wide range of consumer goods, from clothing and footwear through electronic goods and motor vehicles. In 1992 to 1993, only 4.4 percent by value of all home-use imports were in the top 60 percent rate band, and of these, only 34 percent by value paid duty. In 1993 to 1994, the top rate was reduced to 50 percent, but was raised to 62 percent for three-quarters of the year when all duty rates were increased by 25 percent. Imports in the top rate band increased to 6.3 percent of all imports in 1993 to 1994, but only 31 percent were taxpaying. When the top band was lowered to 45 percent in 1994 to 1995, however, the share of imports in this band doubled to 12.3 percent, of which 56 percent paid duty. This increase represents the strong combined price effect of a lower top tax rate and the improved valuation and enforcement effects of the PSI program in conjunction with improved customs import release and examination procedures.

Third, in the income tax, the top marginal tax rate was dropped for the first time in 1987 from 65 percent to 50 percent and simultaneously the process of increasing the taxable value of employer-provided benefits was started. Although no significant increase in revenues was noted at that time, no drop occurred either. Over the subsequent years, the tax rate was systematically lowered and benefit values increased, but from the early 1990s external income tax and pay-as-you-earn (PAYE) audits started with marked effect. By mid-1993, the top rate was down to 40 percent, benefits were nearly fully taxable, and more vigorous PAYE audits were under way. The risks of PAYE audits for major corporations were becoming so significant that when a PAYE amnesty was offered for back taxes in mid-1993, some two-thirds of the major corporations took up the offer in exchange for full compliance. PAYE revenues immediately jumped by approximately 20 percent.

In general, lower tax rates make the tougher enforcement measures to widen the tax net more politically palatable. To bring potential taxpayers into the tax net requires active programs to identify taxpayers. The introduction of the PIN in 1993 was one such effort. The effectiveness of a PIN system stemmed from its important role in allowing comprehensive computerized tax accounts to be implemented. Also, the use of the PIN could be linked to other events that would indicate high economic activity or wealth, such as the large-volume imports or the registration of motor vehicles or real property.

A key to the success of the TMP has been the combined support-ive effects of tax policy reforms and capacity building in the revenue departments. Either effort on its own clearly would have been sig-nificantly less effective.

Contracting Out Administrative Functions

Aside from computer systems development, the government under-took two major contracts to support customs operations. One was the new PSI arrangement to support customs collections initiated in May 1994. The other was the verification and reconciliation program to support duty/VAT exemptions for imported inputs for exports production under the EPPO program, and the MUB for export pro-gram that was contracted out from mid-1995.[24] As described in the conceptual framework, contracting out of routine operations should be analyzed in terms of both its contribution to the organizational output and to capacity building in the organization.

At the level of productivity analysis, the success of the PSI pro-grams can be readily judged in terms of the ultimate objectives of tax reform. Based on the first six months of the PSI program, analysis of collection efforts from non-oil imports shows that revenues were about 20 percent higher than would have been predicted taking into consideration changes in import volumes, prices, and duty rates. What did the PSI system add to the customs system? It provided an inde-pendent and objective source of import values (and in some cases quality); it contributed to the control of imports in that imports are pre-identified, and the reconciliation of customs and PSI documents identifies "missing" or undervalued imports; and it added a level of integrity control given that the reconciliation of PSI and customs activities allows either side to police the other. Finally, it provided readily usable information on imports in electronic form. This infor-mation is useful to both the customs administration and the makers of trade and tax policy.[25]

In the future, the PSI program also should add to capacity build-ing in customs. Can customs recapture the functions being supplied by the PSI program? From some perspectives, this might be possible. The integrity and professionalism of the customs staff would be en-hanced by the changes in the organization envisaged under the KRA and by appropriate training. Computerization of the customs system would, for the most part, provide similar information to the PSI pro-gram for customs, tax, and trade policy purposes. The valuation of imports would be assisted by development of valuation databases and valuation skills among customs officials. Ultimately, however, the pure information on country-of-export price and quality cannot be fully replaced without incurring the costs of obtaining the information in a similar way to the PSI companies. From a capacity-building perspective, therefore, the PSI contract assisted by regaining customs integrity and performance; by providing objective import values to start an import valuation database; and by assisting with the development of a computerized customs system.

The second function contracted out by the government in mid-1995 was the verification and reconciliation of the imports exempted under the EPPO or MUB programs with the exports produced with these imports. As background, between 1988 and 1991, MUB, EPZ, and EPPO legislation was enacted to promote export growth. Export development was a major objective of the government starting in the mid-1980s. These export programs were designed to replace the export compensation program that had been in place since 1974. The export compensation program was designed to be a simplified replacement for a duty exemption or a drawback for the import duty content of inputs into the production of exports. This simplified export compensation program was introduced to compensate for the inadequacies of the customs system to administer the duty drawback program in place in the early 1970s. In the early 1990s, it paid 20 percent on most manufactured exports. Given its crude flat-rate approach, it was cost-ineffective and was also ostensibly a prohibited export subsidy under the General Agreement on Tariffs and Trade (and subsequently the World Trade Organization). The EPPO program was designed as the primary replacement of export compensation. Duty exemption programs for inputs-into-export production, however, require sophisticated and active administration. Many of the skills required to administer duty exemption and drawback-type programs had disappeared from customs after nearly twenty years of the export compensation program. The export compensation program was gradually phased out over a few years, ending in September 1993 to allow time to establish an effective capacity to administer the EPPO programs. However, the government was unable to mobilize an effective office to support the program despite a special program of aid-funded technical assistance and training.

Key to the possible effective administration of the EPPO programs was the training and organization of customs officers to conduct the verification and reconciliation program in a manner that facilitated exports, while also protecting the customs revenues. Although export development was presented as a top policy priority, the government was unable to allocate adequate staff in terms of numbers or quality to effectively run the program. Hence, while, on the one hand, the genuine exporter did not get the required quality of service, on the other hand, the fraudulent importer who used the program to leak duty-exempt goods into the market was not adequately policed. The MUB program similarly was being poorly administered. By the time the export compensation program was being terminated in 1993, it was clear that a crisis was looming because most users of export compensation were expected to switch to the EPPO program. Despite the evident crisis and growing complaints from the business community of poor service from the EPPO, it took close to two years to complete the contractual arrangements. Contracting out can supplement the government administration, yet contracts still require active and able management by the principals to ensure effectiveness. This type of management was not forthcoming given the weak state of EPPO administration and leadership.

The underperformance of EPPO can be viewed with some surprise given that the same organizations and leadership in the Ministry of Finance and revenue departments that were succeeding in strengthening the tax system were struggling to implement the export programs.[26] Some of the following contributed to the differences in outcomes. Export programs are more complex to administer than most types of tax collection. Both are generally administered by two organizations: one sets policy, the other administers. Taxes, however, are generally administered in a linear fashion, whereas export programs are circular. Ministries of finance hand down policy to tax administrations to implement, whereas under EPPO-type programs the import duty exemptions being granted by policy makers are continuously being modified as administrators verify and reconcile exporters' activities. Thus a close and continuous working relationship is required between the two organizations. Inter-organizational coordination was generally more difficult than administering a program contained within one organization, especially where organizations were relatively weak. In the area of tax administration, the development of joint audits and tax information sharing across revenue departments were similarly weak components of the TMP. In addition, the success and importance of tax administration was immediately evident to policy makers. Tax collections were immediately evident and supported government expenditures under the control of the same policy makers, whereas the success and importance of improved export performance were neither immediately evident nor necessarily directly beneficial to policy makers. This added complexity of export programs made specific capacity building that much more difficult than for basic revenue collection.

Conclusions

The TMP in Kenya was a successful product-oriented capacity-building program. It successfully promoted the goals of increased revenue effort (reaching record highs in 1993 to 1994 and 1994 to 1995 of more than 29 percent of GDP), improved efficiency and equity of tax collections, enhanced stability of revenues, and good prospects of sustainability of tax collection capacity and performance. This sustainability was supported by specific and general capacity-building efforts: a broad-based program for all policy and administration innovations; the strengthening of schools to continue training in the new policies and procedures; increases in the operating and maintenance budgets of the revenue departments; and the establishment of the KRA in the late stages of the TMP. The KRA aimed at improving the conditions of employment of revenue officials, providing a stable resource base, and allowing for greater organizational flexibility in tax administration.

The success of the TMP reflected a comprehensive and coordinated approach to tax reform. Careful attention was paid to the appropriate sequencing, timing, pace, and scale of interventions, particularly given the weak to moderate strength of the organizations.

Capacity building employed a full range of interventions from policy and systems reform to training and organizational development. A range of approaches was used to deliver the interventions, including organization-wide incremental systems improvements, contracting out functions such as PSI of imports, and the development of limited centers of excellence to form the seedbed of the future by spreading out specialized skills in the organization.

A key finding of the TMP was the importance of reinforcing interactions between tax structure reforms and tax systems reforms. Tax policy reforms without supportive tax administration, or strengthening the administration of tax structures with perverse tax incentives still in place have limited effects. Reducing and rationalizing tax rates along with tax base broadening can have marked positive effects on revenue performance if the base broadening is backed up by well-designed and implemented control systems. While lower tax rates reduce tax avoidance and evasion by existing taxpayers, bringing potential taxpayers into the tax net requires more active enforcement measures and administrative effort.

Another lesson learned was that capacity-building programs in complex areas such as tax administration in large, relatively weak bureaucracies require lengthy time frames to allow time for training and to fit the pace of innovation to the absorption capacities of the revenue departments. Significant success in the TMP was only achieved after three years of consistent and concerted efforts to improve the tax structure in conjunction with reforms and strengthening of administrative systems. More than three more years were required to ensure sustainability of the reforms by establishing the training to support the new systems and reforming the organizations to retain and attract suitable professional staff. These time frames to obtain true capacity building exceeded the planning horizons of most donor organizations. It was only the persistent commitment of the leaders of the Ministry of Finance that allowed the program to be supported for long enough to achieve successful product-oriented capacity building in the tax system.

NOTES

1   For example, Edward V. K. Jaycox ("Capacity Building: The Missing Link in African Development," [transcript of address to the African-American Institute Conference, African Capacity Building: Effective and Enduring Partnerships, Reston, VA [May 20, 1993]) sees development assistance in sub-Saharan Africa as having been generally unsuccessful.

2   See for example Arthur A. Goldsmith, "Institutions and Planned Socio-economic Change: Four Approaches," *Public Administration Review* 52 (November–December 1992): 6, and Douglass C. North, "Transactions Costs, Institutions and Economic Performance" *ICEG Occasional Paper* 30 (San Francisco: ICS Press, 1992).

3   Much of the criticism of aid-funded technical assistance argues that although beneficial outputs may be achieved during the period of assistance, these outputs are not often sustained when the assistance is withdrawn.

4   The objectives of taxation as stated here follow the traditional approach in public finance of separating the revenue-raising function from the expenditure function except where tax expenditures are involved (such as investment incentives), and where the contribution of the tax structure to the overall net distribution impact of the public sector is being analyzed. The analysis of the TMP excludes analysis of the expenditure side of government as well as debt and other financing mechanisms. Although a major concern in Kenya and, in fact, in many sub-Saharan African countries is the low quality and quantity of public sector goods and services, to include objectives of improving the efficiency of the expenditure function in a tax reform program would widen its scope to an overall public sector reform program. However, poor-quality public sector production does adversely affect the willingness of taxpayers to bear the burden of taxes and may undermine their voluntary compliance.

5   Specific and general capacity building are analogous to the economic concepts of specific and general training or education. Specific training means the skills and experience that raise the value of the marginal product of a worker in a specific skill area, industry, or company. General training enhances the productivity of a worker across a wide range of employment situations.

6   Malcolm Gillis, "Towards a Taxonomy for Tax Reform," in M. Gillis, ed., *Tax Reform in Developing Countries* (Durham, NC: Duke University Press, 1989), Chapter 1. He defines the concept of a "comprehensive reform" to mean the full coverage of all types of taxes. With the focus here on capacity building, the primary concern is the depth of coverage of all facets involved in the structure and administration of a tax. The breadth of coverage of the types of taxes in a tax reform is key to gaining the desired revenue and efficiency effects through *coordinated* changes in the rate structures.

7   Analogies can be drawn from capital investment projects that illustrate the synergies or multiplicative relationships among project components. Investment projects can fail because the supply of some critical input is lacking or its price is unexpectedly increasing, there is a delay in gaining some key authorization, management is underperforming, there are labor disputes, or the product market is weaker than expected. Successful or profitable projects generally need to have all components of the project functioning within acceptable ranges.

8   For example, in the tax reforms undertaken in Uganda in recent years, the establishment of a revenue authority was an early step because the staff levels and incentives were at the outset so weak that any structural or administrative reform was unlikely to succeed. In addition, in the initial reform stages many top management positions were filled by expatriate experts.

9   The cost-saving or productivity gains from contracting out can arise for many reasons. The contractor may have access to specialized technology or knowledge to produce a higher-quality, more valuable product; the principal in the contract may be avoiding a large fixed investment in physical or human capital by effectively renting the capital of the contractor for a temporary period; or the contractor may simply be able to produce at a lower cost than the principal.

10 Typically, analyses of successful development projects and programs point to the requirement for: committed leadership; well-defined and attainable goals supported by the organizational policies; well-developed administrative support systems; available human capacity and other resources; and the organizational support to maintain the system. See for example David K. Leonard, "The Political Realities of African Management," *World Development* 15 (1987): 899–910, for a development of this framework.

11 For a more detailed review of the accomplishments of the TMP through June 1994, see *Kenya Tax Modernization Programme: Completion Report for the Institutional Support Project for Tax Modernization in Kenya, Phase I* (Nairobi: Ministry of Finance Government of Kenya, September 1994). An appendix is also available on request from the author. It is entitled, "Tax Policy and Administration Achievements of the Tax Modernization Program in Kenya, January 1990–June 1995."

12 In 1995 and 1996 the rates were free, 5 percent, 10 percent, 15 percent, 20 percent, 25 percent, and 40 percent.

13 For a description of the conversion from sales tax to VAT, see Graham Glenday, "On Safari in Kenya: from Sales Tax to Value Added Tax," *International VAT Monitor* (December 1991).

14 For a more extensive discussion of the modernization efforts and capacity-building experience in the Customs and Excise Department, see Vince Castonguay, "Capacity Building in the Kenya Customs and Excise Department" (paper prepared for the Harvard Institute for International Development conference on capacity building, Bermuda, March 1995).

15 See Government of Kenya, sessional paper no. 1 of 1986.

16 For example, the Government of Kenya, policy framework paper (1994) proposes that tariff rate reductions and rationalizations will continue through 1997 to 1998 by which time the tariff bands should be reduced to four (including duty-free) with a top rate of 30 percent. The tariff structure thus would be brought further in line with the proposals for a common external tariff under the Cross Border Initiative of the Common Market for Eastern and Southern Africa (COMESA). Full implementation of COMESA is targeted for 2010.

17 Failure to reach the recurrent budget targets of 1 percent of revenues arose because the budget officers persisted in their habit of cutting back any funding request, and tax collections of the revenue departments started to exceed budgeted revenue targets that formed the basis of the 1 per cent funding estimates. Budget officers persistently resisted the notion that increased funding for tax administration would result in increased revenue yields in excess of the increased expenditures that would decrease the deficit. In the budget estimates for 1993 to 1994, the recurrent budget for income tax, VAT, and customs and excise was K£22.3 million or only 0.54 percent of the expected revenues from these departments of K£4.1 billion. In the course of the year, recurrent budgets were increased by K£4.9 million, or 22.2 percent, but revenues exceeded target by K£780 million, or 17.9 percent. The increased funding was associated with a 149-to-1 revenue yield.

18 In aggregate across all Government of Kenya ministries, the share of O&M expenditures out of recurrent expenditures (excluding interest payments) in the early 1990s were in the 30 to 45 percent range compared to approximately 50 percent in the early 1980s. In contrast to the revenue departments, however, which experienced increases in O&M expenditures from 1991 to 1992 onward, O&M expenditures in the remainder of government declined from 44 percent in 1991 to 1992 to 30 percent in 1994 to 1995, but were expected to recover again starting in 1995 to 1996.

19 See Government of Kenya, Kenya Revenue Authority Act (1995).

20 The establishment of a revenue authority is somewhat analogous to an EPZ. An EPZ allows a liberalized, export-oriented enclave economy within an economy that has been unable to implement the general economic improvements required to support export development. Similarly, a revenue authority provides an "enclave organization" with the organizational resources and flexibility within a government which has been unable to implement a sufficiently strong civil service reform program to have attained the general capacity building required to operate a modern and effective tax system.

21 The motivations for the establishment of the KRA fall within the "new institutional theory" discussed by Goldsmith, "Institutions and Planned Socioeconomic Change," or "Model III" analysis of organizational behavior in Graham Allison, *Essence of Decision: Explaining the Cuban Missile Crisis* (Boston: Little, Brown, 1971).

22 See, for example, C. Eugene Steurele, *Who Should Pay for Collecting Taxes: Financing the IRS,* American Enterprise Institute Studies in Fiscal Policy Series (Washington, DC: American Enterprise Institute for Public Policy Research, 1986) for a discussion of methods of improving the cost-effectiveness of tax administration.

23 See Graham Glenday, "Perspectives on the Computerization of Tax Systems in Sub-Saharan Africa," in Glenn P. Jenkins, ed., *Information Technology and Innovation in Tax Administration* (The Hague: Kluwer Law International, 1996) for a discussion of the computerization strategies of tax systems in Kenya.

24 The PSI program is described in more detail in Castonguay, "Capacity Building in the Kenya Customs and Excise Department."

25 The PSI contract has elements of both competition and cooperation. The competitive elements are required to keep both sides honest and to improve their performance. The cooperative elements are required so that there is sharing of information on importers to improve the performance of both organizations and to build the valuation capacity within customs.

26 The MUB and EPZ programs suffered poor administration along with the EPPO programs. For example, after passing EPZ legislation in 1990, it took more than two years before an operation EPZ authority could be properly established. Moreover, although several privately developed EPZs became operational quickly, it took approximately four years to get the first publicly developed EPZ to an operational state.

Part III

The Role of Technical Assistance in Capacity Building

13 PARTICIPATION, OWNERSHIP, AND SUSTAINABLE DEVELOPMENT

Albert R. Wight

The most neglected and least understood aspect of development assistance—facilitating recipient participation in the development process—is the most critical with respect to sustainable development. Much has been written on the need for participation, but very little on how it is achieved—the strategies, approach, methodology, techniques, and activities associated with the process of donor facilitation and support of recipient participation. Too often donors assume that the process will take care of itself. Too often they assume that transfer of knowledge and understanding, recipient acceptance of technology, and recipient commitment to further development will occur automatically with development projects. Projects such as building a road, a water supply system, or a school or introducing a computerized accounting system are certainly important, but they may contribute little to long-term development, sustainability of the improvement introduced, or achievement of the ultimate aims of recipient ownership: self-reliance, self-sufficiency, and responsibility and capacity for their own development. Projects may instead do the opposite—reinforce dependency on the donor—if the recipients do not participate meaningfully in their planning and implementation.

This chapter presents a model of donor role behavior, skills, and attitudes necessary for effective facilitation of the development process. This model was tested in World Bank projects in Pakistan (1987–1994). In spite of policy statements to the contrary, most donor agencies and staff approach development with a traditional orientation that is diametrically opposed to that required to achieve recipient participation, ownership, and commitment. Effective change and capacity building require a long-range program orientation, not a focus on short-term projects. Programs must be broad-based, because changes in a narrow sphere of activity are not likely to survive in a system that does not accommodate change. Finally, obstacles to change, and to meaningful and productive recipient participation in development, are inherent in the culture, organizations, and institutions of most, if not all countries. All of these factors must be taken into account in planning, implementing, and supporting programs to achieve recipient participation, ownership, and sustainable development.

Participation and Development Policy

Participation in development undoubtedly has its foundations in a global evolution in governance toward participatory democracy. This study is interesting in itself but not the purpose of this chapter.[1] The philosophy and approach to participation reported herein derive primarily from the writings of Rensis Likert, John Dewey, Kurt Lewin, Carl Rogers, and early work of the National Training Laboratories, with which few donor staff and development specialists are likely to be conversant.[2] The professions that contribute most staff and consultants to the development field are not likely to include the works of these authors in their curricula. Those professions more closely associated with the behavioral and social sciences (i.e., management and organizational development, training, and counseling) are more likely to draw on this literature.

Research for the U.S. Peace Corps in the early 1960s showed that community development volunteers with a "project orientation" were not as effective as those with a "human development-orientation." Project-oriented volunteers identified the needs of their host communities and mobilized the resources to meet these needs, whereas human development-oriented volunteers worked with their hosts to help them learn to identify and solve their own problems. The human development (participatory) orientation was more likely to result in ownership and commitment on the part of the community and in sustainability of the development efforts. Volunteers with a project orientation were more likely to become frustrated, dissatisfied, disillusioned, and resentful because of the lack of appreciation of their efforts and lack of commitment to their "Peace Corps" projects.[3]

An abundance of literature suggests the need for more effective participation of recipients in their development programs and for change in donor policies and practices to promote participation. With the enactment of Title IX in 1966, the U.S. Congress called for more participatory approaches in foreign assistance. Over the years, the development literature has reiterated the need for participation, and in their current policies, many donor agencies—for example, the United Nations, the World Bank, the U.S. Agency for International Development (USAID), the Finnish International Development Agency, and the Canadian International Development Agency (CIDA)—call for participation in their development activities.[4]

The primary emphasis in participation, as reported in the literature, has been on "popular participation," or involvement of the intended beneficiaries of development programs in some aspects of planning, preparation, and implementation of these programs.[5] The focus on beneficiaries does not necessarily build local capacity for development, however. Consultants or donor staff can plan and implement programs involving beneficiary participation with little involvement of the government officials who would be expected to carry out such programs in the future. Much of the development activity involving popular participation makes use of nongovernmental organizations (NGOs) as intermediaries, but NGOs too often operate in an adversarial relationship with government—often out of necessity—and such programs thus can essentially bypass government officials and institutions. This should not be interpreted as a criticism of popular participation. The point is that popular participation is important but not sufficient for sustainable development. More attention must be given to the participation of government, not just beneficiaries.[6]

Landell-Mills and Serageldin observed that "While the ultimate beneficiaries may be 'the people' or 'the poor,' given that international institutions are constructed as associations of member states, the channel of communication remains the government concerned."[7] They added, "There is a growing appreciation among donors that improved governance is central to achieving development goals and that external aid will never yield lasting benefits unless concrete steps are taken to tackle the systematic causes of poor governance. But the right—and the willingness—to be proactive does not in itself ensure effectiveness. Modes of intervention that seem both justifiable and promising need to be explored." This chapter is concerned with these modes of intervention.

IMPLEMENTATION OF PARTICIPATION POLICY

By their own evaluations, donor organizations report a low success rate in transfer of technology, implementation of programs, and sustainability. They attribute much of this lack of success to failure to achieve commitment through stakeholder participation and local "ownership."[8] Because of the low success rate in technology transfer, CIDA implemented an orientation program to provide better preparation for advisors involved in technical cooperation.[9] The Finnish International Development Agency developed manuals for project preparation and design following an approach to elicit participation of the target organizations and beneficiaries.[10] USAID started a participation forum to explore ways of putting into practice Administrator J. Brian Atwood's mandate to "build opportunities for participation into USAID's development processes."[11] The World Bank reported that it was taking action in staff recruitment and training, performance management, and promotion criteria to promote participation; that it would augment the skills of its staff in institution building, public sector management, and social sciences other than economics; and that it would provide new training programs for staff which would include participatory development.[12]

These intentions are encouraging, but good intentions do not always lead to realization. We should ask why, given that the need for participation has been recognized for at least the past thirty years, so little has been done to implement it up to this time. One needs only to visit programs in the field to see that staff and consultants in most development agencies and programs are more likely to have been selected for their technical specialty—i.e., economists, engineers, financial analysts, computer specialists—than for managerial, institutional development, or process and people skills. For the most part they have little understanding of their role and responsibilities in promoting ownership and commitment, and they are given little if any training, preparation, or support in performing this role. Many of the staff and consultants who are effective perform the role intuitively. Most would not have received training or instruction in facilitating participation, either by their employer or in their professional education. It is safe to surmise that most donor agencies are not structured to support participative activities in the field.[13]

This is not an accusation of lack of responsibility on the part of donors. The probability is that persons in policy-making positions themselves have not had a sufficient understanding of the role to prescribe training, planning, and institutional support for its implementation. It is not enough to say that programs should involve participation of recipients. The question is, What can and should donors do to involve them? What skills are required? What kind of institutional support is needed? In planning development programs, selecting and training staff and consultants, and providing a support system, the dynamics of interaction at the behavioral level between donors from one culture (developed) and recipients from another (developing or transitional) must be taken into account. This process of interaction may determine the success or failure, effectiveness or ineffectiveness of programs, and, ultimately, achievement or lack of achievement of sustainable development. To implement the objective of a redefined donor role in promoting sustainable development, donor agencies need a better understanding of what is required at the level of interaction between donor and recipient to promote active participation by the recipient in the development process.

Pakistan Experience: Karachi Water and Sewage Board and Sindh Special Development Project

An approach to development based on the participatory model was implemented in 1987 in selected projects in the province of Sindh, Pakistan.[14] The strategy was to test and demonstrate the approach with the first project and use this as a base to expand to subsequent projects. The first project was the Second Water Supply and Sanitation project of the Karachi Water and Sewage Board (KWSB), jointly funded by the World Bank and the Asian Development Bank. The subsequent project was the World Bank-funded Sindh Special Development project (SSDP). The World Bank assigned the author as a consultant to work in the field as "participant observer/process facilitator," with the Bank task manager providing backup support and reinforcement from Washington and during Bank missions.

Role of Process Facilitator

The consultant and task manager were convinced that any meaningful institutional change, necessary for success of the project, would have to be initiated at the behavioral and attitudinal level, through involvement of local staff in the process of problem solving, decision making, planning, implementing, monitoring, and evaluating. The role of the consultant was to serve as "process facilitator," focusing on the tasks to be performed in preparing the project as well as those involved with institutional strengthening and capacity building. Process facilitation as used here is different from the conventional process facilitation in group work or "sensitivity training," in that it is broader in scope, is more task oriented, and follows an "instrumented" orientation, in which many of the tools and concepts used by the facilitator are gradually transferred to the recipients to promote development of competence, self-confidence, self-reliance, and independence.[15]

In this program, the facilitator engaged the staff in identification of problems and examination and evaluation of what was being done, how, and by whom, against agreed targets or action plans. A typical list of tasks for the facilitator included:

- Attending and facilitating meetings

- Assisting in identifying needs and tasks

- Clarifying and recording agreements

- Developing task lists

- Monitoring progress

- Confronting the staff when agreements were not honored or targets were not met

- Facilitating identification and clarification of problems and exploration of possible solutions

- Facilitating communication with the World Bank

- Expediting decisions by both the KWSB and the Bank

- Holding informal discussions

- Making sure information was disseminated

- Building trust

- Reinforcing productive behavior.

The objective was to use these activities and others like them to involve the client staff in ways that contributed to their sense of meaningful participation, accountability, ownership of any outcomes or decisions, and pride in their achievements; to improve the process of getting the job done (preparing and implementing the project); and to help participants learn new skills and practice and internalize effective behavior and actions.

In a simple but effective example of facilitating the process and providing the tools to the recipient, a facilitator took notes in meetings, then gave the Pakistani coordinator a typed set of those tasks he had agreed to. The next time, he suggested that he might want to take notes himself, and he got a smile in response. The third time he handed the coordinator a sheet of paper and a pencil. Eventually the coordinator was bringing his own notepad and pen and taking notes himself. The coordinator later attended time management training, began applying it, and stated that he would like to conduct the training for the other managers in KWSB.

Role of Participant Observer

The rationale of participant observation (action learning)[16] is that staff and consultants cannot plan in detail and with certainty what will be done in the future. Participatory development is an evolving, learning process. In Pakistan, it involved learning through direct participation of the consultant in various activities, observing both process and outcomes, and acting on what was learned. Interventions were designed and implemented as they were needed. Change efforts were observed and evaluated and became the basis for additional change. With recipient staff and the participant observer involved in this process together, barriers and defenses were broken down over time and trust and openness developed between recipients and donor staff and consultants. Participation of local staff in decision making pertaining to their institution's needs resulted in improved communication with the Bank and the adoption of appropriately tailored solutions to problems, with the associated benefit of capacity building through on-the-job training.[17]

Context

KWSB was a relatively new organization, formed only four years earlier from three different organizations in Karachi. The three groups still functioned under different service rules, with different benefits programs, including promotion, retirement, and different grade levels for given positions, which caused considerable resentment. Personnel in the different groups still identified with their own group, not with KWSB as a whole, and there was conflict and competition among the groups. There was a serious water shortage, with households on the average receiving water only two to three hours a day, if they were lucky. The water distribution system was old and dilapidated, leaked badly, and frequently ruptured. The groundwater was highly contaminated with sewage and industrial effluent, which seeped into the leaky pipes when they were empty. The sewerage system was grossly inadequate, with virtually no sewage treatment. Raw sewage emptied into stream or river channels and ultimately into the sea. With only a light rain, the sewage lines and storm sewers would plug up and sewage would flow into the streets. Waterborne diseases were rampant. KWSB management would be called out at all hours to deal with crisis after crisis. The organization was greatly overstaffed, but with only a thin layer of management at the top. There were water riots and near riots by unhappy customers. Customer records were in poor shape, and a large percentage of consumers did not pay their water bills, particularly the large government consumers.

Nearly half of the city of 10 million persons lived in slums, without water supply except through standpipes or tankers, supplied free by KWSB. There were allegations that KWSB management and staff were associated with the tanker mafia who took the water for the slum areas and sold it to persons who could afford to buy it. There were other allegations of kickbacks from contractors, and contracts that were on paper only, with nothing actually built, homes of well-to-do persons that were not on the rolls, water payments that never made it to the bank, and ghost employees who nevertheless received their pay every month. Contractors and consultants often had to wait for payments for a year or more. One hundred and seventy-four steps were involved from invoice to payment.

Initial Activities

The initial project goal, in May and June 1987, was to learn as much as possible about KWSB in the shortest possible time. This knowledge would be used as a basis for designing and developing a comprehensive institutional strengthening program. The process consultant conducted interviews with all senior managers and some managers at lower levels to identify the problems in the organization as they saw them. The notes taken were edited to eliminate references to individuals other than the managing director and problems that could not be dealt with constructively at that time. Individual sessions were held with the managing director to prepare him for the criticism he would receive. The notes were then rewritten as one- or two-line problem statements and fed back in a large group setting to all persons interviewed, with World Bank and Asian Development Bank staff participating or observing.

The first reaction in this meeting, as expected, was one of denial, and attacking the consultant. The consultant responded that all of the problems had come from the group, not from him, and that if any issues really were not problems they should be taken off the list. None were removed. The consultant then asked the group to individually check the four or five problems they felt were most critical so they could begin with those. Hamid (not his real name), a senior manager with considerable power in KWSB, then responded, saying they would discuss the problems one at a time, starting from the top. The consultant said: "No, we don't have time in this session to deal with all problems, so we will take only those you as a group feel are most important." Hamid again said they would start from the top, but the consultant pointed out that he was conducting the session and the group would proceed as he had indicated, whereupon the group, including Hamid, complied and checked those on their lists which they felt were most critical.

This was the first time the group of senior managers had ever met together. The consultant had already determined that in some instances and in some forms confrontation was acceptable in this culture and that Hamid tended to dominate, so the consultant was modeling behavior that communicated to the group that confrontation and disagreement with powerful persons were acceptable in this setting. This behavior was reinforced by acknowledging and supporting others who were willing to speak out.

The individual scores were quickly tabulated, and the six problems receiving the largest number of check marks were written on the whiteboard where they could be seen by the entire group. The consultant then asked the group to discuss the problems one at a time, to elaborate and clarify as a basis for deciding what action needed to be taken. Again, Hamid said these really were not problems. The consultant asked why they were given the largest number of check marks by the group if they were not. There was no response, and a very fruitful discussion began.

Some of these problems concerned the managing director, who was generally perceived as being weak because he did not live up to the staff's expectations of being a strong, autocratic leader. He preferred a more participative style, did not like to dominate, and wanted the input and contributions of his subordinates, which they did not understand. When asked by the consultant for his opinions or reactions to one of the problems involving him as managing director, he would begin to respond only to be cut off by Hamid or another senior manager, Rafique, who would then speak for him. After this happened a few times, the consultant stopped Rafique, saying "I wasn't talking to you, I want to hear from the managing director." The managing director was thus allowed to speak, and had some very good things to say.

The general consensus was that this was a very productive session. It was followed by a series of sessions with this same group, in which, with the assistance of the process consultant, they defined the institutional-strengthening needs of KWSB and prepared terms of reference for a comprehensive institutional-strengthening program to be included in the loan package, along with the large physical works program.

KWSB management typically agreed to whatever the World Bank mission asked during the mission, but did nothing until a couple weeks prior to the next mission. Thus, the process facilitator remained in Karachi following the appraisal mission in June 1988 to help KWSB meet the conditionalities agreed to with the Bank in preparation for negotiations, Bank board approval, and loan effectiveness. The facilitator met regularly with the persons involved to develop checklists of tasks required and to monitor to see that they were carried out, and he gradually handed the monitoring tools and responsibility over to the local counterparts. The KWSB officer assigned as project manager to coordinate this work started using the checklists and bar charts himself, and began reading management literature to identify additional tools and concepts that would be useful to him.

More Context

During preparation of the project, General Zia was killed, martial law ended, and elections were held. A shaky coalition was formed between the Pakistan People's Party (PPP) national government and the Muhajir Quami Movement (MQM) party in Sindh. The coalition soon deteriorated to open warfare, with people killing one another in the streets. The MQM represented immigrants from India following partition, or their descendants, living mainly in Karachi and the interior cities, whereas the PPP for the most part represented the peoples who were native to the territory of Pakistan. In Sindh, this group included the Sindhis, who were mostly from rural, feudal Sindh. Many of the MQM were responsible and respected businessmen or professionals, but a large percentage were unemployed and dissatisfied youth of the cities. The newly elected mayor of Karachi was an unemployed medical doctor and the minister of planning and development managed his own accounting firm. The Sindhis largely resented the MQM, who they felt controlled most of the businesses and employment in the cities. The MQM resented the Sindhis, who they felt kept them out of government.

KWSB was placed under the chairmanship of the mayor of Karachi, who in turn could make no major decisions without consulting the MQM high command. Two MQM officers were assigned to the mayor as members of the KWSB board, essentially to run KWSB, reporting primarily to an MQM official over the mayor.[18] One officer was on the personnel committee and made all decisions regarding appointment, promotion, and transfer of personnel. Nearly a thousand persons were added to the payroll of KWSB the first year they were in power, to change the membership of the union and give the MQM control, in spite of an agreement with the World Bank and Asian Development Bank to freeze new employment. MQM councillors throughout the city took over operation of the valves for water distribution. The law-and-order situation deteriorated, particularly in rural Sindh, where bandits roamed the countryside at will, robbing, kidnapping, and extorting money from villages. During the Gulf War, a good part of the Pakistani population sided with Saddam Hussein, and strong anti-Western, particularly anti-American, feelings developed.

This was the environment within which KWSB had to operate and within which the project and institutional strengthening had to be implemented. Moreover, KWSB did not have the capacity to manage the project or to operate and maintain the system, let alone get its finances under control and increase its revenues so it would be able to pay off the large debt it was taking on. Why undertake such a project under these conditions? Primarily because of the problems in the water sector itself. Water is necessary for life, and Karachi was a rapidly growing city of 10 million persons, with a serious water shortage.

Procurement and Reorientation of Consultants

The process facilitator assisted in procurement of consultants for a range of institutional-strengthening activities designed with the senior managers of KWSB, and assisted in supervising the consultants' activities. One of the problems encountered was finding consultants with the participatory orientation or the ability to adapt to it.

The first consultancy was a human resources study to identify the actual number of persons and their location in KWSB, and to reconcile this number with the payroll. The second consultancy was a comprehensive organization study of KWSB. Local Pakistani consulting firms were asked to undertake these activities. It was agreed with the organization study consultants that they would not follow the typical expert auditing approach that they were accustomed to but would work closely with KWSB management to help them identify their problems and develop and implement their solutions. The person assigned as lead consultant for the consulting firm approached the study as an audit, however, collecting his own information, arriving at his own conclusions, and preparing his recommendations. When confronted by the process facilitator, who explained that he should be working in a participatory manner with management, he responded, "We don't work that way." The facilitator replied, "We have a contract that says you will work this way," after which a meeting was held with the lead consultant and his superior to make sure he did.

Although this approach was foreign to the way they normally worked, the consultants made a sincere effort and over time were successful. This was not easy, because managers too were accustomed to having studies done of them, not with them; they thus were not used to accepting or being accountable for implementing them. Subsequently, because of the trust that developed between the consultants and KWSB, they were hired on a sole-source basis by KWSB for additional work.

The expatriate project management consultant was hired to help implement the new development wing (for management of the large foreign-aided development works). He was accustomed to running projects for clients, not building the capacity of clients to manage their own projects. He resisted making the change, and resented being held accountable for training and capacity building, although this requirement was made clear to him when he was hired. The process facilitator had to develop a list of objectives and tasks with the consultant and the director of the development wing that could be monitored on a regular basis and reported on formally each month. Over time, the consultant became quite effective in working with management in a way that transferred the skills and responsibility to them, and he became committed to the process.

A new temporary position was created for a KWSB staff member to develop a consumer education program as a part of institutional strengthening, but the brother of one of the senior MQM officials was appointed to the position as soon as it was opened. He was given a house, an office, and a personal car, but did virtually nothing. He was away from the office for months at a time, and KWSB management could do nothing about it. In fairness to him, he was an outsider and received virtually no support from senior KWSB management.

The temporary position of training director was also filled by an MQM appointee, the brother of a high official, but he proved to be conscientious and hardworking. He genuinely appreciated what he could learn from specialists in the field, took the responsibility for his own professional development, attended several courses on training and training management, and worked conscientiously with a highly skilled participative training management consultant hired for a short time to help organize the training department. Unfortunately, the training director too was isolated to a considerable extent by the other managers.

Tom, a retired manager from the water sector in a developed country, was hired to work with the organization study as technical advisor, but used every excuse to avoid having to meet with the Pakistani managers. He preferred to sit at his desk and keep busy with unnecessary paper work. When confronted, he said they knew he was there, that he was a resource, and if there was anything they needed from him they knew where to find him. After considerable time and eventually assignment of specific tasks with a Pakistani consultant to assist him (and a lot of pressure from the process consultant) he became reasonably effective in working with the managers.

The manpower study consultants obtained conflicting sets of human resources data, which management would not confirm or accept. The consultants thus were not able to complete the assignment. The task was turned over to the organization study for completion, but after some time the KWSB finance director and the lead consultant on the study were told that if they did not want to end up on a trash heap some morning with broken legs or worse, they should back off and quit trying to get the numbers. In the meantime, the union, which was closely allied with the MQM high command, commandeered vehicles assigned to managers, took over offices for itself, and continued to force management to hire more staff. KWSB grew in size with each month.

Eventually, following a major restructuring of KWSB through the organization study, the restructuring activity was carried down through the organization, particularly within the newly formed technical services department, where the bulk of the personnel were assigned, and a reasonably accurate accounting of personnel and their locations was obtained. This accounting was accomplished largely through the efforts of Tom and his Pakistani assistant. Under the direction of the process consultant and with the support of the deputy managing director of technical services, they worked alongside the supervising engineers down to the lowest level of the organization to help them determine what activities and tasks were required, the number and types of persons needed to carry out the tasks, the logical grouping of activities and work groups within the evolving organizational structure, and the existing locations and job assignments of persons who would be assigned to these positions. KWSB was declared an essential service, and the negative activities of the union were curtailed to an extent.

Further Activities

In their first report, the organization study consultants said that managers were not allowed to manage, that the board, and, if not the board, the Government of Sindh (GOS), made essentially all decisions that management should be making. They recommended that the roles and responsibilities of the board and management be defined, that authority be delegated, and that management be allowed to manage. A copy of the report was given to the mayor, who was furious. He called a meeting of senior management and angrily demanded that the persons who had given this information to the consultants be identified. When no one spoke up, he directed the senior manager who was assigned as organization study coordinator, Wajid, to get the information from the consultants and to see to it that this information was removed from the report before it was disseminated.

The process facilitator was with the consultants when Wajid came in, visibly shaken, and asked for the names, saying the mayor wanted to see the original interview notes. The process facilitator interceded, saying that the managers had been guaranteed anonymity and the names would not be given to anyone. He told the consultants to remove the interview notes from their KWSB office and either destroy them or keep them under lock and key. Then he met with the managing director and senior managers and assured them that the information would not be given to the mayor. He met with the mayor and explained to him that if he wanted to build an institutional-strengthening program to correct the real problems of the organization, it was necessary to find out what these problems were and that the only way to find out was to assure the staff that they would not be punished for sharing their perceptions of the problems, which, right or wrong, were a part of the reality that the organization had to deal with. He said, also, that this same problem had been reported in other studies, before the mayor was in office. The mayor listened and agreed, but said that the main problem was that he had weak managers, he did not trust them to manage. This was the beginning of a series of meetings with the mayor to keep him informed and involved in the process in a constructive way.

Each time the facilitator met with the mayor, who was very bright but liked to talk and tended to ramble, he handed him a sheet of paper with an agenda, which the mayor genuinely appreciated. This agenda forced him to deal with the issues one at a time, to make decisions, and to make good use of his time. As chairman of the KWSB board, the mayor influenced the councillors in the city to ask their constituencies to support KWSB in its efforts to bring additional water into the city and improve delivery. There were no more water riots. With his support and through the efforts of KWSB management, collections were improved, significant increases in water tariffs were implemented, and efforts were implemented to contain expenditures, including a freeze on employment of new personnel. The mayor supported management in preparing and submitting recommendations for restructuring of KWSB and for delegation of authority, and the board approved both, with only minor modifications. When it came time to appoint the managers of the new departments and the managing director, he invited the process facilitator to join in the review of qualifications, partly because of the facilitator's knowledge of their capabilities from his close working relationship with them, and partly because the loan agreement specified that appointment of senior managers would require the Bank's acquiescence. In this case, appointments were made on the basis of merit. Hamid, by the way, was appointed managing director.

Eventually, the mayor said he would like a similar program for the Karachi Metropolitan Corporation (KMC) and he formed a steering committee to work with the facilitator to identify the problems and develop terms of reference for a similar comprehensive institutional-strengthening program in KMC. This program was later incorporated into the SSDP.

SINDH SPECIAL DEVELOPMENT PROJECT

With the KWSB project being implemented successfully, the GOS asked for assistance with other urban infrastructure projects in Sindh Province. This effort evolved into the SSDP. The World Bank, through its task manager, indicated to the government that it would not be interested in financing physical investments without corresponding policy and institutional change, because it was questionable whether the government had the capacity to implement the projects or the resources to pay for them. Thus began a series of missions and studies to agree on the physical investments and the policy and institutional change program, which was concerned basically with development planning and administration, financial management, revenue generation, and municipal governance, and involved the core departments of the GOS—services and general administration, planning and development, finance, excise and taxation, local government, housing and town planning, transportation, and the board of revenue. The GOS selected four interior cities to be included in SSDP along with the KMC. Since the Karachi Development Authority (KDA) would be involved in much of the physical work under the project in Karachi, it also was included.

The experience was similar to that in KWSB in that the concerned persons in the GOS dutifully met with the Bank missions, but would do virtually nothing between missions. The process facilitator then cut back on his work with KWSB and began working part-time with

SSDP to assist in preparation of the project and to help the GOS to prepare for productive interaction with the Bank missions. The most difficult aspect of the assignment was dealing with the conflict between the PPP and the MQM, which was seldom confronted directly but very much present in the background. It was difficult to remain apolitical in a highly politicized environment, particularly when each side was trying to obtain the facilitator's support and suspicious that he might be sympathetic to the other.

The most obvious problem was the conflict between the MQM minister for planning and development and his additional chief secretary (the senior bureaucrat in the department); this department was most centrally involved in preparing the project. The minister took a personal interest in and wanted control of the project. This was resented by the additional chief secretary, who felt the project should be under his control and that he represented the government. Each put considerable pressure on the process facilitator to side with him against the other, and each at times considered the facilitator to be in the enemy camp. It was difficult to keep both doors open, and required a constant focus on issues related to the project and avoidance of political issues or issues related to the conflict. A local consultant with excellent credentials, hired to work with the facilitator, was not able to do this, and ended up alienating both the additional chief secretary and the minister, who demanded that he be taken off the project.

In his frequent meetings with the additional chief secretary, the process consultant had to listen patiently to a twenty- or thirty-minute harangue against the World Bank for interfering in government, using expensive foreign consultants, selecting the wrong local consultants, and focusing too much on Karachi while neglecting the interior cities. The additional chief secretary also complained about being overworked and having an incompetent staff. Only then could attention be given to the issues and tasks at hand. The finance department and the finance director of KDA strongly resisted attempts to determine the financial condition of the GOS and KDA. KDA finances were in shambles. The GOS was reporting a surplus each year, whereas in reality it was running a large deficit. The development allocation from the central government was largely allocated to ministers for pet projects in their constituencies, with no systematic planning, monitoring of projects, or consideration of province-wide priorities, or the effect of the projects on recurrent expenditures and future debt servicing. Land records were inaccurate, incomplete, and sometimes nonexistent. Revenues from property taxes were only a fraction of what they should have been. Studies of the fiscal and financial condition and institutional-strengthening needs of the GOS, KDA, KMC, and the interior cities, conducted by a combination of local and foreign consultants, were largely rejected, particularly by the additional chief secretary and the director general of KDA.

Policy Formulation

Because of the size of the project, the services of a second process facilitator were engaged to assist in its preparation. Their role was legitimized by the Bank and considerable success had been achieved with KWSB, so the process facilitators were accepted within the government. There was difficulty in obtaining decisions within the government and most issues involved more than one department, with virtually no communication among departments, so a structure for policy formulation was proposed by the process facilitators and the Bank task manager. This structure consisted of interdepartmental working groups, a secretarial committee, and a cabinet committee. Before this time there had been no formal procedure or mechanism in the government for policy formulation.

Interdepartmental working groups consisting of staff below the level of secretary and representatives of KMC and KDA were formed to deal with particular policy issues. The facilitators met with the working groups, but analysis of problems, exploration of possible solutions, and preparation of recommendations were left up to the groups. The groups were encouraged to maintain close contact with their secretaries, the mayor, and the director general of KDA. The working groups presented their findings and recommendations to the secretarial committee, which was chaired by the chief secretary (the senior bureaucrat in provincial government) and consisted of secretaries of the core departments, the mayor, and the directors general of the KDA, Sindh Katchi Abadi (slum areas) Authority, and Sindh Environmental Protection Agency. Their recommendations were in turn taken to the cabinet committee, which consisted of the ministers from the same departments and was chaired by the chief minister.

Beginning steps were taken to include other groups and beneficiaries. NGOs were involved in environmental and resettlement assessments. The Orangi Pilot project (an NGO) was included in discussions of physical works projects being considered for the Orangi area of Karachi. A citizens' advisory group was formed to work with the transport working group to discuss issues related to mass transit in Karachi. Representatives from federally owned areas and industrial estates in Karachi participated in the land management working group.

More Political Turmoil

During preparation of SSDP, one faction of the MQM attempted a coup of the party, which was quickly put down. The leaders of the coup left the country, only to come back later through another province. Partly because of strong opposition in the central government and, allegedly because of inexperience and incompetence, the prime minister was relieved of her post by the president. Her husband was charged with serious crimes and jailed. Her government was replaced by an interim government. She then lost the election, and immediately proceeded with attempts to bring down the new prime minister. She eventually succeeded. Another interim government was in place until she won the next election and was back in power. The army was called in by the central government to get the law-and-order situation under control in Sindh, but also, allegedly, to control the MQM. All MQM ministers and the mayor resigned and most went into hiding. Warrants were issued for the arrest of several senior party officials. The chairman of the party left the country. The army then lent its support to members of the dissident group, who were now back in the province. The mayor was replaced by a succession of administrators. The MQM minister positions eventually were filled by either the PPP or members of the dissident MQM group. Some of the MQM officials resurfaced and began negotiations with the army and central government. The vice-chairman of the party attempted to bring the different MQM factions together and was assassinated. Fighting accelerated between the main faction of the MQM and the dissident faction.

Results of the Project

In spite of the political turmoil, the working groups and the secretarial committee continued their work, with the active interest and involvement of the chief secretary, and through him the chief minister and the cabinet committee. The mechanism and process established managed to transcend changes in key political and government personnel. Good relations developed between the Bank and the secretaries, and even with the additional chief secretary, who became a strong supporter of the project. He said he would insist that consultants on SSDP work with management as they did in KWSB, not in their usual way. The findings and recommendations of the studies, earlier rejected, were accepted as valid for the most part and were incorporated into the work and recommendations of the working groups. In its annual report on the budget in 1993, the GOS admitted that it was running a large deficit, not a surplus, and that expenditures would have to be brought under control. KDA admitted that it had serious financial problems and was greatly overstaffed, and developed terms of reference for restructuring and institutional strengthening. Through a long process of analysis, discussion, and interaction, and in spite of many changes in personnel, agreement was finally reached on the physical projects and a comprehensive policy and institutional reform package. Agreement was also reached to establish a semi-autonomous cell (EXPACO), reporting to the chief secretary, to facilitate the policy formulation process in the future and serve as secretariat to the secretarial committee and cabinet committee, as well as to manage implementation of SSDP and coordinate preparation of future projects.

Negotiations in Washington were attended by the chief secretary, the additional chief secretary, and the secretary of finance, as well as the KMC administrator and director general of KDA, with the process consultants also participating. Most agreements had been worked out previously, so the negotiations went smoothly, and the chief secretary (who later became the personal secretary to the prime minister) commented on the good relations with the Bank. Following negotiations, highly competent individuals were selected by the government, with the Bank's approval, for the director general and director positions in EXPACO, and began, with minimal guidance by the process consultants, taking over implementation of SSDP and management of the policy formulation process. Two of these persons had had extensive involvement with the consultants during preparation of SSDP. The government proposed to expand EXPACO's role and to include other departments in the policy formulation process.

DIFFERENCES IN APPROACH:
TRADITIONAL VERSUS PARTICIPATIVE

Based on the Pakistan experience, it is now possible to define more clearly the role of donor staff and consultants in facilitation and support of participation as well as the kinds of problems one can expect to encounter in implementing the role. A fairly detailed description of findings and conclusions will be presented, as a basis for further research, comparison with other programs, and for planning and design of participatory development, selection, training, and institutional support systems and programs.

There are underlying philosophical differences between the participative and traditional approaches to development. The fundamental orientation an individual carries into the development situation, whether donor or recipient—a complex combination of objectives, expectations, role definitions, attitudes, needs, behavior, and beliefs or assumptions about human nature—is the critical factor in the development process. The orientation of the donor staff members, consultants, or advisors will determine, to a great extent, the way they will interpret their role and responsibilities, the approach they will take in carrying out this role, and the nature of their interaction with recipients.

There are two basic orientations—the traditional and the participative—in development. Both are internally consistent but diametrically opposed, and based on very different assumptions, expectations, and theories of human nature. The theories are self-reinforcing and self-fulfilling, in that persons who hold one theory or the other will behave in ways that contribute to the outcomes they expect and will perceive events and situations in ways that reinforce their assumptions and expectations. The two basic orientations are consistent with management theory, particularly Douglas McGregor's Theory X and Theory Y.[19] Theory X holds that people are basically lazy, undependable, and self-serving, and have to be directed, controlled, motivated, and watched. Theory Y holds that people are basically interested in growth and development, are goal oriented, concerned for the welfare of others, self-motivating, self-regulating, and responsible, *if given the opportunity to be so.*

An orientation toward engaging recipients in the process of development and facilitating active participation is fundamentally different from the traditional orientation toward provision of development assistance and transfer of technology and information. For clarification, differences in the traditional and participative positions are presented in Table 13-1. Although the participative orientation is likely to be advocated in the current development literature, the traditional orientation is more likely to be found in practice. For the

TABLE 13-1

Comparison of Orientations

Traditional	Participative
Universal principles, standards, goals and priorities that apply to all peoples and countries of the world should take precedence in development programs, for the greater good of all mankind.	People have to come to terms with their own felt needs, perceived priorities, and traditional beliefs and practices before they can be expected to take a global view.
If people in developing countries are wise and responsible they will readily accept modern approaches to governance and systems and technology that will allow them to become more active participants in the global economy and global society.	People generally understand and prefer that which is familiar to them. Things that are foreign are not readily understood or accepted. People are more likely to accept new ideas and technology if given the opportunity to study them and modify them to suit their needs.
Western systems and technology are superior and generally applicable throughout the world.	Western systems and technology are themselves constantly changing. Solutions that combine the new with the traditional may be superior, particularly for those who do the combining.
Experts with experience in developed countries are in a better position to decide what is needed for development than persons in developing countries with little outside experience.	People in developing countries are generally aware of their needs and should themselves decide their priorities for development.
It is more efficient, less time consuming, and less costly to provide direct transfer of technology and information by experts, primarily through one-way communication. The expert has little to learn from the recipients in his or her area of expertise.	If technology and information are applied with lack of understanding, enthusiasm, or commitment, the transfer has been neither efficient nor effective. All human beings approach new information from their own frame of reference, understanding, and customary way of doing things.
For maximum impact, development efforts should be focused on specific projects with a given time frame and clear, limited objectives.	Given the difficulty and time required to change entrenched, complex systems, it is necessary to take a long-term, broad-based approach to development.
It is best to limit institutional development projects to objectives where achievement is relatively certain, rather than to dissipate efforts by trying to change the whole system.	Limited changes within a system and an environment that do not change have little impact or chance of survival. The broader system and environment must be taken into account.

TABLE 13-1

Comparison of Orientations (continued)

Traditional	Participative
To make effective use of limited funds available for development, persons or firms with the necessary expertise should be engaged to complete projects for recipients in the shortest time and most efficient manner possible.	Development of local capacity to implement and manage projects should be a major objective of development assistance and will be more cost-effective in the long term.
Experts with the requisite expertise should be hired to plan and implement projects for developing countries, which are generally lacking in planning and project management skills.	Experts should be employed who have the requisite expertise in their specialty and the understanding and skills required to engage recipients in a process of joint planning and implementation of projects.
Assistance should be provided through well-planned programs with clearly defined objectives and activities at the outset, against which the program is evaluated. The program should adhere to targets and time lines established in the plan.	Programs should be developed through active participation of recipients and stakeholders, with objectives and plans evolving through the interactive process, modified with increased understanding of needs and problems, and adapted to changing conditions and circumstances.
Experts should evaluate projects and programs on the basis of established international standards and criteria.	Donors and recipients together should evaluate projects and programs on the basis of jointly developed objectives, targets, and standards.
Work should be done with and through the formal organizational structure, established procedures, and designated officials.	Particularly in a developing country, many of the decisions are made and much of the work is done within the informal system and organization.
Personal and cultural differences should not be allowed to stand in the way of efficient project planning and implementation and transfer of technology.	Project planning and implementation and transfer of technology are unlikely to take place effectively if a relationship of respect, understanding, trust, and acceptance among the various actors is not achieved.
People generally are motivated by the carrot and the stick, and cannot be expected to be responsible or dependable unless they are controlled or see something in it for themselves.	Initial motivation may have to be carrot and stick, but people generally are self-motivated and conscientious when allowed to take responsibility and not punished for doing so.
People in need will appreciate what is given to them.	People seldom appreciate what is given to them. Too often this leads to dependence; lack of self-reliance, self-sufficiency, and self-esteem; and resentment of the donor.

most part, selection, training, reward systems, and operational policies and directives have not yet been modified to support the participative orientation, in part because the role, process, and skills of facilitating active participation in the development process have not been clearly defined. Another major factor in the discrepancy between what is advocated and what is done is that persons with a traditional orientation are more likely to gravitate to positions of control in a traditional organization, where they continue to establish the rules and select and evaluate their staff and consultants. It is difficult for a staff member or consultant with a participative orientation to function and survive in such a system, and traditional, control-oriented systems and organizations are highly resistant to change.

Facilitating the development process, as defined herein, assumes that the process facilitator is operating from the participative paradigm. It is impossible to anticipate all situations or encounters and to prescribe appropriate behaviors. When confronted with a given situation, a person must be prepared to react spontaneously with appropriate attitudes and behavior based on the assumptions and objectives inherent in this paradigm. Reactions based on the traditional paradigm would more than likely be dysfunctional or inappropriate. Selection, assignment, and training of donor staff and consultants should take this into account. If staff or consultants do not subscribe to or are not able to genuinely adopt the participative orientation, they are not likely to be effective in facilitating participation in the development process.

Context of Development

Organizational Characteristics

To be effective in their attempts to facilitate active participation of recipients in development programs or to develop programs for capacity building, development facilitators must achieve a good understanding of the people and the organizations with which they work and the larger economic, political, social, and cultural context within which the people and organizations must function. Strategies the facilitators would use in their own culture or in a perfect world might not work. They need to be ready and able to modify their approach based on the conditions they encounter. Some characteristics of people, organizations, and the larger environment might be assumed, based on prior information, and some might be identified in an initial assessment, but others will be identified and clarified in the course of the work (participant observation).

From the initial interviews and through the process of working with KWSB, a picture of the organization and the environment within which it had to function emerged. This view was further elaborated and defined in work with SSDP and in other projects in Pakistan. It became apparent that the findings were typical of most parts of Pakistan, and not unlike conditions in many developing countries. Box 13-1 presents an outline of the most significant characteristics of the organization and larger environment.

The persons with whom the process consultant and Bank staff had to work on the project were operating within this system, were themselves a part of the system, and held many of the values, assumptions, and expectations of the system. To work effectively with these persons, and to implement change, this had to be understood. Donor staff and consultants and the local counterparts have to work within and adapt to this context while introducing the changes required for development. This is not easy. There are a great many obstacles, as can be seen from reading through the list. It would be naive to assume that they could be ignored. They have to be overcome, accommodated, or worked around, but this cannot be done without understanding. It would also be a mistake to say, as some persons have, that development must wait until the country and people are ready. These cultural characteristics have been developing for thousands of years. Perhaps the main point of this chapter is that even within this context, change and development can occur, providing the people themselves see the need and commit to finding a way to make the change. The development specialist only provides the structure and facilitates the process.

As an example, KWSB held up payment of the organization study consultants, whose stated policy was that they would not pay kickbacks or bribes under any circumstances. The finance director said he would not release payment until the organization study coordinator, Wajid, certified that their work was satisfactory. The process consultant asked Wajid several times why the payment had not been made. Finally, the process consultant confronted him and told him that because he was working closely with the consultants and knew they were doing satisfactory work, it was his responsibility to certify their payment. Wajid began shaking and in a loud, shrill voice, said "But there is money involved!" Then he explained that the mayor had di-

BOX 13-1

Frequently Encountered Characteristics of Organizations, Officials, and Their Environments

System Based on Relationships, not Rules, Procedures, or Performance

■ Political patronage, nepotism, cronyism

■ Networking—orientation to building a network of relationships and obligations

■ General expectation of going around the system to get anything done, through personal influence, favoritism, mutual obligations, and mutual blackmailing

■ Little respect for rules, laws, or authority; dependence on connections

■ Job assignments and promotions based on connections, not merit

■ Little control of managers over subordinates with political appointments; lack of discipline

■ External pressure on management; imposed constraints, expectations, and requirements

■ Managers squeezed between the political party and the union

■ Political instability—changes in personnel and policies based on political group in power

■ Opportunism—expectation of capitalizing on political position for personal gain and to meet family and network obligations

Clannish, Tribalistic, Feudalistic Orientation

■ Tendency to form exclusive, mutually supportive groups, cliques

■ Lack of communication; information shared selectively, used as power

■ Lack of trust of or concern for those outside one's group

■ Tendency to maintain cordial, superficial, safe relations with those outside one's group

■ Tendency to keep interaction on a safe level; disdainful of display of impatience, disrespect, temper, lack of control (except with persons of lower status)

■ Tendency to take things personally and to hold a grudge; vindictive, revenge seeking

■ Selective confrontation, usually with persons of lower, sometimes equal, status

■ Given to gossiping, backbiting, negative criticism of others

■ Given to seeking alliances against other groups

■ Resist group problem solving and decision making. Prefer one-on-one interaction

■ Lack of coordination with other groups.

Authoritarian, Top-Down Management, Hierarchical System

■ Centralized governance and decision-making

■ Senior person has the power and the authority

■ Managers not allowed to manage—management by the board or senior government officials

(continued on next page)

BOX 13-1

Frequently Encountered Characteristics of Organizations, Officials, and Their Environments (continued)

- Lack of delegation of authority or shared decision-making
- Punishment orientation, little reward or recognition
- Survival orientation, fear of making mistakes, lack of risk taking; play it safe
- Reluctance to communicate upward; tendency to tell superiors what they want to hear
- Reluctance to make decisions or take responsibility
- Push decisions upward or obtain many signatures to avoid being held accountable
- Management by sequential processing of files, from one desk or office to another
- Bureaucratic procedures strictly followed
- Lack of a work ethic, little incentive to work or do a good job; it is safer to do nothing
- Submissiveness toward superiors
- Expectation of being told or taught, not thinking for oneself or asking questions or challenging the superior or expert; rote learning
- Negative, pessimistic

Concern for Form versus Substance

- Overriding concern for status, position, titles, power, paper qualifications
- Expectations of treatment befitting one's status—recognition, respect, perks, prerogatives
- Concern for protocol, proper behavior
- Deference to age, seniority, status
- Promotions based on seniority (or connections), not merit
- Concern for appearance of reports, etc., meeting requirements, more than content

Low Need for Achievement or Efficiency

- Little planning—orientation toward crisis management, ad-hocism
- Tendency to avoid, not to confront, problems
- Little commitment to decisions or agreements (which are easily reversed)
- Lack of follow-through on plans and agreements
- Lack of organization of time or activities
- Continuous interruptions in meetings
- Few if any job descriptions, lack of clear job assignments
- Few written procedures
- Little or no monitoring of activities; lack of feedback; lack of control
- Too many people, working only a few hours a day if at all (but showing up for pay)
- Little concern for training or employee development

(continued on next page)

B O X   1 3 - 1

Frequently Encountered Characteristics of Organizations,
Officials, and Their Environments (continued)

Informal System and Organization

- Develop informal system that does not follow established formal procedures or lines of communication, in order to get things done
- Establish and work through informal networks of connections and contacts
- Establish informal, unwritten procedures, expectations, rules, and sanctions
- Personal or network needs, objectives, and procedures take precedence over those of the formal organization
- Low pay scales contribute to expectation of augmenting pay through corruption
- Alleged distribution (sharing) of money within networks from corruption
- Permits or permissions given with expectation of payment, even for routine processing

---

rected him not to make the payment, that if he disobeyed the mayor he could be charge sheeted (receive a negative letter in his personnel file which would be there for the rest of his career), and if anyone should decide later that the money should not have been paid, he would be held responsible for repaying it. Wajid was caught in a vise between the Bank, represented by the process consultant, and the mayor. The process consultant then met with the mayor and discussed the problem with him, explaining that he too had been observing the consultants and that they were doing a good job, and pointing out that the Bank was concerned about the length of time it took to pay these and other consultants. The consultants were paid, and, as a part of the organizational study, the steps involved in effecting payment of consultants or contractors and the time required were greatly reduced, and the process became much more transparent.

Box 13-1 focuses on characteristics that could create obstacles to development and that would be perceived as negative by most persons from Western cultures. It is not meant to be an exhaustive description of the culture. There is a positive side to most of the categories presented. The focus on relationships includes close extended family ties, with people genuinely caring for one another and looking out for one another's welfare. This focus extends to friendships, with a loyalty and willingness to help that is not found in many Western societies. An openness to friendship with persons who show a sincere interest in becoming friends and a warmth and hospitality on a level seldom encountered in the West, make working with Pakistanis rewarding. The respect shown for authority and age result in a more orderly system. The concern for social obligations and pleasant interpersonal relations may not support efficiency on the job, but certainly has its merits. The social welfare system is designed to provide a living wage and security to a large percentage of society, and extends to institutionalized corruption, which is another way of increasing the distribution of wealth to a larger part of the population, supplementing the low wages most government employees are paid. The development facilitator who appreciates all this can participate in and support the positive aspects of the culture while promoting more effective work attitudes and behavior. He or she can argue and confront, so long as respect and caring are shown for the person confronted. Change agents within the culture can use the positive aspects to counter the negative. For example, the managing director of KWSB who replaced Hamid initiated team building at all levels of management, with the assistance of a consultant facilitator, and appealed to his managers' religious values to reduce the corruption.

Attitudinal and Behavioral Differences

Perhaps the most difficult problems donors face in development programs, and the primary source of frustration, come from the conflict of values, concerns, and priorities. The differences in needs and goals of donors and recipients are not always clear, because for the most part they derive from underlying and possibly unconscious values, assumptions, and expectations. Donors and recipients may not articulate their positions, even to themselves. Recipients are not likely to share their position openly with the donors, particularly when they feel they may encounter negative reactions. It may take some time, careful observation, and building of trust before the donors learn what the recipients' position is, and they may never know completely.

Table 13-2 lists examples of differences commonly encountered when donor and recipient personnel interact, although they are seldom recognized and discussed. The concerns and attitudes on the left are typical of donor staff and consultants operating from an achievement, "let's get things done" orientation; those on the right are typical of recipient persons who are functioning and surviving in organizations and institutions with the characteristics identified in

TABLE 13-2

Differing Assumptions and Attitudes

Donors	Recipients
Concerned with the practical requirements of planning, designing, implementing, and completing projects and with building the institutional capacity for continuation of such activities.	More concerned with political realities and personal survival than with change or improvement, and with immediate, visible projects than with building a future capability.
Expect people to commit themselves to the objectives of the project and to take the initiative to get things done.	Often do not identify with the objectives of the project and are not willing to take risk-taking initiative, because they are likely to be punished for doing so.
Expect people to subordinate their personal needs and objectives to those of the project for the good of the project, the organization, and their country.	Feel they have responsibilities to support their families, often extended families, and have to look after their own personal and survival needs first.
Expect managers to make decisions to expedite implementing and carrying out the project.	Resist making decisions that involve taking risks, and for which they may be held accountable.
Concerned about effective use of time and resources, careful planning and preparation, and organizing of activities.	May have little concept of time or concern for planning, tend to deal with things as they come.
Expect recipients to follow through on agreements, adhere to timetables, and achieve targets and objectives; time is seen in terms of what needs to be achieved during the consultancy or project; what happens today or tomorrow is extremely important; there is a sense of urgency.	May feel little need to follow through with plans or adhere to targets and timetables; consider agreements to be part of discussion and interaction today which may have little relevance tomorrow; what happens today on the project is of comparatively little importance.
Expect everyone involved to focus on work to be done, and to obtain staff, space, equipment, vehicles, and other requirements as needed, without delaying the work.	Tend to focus on positions and job titles, support staff, office space, equipment, vehicles, etc., first, and only then on the work to be done.
Focus on expedience, getting things done, working within the system through increased efficiency or legitimate shortcuts, or changing the system, but avoiding use of personal contacts or influence.	Focus on bureaucratic procedures, with no deviation unless through intervention as a personal favor by someone in one's network of connections.

TABLE 13-2

Differing Assumptions and Attitudes (continued)

Donors	Recipients
Prefer to confront problems, issues, and differences directly, with a focus on understanding problems so that solutions can be found. People involved should not take things personally.	Tend to avoid facing problems directly or revealing the real problems, which often tend to be personal or political and not solvable through direct confrontation. Take things personally.
Focus on open communication, sharing information with those involved in any aspect of a program or project, assuming the more information persons receive the better their understanding and the more they will be able to contribute.	Tend to withhold information or to share selectively, because it is risky to share information that might be misused or used against one. Information is power, giving one an advantage over those who do not have the information.
Attempt to work with persons at any level who might have a stake in the project or program to gain their commitment and active support or assistance, or to obtain decisions.	Tend to operate with top-down authority or through connections, and those in authority may resent or even attempt to prevent donors' involvement with others.
Select or encourage selection of persons to work on projects or programs on the basis of merit—the best-qualified persons for the particular job.	May accept the value of merit, but in practice support posting of persons on the basis of political or personal patronage.
Expect people to have a positive, optimistic attitude; confidence that goals will be achieved and that the project will be a success.	Tend to be negative, pessimistic, and cautious; it is safer to assume things will not work as planned, because they seldom do.
View relationships with recipients in terms of respective roles in carrying out tasks and achieving objectives; expect cordial relations, cooperation, responsiveness, commitment, interest, active involvement, dependability, responsibility, honoring of agreements, industriousness, resourcefulness, initiative, leadership, and teamwork.	View relationships with donors in terms of whether they will enhance or reduce their status and prestige, or place them at risk politically or professionally; whether donor staff and consultants have proper credentials and sufficient age to command respect; whether they observe protocol; how they relate to one personally; and perhaps in terms of cultural expectations regarding host/guest obligations.

Box 13-1. Recipients with attitudes like those on the left more than likely would be out of step with the society at large in which they had to function and if so might be subjected to considerable pressure to conform, particularly from the informal system. In comparing the two columns, consider the consequences when persons operating from the different sets of assumptions, attitudes, and expectations interact; the reactions of each to the other, both attitudinally and behaviorally, when such differences are encountered; and the implications for development programs.

These differences can lead to frustration, irritation, impatience, breakdown of communication, ineffective working relationships, and sometimes anger and resentment on both sides. Donors need to adopt a strategy for managing these differences in ways that help recipients identify and make the changes that are necessary for development. Change is difficult, particularly change in attitudes and values that are continuously reinforced by the system as a whole. People learn to function within a system. The more effective they are, the greater the rewards and the more they support maintaining the system; the more powerless they are, the more they feel they are controlled by a system they can do nothing about.

Change may be required not just in recipients' attitudes and behavior but ultimately in the system as a whole, which may require a consistent, collaborative effort on many fronts over a long period of time. A narrowly focused, short-term project orientation on the part of donors is not likely to achieve meaningful, sustainable change. It is highly likely that this project would have enjoyed only limited success if it had had a narrow focus within KWSB and had been concerned only with the one project. Even with the SSDP project, the focus was on a series of projects within an overall, long-range program approach.

PROCESS FACILITATION: ROLE, SKILLS, AND ATTITUDES

Objectives and Activities

The development process facilitator may be anyone involved in managing direct development assistance. He or she manages the process with the various actors, with an aim toward achieving active and responsible recipient involvement; teamwork and partnership between donor and recipient; recipient ownership and commitment; consideration and accommodation of the context within which the project or program must be prepared, implemented, and maintained; and effectiveness in working through the project cycle of identification, definition, preparation, implementation, and evaluation. He or she focuses on strategies for promoting achievement of the dual objectives of realistic, affordable, sustainable projects or programs that meet priority needs of the country and building recipient capacity for development. The facilitator also assists recipients in learning to make effective use of those technical specialists or advisors who can not be expected to assume the facilitator role. Space does not permit elaboration of the activities associated with development process facilitation, but the main activities are outlined in Box 13-2.

Development process facilitation is not an easy role. It is quite different from what is usually expected or rewarded, and from what is normally taught in or out of schools and universities. In Western societies, individuals learn to compete more than to collaborate, to speak more than to listen, to be leaders or followers rather than participants, to be dominant or submissive rather than egalitarian, and to direct or control rather than to promote self-direction and independence. Changing this fundamental orientation and learning the attendant skills is not easy, but it can be done. Most of the consultants in the KWSB and SSDP projects did not come with the orientation or the skills for facilitation of participation, but many of those who stayed with the project for some time were able to adopt the orientation and learn many of the skills.

Requisite Attitudes and Attributes

The activities of the development process facilitator not only require a participative orientation and associated understanding and skills, but particular personal attitudes and attributes. Donor staff and consultants are quite likely to have power that is easy to abuse; to find themselves in situations that try their patience; to find their aims and activities frustrated; to be faced with ambiguity and confusion; to feel that their values, principles, standards, and expectations have been violated; to feel that others have failed to honor their agreements and commitments; and to feel that they will be held accountable for failure to achieve the objectives of the program. The ways in which they cope with these feelings and respond to the situations will have a major impact on their relations with the recipients and their effectiveness in achieving their objectives.

BOX 13-2

Activities of the Process Facilitator

Engages Participants and Structures Participation

- Engages recipients in the process of confronting issues, identifying and solving problems, establishing objectives, planning, decision making, implementing plans and decisions, monitoring, evaluating, and making corrections
- Provides structure for and facilitates these activities
- Assists in clarifying roles and responsibilities of the various actors involved, including his or her own

Promotes Involvement of Stakeholders and Beneficiaries

- Assists in identification of persons, groups, and institutions that should be involved
- Promotes inclusion of appropriate persons at appropriate times
- Facilitates communication and promotes productive interaction among various actors
- Promotes coordination with other groups or activities

Facilitates Involvement and Communication

- Participates without dominating
- Promotes openness to suggestions, ideas, and alternatives
- Legitimizes involvement, initiative, contribution, disagreement
- Empowers recipients, particularly those of lower status
- Protects recipients from donors and subordinates from superiors
- Blocks attempts at dominance or control in group activities
- Models sharing, openness
- Provides encouragement, support, recognition
- Challenges and assists with testing of assumptions, beliefs, conventions, traditions, and the status quo
- Manages and helps resolve conflicts and disagreements
- Facilitates negotiation and agreements
- Promotes and facilitates decision making through consensus
- Promotes and facilitates team building

Observes and Reports

- Documents agreements
- Observes, monitors, and reports process and progress
- Holds participants accountable for following through with agreements
- Provides feedback, confronts (constructively)
- Assists in identifying and overcoming obstacles
- Expedites decision making and action taking

(continued on next page)

BOX 13-2

Activities of the Process Facilitator (continued)

Listens and Counsels
- Serves as sounding board, listens, genuinely tries to understand
- Communicates respect, acceptance, trust, and personal regard
- Coaches and counsels as appropriate
- Supports attempts to change or improve

Helps Recipients Learn, through Involvement in the Process
- Needs assessment, goal and priority setting
- Planning and organization
- Participative problem solving and decision making
- Time management
- Accountability for results
- Learning how to learn
- Management of change
- Structuring and facilitation of stakeholder and beneficiary participation

---

Although it could be argued that dysfunctional attitudes and behavior in such situations are more likely to be found with persons who have the traditional orientation, persons who subscribe to and articulate the participative orientation would be unable to perform the role if they were not able to cope effectively with their frustration and disappointment, or if they had personal needs and characteristics that conflict with their role as facilitators. A person with high needs for status and recognition, for example, can suffer from role confusion, wanting to be perceived as an expert advisor who is knowledgeable about technical areas in which he or she does not have the experience and expertise. A person who is impatient, has difficulty listening, is quick tempered, or communicates arrogance, superiority, disrespect, or condescension would not be able to perform this role. Instead, attitudes and attributes such as those indicated in Box 13-3 are considered to be essential for effective facilitation of participation.

The meaning of most of these characteristics is self-evident, but some require explanation. *Power*, for example, is a combination of perceived influence, credentials, knowledge, and expertise. The donor staff member or consultant must be perceived as having power if he or she is to be taken seriously by the recipient. People are quite likely to be ignored or at best tolerated if they are not in a position to help the recipients get something they want, or if they do not have

BOX 13 - 3

Attitudes and Attributes of Effective Process Facilitators

Goal Commitment and Goal Behavior

■ Genuine commitment to the goals of participation, development, and capacity building
■ Need for achievement but with corresponding ability to lower standards and expectations
■ Ability to delay gratification, while keeping the goals in sight
■ Perseverance; persistence that is task oriented, steady, consistent, and respectful
■ Positive, optimistic attitude

Power

■ Low need for dominance or power
■ Ability to use power constructively
■ Low need to be right; nonargumentative
■ Low need for recognition or status
■ Humility, lack of arrogance or superiority

Openness to Different Views and Opinions

■ Willingness and ability to listen
■ Tolerance of differences; respect for differing ideas, views, opinions
■ Recognition of the contribution or potential contribution of others
■ Willingness and ability to understand the other person's position
■ Acceptance of the validity of others' views and perceptions from their perspective
■ Ability to adapt without compromising one's values

Personal Control

■ Patience
■ Ability to control one's temper
■ Ability to absorb hostility and to manage conflict
■ Nondefensive
■ Lack of vindictiveness, ability to forgive and forget
■ Ability to communicate acceptance of the person while disagreeing with his or her behavior
■ Confidence and personal security
■ Sense of humor

Concern for Others

■ Genuine concern for others and ability to develop personal relationships
■ Sensitivity to others' feelings and reactions
■ Nonjudgmental; noncritical
■ Trust, but not to the point of gullibility

the required status. Donor agencies must select staff and consultants with credentials the recipients will respect, then empower them by giving them the authority, recognition, and support that the recipient will appreciate.

With power, however, comes responsibility. Power too often and too easily is misused, often unconsciously, to enhance one's own status or to curry favor, humiliate or diminish the status of others, place others in a position of dependency and deference, or simply to impose one's will on others. It can just as well be handled, as it should be, to empower others, to enhance the status of others, to protect persons when they need protection, and to promote interdependence and independence, mutual respect, cooperation, and personal growth and development, as well as to facilitate communication, secure cooperation, and expedite decisions or approvals where it is mutually agreed that these are desirable for the program.

Willingness and ability to understand the other person's position and *acceptance of the validity of others' views, concerns, and perceptions*, require some explanation. Donors must genuinely understand, not just superficially, that their perceptions of needs, goals, priorities, methods, procedures, practices, values, and standards may be very different from those of the recipients with whom they are working. Such differences are not always easy to identify or resolve. Persons from different backgrounds, particularly from very different cultures, are quite likely to confront the same situations from a very different frame of reference. It is not easy, but these differences need to be identified, clarified, accommodated, and perhaps confronted. Disagreements have to be dealt with, but with understanding, acceptance, tolerance, and, *if appropriate*, a sense of humor. Here also the pressures to which the recipients are subjected must be recognized. Recipients operate within an informal system the donors may know little about, and this system makes demands on them that the donors may not comprehend. Insensitivity to or lack of understanding of these demands can create obstacles to communication, problem solving, and identification and implementation of effective strategies for development.

CONCLUSIONS

The strategy to test and demonstrate facilitation of recipient participation in the development process with the first project, KWSB, and to use this experience to expand to subsequent projects, beginning with SSDP, was successful. Meaningful borrower participation, contribution, understanding, ownership, and commitment were achieved, and considerable progress was made in building the capacity of GOS and KWSB for their own development. The development wing of KWSB, in particular, became a showpiece of project management and associated procurement, disbursement, project monitoring and accounting, and construction supervision. The GOS committed to major policy and institutional reform. EXPACO acquired the capacity to manage policy formulation and implementation within the government, with a good chance of continuing in this role beyond SSDP and the follow-on projects that were already in the Bank's lending program.

The KWSB/SSDP project captured the attention of: the World Bank, which singled it out as one of six projects to be examined in a Bank study of applications of participative methodology; the Pakistan government, which suggested that the Bank follow a similar approach in other provinces of Pakistan; and the UNDP, which proposed that a similar model be adopted in its projects in other countries. According to Holmes and Krishna, "arguably the best recent example of governmentwide institutional reform being driven 'bottom-up,' beginning with a traditional sector specific project, is provided by the…work done in Sindh Province, Pakistan."[20]

The value of active participation in development programs by recipients, which is now widely accepted in principle, was reaffirmed in these projects, along with the value of process facilitation by donor staff and consultants. These projects demonstrate that participation works, even under very difficult conditions.

Skill is required in process facilitation. Process facilitation skills and attending behavioral and attitudinal characteristics are in short supply, are seldom considered in selection and assignment, and are seldom rewarded. They can be developed through training, however, and should be, along with modification of policies for selection, assignment, promotion, and support of staff, as recommended by the World Bank's Wapenhans Report.[21] Given the entrenched institutional bureaucracy and resistance to change in most donor organizations, however, this would require a major reorientation and concerted change effort. Making the transition from a focus on projects to a focus on sustainable development would entail some cost, but in the long run, as donors became more skilled in their redefined role and recipients became more accustomed to participating and taking more responsibility, the cost would be expected to be reduced. If cost-effectiveness is assessed in terms of recipient ownership, project impact, and sustainable development, however, use of development facilitators and reorientation of staff and consultants would undoubtedly be more cost-effective than prevailing practices in most other donor agencies.

Notes

1   For a discussion of the historical and theoretical context of governance, see Deborah Brautigan, "Governance, Economy, and Foreign Aid," *Studies in Comparative International Development* 27, 3, (Fall 1992): 3–25.

2   The participatory methodology on which the activities in Pakistan were based is largely an outgrowth of the work of Kurt Lewin and his associates. Lewin was influenced by earlier work of John Dewey, particularly Dewey's "reflective learning," "learning by doing," and view that much of what man considers to be individual is in fact incorporated and internalized from his social and cultural surround. He was also influenced by contemporaries such as Douglas McGregor, Abraham Maslow, Rensis Likert, Gordon Allport, Carl Rogers, and others who looked on human beings as potentially rational and responsible creatures, but influenced by unconscious or preconscious attitudes, values, norms, assumptions, and motivations. Lewin introduced the concept of "action research," in which a person learns from experience, largely through a process of "unfreezing" old beliefs, attitudes, or assumptions; followed by a period of "experimentation and change"; followed by "refreezing." He felt that information alone is not effective for learning that involves change, that man must participate in his own re-education if he is to be re-educated at all. Rensis Likert is generally accepted as the father of participative management, and Carl Rogers was possibly most influential in defining the "helping relationship" to promote and facilitate mutual growth and development.

3   Calvin W. Taylor, Gary de Mik, Michael F. Tucker, Albert R. Wight, and Kan Yagi, "Development of Situational Tests for the Peace Corps" (Salt Lake City, UT: Department of Psychology, University of Utah, 1965, under Peace Corps contract). The term "human development orientation" was coined by Wight, a member of the research team, who beginning in 1965, developed and conducted community development training based on the research and situational tests to prepare Peace Corps volunteers to engage their host community in participation in their own development.

4   For a review of the early literature on this topic, see J. M. Cohen, G. Culagovski, N. T. Uphoff, and D. Wolf, *Participation at the Local Level: A*

Working Bibliography (Ithaca, NY: Cornell University, Center for International Studies, Rural Development Committee, 1978) and J. M. Cohen and N. T. Uphoff, "Participation's Place in Rural Development: Seeking Clarity through Specificity," *World Development* 8 (1980): 213–235. In his "Statement of Principles on Participatory Development" (November 16, 1993) J. Brian Atwood, Administrator, USAID, said: "there is nothing more basic to the development process than participation," and added that "we must build opportunities for participation into the development processes in which we are involved." The Helsinki University Knowledge Services Ltd. reported that it had helped the Finnish International Development Agency develop manuals based on participatory methods for work with target organizations and beneficiaries. In its evaluation of World Bank performance "Effective Implementation: Key to Development Impact: Report of the World Bank's Portfolio Management Task Force, The World Bank, September 1992, commonly known as the Wapenhans Report), the Portfolio Management Task Force reported, inter alia, that:

- The Bank's success is (should be) determined by benefits "on-the-ground"—sustainable development impact—not by loan approvals, good reports, or disbursements (p. ii);

- Successful implementation requires commitment, built on stakeholder participation and local "ownership" (p. ii);

- The focus in the past has been on technical soundness of projects, with local commitment and "ownership" receiving little attention (p. 6); and

- The most satisfactory projects tend to be those in which there has been the most borrower participation during preparation and, as a result, the greatest likelihood of high borrower commitment (p. 9).

The task force recommended that the bank's role should be defined to promote borrower commitment and accountability, through adequate participation in the identification, preparation, and implementation of projects. Robert Picciotto ("Institutional Learning and Bank Operations: The New Project Cycle," draft paper, The World Bank, 1994) suggested that the World Bank's Project Cycle be changed to "put the *borrower and the beneficiary*—not the Bank—at the center of the cycle," and "incorporate ownership, participation and capacity building features *within* the cycle."

5   See in particular Bhuvan Bhatnagar and Aubrey C. Williams, eds., "Participatory Development and the World Bank: Potential Directions for Change," *World Bank Discussion Paper 183* (Washington, DC: The World Bank, 1992), and Michael M. Cernea, "The Building Blocks of Participation: Testing Bottom-up Planning," *World Bank Discussion Paper 166* (Washington, DC : The World Bank, 1992). In his paper on "Participatory

Development," Robert Picciotto ("Participatory Development: Myths and Dilemmas," *A Policy Research Working Paper* [Washington, DC : The World Bank, 1992], 3) said that "the direct involvement of individuals in the resource allocation decisions that affect their lives has become a central theme of development. Thus, the "broader participation of all people in productive processes and a more equitable sharing of their benefits" are major thrusts of the Development Assistance Committee's (OECD) Policy Statement on Development Cooperation in the 1990s." People's participation was the special focus of *Human Development Report 1993* of the United Nations Development Programme. The "Participatory Sourcebook Technical Paper" being prepared for the World Bank by Mary Schmidt and Tom Carroll focuses on intermediary NGOs and participations.

6   In his closing remarks following the workshop on participatory development and the World Bank, where the focus was on popular participation (Bhatnagar and Williams, "Participatory Development," 8), Sven Sandstrom stated that: "We need to look at participation with all other elements of the Bank's work in each country. If we can get participation into this broader framework, we can mainstream participation throughout the Bank." In his introduction to the Wapenhans Report (World Bank, 1992) Lewis Preston, then World Bank president, said that the Bank "must rely more on borrower leadership and foster borrower commitment and strengthen participation by project agencies and, as appropriate, beneficiaries." In a paper that does not necessarily represent the views of the World Bank, Holmes and Krishna commented that "most of the discussion on participation has been focused at the level of the grassroots and the immediate impact on project-level beneficiaries," but "the public sector dimension of participation is of crucial importance because of the central role of government in sustainable development," and "attempts to facilitate participation without bringing government along would have very limited consequences" (Malcolm Holmes and Anirudh Krishna, "Public Sector Management and Participation: Institutional Support for Sustainable Development," draft paper, The World Bank, December 15, 1994). In the report of the Tenth USAID Participation Forum, February 23, 1995, discussing the question of how donors can promote participatory development in urban communities, Sigifredo Ramírez said that there is a need "to place more trust in the local authorities (as opposed to NGOs), provide them with the necessary training and technical assistance, and teach them how to work with their communities in a more effective manner."

7   Pierre Landell-Mills and Ismail Serageldin, "Governance and the External Factor," *Proceedings of the World Bank Annual Conference on Development Economics* (Washington, DC: The World Bank 1991: 309–310).

8   For example, in research with the Canadian International Development Agency (CIDA) (reported in Daniel J. Kealey and David R. Protheroe,

"People in Development: Towards More Effective North-South Collaborations," study for the Canadian International Development Agency, October 1993), estimates of the success of expatriate technical assistance ranged from 10 to 20 percent with respect to facilitating acquisition of skills and knowledge by national counterparts. Robert Picciotto ("Institutional Learning") reported that about a third of the World Bank lending operations yield unsatisfactory outcomes (i.e., do not reach their major relevant objectives and do not produce a satisfactory development impact) and that not much more than half of completed projects are currently rated as sustainable (i.e., likely to sustain their benefits over time). The recent evaluation of World Bank performance by its Portfolio Management Task Force, commonly known as the Wapenhans report (World Bank, 1992) revealed that approximately 20 percent of the Bank's projects were considered to be problem projects, that is, experiencing major difficulties in implementation.

9   Personal communication from Dan Kealey. Efforts to develop such a program were reported in Kealey and Protheroe, "People in Development."

10   Communication from the Helsinki University Knowledge Services, Ltd.

11   The participation forum is a series of meetings for USAID personnel beginning in February 1994 to explore ways of implementing the Administrator's Principles of Participatory Development.

12   Follow-up summary of the World Bank's 1992 evaluation of its performance reported in the Wapenhans Report: World Bank, *Getting Results: The World Bank's Agenda for Improving Development Effectiveness* (Washington, DC: The World Bank, 1993).

13   The report of the session on "Strategy for Change Within the Bank," in the session summaries from the World Bank Participatory Project Planning Learning Event, held in Washington, DC, February 23–24, 1994, stated that "Bank effectiveness is tremendously constrained by the top-down, expert-mode approach to development. Even Bank staff committed to participation still lack confidence and competence necessary to act on this commitment. Nor are the incentives in place to be participatory. Staff need knowledge and skill; resources and time; and a more enabling environment for such work," 78.

14   Neil Boyle, a World Bank financial analyst and task manager, and Al Wight, who had worked together in Peace Corps training in Brazil and shared the opinion that the usual focus on projects in development assistance should be replaced by a focus on sustainable development through participation of recipients, proposed testing the idea in Pakistan. This opinion was supported by then Division Chief Yoshiaki Abe.

15 This approach owes a great deal to Robert Blake's innovation of instrumented laboratory training, in which trainers in small groups were replaced, reportedly at the suggestion of social psychologist Muzafer Sherif, by instruments designed to provide group participants with the tools and concepts usually used by the trainer to manage the group. Blake's approach was later applied in participative management training by Morton and Wight (Robert B. Morton and Albert R. Wight, *Proceedings Manual for the Organizational Training Laboratory*, [Sacramento, CA: Aerojet-General Corporation,1963]). It was further adapted by Wight for training of institutionalized delinquents (1963–1964), and for community development and cross-cultural training for the Peace Corps (Albert R. Wight, *Trainers' Manual for an Instrumented Experiential Laboratory for Peace Corps Training*, U.S. Peace Corps contract, 1968; and Albert R. Wight and Mary Anne Hammons, *Guidelines for Peace Corps Cross-Cultural Training* [Washington, DC: Office of Training Support, U.S. Peace Corps, 1970]). It was also proposed for education (Albert R. Wight, "Participative Education and the Inevitable Revolution," *The Journal of Creative Behavior* 4, 4, [Fall 1970]: 234–282).

16 For a more complete description of participant observation, see William F. Whyte, *Learning from the Field: A Guide from Experience* (Beverly Hills: Sage Publications, 1984) and Lawrence F. Salmen, *Listen to the People: Participant Observation in Development Projects* (New York: Oxford University Press, 1987).

17 Neil Boyle and Albert R. Wight, "Policy Reform: The Role of Informal Organizations," *Infrastructure Notes*, Urban No. OU-5, (Washington, DC: The World Bank, Infrastructure and Urban Development Department, September 1992).

18 One of these board members was captured and imprisoned for murder following a shoot-out with the PPP. The other, allegedly accused of pocketing money that should have gone to the MQM, was stripped, hung upside down, and given a severe lashing in one of the MQM torture cells, after which he fled the country. Both later reappeared and were reinstated.

19 Douglas M. McGregor, *The Human Side of Enterprise* (New York: McGraw-Hill, 1960).

20 Holmes and Krishna, "Public Sector Management and Participation".

21 See endnote 4.

14 Technical Assistance and Capacity Building for Policy Analysis and Implementation

Clive S. Gray

In a celebrated mea culpa in 1993, Edward Jaycox, vice president of the World Bank's Africa region, described the use of expatriate resident technical assistance by aid donors as "a systematic destructive force which is undermining the development of capacity in Africa."[1]

Jaycox did not blame the donors alone; he also accused African governments of "pushing away" indigenous professional talent. He attributed this rejection to poor economic performance that deprived government budgets of resources with which to pay competitive salaries; ethnicity; and monopolization of political power that allowed "in-groups" to enforce their jealousy of trained newcomers.

Close to the time of Jaycox's speech, the Regional Bureau for Africa of the United Nations Development Programme (UNDP) and Development Alternatives International, Inc. published a report referring to "the failure of the resident expert-counterpart model." A foreword by the then director of UNDP's Regional Bureau for Africa describes the report, which was prepared in coordination with the prominent development economist Eliot Berg, as an outgrowth of UNDP's trademark National Technical Cooperation Assessment and Programme (NaTCAP) process. According to Berg:

The expert concentrates on getting the work done rather than on training, is often good at his job but bad as a trainer, upstages the counterpart in influence, and sometimes blocks the counterpart's career progress by staying too long. Counterparts are too few and often not right for the job, are selected too late in the life of the project, are too lightly trained, or quit for better jobs.[2]

The solutions propounded by Jaycox and Berg include closing down or at least greatly reducing resident technical assistance; abandoning the project implementation units to which donors have lured local administrative talent in order to increase the chances for efficient execution of their capital projects; and "projectizing civil service reform,"[3] implying that the World Bank would underwrite compensation for civil servants in upper-skill categories as well as pay for training and equipment.

In forty years of trying to build capacity for policy analysis and implementation in all regions of the developing world, not only in Africa, the Harvard Institute for International Development (HIID) and its predecessor agencies at Harvard have observed many instances of the shortcomings identified by Jaycox, Berg, and others. On the other hand, as an implementer—a cynic might even say beneficiary— of some of the resident technical assistance they denounce, HIID has shied away from accepting a significant share of the blame for these failures and has expressed reservations about some of the more draconian solutions that have been proposed. The same can be said of several other organizations providing assistance in this field, sometimes in competition with HIID for technical assistance contracts, sometimes in collaboration with it.

The object of this chapter is to propose realistic options for using technical assistance to build indigenous capacity in the domain of policy analysis and implementation. I begin by defining such capacity. Next, I endeavor to put the relationship between technical assistance and capacity building in context by considering whether capacity building is properly regarded as the sole objective of technical assistance in our chosen domain, and if not, what other objectives should be taken into account in evaluating technical assistance interventions.

Given alternative vehicles for technical assistance—resident advisors, short-term consultants, and various modes of training for local staff—the allocation of fungible resources among them raises complicated issues. I illustrate the trade-off between use of expatriate policy advisors and capacity building through foreign training of counterparts.

I then review selected project experiences of purveyors of technical assistance, notably HIID, describing instances of success and failure in building temporary indigenous capacity. I look for the causes of failure; review what the purveyors, whether institutionally or as individual policy advisors, have done to try to counteract these; and draw lessons from that experience. A concluding section describes approaches in designing and implementing future technical assistance interventions that might augment their contribution to capacity building.

Defining Indigenous Capacity for Policy Analysis and Implementation

An indivisible unit of indigenous capacity for policy analysis and implementation can be said to exist in Country X when at least one national of the country, employed by government or available to advise the government when invited by policy makers, has sufficient training and intuition to analyze economic problems; predict the approximate outcomes of alternative solutions; and propose policy measures that, if implemented, will augment rather than diminish social welfare. Indeed, it is not necessary that the individual in question have the technical skills to analyze every conceivable issue. Rather, an understanding that a given problem outstrips his or her knowledge and requires bringing in outside expertise may itself be regarded as part and parcel of capacity for policy analysis and implementation.

The more such people exist, the greater Country X's indigenous capacity. At the same time, presence within X's boundaries of a set of qualified analysts obviously does not ensure that government will review or implement welfare-enhancing policies. Possession of "adequate" capacity presupposes fulfillment of organizational and institutional conditions as well:

- There must be one or more organizations that mobilize analysts' talents, apply them to significant issues, and ensure that their findings and recommendations are presented to policy makers in an intelligible form; and

- The country's institutional framework must ensure that policy makers consult such organizations and consider their findings and recommendations, even if political circumstances ultimately entail different policy outcomes.

Multiple Goals of Technical Assistance

Jaycox, Berg, and others commit a fallacy in treating capacity building by implication as the exclusive goal of technical assistance, at least in the sphere of policy analysis and implementation. It is perfectly normal, when invited to address a conference on capacity building, or when paid to prepare a report on the subject, to attribute nontrivial importance to capacity building. At the same time, it need not be treated as the be-all and end-all of development aid.

The stated goal of most instruments of development assistance is to maximize net present value (NPV), taking as a point of departure the target country's stream of future gross domestic product (GDP). Foreign technical assistance for policy analysis and implementation can increase GDP simultaneously or alternatively in two major ways. First, persons serving as a vehicle for the technical assistance—usually but not necessarily expatriates—create indigenous capacity to design and implement economic and social policies that make the NPV of the future stream of GDP higher than it would otherwise be. Also, irrespective of whether they create indigenous capacity that persists after their departure, while in residence such persons, acting as advisors, design and secure implementation of policies that raise GDP over a limited period.

In other words, the vehicles of the assistance may apply their expertise to analyze macroeconomic issues—fiscal, monetary, trade, etc.—as well as problems of sectoral development, and design policy measures, public investments, and other interventions the implementation of which will improve economic performance. Moreover, the advisors themselves, with or without leverage from third parties such as the International Monetary Fund (IMF) or the World Bank, may persuade the national authorities to implement these measures during a discrete period of time that may extend beyond the advisors' departure.

Unless the advisors have improved indigenous capacity, the authorities' policy response to changing circumstances once the advisors have departed will be no better than it would have been without the technical assistance in question. Even so, during their period of implementation, the recommended policy measures may succeed in raising the stream of GDP sufficiently to create a positive NPV, taking into account the cost of the technical assistance.

In effect, therefore, in evaluating a given technical assistance intervention in policy analysis and implementation ex post facto, one has to take into account both its direct impact on economic performance and its indirect impact on performance through enhancing local capacity. Measurement of either impact is a highly subjective exercise, characterized by great uncertainty. How does one go about assessing how much greater a country's GDP, exports, and employment will be over time because of the intervention of one or more foreign advisors than they would have been without the advisors? How does one distinguish between the advisors' direct and indirect impacts, and forecast the improvement in economic performance that will be forthcoming because local analysts design better policies as a result of having been associated with or trained by the advisors?

Direct and indirect impacts are equally relevant at the stage of designing a technical assistance intervention. A necessary, though by no means sufficient, condition for a country to attain self-sustaining growth is that it must have an indigenous corps of policy analysts who will show the policy makers (i.e., political leaders) at the very least how to avoid serious mistakes such as those that led the communist world and many developing countries into sharp economic decline. Accordingly, to be worthy of consideration by either donors or recipients, the scope of work of any long-term policy advisory intervention must envisage efforts to transfer skills and experience to local professionals.[4]

The reverse side of the coin is not obvious. That is, country situations exist in which the human capital available to foreign advisors to work with is sufficiently advanced to make any effort by advisors to design and implement policies without working through local technical counterparts less beneficial than the alternative of working through the counterparts, even at the cost of some delay in implementation.[5]

More typically, though, occasional situations arise in policy advisory projects in which the NPV of an advisor's direct intervention in policy analysis, design, and presentation to decision makers is greater than the NPV of delaying the intervention in order to associate local technicians with the process. The key operational question facing project designers is to determine the relative weights of direct advisory work and capacity building for policy analysis and implementation in the design of a technical assistance project for a given country.

The author has served as a resident policy advisor in five developing countries in three continents and has observed, from the viewpoint of a short-term visitor, resident policy advisors at work in many other countries.[6] It is difficult, if not impossible to estimate the NPV of any of these interventions, and in most cases I suspect it would be difficult to establish convincingly whether the NPV was even positive or negative. I do, however, conclude from my experiences that it is highly desirable to build a high degree of flexibility into any technical assistance project in policy analysis and implementation to shift the emphasis between direct advisory work and capacity building in response to changing local circumstances.

Using Expatriate Advisors versus Training Counterparts

An obvious dimension of the trade-off between direct advisory assistance and capacity building is the division of a technical assistance project's budget between expatriate resident or short-term advisors and training investments. It is a simple matter to calculate how many counterparts can receive one or another type of foreign training if planned expenditure on expatriate technical assistance is reallocated to training.

As a UNDP consultant in 1992, I incorporated such an analysis in a paper on a technical cooperation policy framework for Mongolia.[7] Because Mongolia was new to the business of Western technical assistance, local counterparts described the analysis as an eye-opener. Particularly intriguing to them was the finding that four Mongolians could obtain foreign diplomas or one-year master's degrees for the approximate cost of one year of resident advisory services (see Table 14-1).

If the financial cost side is relatively easy to compute, the benefits side is a different matter. Among the issues raised in trying to compare benefits of alternative uses of technical assistance resources are the following:

- Expatriate advisors' scope of work normally calls for them to devote time to training, and advisors who take this function seriously can, if given trainable people to work with, contribute effectively to capacity building. This is so regardless of whether their

TABLE 14-1

Cost Equivalencies between Foreign Advisor/Trainers and Overseas Training of Mongolian Staff

I. Unit cost estimates obtained from donor agencies ($'000)[a]

	Unit	Minimum	Maximum	Midpoint
Expatriate staff				
Resident advisor/trainer	1 yr	100,000	180,000	140,000
Resident volunteer	1 yr			21,000
Short-term consultant	1 mo	10,000	20,000	15,000
Overseas training of Mongolian staff				
One-year degree/diploma course:				
Western university	1 yr	35,000	40,000	37,500
Philippines	1 yr			10,000
Foreign internship	2 mos			7,500
Foreign short course	2 mos	12,500	15,000	13,750

II. Number of Mongolian staff trained for cost of 1 unit of foreign advisor/ consultant staff time (midpoint figures)

Type of Training	Unit	Resident advisor/ trainer	Resident volunteer[b]	Short-term consultant
One-year degree-diploma course:				
Western university	1 yr	3.7	0.6	0.4
Philippines	1 yr	14.0	2.1	1.5
Foreign internship	2 mos	18.7	2.8	2.0
Foreign short course	2 mos	10.2	1.5	1.1

[a] Cost estimates for expatriate staff indicate ranges within which most assignments—but not all of them—fall. Where ranges are indicated, midpoints were calculated by the author. Otherwise, midpoints represent single estimates supplied by UNDP.

[b] Peace Corps, U.N. Volunteer, British Volunteer Service Organisation (VSO), etc.

activity is labeled as such, or whether they merely function as models with a positive demonstration/effect on counterparts.

■ The return on alternative training investments, measured in terms of creation of capacity for policy analysis and implementation, is hard enough to measure ex post facto, let alone predict. The individuals who win the customary scramble for foreign scholarships may or may not be the most qualified in their milieu to put the training to its intended use. Indeed, there is no guarantee that their future work will be improved by the training, and there is a high probability that they will soon be doing work other than policy analysis and implementation, as I suggest later in this chapter.

PROJECT EXPERIENCE OF TECHNICAL ASSISTANCE PURVEYORS

The agencies that fund most technical assistance interventions in policy analysis and implementation act on the basis of legislative or other guidelines that direct them *inter alia* to help organizations in developing countries and countries in transition to establish indigenous capacity to design and implement public policies that will promote sustainable economic and social development.[8] HIID, with its primary goal to "mobilize the knowledge and experience gained in…development efforts throughout the world and make that knowledge and experience available to those who must ultimately decide what is to be done,"[9] is a major purveyor of technical assistance in this area, though by no means the only one.

Given the objectives of the funding agencies and purveyors such as HIID, what a frustrating experience it has been for them so often to encounter government leaders or managers of host agencies behaving as though building sustainable capacity for policy analysis and implementation was the last thing on their minds. In some cases, for example, HIID and other purveyors have worked under venal political leaders who were driven by personal ambition, nepotism, tribalism, or corruption much more than by a desire to promote national development or bequeath an improved public service to their successors. Such leaders not only refrain from attracting and motivating competent staff, their very presence discourages them. Such a situation prevailed in Kenya, where the finance ministry and the economic planning organization, which was united with it from time to time, ended up with less capacity for policy analysis than when HIID first started working in Kenya in 1976.[10]

In other cases, and one step up the ladder of virtue, purveyors frequently have to deal with another group of leaders whose posture vis-à-vis organizational development is more one of benign neglect than outright despoliation. These individuals, petty opportunists rather than brigands, are typically jockeying for influence by currying short-run favor with superiors, on up to the monarch, president, or prime minister. Their perception of staff requirements is limited to a small coterie—sometimes just one person—capable of running errands in fulfillment of requests from above.

Such leaders have no vision of, or see no interest in, development of a professional staff with sufficient competence, for example, to deal as peers with missions from international financial institutions. Thus they fend off efforts of donors and foreign advisors to build such a staff. A good example of this type of manager is the individual who held the post of minister of economic affairs while the author headed a resident advisory project in Morocco from 1986 to 1990.[11] Another example is the chairman of Mongolia's National Development Board (NDB) during the brief term (July 1993–December 1994) of an HIID advisory project in that country.[12]

Finally, mention has to be made of the army of lower-level managers with responsibilities touching on personnel management for whom giving differential treatment to capable *versus* incompetent technical staff involves contravening seniority, creating invidious comparisons, and otherwise stepping on toes.

In every field of human endeavor, doing a job well requires more effort and imposes heavier stress than doing it poorly. Competent personnel administration involves seizing initiative, exercising judgment, taking risks, and justifying one's actions before superiors. In the absence of a political leadership that enforces incentives on the personnel administrators, these individuals secure a peaceful existence for themselves by withholding support from, and even blocking, efforts of serious managers and their foreign colleagues to create the incentives needed to attract and retain competent policy analysts.[13]

Clearly, the organizational and institutional prerequisites for capacity for policy analysis and implementation are vitiated by conditions such as the foregoing. Latent capacity may still exist in the form of qualified human resources that can be drawn into policy analysis in the future, but the disincentives created by such conditions make this less likely and also hamper the development of new talent.

On the other hand, positive chapters in the history of technical assistance for policy analysis and implementation suggest that political leaders and agency managers in developing countries are not generically bound to obstruct capacity building. For example, as planning minister in Kenya from late 1964 until his assassination in 1969, Tom Mboya aspired to design progrowth policies, showed that he cared about the difference between good and bad staff work, and actively supported efforts by his senior foreign advisor to build up a competent Kenyan staff.[14] This effort resulted early on in the recruitment of the then most qualified Kenyan economist, Philip Ndegwa, and subsequently the foreign training and rapid promotion of Harris Mule, who was later seen by Kenya's donor community and foreign advisors as Kenya's foremost technocrat.[15] The introduction of a special scheme of service for economists narrowed the gap between compensation of qualified staff in and outside government. Into the 1970s, the ministry's local assets gave it a constructive role in policy making, but under the pressures cited above, that capacity was eventually dissipated, notwithstanding millions of dollars in technical assistance from the U.S. Agency for International Development (USAID), Britain, Canada, the European Community, UNDP, and others.

Another positive example is that of one of Latin America's early liberalizers, Carlos Lleras Restrepo, who was elected president of Colombia in 1966. He appointed Edgar Gutierrez to head the National Planning Department (NPD). Gutierrez held a master's degree in economic development from Harvard, as did Harris Mule. After ousting ineffective personnel from the NPD, Gutierrez launched a serious recruitment effort and invested heavily in training Ph.D.s in the United States. The NPD soon became one of the most professional economic policy agencies in the developing world. It was allowed moderate flexibility vis-à-vis civil service rules in designing its staff compensation package, and was able to keep itself more or less competitive with the private sector. Although the department continued to face rapid turnover, the stock of trained Colombian economists became large enough so that any serious new NPD chief could rapidly assemble a competent staff.

In another case, two successive Ethiopian planning ministers between 1970 and 1975, Belai Abbai and Tekalign Gedamu, both with master's degrees in economic development from Harvard, took capacity building seriously, conducting annual interviews of local economics graduates and supporting a major foreign training effort.[16] This capacity was partly dissipated and partly diverted into service of dubious national benefit under the communist Dergue during the ensuing fifteen years. The new government continued to be saddled with an unwieldy planning agency (reportedly staffed by two hundred professionals, most with training of dubious merit from a local university ravaged by the Dergue or from Eastern Europe), but the minister in office in mid-1995, economist Duri Mohamed, was taking concrete steps to build bona fide capacity.[17]

In the aftermath of Indonesia's hyperinflation in the 1960s, agencies were left more or less on their own to construct ad hoc compensation packages, with heavy proportions of benefits in kind, project bonuses, and moonlighting.[18] Several of the technocrats installed by President Suharto took advantage of this bureaucratic space, not to mention a key role in the budget process, to attract and retain competent staff. Likewise, they took advantage of the country's favorable resource situation, which itself was protected by their ability to prevent diversion of oil revenues à la Nigeria, to arrange massive investments in professional training abroad.[19] Post- Sukarno capacity building in Indonesia has also been greatly helped by political stability and a cultural environment that limits brain drain and staff turnover.

In 1983, The Gambia's finance minister, Sheriff Sisay, commissioned me to survey the potential of his professional staff and propose a comprehensive training program. The minister reviewed the resulting recommendations in detail, expressed a keen sense of the differences in performance and potential among staff members, and accepted sacrifices in short-run output to get the best ones trained. In conjunction with an HIID advisory project that started in 1985, Sisay supported establishment of an economic analysis unit. These accomplishments were dissipated following Sisay's withdrawal in 1988 because of illness and his succession by officials who cared little about capacity. The coup de grâce came in July 1994 with a takeover by the army.

In a final example, the pre-1986 Moroccan economic affairs minister, Taieb Bencheikh, gave strong indications when negotiating with the USAID-funded advisory team that he was serious about developing analytical capacity. Although he was transferred to another ministry before the project began, he later made himself accessible to HIID staff and spoke knowledgeably about issues of capacity building, notwithstanding his inability to intervene in his old ministry.

To be sure, not all of the positive cases cited here met all three prerequisites of "adequate" capacity, i.e., qualified human resources, functioning organizations, and a favorable institutional environment. More often than not, talented staff were available but poorly organized, or policies were imposed by vested interests while technocratic recommendations were ignored.

Apart from the cases mentioned above, other developing countries have undergone substantial deterioration of capacity for policy analysis—in some cases followed by partial rehabilitation and in others not.[20] In sub-Saharan Africa, these countries include the Central African Republic, Ghana, Tanzania, and Zambia, not to mention countries racked by civil strife, such as Angola, Mozambique, Somalia, Sudan, Uganda, and Zaire. An important new study presents case material on deterioration of capacity in the Central African Republic, Ghana, Tanzania, Bolivia, and Sri Lanka.[21] Of the report's six case studies, only that for Morocco documents retention and possible strengthening of capacity in selected sectors.

LESSONS OF TECHNICAL ASSISTANCE PROJECT HISTORY

The first lesson that can be extracted from reviewing the foregoing case histories is that development of capacity for policy analysis and implementation in a particular organization is virtually unpredictable. It appears to depend first and foremost on whether the individuals to whom the political leadership entrusts the organization pursue an objective function with a significant degree of altruism, thus fulfilling the definition of enlightened leadership. Another factor, though probably less important, is the managerial skill of these individuals. Persons in visible positions of responsibility who are altruistic, even if not good managers, can attract serious policy analysts to work with them, whereas good managers who lack altruism attract collaborators whose essential role is to help them extract graft or advance to higher positions.

Predilections of the paramount political leaders are no foolproof predictors of the objective functions of the individuals they install to manage agencies operating in the policy arena. That is, whether the leaders have some idea of what professional policy analysis is about, attach positive value to it, and are occasionally willing to implement the policy recommendations it generates, or alternatively ignore the latter and go no further in economic policy making than to tolerate measures dictated by the IMF and donor agencies, seems not to determine the caliber of their appointments.

Thus, national leaders such as Kenya's Jomo Kenyatta, Ethiopia's Haile Selassie, Morocco's King Hassan, and The Gambia's Dawad Jawara installed at various times as ministers of economic planning or finance individuals who could be termed enlightened leaders, succeeded by or alternating with ministers who could not be so described. The composition of cabinets and allocation of ministerial portfolios in most countries are generally more political balancing acts than a scientific matching of skills and job requirements.

The second lesson that emerges from the cases is that capacity for policy analysis, once it has made its appearance in any organization in or with which a technical assistance purveyor such as HIID has worked, is subject to deterioration because of factors that neither the purveyor nor the relevant funding agencies can control. Erosion of capacity may be gradual or sudden, it may be partial or total. In some cases, for example, political control can pass from those who, if not favoring policy analysis, at least tolerate it, to those who actively oppose it as a hindrance to their objectives. Similarly, at any moment enlightened ministers and department heads may leave their positions because of illness, rotation to another post, political disfavor, or attraction into more remunerative employment, and can be replaced by unenlightened ones. This transition may be a result of the political character of the cabinet appointment process, or because an individual with apparent credentials to motivate and manage a policy analysis staff turns out to have a different agenda. In other cases, the economic context within which policy analysts work can deteriorate to such an extent as to induce or even oblige them to seek alternative employment in order to make ends meet. In many African and Latin American countries, acceleration of inflation, ensuing fiscal stress, and plunging real compensation have undercut the sincere desire of enlightened managers to retain competent staff.

In sum, any donor or technical assistance purveyor that thinks it has found a way to design a project guaranteed to build *sustainable* capacity in any specific counterpart organization is deluding itself.

On the other hand, technical assistance purveyors can certainly communicate, to repeat Dwight Perkins' words, "knowledge and experience gained in development efforts throughout the world" to individual counterparts, and those counterparts, even if they then quit the organization in which a purveyor was expected to build capacity, can subsequently bring that knowledge and experience to bear in support of their country's development under other auspices. One can envisage several scenarios in which capacity built with the help of technical assistance may continue to generate social value outside the initial target agency.

- Former counterparts may surface in public institutions, other than those for which they were trained, where their positive contribution to policy making is sufficient—or holds promise of being so—to give a favorable return to the technical assistance investment in them. For example, ex-counterparts may contribute to policy making in successive assignments in the ministries of planning and finance, the central bank, a monetary board, the president's or prime minister's office, or sectoral planning units. In the best of all possible worlds, as the fortunes of a given agency ebb and flow with management's competence and honesty or influence with the national leadership, capable policy analysts will rotate to those agencies currently holding influence over policy formulation.

■ In most countries, a much more common scenario is one in which counterparts leave the public policy arena altogether, taking jobs with international agencies in or outside the country, public enterprises, or the private sector. One variant of the scenario is that they return to the policy arena at some later time, near or distant, attracted by the advent of dynamic management that understands the problem of compensation differentials and arranges special packages to bring any temporary sacrifice of income within tolerable limits.[22]

■ A second variant is that the counterparts leave the public sector policy arena never to return. The question then becomes whether the impact of their association with the technical assistance purveyor generates sufficient social value in their alternative occupations to render a positive return to the human capital investment involved. Outside the framework of a global (worldwide) welfare function, it would be difficult to make that case for a counterpart who emigrates and leaves the country scene permanently. A counterpart who stays in the country may conceivably generate high social value as a private or public enterprise manager or local executive of a donor entity.

■ Finally, even if the present social value of the contribution already made or likely to be made in the future by policy analysts trained by technical assistance purveyors does not cover the cost of the assistance, when added to the social benefit from a technical assistance project's contribution to current policy making, the NPV of the intervention may still turn out to be positive.

Some countries may offer little prospect that the working environment in agencies responsible for policy analysis will improve sufficiently in the foreseeable future to attract and retain competent staff, or, if competent staff can be attracted for limited periods, to draw adequate replacements for those leaving and thus ensure a manageable rotation. This would be the case where tribalism and corruption are institutionalized from the top down; of the case histories mentioned above, Kenya and The Gambia appear to fit this description.

A similar situation is likely to prevail in countries where hyperinflation has undercut staff compensation and a date for recovery of revenues cannot be predicted. This is certainly the case in many transition economies; it appears also to be the case in Zambia, where the finance ministry had not, as of mid-1995, succeeded in recruiting qualified counterparts for an advisory project initiated in 1991.[23]

FUTURE CAPACITY BUILDING FOR POLICY ANALYSIS AND IMPLEMENTATION

Purveyors of technical assistance can enhance their contribution to capacity building in one or both of two ways. First, they can take special measures—if possible with the support of agency managers, but if that is not possible, without it—to motivate competent professionals to remain in counterpart agencies. Second, they can look at capacity for policy analysis in a developing country as something broader than simply a counterpart agency's retention of competent individuals whom the technical assistance purveyor has helped to cultivate. Special measures that have been proposed at various times by observers of the capacity-building scene include the following:[24]

- Influence the finance ministry and the personnel management agency to establish conditions of service attractive to competent personnel;

- Provide infrastructure and equipment to help staff better realize their professional potential;

- Raise morale through improved management practices of supervisors;

- Insulate competent staff from ethnic, religious, and social discrimination;

- For key individuals, design special packages with competitive terms and conditions well in excess of civil service levels;

- Design training programs to promote retention, such as conferring credentials not easily marketable outside government; and

- Induce foreign and multilateral agencies to refrain from recruiting competent staff out of government service.

In the writer's view, the first four items in the list should form an integral part of the work program for any technical assistance project designed to build capacity. Conversely, the last three approaches raise complicated issues:

- Donor agencies often use special packages to ensure special attention for their projects. If a project involves sufficient commitment of resources, such attention may be justified. However, there is also a cost in terms of the diversion of staff resources from other duties and the resentment felt by staff who are excluded from the package.

- The use of nonmarketable credentials carries the aura of luring people into modes of training that will prevent them from realizing their innate economic potential.

- Efforts to reduce "poaching" by foreign agencies in effect institute a blockage in the labor market that will prevent talented individuals from realizing their financial potential. Whether the financial rewards of working for foreign agencies correspond to social returns depends on the value the agencies are contributing and how much the local employees contribute.

Whatever the measures taken and whatever their justification, technical assistance donors and purveyors must be prepared for the eventuality that they will not succeed sufficiently to make it possible, within the organization targeted by a given project, to establish a durable local capacity to do analytical staff work comparable to that performed by the foreign advisors. Given that outcome, donors and purveyors must take a broader view of capacity building.

Based on long experience, donors and technical assistance purveyors must face up to the fact that, in most developing countries and, for the time being, in countries in transition, capacity within any given host agency—indeed within the host government as a whole, will unavoidably be ephemeral, no matter how much is invested in building it. Accordingly, donors and purveyors should be worrying about how to create a stock of capacity for policy analysis that will not be tied to particular agencies, but will nonetheless be available to be channeled, for longer or shorter periods of time, into specific uses when effective demand for talent in such uses comes into being.

Suitable repositories for relevant talent (skills for policy analysis) will differ from one country to another. Universities, independent policy research institutes, and consulting firms are leading candidates for such a role. These institutions, though, no less than government agencies, are subject to vicissitudes causing their own stocks of capacity to rise and fall. At some points in time the most suitable stock of talent to be tapped for a given policy-analytic role may consist of a handful of individuals unaffiliated with any such institutions.

HIID's advisory project in Morocco was a demonstration of the need for donors and technical assistance purveyors to take a broad view of capacity building and to suggest measures, usually omitted from scopes of work spelled out in official project agreements, that can be taken to realize the potential offered by this view. The ablest economists available to interact with the HIID project turned out to be a group of faculty and one graduate student at the Universities of Rabat and Casablanca.[25] Unquestionably, the project's most important research output was a three-year study of the response of a dozen local industries to price control and its relaxation, carried out by a team of three lecturers from the University of Rabat on contract to HIID, and involving regular interaction with the two resident advisors. The study report was published with USAID funding following the project's end.

Securing the minister's consent to this contract notwithstanding opposition from his permanent staff, who eventually cooperated with the team, was a laborious process. Over a three-year period, the minister granted two audiences to the academic team, their expatriate colleagues, and the responsible division chief, and serious interchange took place. Nevertheless, the ministry's leadership ignored HIID's proposals to institutionalize use of academics and other local consultants following the project's end.

As for the graduate student recruited into the host agency, his policy research talents blossomed up to the project's end in 1990, when he entered a foreign Ph.D. program. Again, he was resented by the host agency staff, and no effort was made to retain him. Completing his degree in 1994, he subsequently joined a local economics faculty.

The HIID project also helped promote collaborative research arrangements between the University of Montreal (both its economics faculty and an affiliated research institute) and faculty at both Rabat and Casablanca Universities. Canadian aid, in supporting this collaboration via three different projects, showed substantially greater interest than USAID in building capacity for economic policy analysis in Morocco.[26]

Through all these relationships, I believe that the project made a significant contribution to building capacity for policy-oriented research in Morocco, not to mention economics teaching.[27] If and when the Moroccan political scene gives birth to more demand for technocrats in economic policy making, the talents of these individuals and persons trained by them are likely to come into play.

Conclusions

The contribution that HIID and other purveyors of technical assistance for policy analysis and implementation have made to building policy and analytical capacity in the broad sense has certainly surpassed any achievement by way of establishing capacity likely to be retained for a significant period in immediate counterpart agencies. If HIID and other purveyors had this vision in mind when they started the projects in question, might they have acted differently, to better effect?

The scope of work of a standard technical assistance project calls on the purveyor to arrange fellowships for the best-qualified counterparts in the host agency and send them abroad in time to return as understudies to the advisors and then take over from them. What if the advisors find strong evidence that the existing counterparts are incapable of absorbing training, while there are outsiders whose training would yield a positive return?

Rather than sticking to the letter of project agreements, there have been situations in which HIID advisors made greater contributions to capacity building by torpedoing the foreign-training aspirations of demonstrably incompetent counterparts and diverting the assigned resources to targets of opportunity, regardless of their current affiliation (or lack thereof). If such targets are not available, the best alternative may well be to underspend a project's training budget, limiting foreign training to the odd short-term course or study tour.

In conclusion, the following elements of capacity-building strategy for policy analysis and implementation are proposed to technical assistance donors, purveyors, ministers of finance and planning, and others:

- Training provisions in project agreements and budgets should give flexibility to recruit trainees if candidates with potential to contribute at some future time at any locus in the policy analysis network can be found.

- Drawing on its connections in the host country, a technical assistance purveyor should seek promising candidates wherever they may be found, irrespective of their nominal relationship to the immediate project, and use whatever skills, experience, and connections it has in brokering training opportunities, foreign or local, to help the individuals in question realize their potential.

- Donors and technical assistance purveyors should sensitize agency managers to the advantages of using local policy analysis talent on a contractual basis, part- or full-time depending on needs as well as availability of the talent and funds to pay for it. This strategy is preferable to relying on civil service recruitment, the terms of which will rarely permit hiring talented policy analysts.

- As a complement to, or possibly even in lieu of, resident advisory projects in agencies concerned with policy analysis and implementation, donors should promote and finance policy research activities that can draw on local talent wherever it happens to be situated. The activities may be based in local policy research institutes, or they may be virtually "footloose." Through such activities the donors and expatriate researchers they enlist can enhance local skills and help to develop informal policy analysis networks with participants who may from time to time, as agencies fall into the hands of enlightened managers, be involved in government policy making.[28]

NOTES

1   Edward V. K. Jaycox, "Capacity Building: The Missing Link in African Development" (transcript of address to the African-American Institute Conference, African Capacity Building: Effective and Enduring Partnerships, Reston, VA, May 20, 1993). Distributed by the World Bank's Africa Regional Office. Washington DC (May 20, 1993): 2.

2   Elliot J. Berg, *Rethinking Technical Cooperation: Reforms for Capacity Building in Africa* (Washington, DC: United Nations Development Programme/Development Alternatives, Inc., 1993), 101.

3   Jaycox, "Capacity Building," 6.

4   This does not exclude short-term technical assistance interventions with the objective of providing an immediate solution to a crisis, and where substantial opportunity costs would be incurred by having the advisor(s) focus on training local analysts rather than designing measures for immediate implementation.

5   By "working through" the counterparts we mean associating them in the analysis and leading them to understand the resulting policy recommendations as well as justifying these in front of the policy makers.

6   The countries were Kenya, Colombia, Ethiopia, Indonesia, and Morocco.

7   UNDP/New York commissioned the paper as part of the same NaTCAP process that gave birth to the Berg study, but was very uncomfortable with the trade-off analysis. For that and other reasons, the report was not published by the UNDP.

8   Countries in transition are those that are moving from centrally planned to market economies.

9   Dwight Perkins, "Director's Statement," *1991–1993 Biennial Report* (Cambridge: Harvard Institute for International Development), 1.

10 See the tabulation of wastage of trained Kenyan staff in Cohen and Wheeler, Chapter 5. Diplomatically, the authors abstain from probing two factors that, based on the author's personal observation, could help explain retention rates exceeding, say, 25 percent in some agencies: namely the presence of opportunities for graft in certain agencies and the possibility that some retainees lack the initiative or competence to find alternative employment notwithstanding low (nominal) emoluments in the public sector. Retention of such staff is scarcely tantamount to building capacity for policy analysis and implementation.

11 One anecdote suffices to symbolize this minister's posture: concluding a meeting with the HIID host unit's staff—the only one he consented to hold during the project's four years—the minister was reminded of a request to assign back to the unit its only trained local economist, hired at HIID's behest, who soon after his recruitment had been reassigned to administrative tasks. Responding to a comment that the unit needed someone with econometric skills, the minister waved at a recently hired commerce graduate and said, "You there, you can do econometrics," at which the subject nervously demurred. The minister let us dangle for another two months before finally assigning the economist back to the unit. When the

project ended, no effort was made to retain this individual, and the process of upgrading of the unit from a price control to an economic studies group, which had been the primary objective of expenditure of $1.5 million of U.S. aid funds, was once again devoid of professional economists.

12 A very similar anecdote applies to that situation. HIID's project director succeeded in attracting to the NDB a talented local who was one of the first Mongolians to obtain U.S. master's training in economics. Management virtually ignored her, and when the project director returned from home leave, he found her gone from the agency.

13 For a recent (and rich) documentation of such bureaucratic behavior in six disparate developing countries—Bolivia, Central African Republic, Ghana, Morocco, Sri Lanka, and Tanzania, see Mary E. Hilderbrand and Merilee S. Grindle, "Building Sustainable Capacity: Challenges for the Public Sector."

14 Professor Edgar O. Edwards, then of the Rice University economics department.

15 Philip Ndegwa's last Kenya Government post was as central bank governor. The Kenya Planning Ministry's gain was, unavoidably, Makerere University's loss. See David K. Leonard, *African Successes: Four Public Managers of Kenyan Rural Development* (Berkeley: University of California Press, 1991) for a perceptive analysis of Harris Mule's rise in the Kenya meritocracy. Mule left the government in 1986 over the issue of a rapacious so-called public investment orchestrated by Moi, Saitoti, and associates (the Turkwell Dam project).

16 HIID's predecessor agency, the Development Advisory Service, fielded a resident advisory team during this period, and was closely involved in the capacity building effort. The author served for eighteen months as the project's initial field director.

17 For example, he applied for assistance from the African Capacity Building Foundation (ACBF) in Harare.

18 See Clive Gray, "Civil Service Compensation in Indonesia," *Bulletin of Indonesian Economic Studies* (March 1979).

19 See Brian Pinto, "Nigeria Before and After the Oil Boom: A Policy Comparison with Indonesia," *World Bank Economic Review* 1, 3, (1987) :419–446. Some of the training was financed by aid donors, but the largest single source was the government budget. HIID has had the privilege of managing some $45 million of government investment in degree training of Indonesian public sector economists since 1982. For details, see Lippincott, Chapter 4.

20 See Jaycox, "Capacity Building," and Berg, *Rethinking Technical Cooperation*.

21 Hilderbrand and Grindle, "Building Sustainable Capacity."

22 L. S. Wilson, in "Kenyanisation and African Capacity Shuffling," *Public Administration and Development* XIII, 4 (1993), describes the costs and benefits of such packages in the Kenyan context. He devotes particular attention to the World Bank's funding of Kenyan professionals in the ministry of agriculture as HIID's eighteen-year intervention in that agency wound down.

23 Based on the author's review of project documents as well as discussions with project staff and outside observers.

24 Several of these measures are suggested by John M. Cohen's and John R. Wheeler's diagnosis in Chapter 5.

25 One of the faculty members simultaneously held a senior post in the finance ministry, and the graduate student was recruited into the project's host agency.

26 The Canadian International Development Agency (CIDA) and the International Development Research Centre (IDRC).

27 This project was complemented by HIID's Cambridge training program. Two members of the Rabat team participated in an HIID summer workshop just before beginning the industry study and one of these members obtained a master's degree in economic development at Harvard midway through it.

28 Canada's IDRC has systematically performed such a function in its more than twenty-five plus years of existence. The Nairobi-based African Economic Research Consortium (AERC), established in 1988 with multidonor support, is facilitating the development of such networks in several African countries. USAID's support for policy research institutes in Asia, notably the Korea Development Institute and the Thai Development Research Institute, has served a similar purpose. At the time of writing, USAID is launching a four-year, $10 million program on the "footloose" model, known by the acronym EAGER (Equity And Growth through Economic Research).

15 Capacity Building in a Transition Country

Lessons from Mongolia

William G. Bikales

A country moving from a command economy to a market economy should be the ideal setting for effective capacity-building projects, particularly in the very challenging area of macroeconomic policy making. Many of the difficulties that have frustrated this work in other developing countries should be avoidable in transition settings.

First of all, one of the most serious underlying problems in many capacity-building projects is that they do not take into account that contextual factors are an important part of the picture and that attention to human resources (or even organizations) without a view of the context is too narrow.[1] In a transition setting, though, context is everything—donors and recipients alike frame virtually all their analyses, project documents, and requests for assistance in terms of the problematic legacies of the old regime and the trauma and challenges of the shift to a new regime. The distinction between capacity building and "institutional strengthening," with its narrower focus on particular target agencies, is nowhere more relevant than in a transition country in which the entire scope of government operations is on the table.

Second, capacity-building projects in developing countries have tended to be supply driven, and not taken seriously by the recipients.

As one observer of aid to Africa has noted, "Most disturbing was that it [technical cooperation] was not managed seriously by the African governments because it is largely perceived, at best, as a free good and, at worst, as something imposed by the donors."[2] In transition countries, however, donors are working with nations that, in the face of a massive macroeconomic shock, have voluntarily chosen the path of sweeping reform. The need for outside technical assistance is indisputable. Problems on the recipient side that we associate with a supply-driven aid process, such as unwillingness to commit the necessary resources, even if these are only staff time and effort, a lack of interest in monitoring project results and making (or demanding) adjustments in the project to improve them, and stakeholder resistance, should be less serious than elsewhere.[3] The simultaneous political reforms that these nations are undergoing also should aid in weakening stakeholders' ability to obstruct necessary changes.

Transition countries should be suitable ground for capacity building for other reasons as well. The training component of technical assistance projects, often neglected by donors even when their nominal goal is capacity building, is difficult to overlook under these conditions.[4] Virtually every government employee, from a policeman to the governor of the central bank, has to develop new skills to handle drastically redefined work. The need for training is highlighted prominently in virtually all technical assistance projects. This training starts with a great advantage: the high level of education that is characteristic of postsocialist societies. Literacy rates and the percentage of the population with higher education are typically very high compared to those in other countries that receive large amounts of foreign assistance. This educated population provides a large pool of potential beneficiaries from projects, and somewhat mitigates one problem that plagues capacity-building projects in other countries: the tendency for newly trained government staff to leave their low-paying positions immediately and move to lucrative jobs in the private sector.[5] Competition for desirable jobs outside government is quite intense.

For these reasons, an examination of the effectiveness of capacity-building projects in transition countries is of particular significance at a time when the usefulness of these types of projects for capacity building is coming under attack. Although the need for strong governing capacity is widely recognized, the suitability of foreign aid as an instrument for development of that capacity is widely doubted.[6] If the unusual circumstances in transition countries lead to generally superior results, this experience could suggest avenues for improvement of capacity-building projects in other developing countries. On the other hand, if capacity-building programs are still found to be problem-prone and of questionable value even under these favorable circumstances, we may have to recognize that the inherent weaknesses in this entire approach to development assistance are more serious than previously acknowledged. At the very least, such an experience would suggest that the extreme difficulty of capacity building must be noted and scrupulously taken into account in designing or implementing such projects elsewhere.

The experience of the Harvard Institute for International Development (HIID) in capacity building in Mongolia provides disturbing indications that such projects are not only very unlikely to achieve their goals, but they are, in fact, often counterproductive. Some key points of that experience follow.

First, the sense of urgency, which could play a tremendously positive role during the transition period, tends to be blunted by the aid process itself. As the aid process permeates the activities of the government, much more time and effort can be spent simply on handling donors than on developing the capacity to handle problems independently. This situation is particularly likely to occur in a country such as Mongolia, which was traditionally heavily dependent on Soviet aid and advisors. In this sense, aid programs can be inherently destructive to true capacity building.

Second, within the recipient government, even one that has, on the surface, embraced an ambitious reform agenda, a consensus about the goals of the transition process is often lacking. Some of this resistance is ideological; there are still many people, some in high government positions, who are unwilling to accept that markets generally work and that central planning generally does not.

Furthermore, the transition period tends to be marked by fierce turf battles as the roles of government agencies are drastically redefined. Under such circumstances, aid can play an additional counterproductive role. Instead of reinforcing the reforms—that is, instead of truly building the recipient's capacity to "perform appropriate tasks effectively and efficiently"— many aid programs undermine them by indiscriminately lending their support to recalcitrant elements of the government along with those that are truly engaged in reform.[7] In fact, there may be a tendency for organizations that are not seriously committed to reform to receive a disproportionate share of attention from donors, because of their weakness and their willingness to devote an inappropriate amount of their resources to playing the aid game. These problems can be particularly difficult for aid projects in formerly socialist countries because of the deftness with which some conservative officials repeat the correct new slogans to donors; this is a skill that they long ago refined to a level of mastery inconceivable in non-Leninist societies.

Given this lack of consensus, the seeming policy neutrality of the term "capacity building" can be dangerously misleading. In a postsocialist economy, any meaningful capacity building must be linked to the reform agenda and must help the government implement an entirely new approach to its work. Strengthening the wrong institutions can impede the development of true governing capacity. "Strengthening" here not only refers to improving staff skills. By receiving donor support, an organization is strengthened in many other ways as well; it receives an implicit endorsement of its importance, it creates or reinforces a tie to a donor that often develops a stake in the enlargement of the recipient's political power, and it receives a crutch that can help prop it up whether it is pursuing good policies or bad. Under these circumstances, every aid project has a political dimension. Yet many donors, under the guise of political noninterference, ignore this aspect of their programs.

A related problem is the extreme difficulty of designing and implementing projects that achieve the focus on overall context that is the greatest strength of the concept of "capacity building." How can one design a project with a mandate that is broad enough, and who is the proper counterpart for such a project? It should be clear that effective capacity building is not possible without the full commitment of the recipient. How can projects be designed to take this fact into account? What is the proper stance for donors when that commitment is found to be lacking? Or in the more complex situation where there are genuine reformers in certain positions of authority, but opponents of reform in others? Mongolia's experience suggested that many donors, with their strong drive to spend funds and their tendency to specialize in specific sectors or even to form allegiances with specific agencies, are ill-prepared to deal with these situations.

Last, even in transition countries, the capacity-building aid process tends to be largely donor-driven. This tendency leads to two problems. First, within the donor community there is also an astonishing lack of consensus regarding priorities and goals of the transition process. Donors and their teams often do not even make a serious effort to understand the unusual features of postsocialist economies. Although the need to implement deep and broad changes offers a great opportunity to technical assistance projects, many donors ignore this opportunity and focus instead on narrow projects that can produce "outputs" that are easily defined and measured. Second, even when such a consensus exists on paper, there is little evidence of any serious attempt by most donors to design or implement their programs in a way that ensures that they will advance the reforms. Instead we find self-serving donor initiatives, aimed at maintaining influence, cultivating friends, scoring points with bureaucratic superiors, or simply not missing out on involvement in favorite areas. The lack of meaningful conditionality in this process creates quite destructive incentives for recipients.

Much of this description will sound familiar to development practitioners in other countries. What is significant here is that even the clear nature of the transition challenges does not seem to be enough to overcome these tendencies. In addition, given the large stakes in the transition period, unproductive aid projects are not just a waste of resources; they are often downright counterproductive, because they may weaken the thrust toward reform and sustain business as usual. The consequences for Mongolia and for other transition countries could be extremely harmful. We should ask whether this situation occurs in other developing countries as well.

HARVARD INSTITUTE FOR INTERNATIONAL DEVELOPMENT'S MONGOLIA PROJECT: "STRATEGIC INTERVENTION IN SUPPORT OF ECONOMIC REFORM"

The HIID Mongolia project functioned for eighteen months, from June 1993 to December 1994.[8] Although a short time span, this was a critical period for the Mongolian transition process, during which a successful project could have made a major contribution to Mongolian economic development. The Mongolian reforms, which began dramatically in 1990 after hunger strikes staged in midwinter in the central square of Ulan Bator brought down the Communist government, had slowed considerably by mid-1993. The second post-Communist government, elected democratically in June 1992, was formed by the Communist "Mongolian People's Revolutionary Party." Although this regime embraced a reform agenda, its approach was far more cautious than that of the previous coalition government. Although macroeconomic stabilization had made considerable progress under this government, with a drop in average monthly inflation from 12.8 percent in 1992 to 6.9 percent in 1993, and with the creation of a unified floating exchange rate against the dollar in May 1993, essential but difficult steps in structural reform were largely avoided.

The central component of this project was assistance to the National Development Board (NDB), on which this chapter will focus. The NDB is a cabinet-level agency, with a very wide-reaching mandate, covering overall economic policy coordination, investment planning, and foreign-aid coordination.[9] It is the direct descendant of the former State Planning Commission, under which most its staff, including its minister and deputy minister, were recruited and trained. On arrival, the HIID advisor found the overall attitude of the staff toward the reforms and toward a market system to be roughly what one would expect from such an organization; they were uncertain what role they should be playing in the new regime, had lost a tremendous amount of power, and were suspicious and resentful of the transition and its upheavals.

At the administrative level, very little had been done within the NDB to respond to these changes. Although the Planning Commission had undergone two name changes and formal reorganizations since 1990, most staff retained their former responsibilities.[10] These responsibilities were almost always defined sectorally, as in a planning commission. In the NDB's most recent reshuffling, a Macroeconomic Policy Department was created, but that department had no officer assigned to work on fiscal issues and no one working on banking and monetary policy issues, although there was an officer responsible for housing, one for culture, and one for education. Similarly, in the Technology and Investment Policy Department, where the public investment plan was formulated, there were officers responsible for the metal industry, chemical industry, light industry, and other sectors in which public investment should have played a much smaller role than private investment, but no one working on the crucial energy sector, only one person responsible for both roads and transportation, and no one for telecommunications. These assignments were largely determined by inertia; as government wages fell in real terms, and as the NDB's budget (like those of all government organizations) was cut back, several employees either left or were dismissed. Little attention seemed to have been paid to managing this situation carefully, and making sure that important posts were filled. For example, the officer who had previously worked on telecommunications was dismissed during staff cutbacks, largely because of her youth. At the same time, older staff members retained their positions and responsibilities for far less important sectors.

Despite abundant opportunities to travel to donor countries, NDB staff were widely perceived as representatives of the old system, with obsolete skills and attitudes. Most of them had little real work to do. They prepared reports for the minister on questions that were largely beyond their authority, participated in meetings with other ministries to discuss issues about which they knew very little and in which their role was unclear, and in some cases simply continued compiling the planning-era data they had always compiled, although the data were now largely useless. One long-term foreign advisor in Ulan Bator described a meeting with representatives from various ministries at which he could immediately identify the NDB officer—the older one who never said a word. A Mongolian friend of the writer's who was very active in business, finance, and the reform movement, once said that the NDB was the one government organization that he had never had any reason to visit.

This detachment from the reforms was reflected in the NDB's institutional role in the policy-making process. Instead of finding a new and appropriate role, the NDB leadership had largely fought to retain or regain as much of their former authority as possible. Their central role in aid coordination was one area in which they had succeeded.[11] They also retained responsibility for public investment planning, within fiscal guidelines set by the Ministry of Finance. However, even within these two areas, when their authority was clearest, the NDB's role was far smaller in reality than it seemed on paper. The International Monetary Fund (IMF), the World Bank, and the Asian Development Bank (ADB), the three largest multilateral donors, all worked primarily with the Bank of Mongolia (BOM) and the Ministry of Finance (MOF). Several other ministries, including the Ministry of Trade and Industry (MTI) and the Ministry of External Relations, were principal counterparts for key bilateral donors. Line ministries maintained direct links with donors as well. Although the NDB continued to play the central role in public investment planning, the size of this budget was very small, because most investment was financed with external resources.

NDB efforts to maintain and strengthen central control over allocation of capital put it in direct opposition to the reform process and to Mongolia's IMF agreements. Although an end to directed credits was a key government commitment in Mongolia's Enhanced Structural Adjustment Facility agreement with the IMF, in public investment planning they routinely included and arranged low-interest credits from commercial banks to key projects. These included loans to state-owned industrial enterprises, for which the NDB acted as a lobby. Its 1994 work plan included such items as "provide support for technical and technological modernization of factories, including 'Ugalz,' 'Mongolshevro,' 'Buligaar,' 'Gobi,' 'Monnoos,' and 'Eermel'" and "in order to normalize operations of the metallurgical factory, make fiscal investments in order to put into operation factories which produce goods in demand both in domestic and foreign markets, including a syringe enterprise, a horse meat factory in Bagakhangai, a fruit-processing enterprise in Ulaangom, a cement factory in Khovd and a silicate-brick factory in Darkhan."[12] It drafted a new "National Planning Law" with a focus on annual planning and with a provision that would subject organizations violating the plan to legal sanctions.[13]

The most reformist ministries, with whom the NDB frequently fought over these issues, were the MOF and the BOM. Through clear new roles and international norms after which to model themselves, the MOF and BOM leaders and staff developed the clearest grasp of the demands of the transition process.[14] Despite very tight budgets, both also developed a core group of bright young staff working on policy questions. The fourth key macroeconomic policy making organization, the MTI, was in a similar situation to the NDB's. They had also lost a great deal of power since the days when they controlled almost all domestic and foreign commerce. It is not surprising that the most bitter turf struggle within the cabinet was between the NDB and the MTI, both of which had become much less powerful and neither of which had a very clear raison d'être in the new regime.

It was quite clear that major reforms were required if the NDB was to play a meaningful and positive role in economic policy making. After meetings with UNDP and the NDB, the project advisor defined the capacity that they sought to strengthen there as follows:

> One weakness in Mongolian economic policy making is its overwhelming focus on short-term goals: reducing the budget deficit,

controlling inflation, privatizing enterprises, finding ad hoc solutions to the most pressing crises in key industrial and infrastructural sectors. There is an urgent need for a high-level agency that is charged with developing a longer-term perspective on the economic challenges facing Mongolia today. Its work should include:

- analysis of medium- and long-term priorities for Mongolian economic development and formulation of a development strategy;

- integration of public investment planning and foreign aid utilization into that strategy;

- coordination with other key economic agencies, including the Ministry of Finance and Bank of Mongolia, to ensure that fiscal and monetary policy are conducted in a way that is consistent with that strategy; [and]

- coordination of policy research activities to assist in the formulation of sound, consistent policies in different sectors, and to resolve disputes in policy matters that cut across ministerial boundaries.[15]

The report went on to suggest that the NDB could play this role in policy making, but that to do so would require a drastic overhaul. Several specific problems were pointed out. Recommendations included a comprehensive review of the staffing needs of the NDB, including at the management level, followed by steps to develop a core group of younger professionals with strong economic and non-COMECON (Council for Mutual Economic Assistance) language skills; closer coordination of work with other key economic agencies; and a shift away from a focus on annual investment planning and sectoral monitoring to the integration of budgetary investment spending and foreign aid into an overall development strategy developed through economic analysis and using new skills and tools.

The project advisor, in presenting such a critical appraisal of the current state of affairs in the NDB, was consciously trying to avoid the mistake of strengthening an agency that was performing a largely negative role in economic management, unless the agency was prepared first to redefine that role comprehensively.

This report, despite being quite frank about weaknesses and underlying problems of attitude and background at the NDB, was received well by the NDB leadership. A series of steps was undertaken.

These steps included the promotion of younger department deputy directors or directors, the redefinition of staff responsibilities in the NDB's Macroeconomic Policy Department (one of three key departments) so that for the first time officers would be responsible for fiscal and monetary analysis, and, crucially, a decision to begin the preparation of a new type of report—a medium-term development strategy incorporating macroeconomic analysis. A few new younger staff members were hired.

Assistance to the NDB was provided within this framework. This assistance, including training in such issues as inflation analysis and forecasting, external debt questions, help with reports that the NDB was asked to prepare for the government, and so on, was generally quite successful, and this work seemed to maintain the NDB leadership's support for the project.

One and a half years later, however, it was difficult to observe any substantial progress toward the deep changes that were so urgently needed. The medium-term report was postponed several times, and, as of December 1994, had not been started. Instead, the NDB leadership and staff spent a tremendous amount of time on a lengthy long-term development "concept" report to the government, forecasting Mongolian development until the year 2010. This report felt much more like a central planner's document than an economist's, announcing what would happen instead of analyzing and projecting. One of the most promising new young staff, a recently returned M.A. in economics from an American university, who had been assigned to work on banking and monetary issues, resigned after three months. No new person was hired to replace her, and one officer was assigned responsibility for fiscal and monetary issues, along with other work as well.

One reason for these very mixed results was the way the NDB decided to manage the project. The NDB had three policy departments: macroeconomic policy, technology and investment policy, and economic cooperation policy. The HIID advisor, as a macroeconomist, was assigned by the NDB leadership to the first department, although the project documents never defined this post so narrowly. It soon became apparent that the NDB saw this advisor's duties as largely limited to working with that one department, which was the weakest of the three in terms of staff skills and influence, and which had a role within the NDB and within the government's policy making process that was very unclear.

The central goals of the project's work at the NDB should have been to teach macroeconomics to the other two departments, which were doing the major work of the NDB—investment planning and aid coordination—and to integrate macroeconomic analysis into their planning. These goals were not understood within the NDB, however, and were resisted by the other departments, the leadership of which felt their staff were much too busy to spend time learning macroeconomics. This situation led to other problems as well. For example, although the NDB was responsible for providing an interpreter for their advisor, all staff with good English skills were in the Economic Cooperation Department. It proved impossible to arrange for a member of that department to assist "another department's advisor."

More generally, although the need for younger staff and training in new skills was recognized, in the end, the leadership's underlying lack of understanding and sympathy for the reform process was a major obstacle to progress. For example, the NDB agreed that there should be a staff member responsible for banking and monetary issues.

When the long-term development concept report was prepared, though, among all the discussions of biotechnology and electronics and steel there was no mention of the need for financial sector reform and development, until at a fairly late date the project advisor was shown a copy and suggested that addition. Many staff members were unhappy about being expected to project developments in their sectors in the year 2010, when they were experiencing great difficulty in finding out what was going on in 1994. To the NDB leaders, this report was a far higher priority than macroeconomic training for their staff; it was meant to reassert the importance of planning and planners. The total uselessness of this report in any practical sense either did not occur to them or did not matter.

This was a difficult situation for the project. The HIID advisor was determined to keep focused on the overall transition context and gauge progress by the extent to which the project was contributing to the reform process. He was aware from an early date that simply enhancing the NDB's capacity for the work it was doing would not lend any meaningful support to the reform process. In fact, given the NDB's overall stance toward reform issues, there was a very real danger that strengthening them without altering that stance could set back the transition, or serve to steer it in a direction that was incompatible with project goals.

In response to these concerns, the HIID staff adopted the following strategy. First, they tried consistently to refuse to help with inappropriate work, such as the long-term report, while offering clear and constructive explanations for their refusal. Although this approach rarely dissuaded the NDB from doing that work themselves, the refusal was generally accepted. Second, they continued to emphasize to the NDB leadership the points that were presented in the assessment—the need to bring in good young staff, employ new skills in their work, develop a policy research capacity, and so on.

Third, and most important, the HIID advisors at all three agencies expanded the scope of their work to include other government agencies as well. Fortunately, the project terms of reference were broad enough to allow this, because it was a very convenient way to allow the government to take fuller advantage of project staff skills than the NDB or other counterparts were prepared to do. Although both USAID and UNDP initially expressed concern about the "vagueness" of the project's terms of reference, in the end it was that vagueness that allowed the project's most substantial achievements.

For example, shortly after arriving, HIID advisors established an interministerial working group on macroeconomic monitoring and forecasting, in which NDB staff were encouraged to participate. Through this group the project advisors were able to develop working relations with economists and leaders in the MOF, Central Bank, and State Statistical Office. In the course of the year, the HIID team also developed contacts with economic advisors in the Prime Minister's Office, with the Ministry of Fuel and Energy, and with various academic institutions. Their work included assistance with gross domestic product monitoring and forecasting, simple budget forecasting, analysis of monetary issues and reform of the banking sector, issues regarding the measurement of inflation, and analysis of the macroeconomic consequences of energy and agricultural policy and other energy sector problems. This aspect of the HIID team's work was very unusual among projects in Ulan Bator. Most advisors seemed to stick quite closely to the counterpart to whom they'd been assigned, other than having contact with other agency's advisors.

In retrospect, the true capacity building that the HIID project accomplished was not in its primary counterpart agencies, but in the others with which the advisors worked. After an initial flurry of discussion within the NDB of the HIID assessment report and its recommendations, the usefulness of that report proved limited because it was never circulated beyond the NDB. At the time this seemed proper; the report was quite critical and could have been embarrassing for the NDB leadership. Rival ministries could have made use of it, and those other ministries, after all, had not been subjected to the same sort of assessment by the project. For the message of this report to be effective, though, it had to be considered by someone who was concerned with the overall policy making process who could reinforce the need for the NDB to redefine its role in that process and hold the NDB accountable for its progress in meeting the goals set out in the report. It should have been clear at the time that problems in the work of the leadership of the NDB could not be addressed solely through discussions with those same leaders. The involvement of UNDP in the assessment process injected a small amount of external pressure on the NDB to act on its recommendations. UNDP's role as the only major multilateral organization for whom the NDB was principal counterpart gave it some weight with the NDB leadership. However, it became clear after some time that this relationship was one of mutual support and benefit, and that in any case UNDP, which was active in Mongolia even before the collapse of Communism, could not credibly threaten an end of its support to the NDB if sufficient progress was not made.

Underlying Issues

One crucial obstacle to achieving better results at the NDB was that even as the project advisor tried to make a case for reform and change, the massive flow of aid to Mongolia was greatly mitigating any incentive for the NDB to follow his recommendations.[16] On a broad level, this aid created an atmosphere of "business as usual" throughout the government. The leaders of the government were not reformers by instinct. With the economic crisis blunted by aid, and with unconditional support coming from donor countries and agencies, they were not inclined to implement necessary but difficult new reforms. Foreign aid seemed to offer the opportunity to sustain the status quo indefinitely.

The NDB received an astounding amount of multilateral and bilateral donor attention. As the HIID project ended, the NDB had a professional staff of fewer than fifty people (most of whom spoke little or no English), of whom five were away on long-term study, and several others on shorter trips. Despite this small size, the agency counted on an HIID advisor (whose work was extended on a direct contract to UNDP), two UNDP advisors on aid coordination, a Japanese advisor, a new European Union TACIS aid coordination unit, and a one-year ADB technical assistance program that sent three or four consultants for two or three months at a time. In addition, the agency received occasional three-week visits from South Korean economists. How is it possible that one relatively small organization, with widely recognized weaknesses, could receive so many projects at one time, with all the inevitable problems of overlap, confusion, and distraction from other work? This raises serious questions about the project design process.

For example, as previously noted, the HIID macroeconomic policy advisor was assigned to the NDB although there was virtually no role for the NDB in macroeconomic policy making. This choice of counterpart seems to have been motivated largely by UNDP's wish to strengthen the NDB, without any serious consideration to whether this would benefit the government overall. Once the advisor was in place, the possibility of observing a productive, focused work plan was greatly reduced by the many other similarly well-intended but vaguely defined and halfheartedly implemented projects there.

Similar problems could be found in several ministries. One striking phenomenon in Mongolia was that technical cooperation projects tended to go in disproportionate numbers to agencies that, because of limited staff or leaders who were not truly committed to the goals of the assistance, were least able to utilize them effectively. There are several explanations for this phenomenon. First, the supply of technical cooperation projects seemed virtually inexhaustible for agencies that were prepared to accept them, because donors competed to get involved in Mongolia. Thus, the main constraint on the aid that an organization could receive was its willingness to solicit or accommodate it. Although the costs to the recipient of an aid project are often substantial in terms of diversion of scarce staff and other resources from more important work, these costs are not obvious to poorly run agencies or those whose work is not urgent.

This is a particularly relevant problem in a transition setting, where ministries that have not adapted to the new regime have very little real work to do and where internal opportunity costs from handling so many projects are therefore extremely low. Well-run organizations that are serious about their work would never accept the number of aid projects that less focused ones do. Furthermore, those weaker agencies, if one disregards the extent to which their problems reflect underlying attitudes that will make effective utilization of assistance impossible, appear to be the ones that need the aid most badly. Donors also tend to develop links to "their" agencies and "their" sectors and are very reluctant to acknowledge the seriousness of problems that occur in their projects.

The NDB and the Ministry of Food and Agriculture (MFA) were two examples of these syndromes. Agriculture was a vital sector in the Mongolian economy and very popular with donors. However, reforms in agriculture moved extremely slowly, and the MFA often followed policies that impeded progress and weakened the entire Mongolian economy. The ministry's demands for large credits at negative real interest rates for farms and flour mills, many of which remained state controlled and mismanaged, were the single largest problem in Mongolian monetary policy, and blunted pressures on farm management to adjust to market conditions. In another case, in 1993 the ministry issued rules that set a minimum size for new wheat farms, despite considerable evidence that smaller, privately operated farms in the same regions, growing the same crops, were more productive and profitable.

Despite the fact that it was pursuing such policies, the MFA, with a capacity to utilize technical assistance that was drastically weakened through a sharp reduction in staff, received a steady stream of assistance.[17] In part, this continual support reflected the fact that many donors simply ignored these questions in designing their aid programs. They viewed their projects in isolation from the context in which they took place, and didn't concern themselves with the effect that their program may have on the overall reform process. This view reflected the lack of concern with results that is a standard problem in donor-driven projects.

The perverse incentives created by such circumstances are obvious. At the very least, there is no incentive for agencies to take the content of these aid projects seriously, or to take strong steps to implement project recommendations, because there is no evidence that their failure to do so will have any negative consequences, and follow-up on their advisors' recommendations is often difficult or politically risky. In their technical assistance projects, few donors apply any conditionalities under which continued support would be linked to concrete actions by the recipients.

Conditionality is a double-edged sword, and if misused it can do much damage.[18] Nevertheless, in Mongolia's case, the lack of conditionality in most capacity-building projects was a far more serious problem than the conditionality that was imposed by the IMF. Of course, no other donor wields so weighty a stick as the IMF, which may explain the reliance on carrots and then bigger carrots by most donors. It is hard to avoid the impression that those donors recognized that if they imposed a conditionality, or other serious costs, as a price for their assistance, the recipients would simply have said no. This answer did not seem to be what many donors wanted, even if the alternative involved projects that did little good for Mongolia.

From the recipients' view, with most non-project-related technical assistance being provided on a grant basis, and with the inevitable side benefits of trips abroad, office equipment, and other advantages, there was a strong incentive to take on as many technical assistance projects as possible and muddle through them with little genuine effort. Only an extraordinarily serious minister was able to resist these pressures. Some organizations with good leadership and ideas turned away from potentially important work and got completely caught up in playing the aid game. Even when projects were financed by credits, not grants, it was not clear that decision makers considered seriously the costs of credit-financed projects.[19]

The most disturbing issue in the HIID project's work in Mongolia was the possibility that in strengthening the NDB, the project was aiding an organization whose commitment to the reform process was among the very weakest in the government. Of course, there was no easy solution to this problem. The NDB was UNDP's prime government counterpart. It was the government agency with responsibility for investment planning and aid coordination, and it certainly was entitled to assistance in that important work. However, the NDB's outdated approach to this work, its inability to attract and hold bright new staff, and the aloofness from the reform process which it demonstrated repeatedly were all signs that the project's resources would have been better spent elsewhere. Most of these tasks could have been handled in the MOF, for example, where the leadership was considerably more involved in the reform process and would have been more likely to handle them well. There were other options worth considering.

This is the sort of issue that should be on the table in any good capacity-building project, and this is precisely the sort of issue that should be at the top of the capacity-building agenda during the transition period. There were people in the government who recognized this need, and who, given the opportunity, might have suggested changes. It is quite possible that this project's support for the NDB prevented the government from facing up to this problem.

LESSONS FOR CAPACITY BUILDING PROJECTS IN OTHER TRANSITION COUNTRIES

Mongolia's dependence on aid leaves it particularly vulnerable to damage from ineffective and counterproductive aid projects. The potential harm from such projects in other transition states, though, is also very great.

Mongolia is one of the majority of transition countries that are going through an abrupt full economic and political transformation, unlike "gradualist" countries such as China and Vietnam in which the Communist Party retains control. Although many of the same lessons pertain to both settings, there are differences as well. Projects in the gradualist states may have less latitude to suggest institutional changes, and opponents to reform in those states may be less likely to allow the sort of donor involvement in their agencies that was possible in Mongolia.

In one respect the HIID experience in Mongolia was particularly relevant to work in many other postsocialist states. Mongolia was the first such state to replace its original reform government with a government run by conservative Communists and former Communists. This reversal has now occurred in several other states as well, and is quite likely to occur in more in the future. The issues that arise in capacity building in governments or agencies that are attempting to retain or restore an unviable economic system will require attention in those countries. Analogous problems arise in some Commonwealth of Independent States countries, which have skipped the reform government stage altogether, and have kept conservative governments in power.

What are the lessons to be learned from the HIID Mongolia project?

Link capacity building to the policy goals of the transition process.

Capacity building in the transition setting must be understood as having very specific policy content. The seeming innocuousness and policy neutrality of the term must be explicitly rejected. Projects should create and strengthen organizations that will function effectively in a way that is consistent with a market economy, in which direct state involvement is reduced to an optimal level, in which new ideas, new skills, and new management techniques are welcomed, and in which command economy approaches are rejected. Extreme care must be taken to distinguish between actors who are truly committed to reform and those who are only paying lip service to it. Support of the latter type of organization is almost certain to be counterproductive.

It is not enough, for example, to seek to "encourage the growth of the private sector" or to "promote small and medium-size enterprise development." Projects that channel support for the private sector through ministries with close links to old state-owned enterprises and an abiding belief in a large role for the state in allocating inputs are likely to achieve precisely the opposite of what they intend. Yet in Mongolia, most of those programs were directed through either the NDB or the MTI, the two government agencies with the least interest in supporting new private businesses. Most observers in that period would have agreed that abolishing those two organizations would have been one of the most constructive measures possible for promoting private sector development in Mongolia.

Don't disregard the political impact of foreign aid.

The flood of aid coming into transition countries, particularly those with relatively low standards of living and small volumes of private capital inflows, has an enormous impact on domestic politics. The transition period is meant to be one of persistent, deep-reaching change. Aid tends to support the status quo by mitigating the economic pressures for change and by strengthening the government or specific organizations that receive the aid. This is another form of nonneutrality which must be taken into account.

The fact that in the transition period virtually everything about the new regime is on the table is a tremendous opportunity for intelligent capacity building, but it carries dangers as well. The internal political battle that rages during this period is extremely intense, and some of the fiercest struggles will be waged by groups such as managers and employees of large state-owned enterprises, large state farms, planners, and so on, whose positions are deeply threatened by the reforms. These groups always have their political patrons in the parliament, in the cabinet, and in local governments.

Aid programs that do not intelligently factor in impact on the political situation can also lead to results directly opposite of what they intend. In particular, the tendency for donors to develop allegiances to specific agencies and continue on quixotic quests to aid them long after the onesidedness of the relationship has become clear must be avoided.

The key bottlenecks are at the top, not the bottom.

Most capacity building projects tend to take a "bottom-up" approach, focusing on enhancing technical skills of recipient experts and staff.[20] However, in Mongolia, the key bottleneck was most often at the agency leadership level, and the problem was not a readily remediable lack of skills, but a lack of commitment to the goals of the reform process. It is extremely difficult for donors, working within the normal diplomatic parameters of the aid process, to deal with such a problem. Issues of sovereignty and a more self-interested donor reluctance to offend the recipient government are both inhibiting factors to a more positive outcome. The fact remains, though, that a "top-down" approach is essential in postsocialist reform programs, where the staff have a tradition of passivity, and new technical skills will not be utilized as designed without a redefinition and restructuring of the work of the recipient agency.

Focus on the underlying goals, not on any specific counterpart.

The first three points suggest the importance of selecting the proper project counterpart and the harm that results when mistakes are made and reinforced by further aid. In practical terms, given the difficulty of performing such analysis before the project, how does one design a project that can avoid such errors or correct them after it is under way? Given the importance of context, who is the appropriate counterpart with the mandate to deal with the broad issues that may arise?

First, no capacity-building project should be launched without first conducting a realistic assessment of the absorption capacity of the recipient agencies, and a review of other ongoing or planned projects there. At this stage, some government organization higher than the actual user agency must be involved. Ideally, both the donor agency and recipient government should be interested in this assessment as a way of avoiding a lot of bad projects.

Second, the project terms of reference should specify project goals in terms of the broad transition context, not just in terms of the target organization, and should state clearly that one purpose of the project is to assess the capacity of the specific counterpart organization to perform its expected role in the new regime and to offer and evaluate alternative ways of achieving the same ends. The advisors should be asked to propose concrete ways for the target organization to improve its capacity to handle its proper work, if they feel this is possible, and these suggestions, after discussion, should then be written into a detailed work plan. To be effective, such reports must be submitted not only to the organization whose work is being reviewed, but to a higher level of government. Serious efforts should be made to identify and involve a higher office that supports the goals of the project and possesses the authority to deal appropriately with such a report. In some cases, such as assistance with tax administration, there is not likely to be an alternative implementing agency to the finance ministry, but it would still be possible to allow a full evaluation of options within the ministry, and to involve others outside it in reviewing this report.

Third, the HIID project's broad mandate, under which advisors were able to work closely with a range of government organizations, was the key to most of the project's accomplishments. The terms of reference should be clear on this point and set goals that involve coordination with more than one agency whenever possible. The assessment just described will be most effective if it is not done in isolation, but in conjunction with similar analyses of work being done in other relevant agencies. If it is possible to include such a task in the terms of reference, that would be ideal. If not, then coordination with other projects situated in those agencies can also be very helpful.

Recognize the possibility of failure and plan mechanisms to deal with it.

The second way in which concern about counterpart problems can be built into the project is through the use of conditionality. The possibility of failure should be written into the terms of reference for each project, and mechanisms specified to identify and take strong measures to rectify or close down projects that are failing. Project management should be encouraged to consider shifting the work to an alternative organization, suspending the project until certain changes take place, or canceling it altogether. Here, too, the involvement of some office higher up than the principal user would be extremely helpful.

The fact that this goal seems so unlikely to be achieved suggests the seriousness of the problems that capacity-building projects face—who has the incentive to take such strong steps? The self-interest of the project experts pushes them to evaluate progress positively. Donors who tend to pursue their own agendas, whether bureaucratic or strategic, are also unlikely to find it in their interest to face up to problems that may have been inherent in their project's choice of counterpart, definition of goals, and so on. Of course, it should be incumbent on the recipient government, the representatives of the people who will bear the consequences of successful or failed aid programs, to take responsibility for making the best use of donor support. However, as we have seen, even in a transition setting we cannot take for granted the recipient's incentive to focus on long-term national goals.

Nevertheless, for all the likely difficulties, a failed project that is acknowledged as such, and that is terminated or altered as a result, could serve as an outstanding example of capacity building, because it could teach precisely the right lessons to recipients. It could also contribute to the laudable goal of capacity building in the donor and consultant community.

Inability to retain good staff is often a sign of mismanagement, not low wages.

One common problem in capacity-building projects, the inability to keep capable people in government because of tight fiscal constraints on wages, was not as serious a problem in Mongolia as its shrinking government budget would suggest. For several reasons, many government agencies were able to attract and retain good personnel. These reasons include: relative job security; traditional attitudes in which government work is regarded as more respectable than private sector work; the benefits available to government employees from aid projects, such as study tours abroad (a major source of income); the chance to acquire new language and technical skills; and the many educated people in the society competing for the most desirable private sector jobs. Well-run organizations with enough challenging work to keep serious staff busy were surprisingly successful at locating and retaining good people.

A far more frequent and serious problem than the quality of personnel was the inability of many government agencies to utilize their personnel to the fullest. When assessing counterparts' staff situations, projects in postsocialist countries should try to distinguish carefully between problems caused by exogenous fiscal constraints and those caused by endogenous mismanagement and lack of clarity of organizational purpose. The second is often mistaken for the first.

The selection of proper individuals as advisors is also essential.

In numerous projects in Mongolia, the quality of the foreign advisors was the major obstacle to success. One Mongolian policy maker, a dedicated reformer working under quite difficult conditions, made the following observation in discussing some of the new experts with whom he was working:

> Mongolians are used to working with foreign advisors. We had 70 years' experience with the Russians. The first ones were very good, but as time passed they got worse and worse. The last ones were worse than the Mongolians. We were teachers of some advisors, to be frank.[21]

Care must be taken to choose the proper people for advisory posts in technical assistance projects—people with skills, and people who can cope with life and work under difficult circumstances, people with drive to accomplish things, and people genuinely interested in sharing their skills with their counterparts. In the transition setting each advisor has a dual role, that of a specialist in his or her area of expertise, and that of an example of the new system that the recipient nation has just embraced. It is distressing, however, to observe projects in which unhelpful advisors are, in effect, communicating to their counterparts the message that "the more things change the more they stay the same," or, "don't expect much of me and I won't expect much of you."

To deal with such situations, conditionality and a strict review process, including the involvement of a higher level of government, are also necessary and appropriate. Insisting on tougher demands on the recipients will only be effective if this is perceived as a fair attempt to increase project effectiveness. This insistence requires similarly high expectations for the foreign staff as well.

Inefficient aid projects undermine, rather than facilitate, the transition process.

With the pervasive influence of aid projects, one of the key lessons that needs to be imparted during the transition—economic analysis of costs and benefits—is constantly undermined by persistent engagement in a process that is marked by great inefficiency and very little responsiveness to market forces.[22] The aid process is so rife with waste, politics, and bureaucracy, and can so easily permeate the entire policy making process in a country that is receiving substantial donor attention, that it requires almost a superhuman focus on the part of the recipient country to avoid being distracted from the lessons it is supposed to be learning. It is difficult to imagine a better example of precisely what governments in transition countries should not be doing than a typical donor-driven aid project. Furthermore, the recipient's role in the aid process is one in which economic cost-benefit analysis is unheard of.

Actually, the situation is even worse. People raised in a socialist society are very finely attuned to differences between rhetoric and reality, and are, in fact, extremely skilled at their own form of cost-benefit calculus. Advisors who teach poorly about efficiency, all the while earning substantial consulting fees, fit very readily into this worldview. The ready response of the recipient is to measure the benefits of a project in terms of its own political advantage, or the chance to acquire new computers, take trips abroad, and so on. In many cases the only costs considered, if there are any, are of a similar nature and are quite nebulous to an observer.

The meaningful costs and benefits are those accruing to the society as a whole. With neither the donors nor the recipients concerning themselves with these factors, it is little wonder that the outcome of these projects tends to be negligible at best, and often counterproductive.

Look for the individuals who will make a contribution no matter what organization they are with.

When all else fails—and even when all else goes beautifully— there is an opportunity for long-term capacity building in finding and encouraging people with energy and new ideas, whatever organization they are with, and whatever their interests. Transition countries, for now at least, abound with such people—ones who are genuinely excited about the changes and eager to learn new skills and apply them to their country's circumstances. An advisor who establishes links with three such people in a year, cultivates their enthusiasm, and helps them put their abilities to use is making a major contribution. These are often, by the way, the people from whom an advisor can learn the most about what is really going on, and how much is really possible, in his or her country of work.

Conclusions

To what extent are the issues raised in this chapter different from those in other developing countries? To what extent are they applicable elsewhere? For many reasons, the lessons of HIID's experience in Mongolia should be relevant to projects in other circumstances.

First of all, every capacity building project is, by definition, a transition project. The abruptness and the comprehensiveness of the shift from central planning to markets throw the transitional element into particularly stark relief, but this is a difference of degree only, not a qualitatively different situation.

Second, there are particularly clear parallels between the HIID experience in Mongolia and those of aid work in any crisis situation, where the alleviation of crisis conditions, without firmly addressing underlying structural problems, can build dependence rather than capacity.

Most important, to return to the opening section of this chapter, our experience in Mongolia suggests that inherent weaknesses in the aid process are even more serious than is generally recognized. Although capacity building, as a concept, is meant to build on and prevent the unfortunate experiences of earlier technical cooperation projects, there is disturbingly little evidence that lessons gained from failed projects in other countries have led to improved results in Mongolia. Many donors seem simply to have seen Mongolia as a new market for their same old products. Within the recipient country, the availability of these resources undermines the drive to reform. As a result, the aid process seems to be recreating in Mongolia familiar problems of other developing countries—cynicism, high levels of debt, a tendency to substitute talk for action, an inappropriately large role for government agencies that control aid money, and the intelligent but socially wasteful choice by a substantial group of local people to channel their abilities into taking advantage of that aid money. Because the stakes are so high in transition countries, I have emphasized the great harm that can be caused by failed projects there. However, here too the difference is one of degree only.

To what extent can foreign aid support change, rather than support the status quo? For reasons that arise mostly from the internal dynamics of large bureaucratic donor organizations and of recipient governments, there seems to be an overwhelming tendency toward the latter. Therefore, we must recognize the very strong danger that aid projects aimed at supporting a transition process, including but not limited to those in formerly planned economies, can be self-defeating. Aid is likely to achieve its desired ends only in the rare case that both the donor and the recipient are truly committed to the change process. If only one or the other has that commitment, and projects are designed to strengthen the hand of the party whose expectations and demands are highest, there is the possibility of significant achievements. Most often, however, both donor and recipient are pursuing other agendas. Without a genuine commitment to reform, capacity building in sensitive areas such as macroeconomic policy making is likely to prove a chimerical goal.

POSTSCRIPT

On June 30, 1996, the Mongolian Democratic Union, a coalition of several opposition parties, scored a smashing victory in parliamentary elections. After holding only six seats out of seventy-six in the previous parliament, the democratic coalition won fifty out of seventy-six in the new one. This is the first time in seventy-five years that the Mongolian People's Revolutionary Party will not be ruling the nation.

As this postscript is written, the new government is taking shape. A sweeping restructuring of the ministries will be undertaken, and the current draft plan includes the elimination of both the NDB and the MTI, with relevant functions being moved elsewhere. The investment budget will be moved from the NDB to the MOF, and the Ministry of External Relations will take over trade and foreign investment policy from the MTI, along with aid coordination from the NDB. Industrial policy from the MTI will be shifted to a new Ministry of Industry and Agriculture, a small agency that is expected to deal with general policy issues relating to these sectors and eschew the control and lobbying roles that both MTI and the MFA previously played in their respective sectors.

In the last year of its existence, the NDB continued to be the center of controversy. First, the eighteen-month first phase of the ADB Public Investment Plan project at the NDB ended, and produced a long and detailed medium-term strategy plan as its key output. However, it was later discovered that the Mongolian-language version of this document, prepared and circulated within the government by the NDB, differed substantially from the original version prepared jointly with the ADB consultants. This discrepancy delayed the start of phase II of this project, although it was not certain whether there would be any long-term impact on assistance to the NDB. Secondly, the joint UNDP-Government of Mongolia Management Development program drafted a reorganization plan for the government, under which the NDB, despite all its widely recognized shortcomings, was to be rechristened as the "Ministry of the Economy," and formally enshrined as "the government's economic advisor," with no important responsibilities removed, and considerable new authority added. The chairman of the NDB was widely seen as the leading candidate for the prime ministership, had the ruling party retained its majority in the new parliament.

These developments add new perspectives to this chapter. First of all, they underline the extent to which so much of the "capacity-building" work done in Mongolia in the last five years has been irrelevant and unproductive. Millions of dollars were allocated to strengthen the NDB, despite the obvious indications that they were producing little. In the end, the former Planning Commission is being abolished. Second, the political ramifications of the support that propped the NDB up for so long gained enormous potential significance for a time. If its chairman had become prime minister, the consequences for Mongolian economic development—if one agrees that market-oriented reforms and acceptance of the relevance of economic principles are necessary in a transition country—would have been extremely serious.

Lastly, however, and on a more cheerful note, in Mongolia's case the political consequences of aid to inappropriate counterparts proved insignificant in the end. The Mongolian people showed themselves perfectly capable of deciding for themselves what path they wished to follow, and donor support for the previous regime did little to influence their views. The destruction wrought by poorly conceived aid projects should not be exaggerated any more than should their benefits. Still, aid organizations aspiring to anything more than irrelevance might take some lessons from developments in Mongolia. These lessons will be particularly relevant if the Mongolian people's recent blunt rejection of rule by ex-Communists proves to be a precursor of similar decisions in other nations, as their 1992 turn to the former Communists proved to be.

Notes

I would like to thank Naomi Chakwin, Lester Gordon, Clive Gray, Merilee Grindle, and Mike Reynolds for very helpful comments on earlier drafts of this paper.

1   Merilee S. Grindle and Mary E. Hilderbrand, Chapter 2 of this volume.

2   Pierre-Claver Damiba, in foreword to Elliot Berg, *Rethinking Technical Co-operation: Reforms for Capacity Building in Africa* (New York: United Nations Development Programme/Development Alternatives, Inc., 1993), vi.

3   Berg, *Rethinking Technical Cooperation*, 94.

4   Berg, *Rethinking Technical Cooperation*, 97.

5   John M. Cohen, "Building Sustainable Public Sector Managerial, Professional, and Technical Capacity: A Framework for Analysis and Intervention," *HIID Development Discussion Paper 473* (Cambridge: Harvard Institute for International Development, 1993): 19–25.

6   See, for example, Grindle and Hilderbrand, "Building Sustainable Capacity," 5–10, and Cohen, "Building Sustainable Public Sector," 4–6.

7   Grindle and Hilderbrand, "Building Sustainable Capacity," 3.

8   The goal of this project, financed by USAID and managed by UNDP, was the strengthening of three important government economic policy making agencies in order to more fully integrate them into the macroeconomic policy making process and smooth the transition. The three agencies were: the National Development Board, a planning agency; the State Privatization Commission; and the Market Research Institute, a nascent think tank and business support organization affiliated with the Ministry of Trade and Industry. A resident advisor was placed in each of these organizations. However, the mandate of the project was quite broad, and allowed HIID staff to work with other government agencies as necessary.

9   "The responsibility and portfolio of the NDB Chairman have been identified as follows: major issues dealing with the formulation of the National Development Concept, long-term development strategies, guidelines of economic and social development, ensuring economic security and balance, macroeconomic coordination, investment, technological transfer, sectoral, multisectoral and regional development policy, external economic cooperation, patent and statistics, standardization and measurement, etc.," Ch. Ulaan, Minister of State and Chairman, National De-

velopment Board, talk on "Policy Formulation, Planning and Resource Allocation" to a workshop on central government processes, March 6, 1995.

10   It was first changed to the "Ministry of National Development," and then, in 1992, to the "National Development Board."

11   Although the 1993 Law on Government, which defined the roles of the various ministries, was unclear about the allocation of responsibilities for aid coordination within the government, Government Resolution #132, issued by the Cabinet in 1993, gave the NDB responsibility for "determining the macroeconomic level of foreign aid and loans; establishing the cardinal areas, priorities, loan and aid utilization schedules; identifying projects in need of technical assistance; making the final choice of projects and presenting it for the government's approval, controlling its implementation, coordinating activities among participating organizations and implementing a common course of action within the foreign investment policy framework."

12   NDB 1994 Workplan, unpublished.

13   In the end this law was not submitted to the Parliament, in part because of concern expressed by our advisors and UNDP. However, new versions have been drafted by the NDB.

14   Mongolia avoided the clash between the Finance Ministry and Central Bank that has thwarted the reform process in many transition countries, and which was a major problem for the previous coalition government. There have been several issues over which the MOF and BOM's interests differed—typically responsibility for financing programs such as bank recapitalization, repayment of official debt, or support of agricultural enterprises. There has been no significant ideological difference between the two organizations, which is one key reason for Mongolia's successful macroeconomic stabilization program since late 1992.

15   William Bikales, "Report on the Operations of the National Development Board of Mongolia with Recommendations," Harvard Institute for International Development, Ulan Bator, 1993.

16   Milton Friedman raised profound questions about the impact of foreign aid, including its tendency to support the status quo and obstruct rather than promote change, in his essay "Foreign Economic Aid: Means and Objectives," first published in 1958 and then collected in G. Ranis, ed., *The United States and the Developing Countries* (New York: W. W. Norton, 1964). I thank Lester Gordon for calling this essay to my attention.

17   In November 1994, it was calculated that the MFA, with fifty three non-administrative staff, had thirty four ongoing technical assistance projects. Although some of these were very small, a foreign advisor there told the author that "it is definitely the case that the ministry cannot cope with

this number of projects." In addition to the scarcity of ministry transla-tors and vehicles, there are many overlaps between projects, and inconsis-tencies among the aims of different projects.

18   Peter Boone, "Grassroots Economic Reform in Mongolia," *Journal of Comparative Economics* 18 (1994): 354 presents an interesting description of the impact of conditionality in Mongolia's first IMF negotiations in 1991.

19   Berg, *Rethinking Technical Cooperation*, Chapter 5, notes that even in credit-financed projects, the users of technical assistance are not the ones who pay and are therefore insensitive to costs. My further point is that even coordinating bodies with overall responsibility for monitoring the utili-zation of aid may perceive the cost of credit-financed projects as negli-gible, at least until so much debt has been accumulated that donors grow concerned. Any measure that reduces the cost of borrowing, such as concessional lending, increases the likelihood of this occurring.

20   See Hilderbrand and Grindle, "Building Sustainable Capacity," 13, and Cohen, "Building Sustainable Public Sector," for descriptions of the sub-stantial body of literature that justify such an approach.

21   This man, a top official in an organization that deals with many donors, understandably requested that his name and position be kept confidential.

22   Berg, *Rethinking Technical Cooperation*, Chapter 5. Although Berg's analysis is extremely interesting, his discussion of the cost to the recipient of un-productive projects focuses on the opportunity cost of wasted resources. In a transition setting, and quite possibly elsewhere, there is often an ad-ditional large cost from such projects; they can retard or reverse the move-ment toward reform.

Bibliography

Abby, H. 1994. Assessment of Capacity Building Needs for Economic Management in Kenya. Nairobi, Kenya: United Nations Development Programme. June.

Adamolekum, L. 1993. A Note on Civil Service Policy Reform in Sub-Saharan Africa. *International Journal of Public Sector Management* 6 (3).

Adams, C. 1994. *The Fiscal Costs of Premature Financial Liberalization: Some Evidence from Zambia.* Oxford: Centre for the Study of African Economies.

Adamu, G. 1994. *Ghana: Pilot Study of Capacity Building.* Cambridge: Harvard Institute for International Development.

"Africa: World Bank." *Oxford Analytica* (June 3, 1993).

Allison, G. 1971. *Essence of Decision: Explaining the Cuban Missile Crisis.* Boston: Little, Brown.

Allman, W. F. 1994. *The Stone Age Present.* New York: Simon and Schuster.

Anand, R., and S. van Wijnbergen. 1989. "Inflation and the Financing of Government Expenditure." *World Bank Economic Review* 3 (1): 17–38.

Atwood, J. B. A. November 16, 1993. Statement of Principles on Participatory Development. USAID.

Avila, G., F. Campero, and J. Patiño. 1992. *Un Puente sobre la crisis. El Fondo Social de Emergencia.* La Paz: Fondo de Inversión Social.

Axelrod, R. M. 1984. *The Evolution of Cooperation.* New York: Basic Books.

Baker, W. E. 1992. "The Network Organization in Theory and Practice." In N. Nohria and R. G. Eccles, eds., *Networks and Organizations: Structure, Form and Action.* Boston: Harvard Business School Press.

Bank of Zambia. various dates. *Main Economic Indicators.*

Barkow, J., L. Cosmides and J. Tooby, eds. 1992. *The Adapted Mind.* New York: Oxford University Press.

Bates, R. 1988. "Contra Contractarianism: Some Reflections on the New Institutionalism." *Politics and Society* 16: 387–401.

Bates, R. H. 1996. "Institutions as Investments." *HIID Development Discussion Paper 527.* Cambridge: Harvard Institute for International Development.

Bayley, D. H. 1966. "The Effects of Corruption in a Developing Nation." *Western Political Quarterly* XIX (4): 719–732. Reproduced in Heidenheimer, et al., 1989, 935–952.

Berg, E. J. 1993. *Rethinking Technical Cooperation: Reforms for Capacity Building in Africa.* New York: UNDP/Development Alternatives Inc.

Bhagwati, J. N. 1978. *Foreign Trade Regimes and Economic Development: Anatomy and Consequences of Exchange Control Regimes.* Cambridge, MA: Ballinger.

Bhatnagar, B., and A. C. Williams, eds. 1992. "Participatory Development and the World Bank: Potential Directions for Change." *World Bank Discussion Paper* 183. Washington, DC: World Bank.

Bikales, W. 1993. Report on the Operations of the National Development Board of Mongolia with Recommendations. Ulaanbaatar.

Binmore, Ken. 1994. *Game Theory and the Social Contract: Playing Fair.* Cambridge: MIT Press.

Birdsall, N., D. Ross, and R. Sabot. 1994. "Inequality and Growth Reconsidered." Paper prepared for the American Economics Association meeting, January, Boston, MA.

Blanchard, O., and S. Fischer. 1989. *Lectures on Macroeconomics.* Cambridge: MIT Press.

Blank, L., M. E. Grosh, and P. Knight. 1995. *Building Analytic Capacity in Conjunction with LSMS Surveys: The Jamaican Story.* Unpublished manuscript. Washington, DC: World Bank.

Blejer, M., and A. Cheasty. 1991. "The Measurement of Fiscal Deficits: Analytical and Methodological Issues." *Journal of Economic Literature* XXIX (4): 1644–1678.

Bolnick, B. 1995. *Early Sequencing of Interest-Rate Liberalization: Interest Rate Policy in Zambia, 1993–94.* Boston: Northeastern University.

Bolnick, B. 1994. *The Macroeconomic Framework for the Budget Program in Zambia.* Boston: Northeastern University.

Boone, P. 1994. "Grassroots Economic Reform in Mongolia." *Journal of Comparative Economics* 18: 329–356.

Bossuyt, J., G. Laporte, and F. van Hoek. 1990. *New Avenues for Technical Co-operation in Africa: Improving the Record in Terms of Capacity Building.* Maastricht: European Centre for Development Policy Management.

Boyd, R., and P. J. Richerson. 1985. *Culture and the Evolutionary Process.* Chicago: University of Chicago Press.

Boyle, N., and A. R. Wight. 1992. "Policy Reform: The Role of Informal Organizations. Infrastructure Notes." Urban No. OU-5. Washington, DC: Infrastructure and Urban Development Department, World Bank. September.

BRAC. 1994a. *The Present and Future of a Research at BRAC.* Deliberations and Recommendations from a Workshop.

BRAC. 1994b. *Building Research Capacity.* A Proposal for BRAC's Research and Evaluation Division.

Brautigan, D. 1992. "Governance, Economy, and Foreign Aid." *Studies in Comparative International Development* 27 (3): 3–25.

Brinkerhoff, D. 1992. "Technical Cooperation and Training in Development Management in the 1990s: Trends, Implications and Recommendations." *Canadian Journal of Development Studies* 20 (3).

Brooks, F. P. 1975. *The Mythical Man-Month: Essays in Software Engineering.* Reading, MA: Addison-Wesley.

Brown, L. D., and D. C. Korten. 1989. "Understanding Voluntary Organizations: Guidelines for Donors." *World Bank Working Paper* 258. Country Economics Department. Washington, DC: World Bank.

Brunner, J. J. 1993. "Investigación social y decisiones políticas." *Sociedad 3* (November): 31–43.

Bureau of Indian Affairs, U. S. Department of the Interior. *Indian Service Population and Labor Force Estimates.* Various Issues.

Burns, T., and G. M. Stalker. 1961. *The Management of Innovation.* London: Tavistock Publications.

Buych, B. 1989. *The Bank's Use of Technical Assistance for Institutional Development.* Washington, DC: World Bank.

Carr, M., and M. Chen. 1992. *Establishment of a WID/Gender Research Programme in BRAC.* Report of a UNIFEM Mission.

Castonguay, V. 1995. *Capacity Building in the Kenya Customs and Excise Department.* Paper prepared for the Harvard Institute for International Development Conference on Capacity Building, March 29–31, Bermuda.

Cernea, M. M., ed. 1985. *Putting People First: Sociological Variables in Rural Development.* New York: Oxford University Press.

Cernea, M. M. 1992. "The Building Blocks of Participation: Testing Bottom-up Planning." *World Bank Discussion Paper* 166. Washington, DC: World Bank.

Chalfant, S. A. 1974. "Aboriginal Territories of the Flathead, Pend d'Oreille and Kutenai Indians of Western Montana." In Horr, D. A., ed., *Interior Salish and Eastern Washington Indians, Vol. II*. New York: Garland.

Chambers, R. 1985. "Shortcut Methods for Gathering Social Information for Rural Development Projects." In M. M. Cernea, ed., *Putting People First: Sociological Variables in Rural Development*. New York: Oxford University Press.

Champy, J. 1995. *Reengineering Management: The Mandate for New Leadership*. New York: HarperBusiness.

Chen, M., and S. Mahmud. 1993. *Assessing Change in Women's Lives*. A Concept Paper for the BRAC-ICDDR,B Collaborative Research Project.

Chen, M., L. Chen, W. Mahmud, and R. Pelto. 1995. *Mid-Term Review of the BRAC-ICDDR,B Collaborative Research Project*. Report of a Mid-Term Review Mission.

Chen, M. 1995. *Report of a Training Workshop*. Gender Research Training Workshop, BRAC, January.

Chen, M. 1995. *Beyond Credit: Promoting the Enterprises of Low-Income Women*. New York and Ottawa: UNIFEM and Aga Khan Foundation Canada.

Chew, D. C. 1990. "Internal Adjustments to Falling Civil Service Salaries: Insights from Uganda." *World Development* XVIII (2): 10003–10014.

Chiluba, F. 1994. *State of the Economy and Wage Policy*. Lusaka: Republic of Zambia.

Chisholm, D. 1989. *Coordination Without Hierarchy: Informal Structures in Multiorganizational Systems*. Berkeley: University of California Press.

Clarke, M., ed. 1983. *Corruption: Causes, Consequences and Control*. New York: St. Martin's Press.

Cohen, J. M. 1995. "Capacity Building in the Public Sector: A Focused Framework for Analysis and Action." *International Review of Administrative Sciences* 61 (3): 407–422.

Cohen, J. M., G. Culagovski, N. T. Uphoff and D. Wolf. 1978. *Participation at the Local Level: A Working Bibliography*. Ithaca: Cornell University, Center for International Studies, Rural Development Committee.

Cohen, J. M. 1993. "Building Sustainable Public Sector Managerial, Professional, and Technical Capacity: A Framework for Analysis and Intervention." *HIID Development Discussion Paper 473.* Cambridge: Harvard Institute for International Development.

Cohen, J. M. 1993. Importance of Public Service Reform: The Case of Kenya. *Journal of Modern African Studies* XXXI (3): 449–476.

Cohen, J. M., and N. T. Uphoff. 1980. "Participation's Place in Rural Development: Seeing Clarity Through Specificity." *World Development* 8: 213–235.

Cohen, J. M. 1993. "Foreign Advisors and Capacity Building: The Case of Kenya." *Public Administration and Development* 12 (5): 493–510.

Cohen, J. M., and S. B. Peterson. 1997. "Kenya: HIID's Advice and Training." In D. H. Perkins, ed., *Assisting Development in a Changing World: The Harvard Institute for International Development, 1980–1995.* Cambridge: Harvard University Press.

Cohen, J. M. 1991. "Expatriate Advisors in the Government of Kenya: Why They are There and What Can Be Done About It." *HIID Development Discussion Paper 376.* Cambridge: Harvard Institute for International Development.

Colander, D. C., ed. 1984. *Neoclassical Political Economy: The Analysis of Rent-Seeking and DUP Activities.* Cambridge, MA: Ballinger.

Coleman, J. S. 1990. *Foundations of Social Theory.* Cambridge: The Belknap Press of Harvard University Press.

Commission on Health Research for Development. 1990. *Health Research: Essential Link to Equity in Development.* New York: Oxford University Press.

Contreras, M. E. 1992. *Social Policy Challenges for the Next Decade.* Paper presented at the Consultative Group Meeting for Bolivia, Paris, October.

Contreras, M. E. 1993. "Universidad que no publica, universidad que no investiga." *Presencia* (February 15).

Contreras, M. E., with M. Urquiola S. 1993. "Educación Superior: Contra el pacto de la mediocridad." *Momento Político (Presencia).* Año III (15) 9 July: 6–7.

Contreras, M. E. 1993. "La Educación Superior en Bolivia: Un desafío por asumir." *Ventana (La Razon).* Año III (10) 30 May: 8–9.

Cooper, R. N. 1991. "Economic Stabilization in Developing Countries." *ICEG Occasional Paper* 14. San Francisco: International Center for Economic Growth, ICS Press.

Cornell, S., and J. P. Kalt. 1995. "Where Does Economic Development Really Come From? Constitutional Rule Among the Contemporary Sioux and Apache." *Economic Inquiry* 33.

Cornell, S., and J. P. Kalt. 1991. "Where's the Glue? Institutional Bases of American Indian Economic Development. Project Report Series." Cambridge: Harvard Project on American Indian Economic Development, John F. Kennedy School of Government.

Cornell, S., and J. P. Kalt. 1994. "The Redefinition of Property Rights in American Indian Reservations: A Comparative Analysis of Native American Economic Development." In L. H. Legters and F. J. Lyden, eds., *American Indian Policy and Economic Development.* Westport, CT: Greenwood Press.

Cornell, S., and J. P. Kalt. 1992. "Culture and Institutions as Public Goods: American Indian Economic Development as a Problem of Collective Action." In T. L. Anderson, ed., *Property Rights and Indian Economies.* Lanham: Rowman & Littlefield Publishers, Inc.

Cornell, S., and J. P. Kalt. 1992. "Reloading the Dice: Improving the Chances for Economic Development on American Indian Reservations." In *What Can Tribes Do? Strategies and Institutions in American Indian Economic Development.* Los Angeles: University of California at Los Angeles.

Cornell, S., and J. P. Kalt. Forthcoming. "Cultural Evolution and Constitutional Public Choice." In J. Long, ed., *Uncertainty and Economic Evolution: Essays in Honor of Armen Alchian.* London: Routledge Press.

Cosmides, L., and J. Tooby. 1989. "Evolutionary Psychology and the Generation of Culture, Part II: A Computational Theory of Social Exchange." *Ethology and Sociobiology* 10.

Cottarelli, C. 1993. "Limiting Central Bank Credit to the Government: Theory and Practice." *Occasional Paper* 110. Washington, DC: International Monetary Fund.

Damiba, P-C. 1993. From foreword to E. Berg, *Rethinking Technical Cooperation.* New York: UNDP/Development Alternatives Inc.

Davenport, T. H. 1993. *Process Innovation: Reengineering Work Through Information Technology.* Boston: Harvard Business School Press.

Davidson, B. 1992. *The Black Man's Burden: Africa and the Curse of the Nation-State.* New York: New York Times Books.

de Merode, L. 1991. "Civil Service Pay and Employment in Africa: Selected Implementation Experiences." *IBRD Staff Paper.* Washington, DC: International Bank for Reconstruction and Development.

Deming, E. W. 1986. *Out of Crisis.* Cambridge: Center for Advanced Engineering Study, Massachusetts Institute of Technology.

Denzau, A. T., and D. C. North. 1993. *Shared Mental Models: Ideologies and Institutions.* St. Louis: Center for the Study of Political Economy. Unpublished (March 3).

Desafíos de la educación superior. 1994. La Paz: UDAPSO.

Dia, M. 1993. *A Governance Approach to Civil Service Reform in Sub-Saharan Africa.* Washington, DC: World Bank.

Diamond, L. 1991. "Nigeria's Perennial Struggle." *Journal of Democracy* II (4): 73–85.

Dornbusch, R., and S. Fischer. 1993. "Moderate Inflation." *World Bank Economic Review* 7 (1): 1–44.

Dornbusch, R. 1990. "Policies to Move from Stabilization to Growth." *Proceedings of the World Bank Annual Conference on Development Economics.*

Dozier, H. E. 1970. *The Pueblo Indians of North America.* Norman: University of Oklahoma Press.

Duesenberry, J., C. Gray, J. Lewis, M. McPherson and S. Younger. 1994. *Improving Exchange Rate Management in Sub-Saharan Africa.* Cambridge: Harvard Institute for International Development (processed).

Dumarest, Fr. Noel. 1919. "Notes on Cochiti, New Mexico." *Memoirs of the American Anthropological Association* 6 (3) July–September: 139–236.

Durham, W. H. 1991. *Coevolution: Genes, Culture and Human Diversity.* Palo Alto, CA: Stanford University Press.

Durrant, F. 1995. "Role of Information in Social Policymaking: Latin America and the Caribbean." In D. Morales-Gómez and M. Torres A., eds., *Social Policy in a Global Society.* Ottawa: IDRC.

Ekpo, M. U., ed. 1977. *Bureaucratic Corruption in Sub-Saharan Africa: Toward a Search for Causes and Consequences.* Washington, DC: University Press of America.

Elster, J. 1989. *The Cement of Society: A Study of Social Order.* Cambridge: Cambridge University Press.

Esman, M. J. 1991. *Management Dimensions of Development: Perspectives and Strategies.* West Hartford, CT: Kumarian Press.

Evans, P. 1992. "The State as Problem and Solution: Predation, Embedded Autonomy, and Structural Change." In S. Haggard and R. Kaufman, eds., *The Politics of Economic Adjustment.* Princeton, NJ: Princeton University Press.

Fahey, J. 1974. *The Flathead Indians.* Norman: University of Oklahoma Press.

Firth, R. 1964. *Essays on Social Organization and Values.* LSE Monographs on Social Anthropology No. 28. London: Athlone Press, University of London.

Foss, K., et al. 1988. *The Effectiveness of Technical Assistance Personnel.* Stockholm: DANIDA, FINIDA, NORAD, SIDA.

Frank, R. H. 1988. *Passions Within Reason.* New York: W. W. Norton & Co.

Frederick, W. H., and R. L. Worden, eds. 1993. *Indonesia: A Country Study.* Washington, DC: U.S. Library of Congress.

Friedland, J. 1994. "Argentine Economy Minister Reassures Fed Official of Currency's Stability." *Wall Street Journal* (December 29).

Friedman, M. 1964. "Foreign Economic Aid: Means and Objectives." First published in 1958. Collected in G. Ranis, ed., *The United States and the Developing Countries.* New York: W. W. Norton & Co.

Galbraith, J. 1994. *Competing with Flexible Lateral Organizations*, 2nd edition. Reading, MA: Addison-Wesley.

Garcia-Zamor, J.-C. 1973. "Micro-Bureaucracies and Development Administration." *International Review of Administrative Sciences* 29: 417–423.

Gillis, M. 1991. *Tax Reform in Developing Countries.* Durham, NC: Duke University Press.

Gillis, M. 1989. "Towards a Taxonomy for Tax Reform." In M. Gillis, ed., *Tax Reform in Developing Countries.* Durham, NC: Duke University Press.

Glenday, G. 1995. "Perspectives on the Computerization of Tax Systems in Sub-Saharan Africa." *HIID Development Discussion Paper 446.* Cambridge: Harvard Institute for International Development. Also in TRS, Taxation Research Series No. 9 (May 1993) and in G. P. Jenkins, ed., *Information Technology and Innovation in Tax Administration.* Norwell, MA: Kluwer Law Publishing.

Glenday, G. 1996. *Tax Policy and Administration Achievements of the Tax Modernization Program in Kenya, January 1990–June 1995.*

Glenday, G. 1991. "On Safari in Kenya: From Sales Tax to Value Added Tax." *International VAT Monitor.* December.

Godoy, R., and M. E. Contreras. 1997. "Bolivia." In D. H. Perkins, ed., *Assisting Development in a Changing World: The Harvard Institute for International Development, 1980–1995.* Cambridge: Harvard University Press.

Goldfrank, E. S. 1927. *The Social and Ceremonial Organization of Cochiti. Memoirs of the American Anthropological Association 33.* Menasha: American Anthropological Association.

Goldsmith, A. A. 1992. "Institutions, Planned Development, and Socioeconomic Change." *Public Administration Review* 42 (6).

Goldsmith, A. A. 1992. "Institutions and Planned Socioeconomic Change: Four Approaches." *Public Administration Review* 52 (6): 582–587.

Goldsmith, A. A. 1993. "Institutional Development in National Agricultural Research: Issues for Impact Assessment." *Public Administration and Development* 13: 195–204.

Goode, R. B. 1984. *Government Finance in Developing Countries.* Washington, DC: Brookings Institution.

Gould, S. 1983. *Hen's Teeth and Horse's Toes.* New York: W. W. Norton & Co.

Gould, D. 1980. *Bureaucratic Corruption and Underdevelopment in the Third World: The Case of Zaire.* New York: Pergamon Press.

Gourman, J. 1993. *The Gourman Report: A Rating of Graduate and Professional Programs in American and International Universities.* Los Angeles: National Education Standards.

Government of Kenya. 1986. "Economic Management for Renewed Growth." Sessional paper No. 1. Nairobi, Kenya: Government Printer.

Government of Kenya. 1995. "The Kenya Revenue Authority Act, 1995." *Kenya Gazette Supplement No. 36* (Acts No. 3) June 5. Nairobi, Kenya: Government Printer.

Government of Kenya. 1986. *Policy Framework Paper.*

Gray, C., L. Khadiagala, and R. Moore. 1990. *Institutional Development Work in the Bank: A Review of 84 Bank Projects.* Washington, DC: World Bank.

Gray, C. S. 1980. "Civil Service Compensation in Indonesia." *Bulletin of Indonesian Economic Studies.* March.

Greene, M. P. 1991. *Research for Development: A Grants Program for the Third World.* Washington, DC: National Academy Press.

Grindle, M. S., and J. W. Thomas. 1991. "Policymakers, Policy Choices, and Policy Outcomes: The Political Economy of Reform in Developing Countries." In D. H. Perkins and M. Roemer, eds., *Reforming Economic Systems in Developing Countries.* Cambridge: Harvard Institute for International Development.

Grindle, M. S. 1994. "Sustaining Economic Recovery in Latin America: State Capacity, Markets, and Politics." In G. Bird and A. Helwege, eds., *Latin America's Economic Future.* London: Academic Press.

Grindle, M. S. 1995. *Las reformas de segunda generación: Hacia la construcción de un estado capaz.* Transcript of lecture presented at the Universidad Católica Boliviana, La Paz, June 23.

Habte, D. 1992. "Building and Strengthening Research Capacity in Health: The Challenge to Africa." *Journal of Diarrhoeal Disease Research* 10: 73–78.

Haddow, P. S. 1982. *The Post-Graduate Training and Utilization of Professional Planners and Economists in the Government of Kenya: Recommendations to the Government and Donor Agencies.* Report prepared for the Ministry of Economic Planning and Development and the Canadian International Development Agency. ANNEX III (July): 118–121.

Hajji, N., L. Jaïdi and M. Zouaoui. 1992. *Prix et Concurrence au Maroc—Douze études sectorielles.* Casablanca: Najah El Jadid.

Hammer, M. 1995. *The Reengineering Revolution: A Handbook.* New York: HarperBusiness.

Hammer, M., and J. Champy. 1993. *Reengineering the Corporation.* New York: HarperBusiness.

Haouach, A. 1994. *Morocco: Pilot Study of Capacity Building.* Cambridge: Harvard Institute for International Development.

Harvard Institute for International Development. 1994. *1991–1993 Biennial Report.* Cambridge: Harvard Institute for International Development.

Heidenheimer, A. J., M. Johnston and V. T. LeVine. 1989. *Political Corruption: A Handbook.* New Brunswick: Transaction Publishers.

Heimer, C. A. 1992. "Doing Your Job and Helping Your Friends: Universalistic Norms about Obligations to Particular Others in Networks." In N. Nohria and R. G. Eccles, eds., *Networks and Organizations: Structure, Form, and Action.* Boston: Harvard Business School Press.

Hilderbrand, M. E., and M. S. Grindle. 1995. "Building Sustainable Capacity in the Public Sector: What Can Be Done?" *Public Administration and Development* 15 (5): 441–463.

Hilderbrand, M. E., and M. S. Grindle. 1994. *Building Sustainable Capacity: Challenges for the Public Sector.* Final report for UNDP Project INT/92/676. Cambridge: Harvard Institute for International Development. March.

Hirschmann, D. 1993. "Institutional Development in the Era of Economic Policy Reform: Contradictions and Illustrations from Malawi." *Public Administration and Development* 13.

Holmes, M., and A. Krishna. 1994. *Public Sector Management and Participation: Institutional Support for Sustainable Development.* Draft paper. Washington, DC: World Bank.

Huberts, L. W. 1989. "The Influence of Social Movements on Government Policy." In B. Klandermans, ed., *International Social Movement Research, Vol. 2.* Greenwich, CT: JAI Press.

Hyden, G. 1983. *No Shortcuts to Progress: African Development Management in Perspective.* London: Heinemann.

International Monetary Fund. 1993. *International Financial Statistics Yearbook.* Washington, DC: IMF.

International Monetary Fund. 1994. *International Financial Statistics Yearbook.* Washington, DC: IMF.

Israel, A. 1987. *Institutional Development: Incentives to Performance.* Baltimore: Johns Hopkins University Press (for the World Bank).

Jarman, A., and A. Kouzmin. 1993. "Public Sector Think Tanks in Inter-Agency Policy-Making: Designing Enhanced Government Capacity." *Canadian Public Administration* 36 (4): 499–529.

Jaycox, E. V. K. 1993. *Capacity Building: The Missing Link in African Development.* Transcript of speech presented to the Conference on African Capacity Building: Effective and Enduring Partnerships at the African-American Institute, May 20, Reston, VA.

Jenkins, R. 1995. Review of *Participando en el crecimiento.* Journal of Latin American Studies 27 (February).

Jorgensen, S., M. Grosh, and M. Schacter. 1992. *Bolivia's Answer to Poverty, Economic Crisis, and Adjustment.* World Bank Regional and Sectoral Studies. Washington, DC: World Bank.

Juma, C., and N. Clark. 1995. "Policy Research in Sub-Saharan Africa: An Exploration." *Public Administration and Development* (May).

Juran, J. 1989. *Juran on Leadership for Quality.* New York: Free Press.

Kabinet Pembangunan VI beserta Buku Alamat Pejabat Negara Republik Indonesia 1994, or "Book of Addresses of State Functionaries of the Republic of Indonesia" (Jakarta: Badan Penerbit Alda, 1994).

Kantner, R. 1983. *The Change Masters.* New York: Simon and Schuster.

Katzenbach, J. R., and D. K. Smith. 1995. *The Wisdom of Teams: Creating the High Performance Organization.* New York: Harper Collins.

Kealey, D. J., and D. R. Protheroe. 1993. *People in Development: Towards More Effective North-South Collaborations.* Study for the Canadian International Development Agency. October.

"Kenya: Donor Alienation." *1995. Oxford Analytica* June 15.

Kenya Training Program. 1989. Ithaca: Institute for African Development, Cornell University. March.

Kiggundu, M. N. 1994. Managing Research Institutions in Developing Countries: Test of a Model. *Public Administration and Development* 14: 201–222.

Killick, T. 1989. *A Reaction Too Far: Economic Theory and the Role of the State in Developing Countries.* London: Overseas Development Institute.

Klitgaard, R. 1991. *Adjusting to Reality: Beyond State versus Market in Economic Development.* San Francisco: International Center for Economic Growth, ICS Press.

Klitgaard, R. 1989. "Incentive Myopia." *World Development* XVII (4): 447–460.

Kolb, D. 1984. *Experiential Learning: Experience as the Source of Learning and Development.* Englewood Cliffs, NJ: Prentice-Hall, Inc.

Krueger, A. O. 1974. "The Political Economy of the Rent-Seeking Society." *American Economic Review* 64 (3).

Krueger, A. 1993. *Political Economy of Policy Reform in Developing Countries.* Cambridge: MIT Press.

Lal, D. 1984. "The Political Economy of the Predatory State." *World Bank Discussion Paper* 105. Washington, DC: World Bank Development Research Department.

Landell-Mills, P., and I. Serageldin. 1991. "Governance and the External Factor." *Proceedings of the World Bank Annual Conference on Development Economics.* Washington, DC: World Bank.

Lange, C. H. 1979. "Cochiti Pueblo." In Ortiz, A., ed. *Handbook of North American Indians.* Washington, DC: Smithsonian Institution. 366–378.

Lange, C. H. 1990 [1959]. *Cochiti: A New Mexico Pueblo, Past and Present.* Albuquerque: University of New Mexico Press.

Leach, Mark. 1993. *Building Capacity Through Action Learning.* IDR Reports. Boston, MA: Institute for Development Research.

Leonard, D. K. 1993. "Professionalism and African Administration." *IDS Bulletin* 24 (1).

Leonard, D. K. 1977. *Reaching the Peasant Farmer: Organization Theory and Practice in Kenya.* Chicago: University of Chicago Press.

Leonard, D. K. 1991. *African Successes: Four Public Managers of Kenyan Rural Development.* Berkeley: University of California Press.

Leonard, D. K. 1987. "The Political Realities of African Management." *World Development* 15 (7): 899–910.

Levy, D. 1996. *Building the Third Sector: Latin America's Private Research Centers,* and *Nonprofit Development.* Pittsburgh: University of Pittsburgh Press.

Levy, D. 1995. Review of *Desafíos de la educación superior.* Comparative Education Review 39 (2) May.

Lindauer, D. L., and B. Nunberg, eds. 1994. *Rehabilitating Government: Pay and Employment Reform in Africa.* Washington, DC: World Bank.

Lindquist. 1993. "Think Tanks or Clubs? Assessing the Influence and Roles of Canadian Policy Institutes." *Canadian Public Administration* 36 (4): 547–579.

Lipset, S. M. 1963. *Political Man: The Social Bases of Politics.* New York: Anchor Press.

Lopach, J. J., M. H. Brown and R. L. Clow. 1990. *Tribal Government Today: Politics on Montana Indian Reservations.* Boulder: Westview Press.

Lovell, C. H. 1992. *Breaking the Cycle of Poverty: The BRAC Strategy.* West Hartford, CT: Kumarian Press.

Majone, G. 1988. "Policy Analysis and Public Deliberation." In R. B. Reich, ed., *The Power of Public Ideas.* Cambridge: Harvard University Press. 156–178.

Marsden, D. 1994. "Indigenous Management: Introduction." In S. Wright, ed., *Anthropology of Organizations.* London: Routledge. 35–40.

Mbuggus, M. 1991. "Kenyans and the 'Chai' Syndrome." *The Daily Nation.* December 18.

Mbuggus, M. 1991. "Bribery and Extortion." *Finance.* November 15: 18–23.

McGregor, D. M. 1960. *The Human Side of Enterprise.* New York: McGraw-Hill.

McKinnon, R. 1991. *The Order of Economic Liberalization.* Baltimore: Johns Hopkins University Press.

Merquior, J. G. 1993. "A Panoramic View of the Rebirth of Liberalism." *World Development* 21 (8).

Minister of Finance. 1993. *Budget Address.* Lusaka: Republic of Zambia.

Ministry of Finance, Government of Kenya. 1994. *Kenya Tax Modernization Programme: Completion Report for the Institutional Support Project for Tax Modernization in Kenya, Phase I.* Nairobi: Ministry of Finance, Government of Kenya. September.

Ministry of Planning and National Development. Undated. *Review of Individuals Departing the Scheme of Service.* Nairobi, Kenya: Ministry of Planning and National Development.

Mohrman, S. A., S. G. Cohen, and A. M. Mohrman. 1995. *Designing Team-Based Organizations: New Forms of Knowledge Work.* San Francisco: Jossey-Bass.

Moore, M. 1995. *Institution Building as a Development Assistance Method: A Review of Literature and Ideas.* Stockholm: Swedish International Development Authority.

Morgan, P. 1993. *Capacity Building: An Overview.* Paper prepared for a Workshop on Capacity Development November 22–23 at the Institute on Governance, Ottawa, Canada.

Moris, J. 1973. "Managerial Structures and Plan Implementation in Colonial and Modern Agricultural Extension: A Comparison of Cotton and Tea Programmes in Central Kenya." In D. K. Leonard, ed., *Rural Administration in Kenya.* Nairobi: East African Literature Bureau.

Moris, J. R. 1977. "The Transferability of Western Management Concepts and Programs: An East African Perspective." In L. D. Stifel, J. S. Coleman, and J. E. Black, eds., *Education and Training for Public Sector Management in Developing Countries.* New York: The Rockefeller Foundation.

Morss, E. R. 1984. "Institutional Destruction Resulting from Donor and Project Proliferation in Sub-Saharan Countries." *World Development* XII (4): 465–470.

Morton, R. B., and A. R. Wight. 1963. *Proceedings Manual for the Organizational Training Laboratory.* Sacramento, CA: Aerojet-General Corporation.

Moser, C. 1989. "Gender Planning in the Third World: Meeting Practical and Strategic Gender Needs." *World Development* 17 (11): 1799–1825.

Mukandala, R. 1994. *Tanzania: Pilot Study of Capacity Building.* Cambridge: Harvard Institute for International Development.

Naím, M. 1995. "Latin America's Journey to the Market: From Macroeconomic Shocks to Institutional Therapy." *ICEG Occasional Paper* 62. San Francisco: International Center for Economic Growth, ICS Press.

Nasution, A. 1983. *Financial Institutions and Policies in Indonesia.* Singapore: Institute of Southeast Asian Studies.

National Development Board 1994 Workplan, unpublished.

Nellis, J. 1989. "Comment on Van Arkadie." In *Proceedings of the World Bank Annual Conference on Development Economics 1989.* Washington, DC: World Bank.

Nelson, J., ed. 1990. "Orthodoxy and its Alternatives: Explaining Approaches to Stabilization and Adjustment." In *Economic Crisis and Policy Choice*. Princeton, NJ: Princeton University Press.

Netherlands Delegation. 1993. *Statement of the Netherlands Delegation*. Bolivia Consultative Group, December 9–11. Mimeo.

Newman, J., S. Jorgensen, and M. Pradhan. 1991. "How Did Workers Benefit from Bolivia's Emergency Social Fund?" *The World Bank Economic Review* 5 (2): 367–393.

Nicholson, T. 1994. "Institution Building: Examining the Fit Between Bureaucracies and Indigenous Systems." In S. Wright, ed., *The Anthropology of Organizations*. London: Routledge. 68–84.

Nogueira, R. M. 1987. "Life Cycle and Learning in Grassroots Development Organizations." *World Development* 15 (Supplement): 169–177.

North, D. C. 1990. *Institutions, Institutional Change, and Economic Performance*. Cambridge: Cambridge University Press.

North, D. C. 1988. "Ideology and Political/Economic Institutions." *Cato Journal* (Spring/Summer): 15–28.

North, D. C., and R. Thomas. 1985. *The Rise of the Western World*. Cambridge: Cambridge University Press.

North, D. C. 1981. *Structure and Change in Economic History*. New York: Norton.

North, D. C. 1992. "Transactions Costs, Institutions and Economic Performance." *ICEG Occasional Paper* 30. San Francisco: International Center for Economic Growth, ICS Press.

North, H. W. 1992. *Capacity Building and Technical Cooperation—Managing the Connection*. New York: NaTCAP/UNDP. June.

Nzapayeke, A. 1994. *Central African Republic: Pilot Study of Capacity Building*. Cambridge: Harvard Institute for International Development.

OECD. 1991. *Principles for New Orientations in Technical Cooperation*. Paris: OECD Development Assistance Committee.

"Office of the Vice President and Ministry of Planning and National Development." 1995. *Economic Review* 1994. Nairobi, Kenya: Government Press.

Olson, M. 1982. *The Rise and Decline of Nations*. New Haven: Yale University Press.

Osborne, D., and T. Gaebler. 1993. *Reinventing Government: How the Entrepreneurial Spirit is Transforming the Public Sector*. New York: Plume.

Ostrom, E. 1992. *Crafting Institutions for Self-Governing Irrigation Systems*. San Francisco: ICS Press.

Ostrom, E. 1990. *Governing the Commons*. Cambridge: Cambridge University Press.

Ostrom, E. 1994. "Neither Markets Nor States: Linking Transformation Processes in Collective Action Arenas." In D. C. Mueller, ed., *The Handbook of Public Choice*. New York: Basil Blackwell.

Pacheco, R. G. 1994. *Bolivia: Pilot Study of Capacity Building*. Cambridge: Harvard Institute for International Development.

Page, J. 1994. "The East Asian Miracle: Four Lessons for Development Policy." In S. Fischer and J. Rotemberg, eds., *NBER Macroeconomics Annual 1994*. Cambridge: MIT Press. 219–268.

Parente, S., and E. Prescott. 1993. "Changes in the Wealth of Nations." *Quarterly Review*. Minneapolis, MN: Federal Reserve Bank of Minneapolis. 3–16.

Perkins, D. H. 1995. *Technical Assistance in the University Context: The HIID Experience*. Paper prepared for the HIID History Conference, March 29–31, Bermuda.

Perlez, J. 1991. "Citing Corruption in Kenya, Western Nations Cancel Aid." *New York Times*. October 21: 1.

Peterson, S. B. 1995. *Hierarchy Versus Networks: Alternative Strategies for Building Administrative Capacity in African Bureaucracies*. Paper prepared for the Harvard Institute for International Development Conference on Capacity Building, March 29–31, Bermuda.

Peterson, S. B. 1991. "From Processing to Analyzing: Intensifying the Use of Microcomputers in Development Bureaucracies." *Public Administration and Development* 11 (September–October): 491–510.

Peterson, S. B. 1994. "Saints, Demons, Wizards and Systems: Why Information Technology Reforms Fail or Underperform in Public Bureaucracies in Africa." *HIID Development Discussion Paper 486*. Cambridge: Harvard Institute for International Development.

Peterson, S. B., C. Kinyeki, J. Mutai, and C. Ndungu. 1995. Computerizing Accounting Systems in Development Bureaucracies: Lessons from Kenya. *HIID Development Discussion Paper 500*. Cambridge: Harvard Institute for International Development.

Peterson, S. B. 1995. "Improving Recurrent Cost Financing of Development Bureaucracies." In N. Caiden, ed., *Public Financial Administration in Developing Countries*. Greenwich, CT: JAI Press.

Peterson, S. B. 1990. "Microcomputer Training for the Government of Kenya: The Case of the Kenya Institute of Administration." *Information Technology for Development* 5 (December): 292–307.

Peterson, S. B. 1990. "Institutionalizing Microcomputers in Developing Bureaucracies: Theory and Practice from Kenya." *Information Technology for Development* 5 (September): 277–326.

Peterson, S. B., C. Kinyeki, J. Mutai, and C. Ndungu. Forthcoming. "Computerizing Personnel Information Systems: Lessons from Kenya." *International Journal of Public Administration.*

Pfaff, W. 1995. "A New Colonialism? Europe Must Go Back into Africa." *Foreign Affairs* LXXIV (1): 2–6.

Phelps, E. S. 1973. "Inflation in the Theory of Public Finance." *Swedish Journal of Economics* 74 (1): 67–82.

Picciotto, R. 1992. "Participatory Development: Myths and Dilemmas." *A Policy Research Working Paper.* Washington, DC: World Bank.

Picciotto, R. 1994. *Institutional Learning and Bank Operations: The New Project Cycle.* Draft paper. Washington, DC: World Bank.

Pinckney, T., J. Cohen, and D. Leonard. 1983. "Microcomputers and Financial Management in Development Ministries: Experience from Kenya." *Agricultural Administration* 14: 151–167.

Presidential Committee on Streamlining the Bureaucracy, Department of Budget and Management. 1995. *Reengineering the Bureaucracy for Better Governance: Principles and Parameters.* Manila: Government of the Philippines. August.

Price, R. M. 1975. *Society and Bureaucracy in Contemporary Ghana.* Berkeley: University of California Press.

Putnam, R. D. 1992. *Making Democracy Work: Civic Traditions in Modern Italy.* Princeton, NJ: Princeton University Press.

Ragin, C. C. 1987. *The Comparative Method.* Berkeley: University of California Press.

Republic of Zambia. 1992, 1993, 1994, 1995. *Budget Address,* presented to the Parliament by the Minister of Finance. Lusaka.

Revans, R. W. 1982. *The Origins and Growth of Action Learning.* Bromley, Kent, UK: Chartwell-Brant.

Rodriguez O., G. 1995. "Políticas públicas y modernización de la universidad boliviana. In Fundación Milenio." *Diálogos de Milenio, no. 15, Educación Superior en Bolivia.* La Paz (April 12).

Roemer, M., and S. Radelet. 1991. "Macroeconomic Reform in Developing Countries." In D.H. Perkins and M. Roemer, eds., *Reforming Economic Systems in Developing Countries.* Cambridge: Harvard Institute for International Development.

Ronan, P. 1890. *History of the Flathead Indians.* Minneapolis: Ross & Haines.

Sachs, J. 1987. "The Bolivian Hyperinflation and Stabilization." *American Economic Review* 77 (2) May: 279–283.

Salmen, L. F. 1987. *Listen to the People: Participant Observation in Development Projects.* New York: Oxford University Press.

Sandbrook, R. 1991. "Development for the People and the Environment." *Journal of International Affairs* 44 (2).

Sanderatne, N. 1994. *Sri Lanka: Pilot Study of Capacity Building.* Cambridge: Harvard Institute for International Development.

Schroeder, A. H. 1972. "Rio Grande Ethnohistory." In A. Ortiz, ed., *New Perspectives on the Pueblos.* Albuquerque: University of New Mexico Press. 42–70.

Selowsky, M. 1990. Comment on Dornbusch. In *Proceedings of the World Bank Annual Conference on Development Economics 1990.* Washington, DC: World Bank. 53–56.

Senge, P. 1990. *The Fifth Discipline: The Art and Practice of the Learning Organization.* New York: Doubleday.

Simon, H. 1984. *Reason in Human Affairs.* Palo Alto: Stanford University Press.

Smithe, J. A. 1991. *The Idea Brokers: Think Tanks and the Rise of the New Policy Elite.* New York: The Free Press.

Srinivasan, T. N. 1985. "Neoclassical Political Economy: The State and Economic Development." *Politics and Society* 17 (2).

Steuerele, C. E. 1986. *Who Should Pay for Collecting Taxes: Financing the IRS.* American Enterprise Institute Studies in Fiscal Policy Series. Washington, DC: American Enterprise Institute for Public Policy Research.

Streeten, P. 1993. "Markets and States: Against Minimalism. *World Development* 21 (8) August.

Strong, M. F. 1991. "ECO '92: Critical Challenges and Global Solutions." *Journal of International Affairs* 44 (2).

Tatto, M. T. 1987. *An Assessment of the LASPAU/AID Training for Development Programs in Latin American and Caribbean Universities.* Harvard University Ph.D. Dissertation.

Taylor, C. W., G. de Mik, M. F. Tucker, A. R. Wight, and K. Yagi. 1965. *Development of Situational Tests for the Peace Corps.* Salt Lake City, Utah: Department of Psychology, University of Utah under Peace Corps Contract.

Tendler, J., and S. Freedheim. 1994. "Trust in a Rent-Seeking World: Health and Government Transformed in Northeast Brazil." *World Development* 22 (12): 1771–1791.

Thompson, J. D. 1967. *Organizations in Action: Social Science Basis of Administration Theory.* New York: McGraw-Hill.

Trosper, R. L. 1976. "Native American Boundary Maintenance: The Flathead Indian Reservation, Montana, 1860–1970." *Ethnicity* 3 (3) September: 256–274.

Trostle, J., and J. Simon. 1992. "Building Applied Health Research Capacity in Less-Developed Countries: Problems Encountered by the ADDR Project." *Social Science Medicine* 35 (11): 1379–1387.

Turney-High, H. H. 1937. *The Flathead Indians of Montana: Memoirs of the American Anthropological Association,* No. 48. Menasha, Wisconsin: American Anthropological Association.

United Nations Development Programme. 1993. *Human Development Report.* New York: Oxford University Press.

United Nations Development Programme. 1992. *Human Development Report.* New York: Oxford University Press.

United Nations Development Programme. 1991. *Human Development Report.* New York: Oxford University Press.

United Nations Development Programme. 1990. *Human Development Report.* New York: Oxford University Press.

United Nations Development Programme. 1993. *National Capacity Building: Report of the Administrator.* New York: UNDP Fortieth Session. March.

Urquiola S., M. 1994. *Participando en el crecimiento. Expansión económica, distribución del ingreso y probreza en el area urbana de Bolivia: 1989–1992 y proyecciones.* La Paz: UDAPSO.

USAID. 1988. *The Effectiveness of Private Voluntary Organizations. Report of the Advisory Committee of Voluntary Foreign Aid.* Washington, DC: USAID.

van Niekirk, Nico. 1993. "La economía va cada vez mejor, pero que pasa con la gente? Deuda o beneficio social." In *Políticas sociales y ajuste estructural. Bolivia 1985–1993.* La Paz: CID-COTESU-MCTH.

Vegh, C. 1989. "Government Spending and Inflationary Finance: A Public Finance Approach." *IMF Staff Papers* 36 (3): 657–677.

Wade, R. 1990. *Governing the Market: Economic Theory and the Role of Government in East Asian Industrialization.* Princeton, NJ: Princeton University Press.

Weiss, C. 1979. "The Many Meanings of Research Utilization." *Public Administration Review*: 426–431.

Wescott, C. 1986. "Microcomputers for Improved Budgeting by the Kenya Government." *HIID Development Discussion Paper 227.* Cambridge: Harvard Institute for International Development.

White, L. A. 1930. "A Comparative Study of Keresan Medecine Societies." In *Proceedings of the 23rd International Congress of Americanists, 1928.* New York. 604–619.

Whitehead, L., ed. 1993. "Special Issue: Economic Liberalization and Democratization: Explorations of the Linkages." *World Development* XXI (8): 1245–1393.

Whyte, W. F. 1984. *Learning from the Field: A Guide from Experience.* Newbury Park, CA: Sage Publications.

Widner, J. 1994. "Reform Bargains: The Politics of Change." In D. S. Lindauer and M. Roemer, eds., *Asia and Africa: Legacies and Opportunities in Development.* San Francisco: ICS Press. 59–97.

Wight, A. R., and M. A. Hammons. 1970. *Guidelines for Peace Corps Cross-Cultural Training.* Washington, DC: Office of Training Support, U.S. Peace Corps.

Wight, A. R. 1968. *Trainers' Manual for an Instrumented Experiential Laboratory for Peace Corps Training.* U.S. Peace Corps Contract. Washington, DC: Office of Training Support, U.S. Peace Corps.

Wight, A. R. 1970. "Participative Education and the Inevitable Revolution." *The Journal of Creative Behavior* 4 (4) Fall: 234–282.

Williamson, O. E. 1985. *The Economic Institutions of Capitalism.* New York: The Free Press.

Wils, F. 1995. *Building Up and Strengthening Research Capacity in Southern Countries.* The Hague: RAWOO.

Wilson, L. S. 1993. "Kenyanisation and African Capacity Building." *Public Administration and Development* XIII (4): 489–499.

World Bank. 1994. *Adjustment in Africa: Reform, Results, and the Road Ahead.* New York: Oxford University Press.

World Bank. 1993. *Zambia: Prospects for Sustainable and Equitable Growth.* Report 11570-ZA. Washington, DC: World Bank.

World Bank Portfolio Management Task Force. 1992. *Effective Implementation: Key to Development Impact (The Wapenhans Report)*. Washington, DC: World Bank.

World Bank. 1989. *Sub-Saharan Africa: From Crisis to Sustainable Growth.* Washington, DC: World Bank.

World Bank. 1991. *World Development Report 1991: The Challenge of Development.* New York: Oxford University Press.

World Bank. 1991. *The Bank's Work on Institutional Development in Sectors: Emerging Tasks and Challenges.* Washington, DC: World Bank Public Sector Management and Private Sector Development Division. May.

World Bank. 1990. *World Development Report.* New York: Oxford University Press.

World Bank. 1993. *World Development Report.* New York: Oxford University Press.

World Bank. 1989. *Sub-Saharan Africa: From Crisis to Sustainable Growth.* Washington, DC: World Bank.

World Bank. 1984. *Towards Sustained Development in Sub-Saharan Africa.* Washington, DC: World Bank.

World Bank. 1993. *Handbook on Technical Assistance.* Washington, DC: World Bank Operations Policy Department.

World Bank. 1993. *Getting Results: The World Bank's Agenda for Improving Development Effectiveness.* Washington, DC: World Bank.

World Bank. 1984. *The Bank's Work on Institutional Development in Sectors: Emerging Tasks and Challenges.* Washington, DC: World Bank Public Sector Management and Private Sector Development Division. May.

World Bank. 1993. *Zambia: Prospects for Sustainable and Equitable Growth.* Washington: World Bank, Report 11570-ZA.

World Commission on Environment and Development. 1987. Brundtland Commission Report. *Our Common Future.* New York: Oxford University Press.

Young, R., and J. Loxley. 1990. *Zambia: An Assessment of Zambia's Structural Adjustment Experience.* Ottawa: North-South Institute.

Zartman, W., ed. 1995. *Collapsed States: The Disintegration and Restoration of Legitimate Authority.* Boulder, CO: Lynne Rienner.

Zuboff, S. 1985. "Automate/Informate: The Two Faces of Intelligent Technology." *Organizational Dynamics* 14 (Autumn).

Index

Page references followed by a bold **t** indicates a table, a bold **f** indicates a figure, and a bold **n** indicates an endnote.

DATE DUE